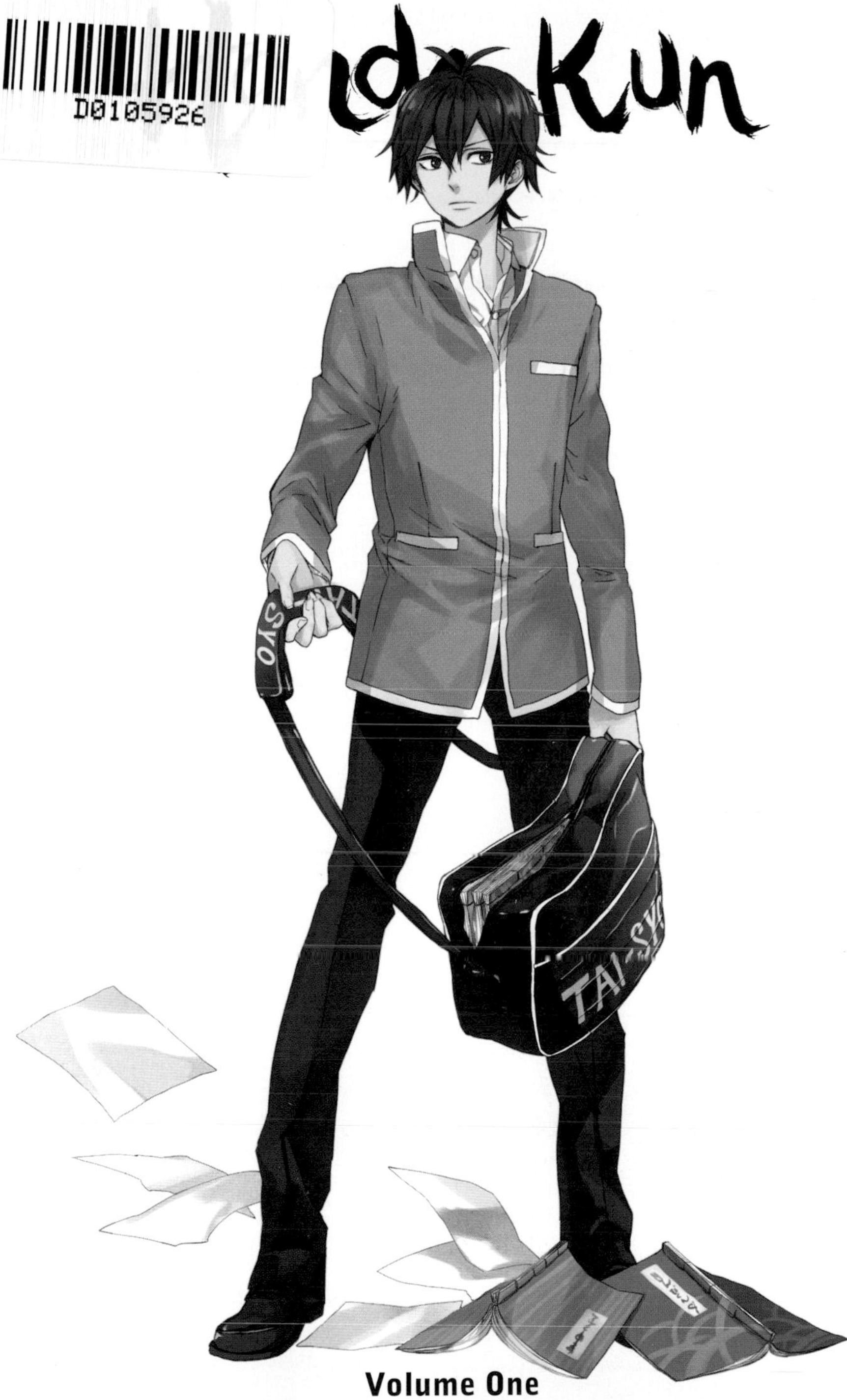
Kun
TAI-SYO
TAI-SYO

Volume One

SATSUKI YOSHINO

Contents

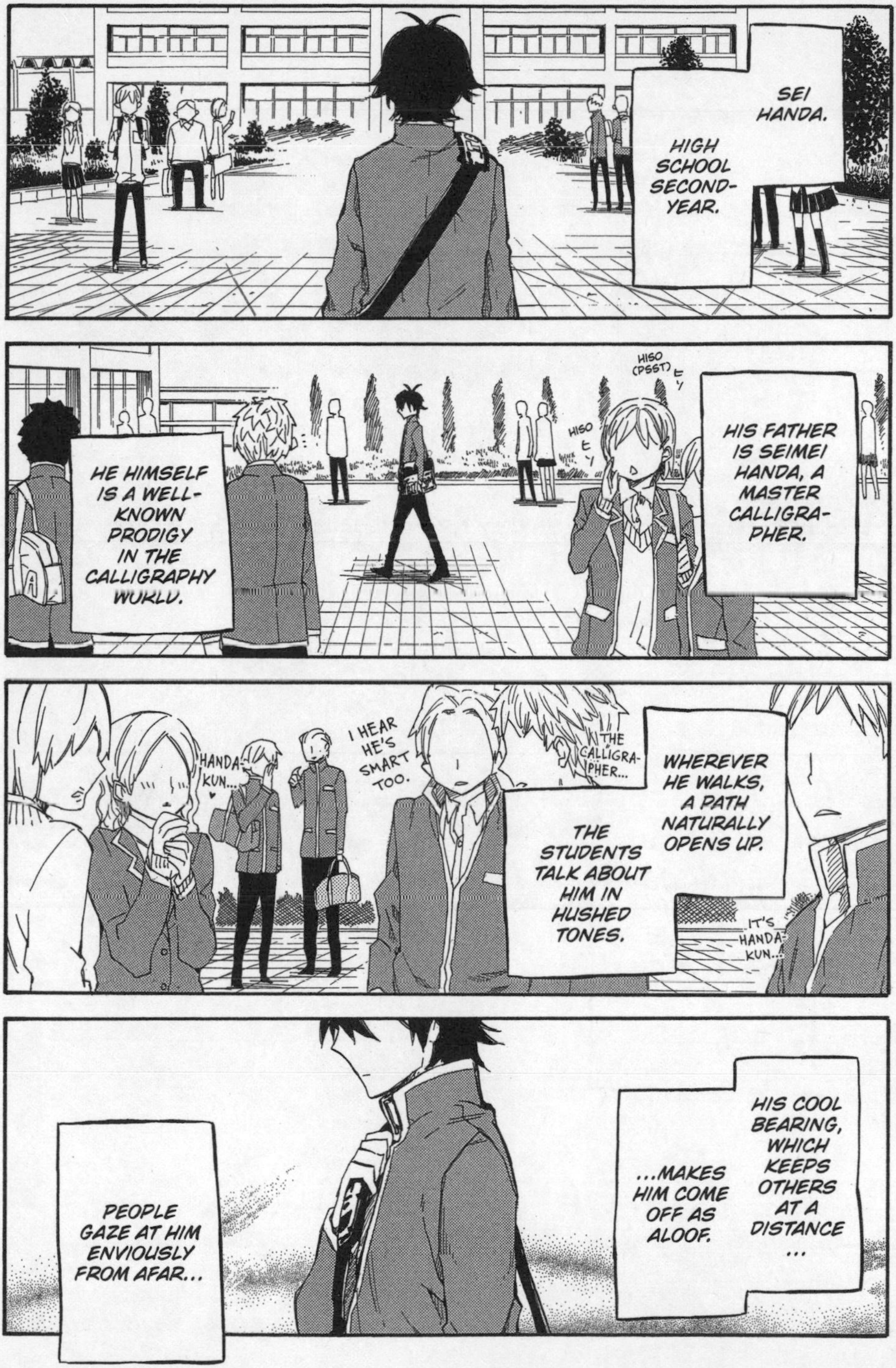
SEI HANDA.
HIGH SCHOOL SECOND-YEAR.
HIS FATHER IS SEIMEI HANDA, A MASTER CALLIGRAPHER.
HISO (PSST) ヒソ
HISO ヒソ
HE HIMSELF IS A WELL-KNOWN PRODIGY IN THE CALLIGRAPHY WORLD.
IT'S HANDA-KUN...
WHEREVER HE WALKS, A PATH NATURALLY OPENS UP.
THE CALLIGRAPHER...
THE STUDENTS TALK ABOUT HIM IN HUSHED TONES.
I HEAR HE'S SMART TOO.
HANDA-KUN...
HIS COOL BEARING, WHICH KEEPS OTHERS AT A DISTANCE...
...MAKES HIM COME OFF AS ALOOF.
PEOPLE GAZE AT HIM ENVIOUSLY FROM AFAR...

Chapter 1: Handa-kun & Girls' Friendship

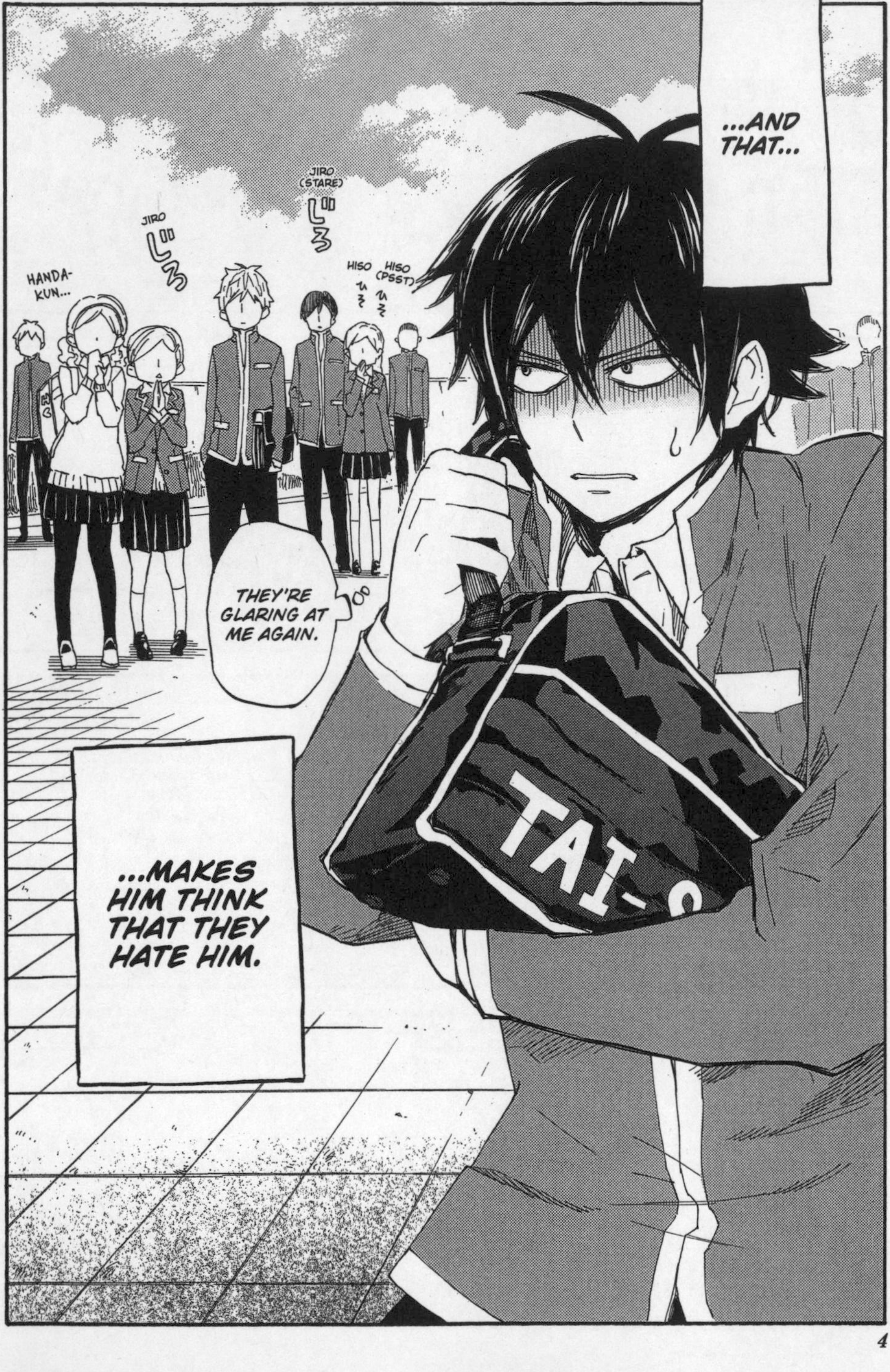

...AND THAT...
HISO HISO (PSST)
JIRO (STARE)
じろ
JIRO
じろ
HANDA-KUN...
THEY'RE GLARING AT ME AGAIN.
...MAKES HIM THINK THAT THEY HATE HIM.
TAI-

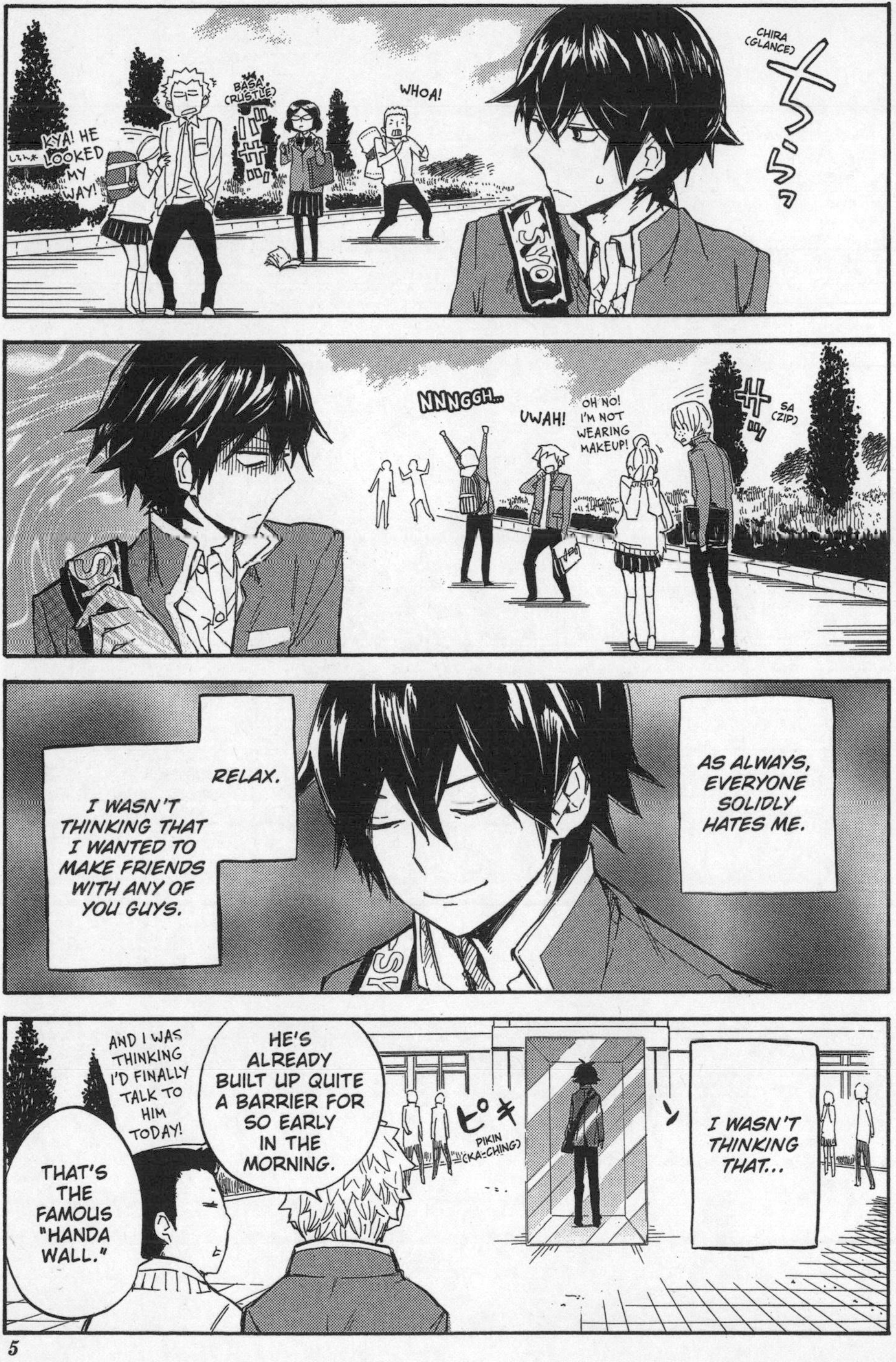
CHIRA (GLANCE)
ちらっ
WHOA!
BASA (RUSTLE)
バサッ
KYA! HE LOOKED MY WAY!
SA (ZIP)
サッ
OH NO! I'M NOT WEARING MAKEUP!
UWAH!
NNNGGH...
AS ALWAYS, EVERYONE SOLIDLY HATES ME.
RELAX.
I WASN'T THINKING THAT I WANTED TO MAKE FRIENDS WITH ANY OF YOU GUYS.
I WASN'T THINKING THAT...
ピキ
PIKIN (KA-CHING)
HE'S ALREADY BUILT UP QUITE A BARRIER FOR SO EARLY IN THE MORNING.
AND I WAS THINKING I'D FINALLY TALK TO HIM TODAY!
THAT'S THE FAMOUS "HANDA WALL."

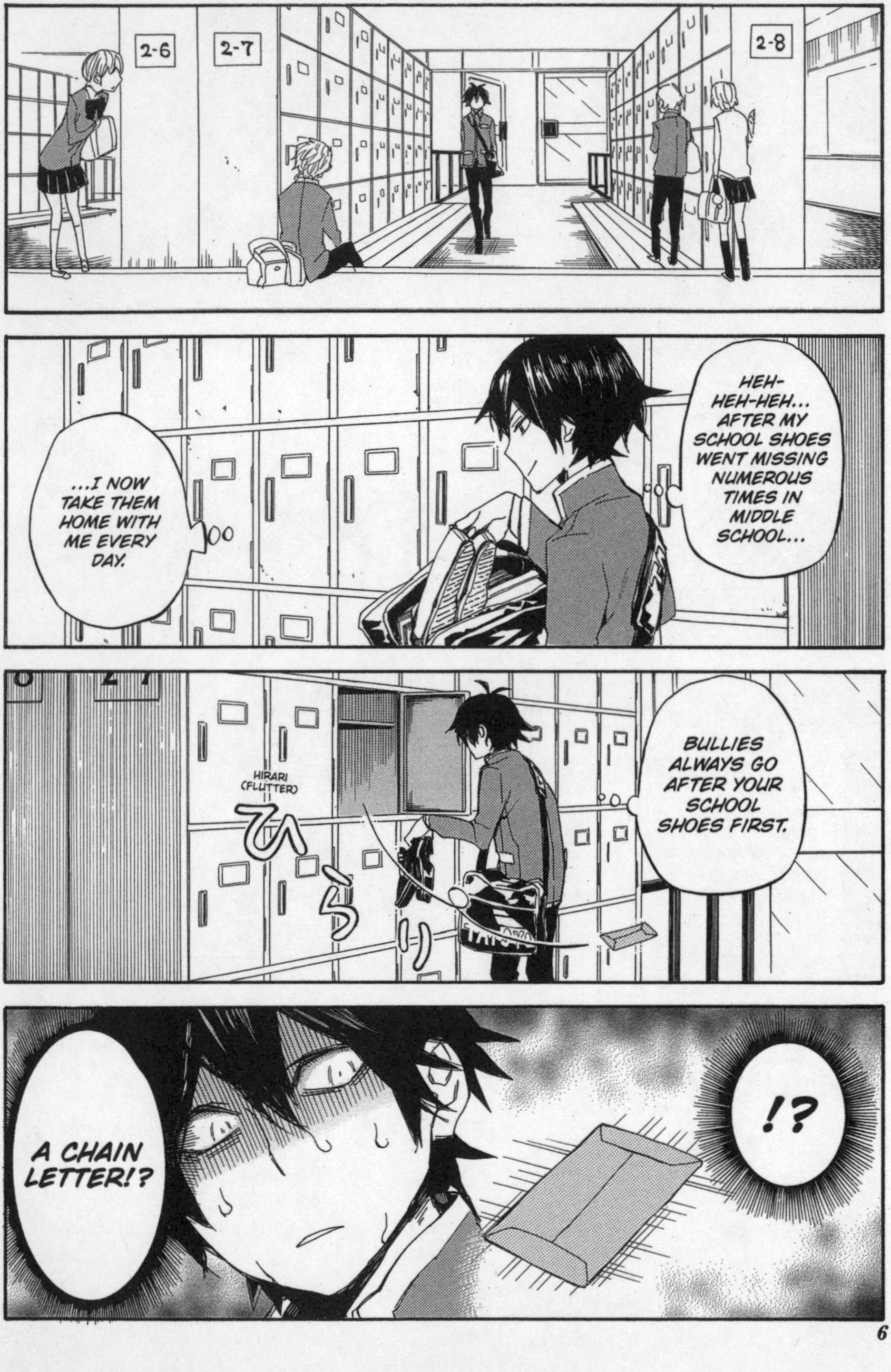
2-8
2-7
2-6
HEH-HEH-HEH... AFTER MY SCHOOL SHOES WENT MISSING NUMEROUS TIMES IN MIDDLE SCHOOL...
...I NOW TAKE THEM HOME WITH ME EVERY DAY.
BULLIES ALWAYS GO AFTER YOUR SCHOOL SHOES FIRST.
HIRARI (FLUTTER)
ひらり
!?
A CHAIN LETTER!?

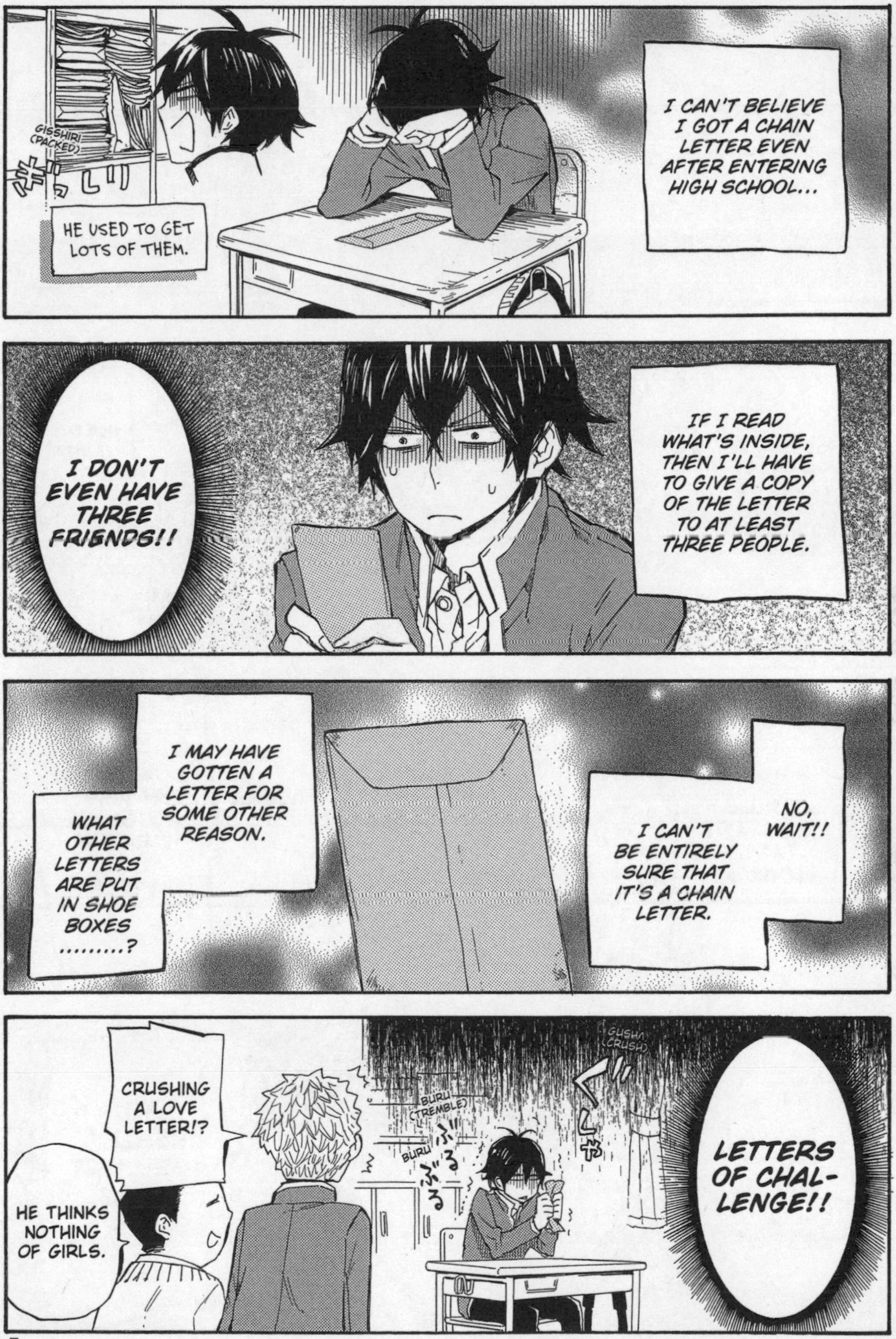
I CAN'T BELIEVE I GOT A CHAIN LETTER EVEN AFTER ENTERING HIGH SCHOOL...
GISSHIRI (PACKED)
HE USED TO GET LOTS OF THEM.
IF I READ WHAT'S INSIDE, THEN I'LL HAVE TO GIVE A COPY OF THE LETTER TO AT LEAST THREE PEOPLE.
I DON'T EVEN HAVE THREE FRIENDS!!
NO, WAIT!!
I CAN'T BE ENTIRELY SURE THAT IT'S A CHAIN LETTER.
I MAY HAVE GOTTEN A LETTER FOR SOME OTHER REASON.
WHAT OTHER LETTERS ARE PUT IN SHOE BOXES ....?
LETTERS OF CHAL-LENGE!!
GUSHA (CRUSH)
BURU (TREMBLE)
BURU
CRUSHING A LOVE LETTER!?
HE THINKS NOTHING OF GIRLS.

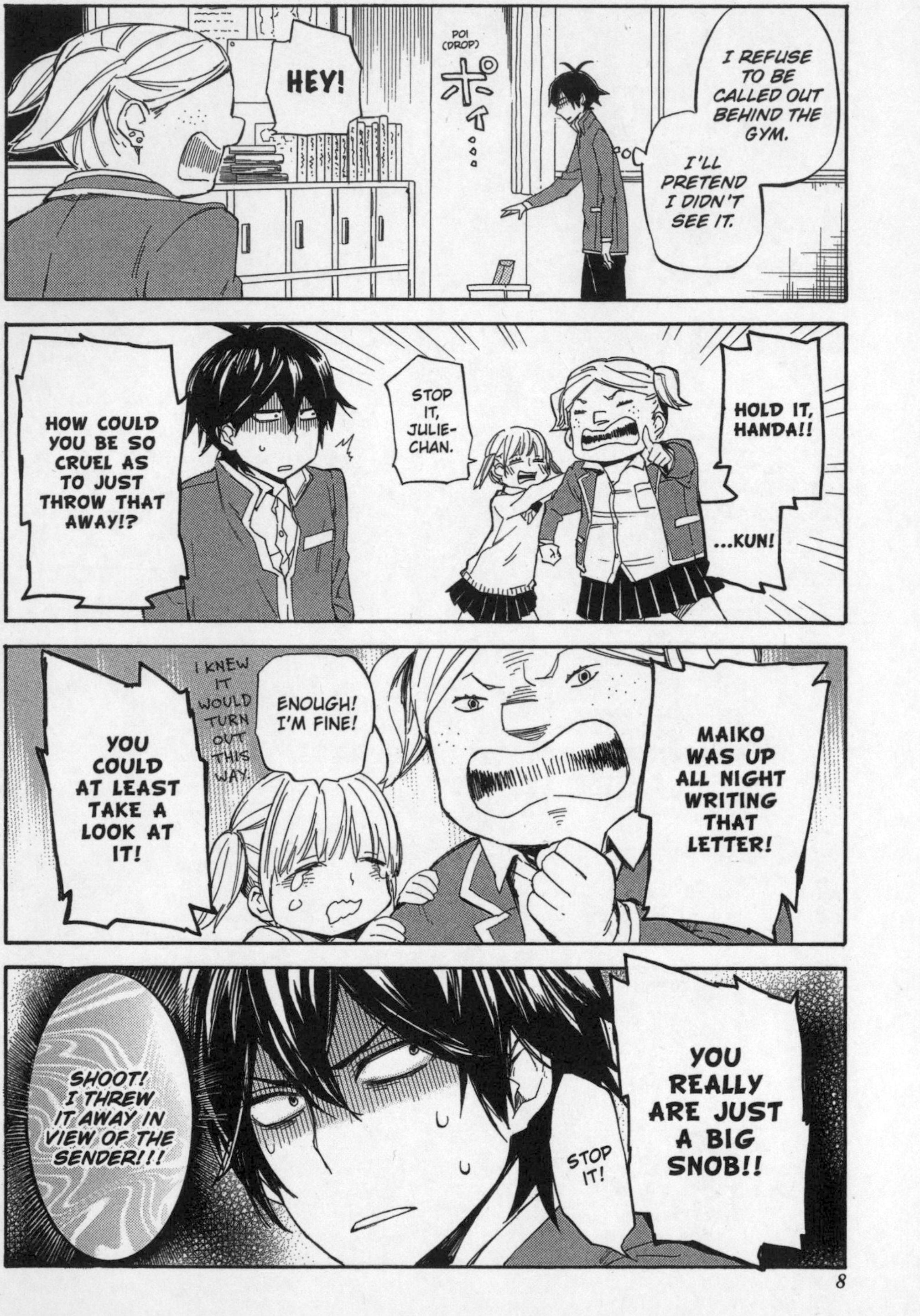
I REFUSE TO BE CALLED OUT BEHIND THE GYM.
I'LL PRETEND I DIDN'T SEE IT.
POI (DROP)
ポイ
HEY!
HOLD IT, HANDA!!
...KUN!
STOP IT, JULIE-CHAN.
HOW COULD YOU BE SO CRUEL AS TO JUST THROW THAT AWAY!?
MAIKO WAS UP ALL NIGHT WRITING THAT LETTER!
ENOUGH! I'M FINE!
I KNEW IT WOULD TURN OUT THIS WAY.
YOU COULD AT LEAST TAKE A LOOK AT IT!
YOU REALLY ARE JUST A BIG SNOB!!
STOP IT!
SHOOT! I THREW IT AWAY IN VIEW OF THE SENDER!!!

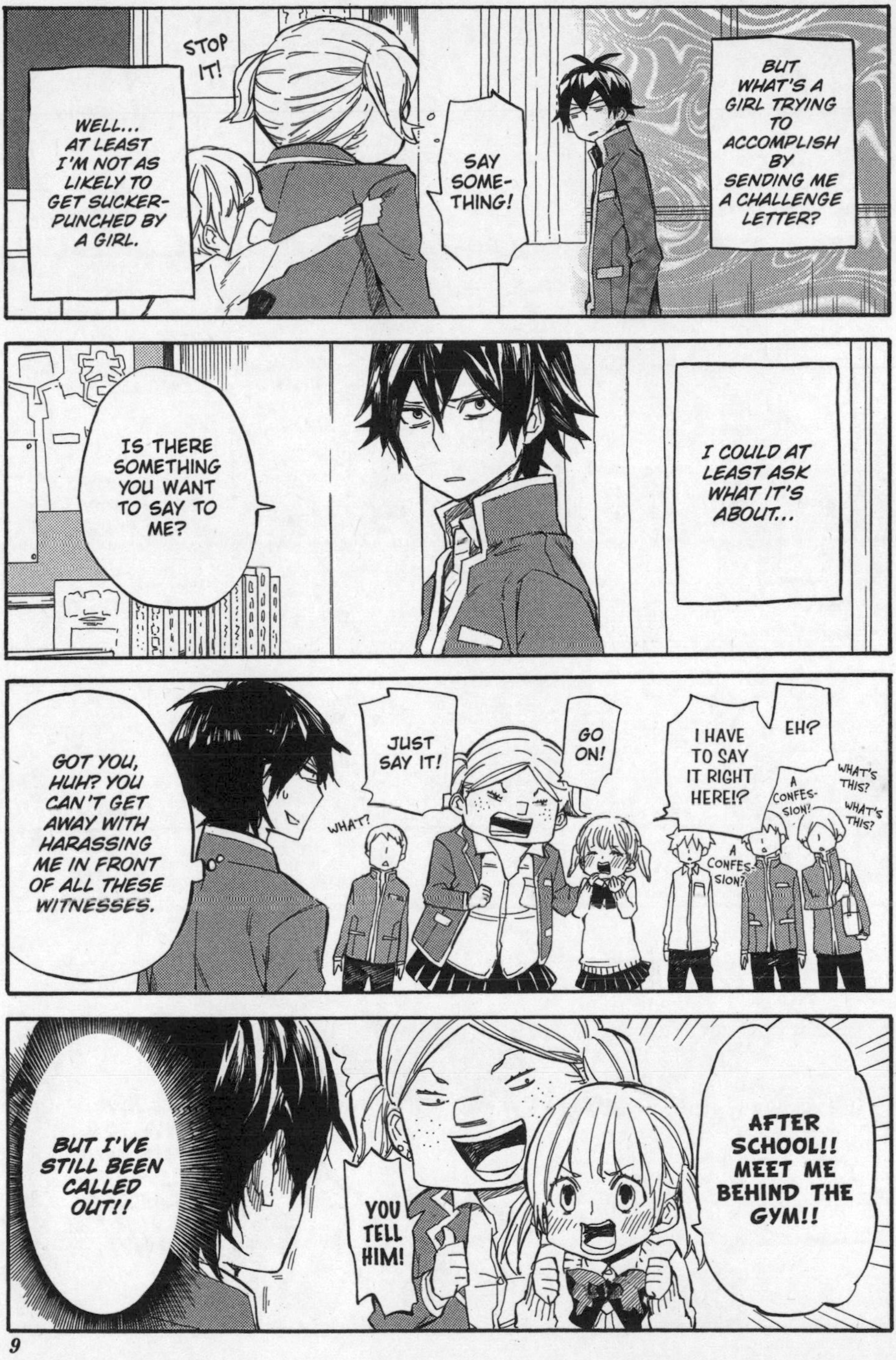
BUT WHAT'S A GIRL TRYING TO ACCOMPLISH BY SENDING ME A CHALLENGE LETTER?
SAY SOME-THING!
STOP IT!
WELL... AT LEAST I'M NOT AS LIKELY TO GET SUCKER-PUNCHED BY A GIRL.
I COULD AT LEAST ASK WHAT IT'S ABOUT...
IS THERE SOMETHING YOU WANT TO SAY TO ME?
EH?
WHAT'S THIS?
WHAT'S THIS?
A CONFES-SION?
A CONFES-SION?
I HAVE TO SAY IT RIGHT HERE!?
GO ON!
JUST SAY IT!
WHAT?
GOT YOU, HUH? YOU CAN'T GET AWAY WITH HARASSING ME IN FRONT OF ALL THESE WITNESSES.
AFTER SCHOOL!! MEET ME BEHIND THE GYM!!
YOU TELL HIM!
BUT I'VE STILL BEEN CALLED OUT!!

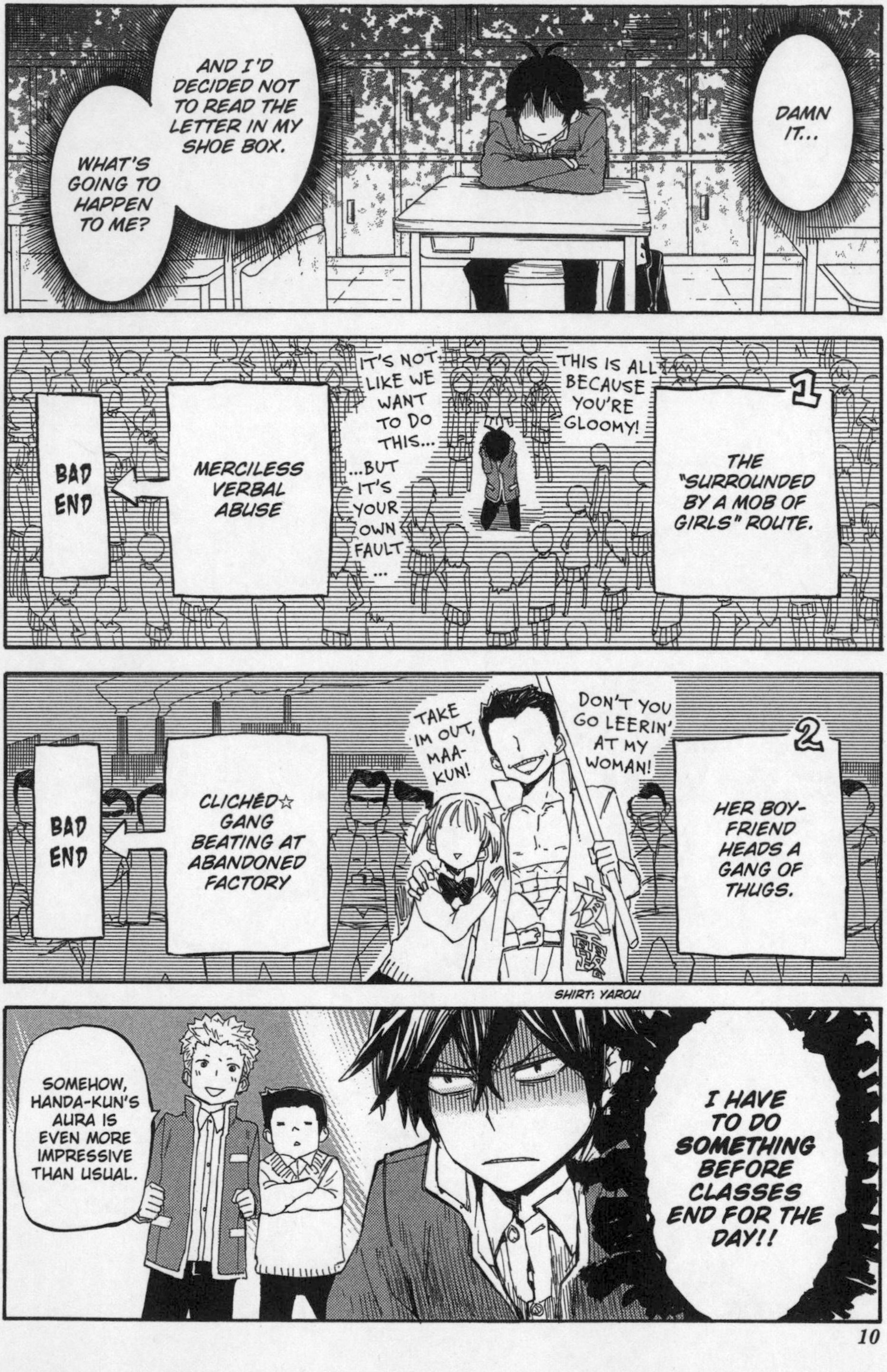
DAMN IT...
AND I'D DECIDED NOT TO READ THE LETTER IN MY SHOE BOX.
WHAT'S GOING TO HAPPEN TO ME?
1
THE "SURROUNDED BY A MOB OF GIRLS" ROUTE.
THIS IS ALL BECAUSE YOU'RE GLOOMY!
IT'S NOT LIKE WE WANT TO DO THIS...
...BUT IT'S YOUR OWN FAULT...
MERCILESS VERBAL ABUSE
BAD END
2
HER BOY-FRIEND HEADS A GANG OF THUGS.
DON'T YOU GO LEERIN' AT MY WOMAN!
TAKE IM OUT, MAA-KUN!
CLICHED☆ GANG BEATING AT ABANDONED FACTORY
BAD END
SHIRT: YAROU
I HAVE TO DO SOMETHING BEFORE CLASSES END FOR THE DAY!!
SOMEHOW, HANDA-KUN'S AURA IS EVEN MORE IMPRESSIVE THAN USUAL.

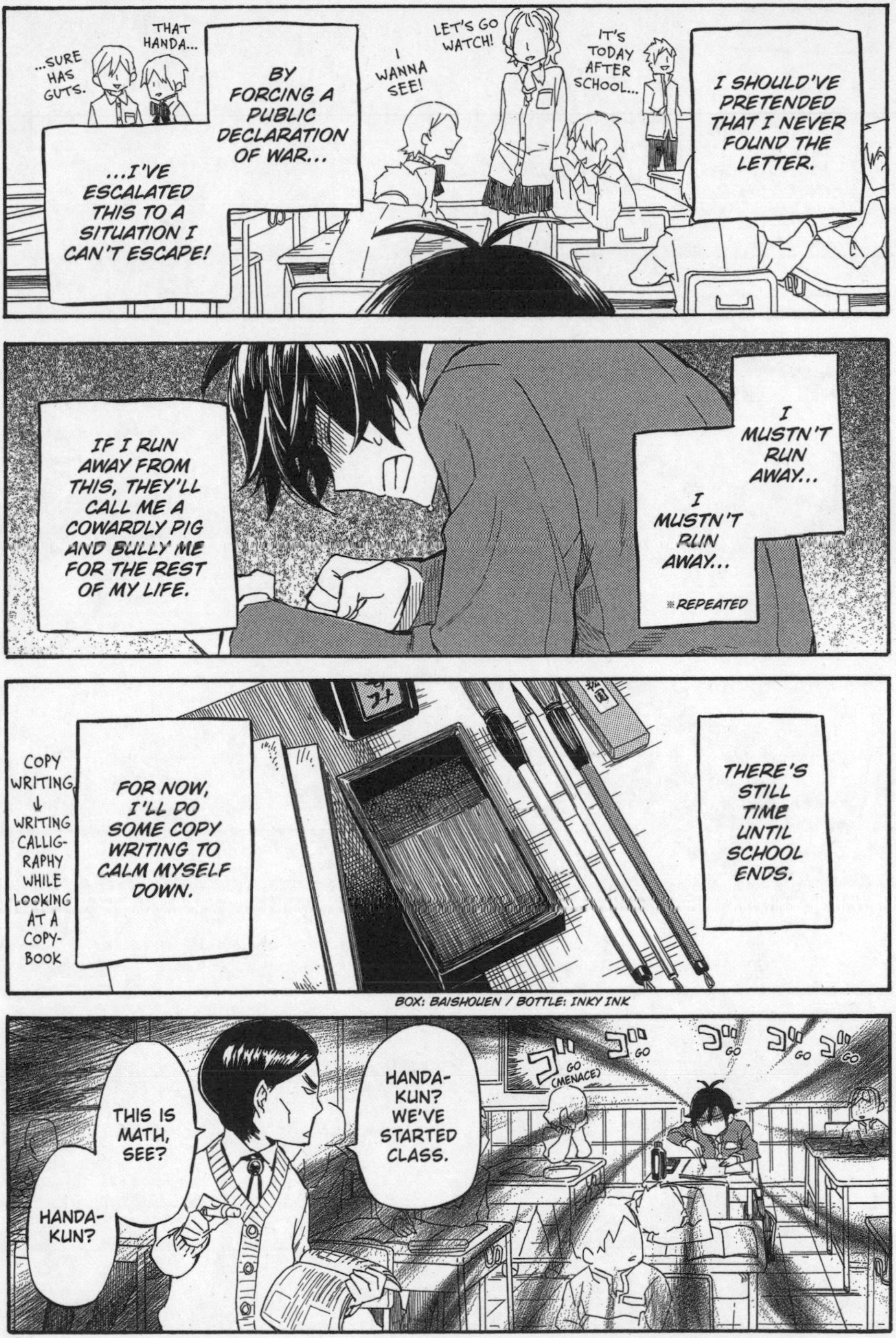
I SHOULD'VE PRETENDED THAT I NEVER FOUND THE LETTER.
IT'S TODAY AFTER SCHOOL...
LET'S GO WATCH!
I WANNA SEE!
BY FORCING A PUBLIC DECLARATION OF WAR...
THAT HANDA...
...SURE HAS GUTS.
...I'VE ESCALATED THIS TO A SITUATION I CAN'T ESCAPE!
I MUSTN'T RUN AWAY...
I MUSTN'T RUN AWAY...
※REPEATED
IF I RUN AWAY FROM THIS, THEY'LL CALL ME A COWARDLY PIG AND BULLY ME FOR THE REST OF MY LIFE.
THERE'S STILL TIME UNTIL SCHOOL ENDS.
FOR NOW, I'LL DO SOME COPY WRITING TO CALM MYSELF DOWN.
COPY WRITING ↓ WRITING CALLIGRAPHY WHILE LOOKING AT A COPYBOOK
BOX: BAISHOUEN / BOTTLE: INKY INK
GO (MENACE)
GO GO GO GO
HANDA-KUN? WE'VE STARTED CLASS.
THIS IS MATH, SEE?
HANDA-KUN?

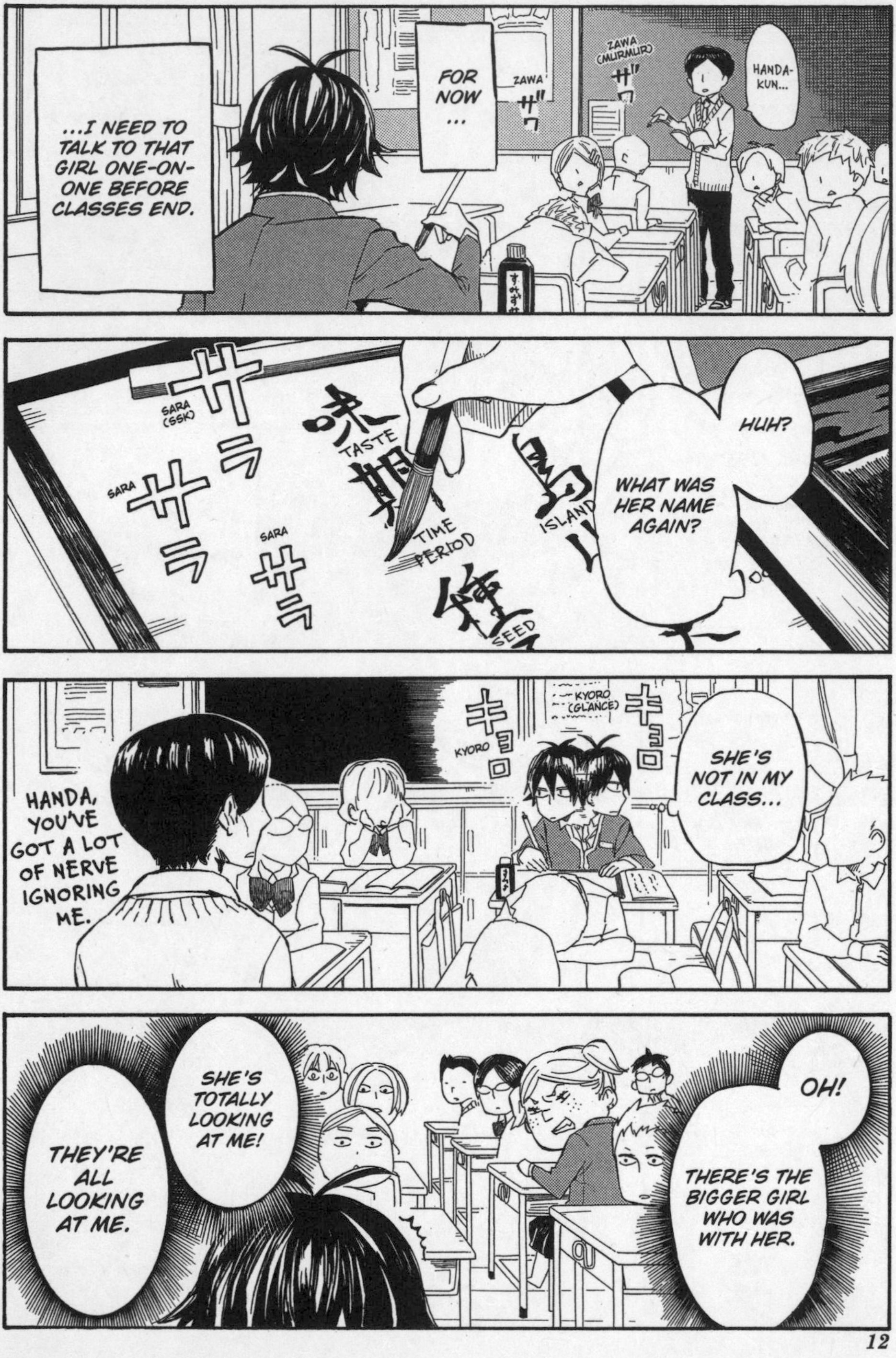
HANDA-KUN...
ZAWA (MURMUR)
ザワ
ZAWA
ザワ
FOR NOW ...
...I NEED TO TALK TO THAT GIRL ONE-ON-ONE BEFORE CLASSES END.
HUH?
WHAT WAS HER NAME AGAIN?
ISLAND
SEED
TIME PERIOD
TASTE
SARA (SSK)
サラ
SARA
サラ
SARA
サラ
SHE'S NOT IN MY CLASS...
KYORO (GLANCE)
キョロ
KYORO
キョロ
HANDA, YOU'VE GOT A LOT OF NERVE IGNORING ME.
OH!
THERE'S THE BIGGER GIRL WHO WAS WITH HER.
SHE'S TOTALLY LOOKING AT ME!
THEY'RE ALL LOOKING AT ME.

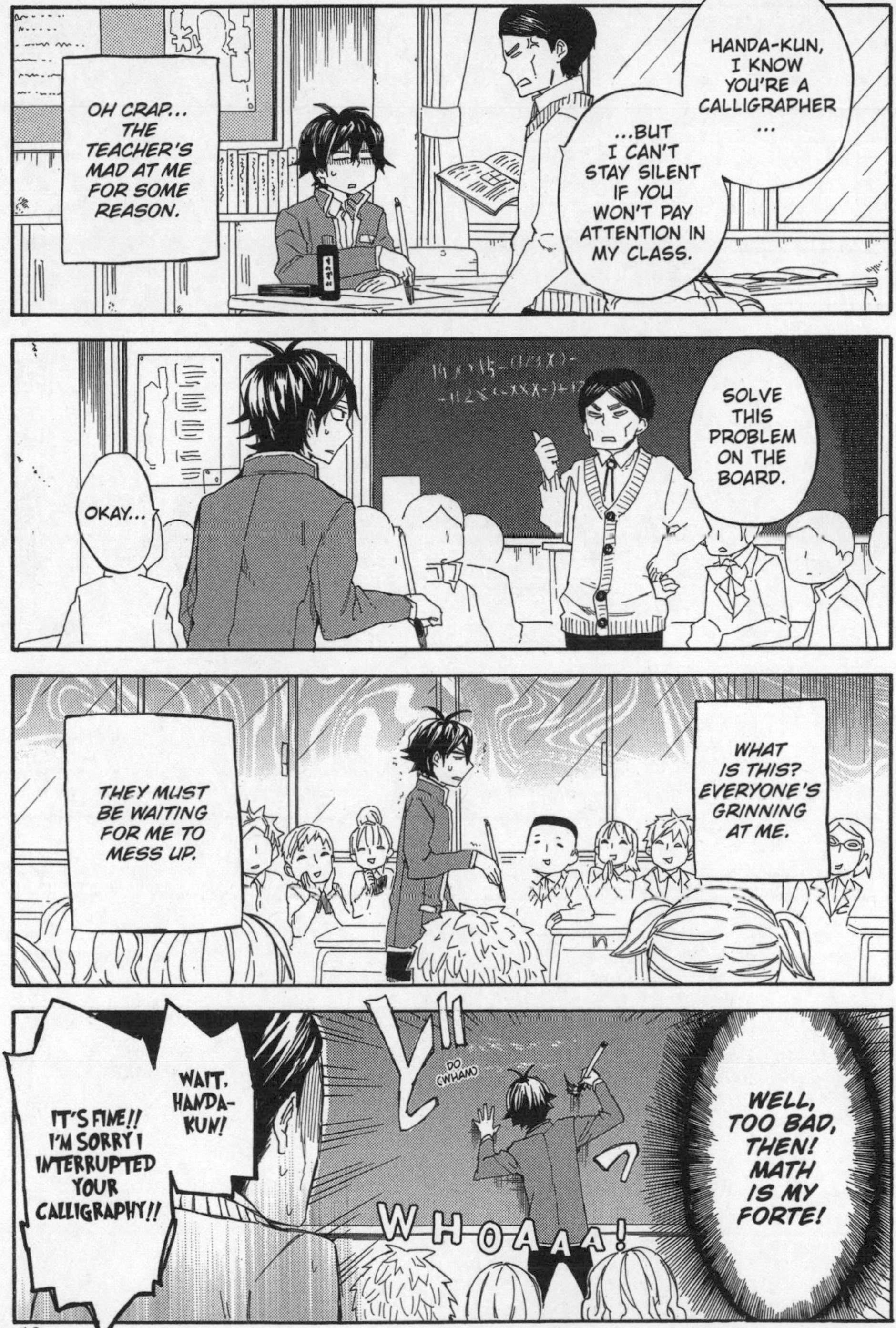
HANDA-KUN, I KNOW YOU'RE A CALLIGRAPHER ...
...BUT I CAN'T STAY SILENT IF YOU WON'T PAY ATTENTION IN MY CLASS.
OH CRAP... THE TEACHER'S MAD AT ME FOR SOME REASON.
SOLVE THIS PROBLEM ON THE BOARD.
OKAY...
WHAT IS THIS? EVERYONE'S GRINNING AT ME.
THEY MUST BE WAITING FOR ME TO MESS UP.
WELL, TOO BAD, THEN! MATH IS MY FORTE!
DO (WHAM)
WHOAAA!
WAIT, HANDA-KUN!
IT'S FINE!! I'M SORRY I INTERRUPTED YOUR CALLIGRAPHY!!

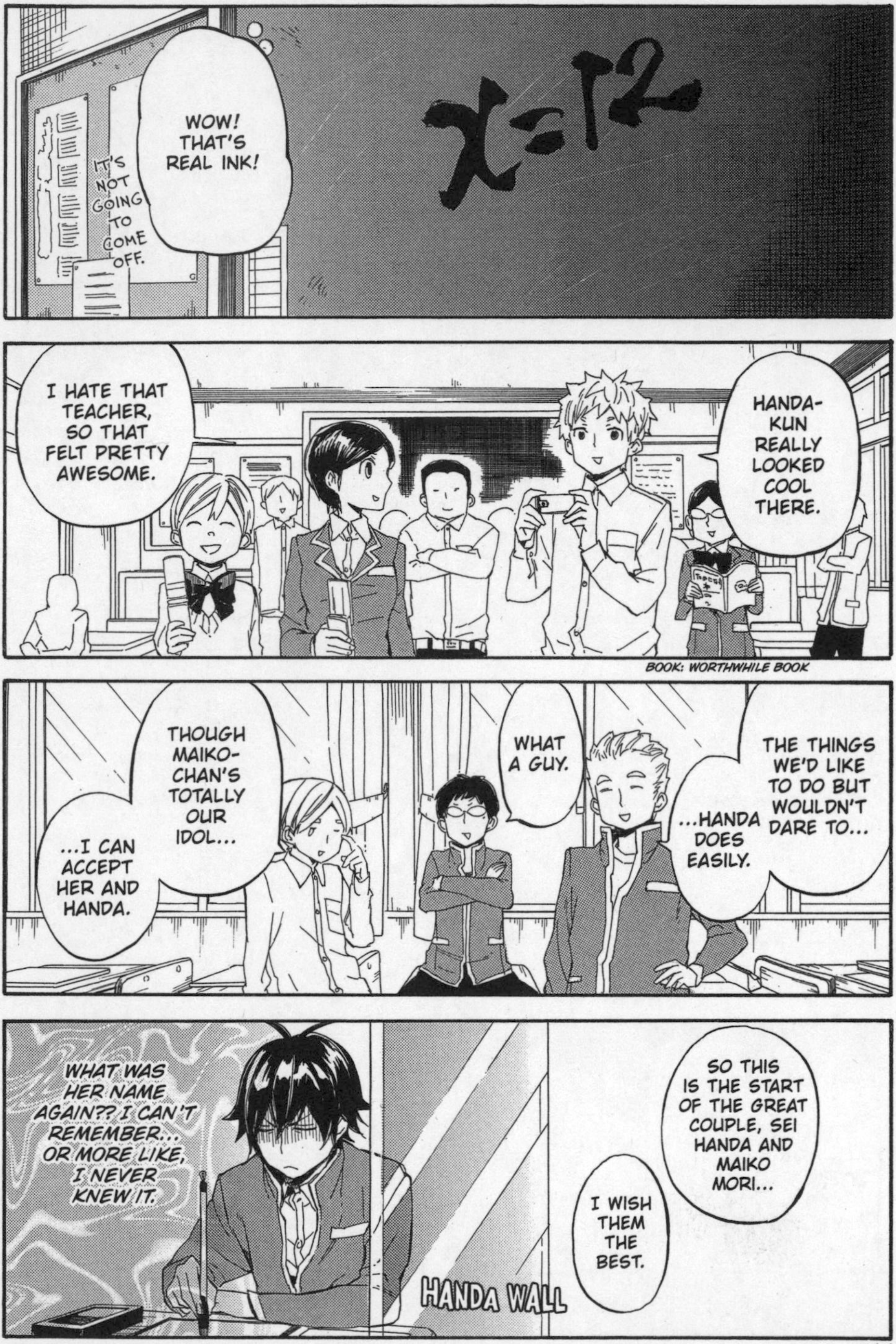
x=12
WOW! THAT'S REAL INK!
IT'S NOT GOING TO COME OFF.
HANDA-KUN REALLY LOOKED COOL THERE.
I HATE THAT TEACHER, SO THAT FELT PRETTY AWESOME.
THE THINGS WE'D LIKE TO DO BUT WOULDN'T DARE TO...
...HANDA DOES EASILY.
WHAT A GUY.
THOUGH MAIKO-CHAN'S TOTALLY OUR IDOL...
...I CAN ACCEPT HER AND HANDA.
SO THIS IS THE START OF THE GREAT COUPLE, SEI HANDA AND MAIKO MORI...
I WISH THEM THE BEST.
HANDA WALL
WHAT WAS HER NAME AGAIN?? I CAN'T REMEMBER... OR MORE LIKE, I NEVER KNEW IT.

BOOK: WORTHWHILE BOOK

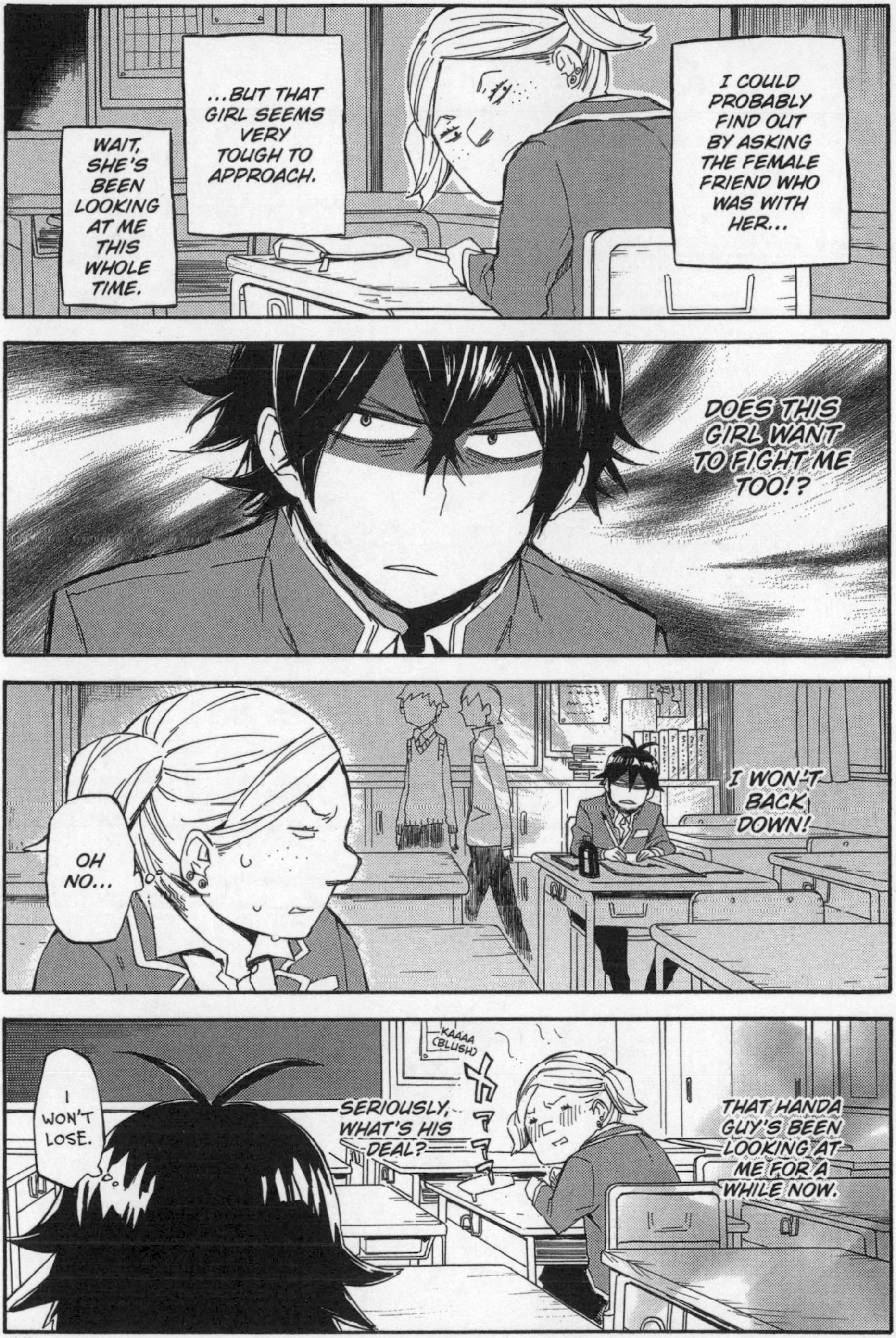
I COULD PROBABLY FIND OUT BY ASKING THE FEMALE FRIEND WHO WAS WITH HER...
...BUT THAT GIRL SEEMS VERY TOUGH TO APPROACH.
WAIT, SHE'S BEEN LOOKING AT ME THIS WHOLE TIME.
DOES THIS GIRL WANT TO FIGHT ME TOO!?
I WON'T BACK DOWN!
OH NO...
THAT HANDA GUY'S BEEN LOOKING AT ME FOR A WHILE NOW.
KAAAA (BLUSH)
SERIOUSLY, WHAT'S HIS DEAL?
I WON'T LOSE.

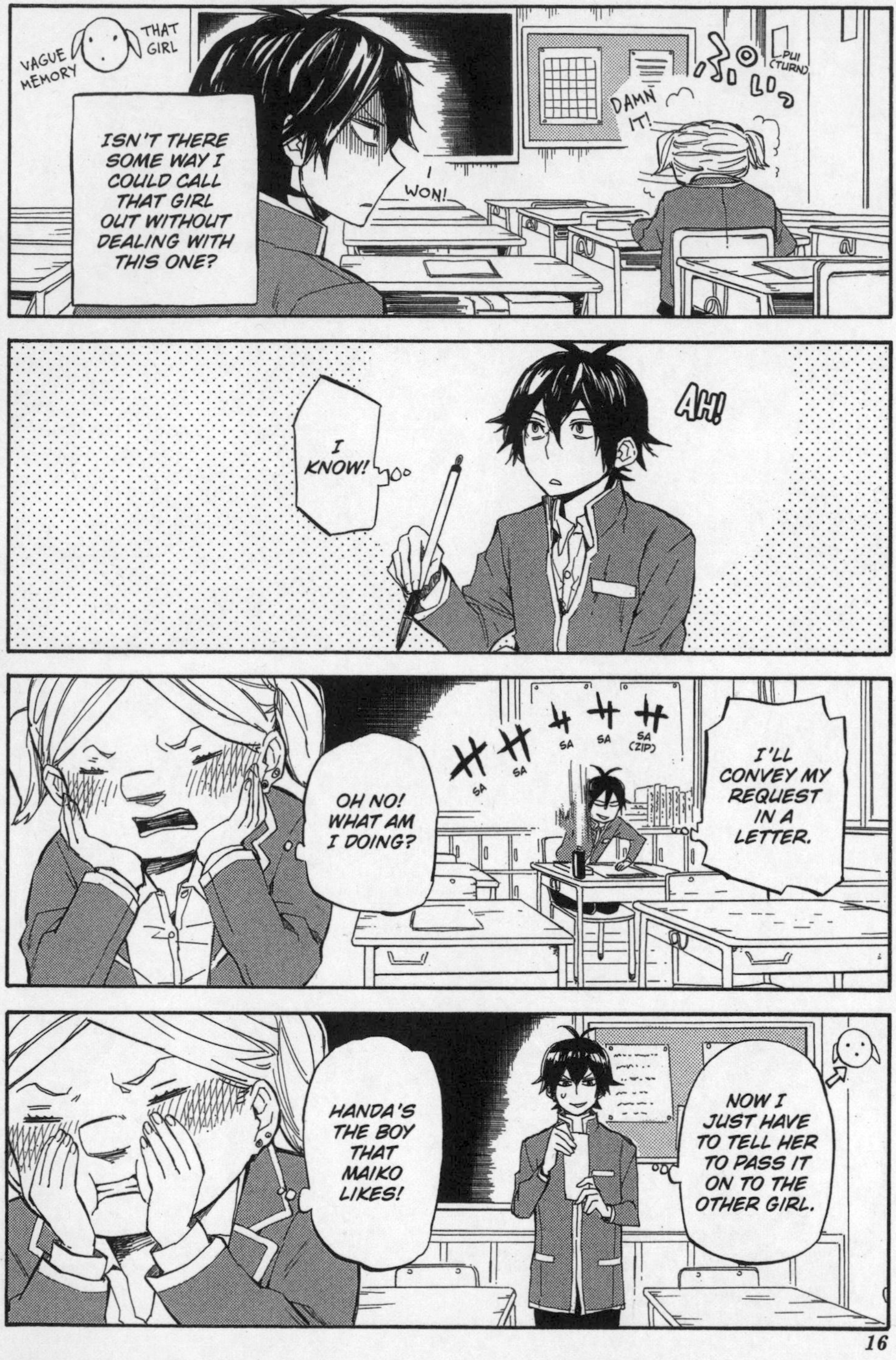
PUI (TURN)
DAMN IT!
I WON!
THAT GIRL
VAGUE MEMORY
ISN'T THERE SOME WAY I COULD CALL THAT GIRL OUT WITHOUT DEALING WITH THIS ONE?
AH!
I KNOW!
I'LL CONVEY MY REQUEST IN A LETTER.
SA (ZIP)
SA
SA
SA
SA
OH NO! WHAT AM I DOING?
NOW I JUST HAVE TO TELL HER TO PASS IT ON TO THE OTHER GIRL.
HANDA'S THE BOY THAT MAIKO LIKES!

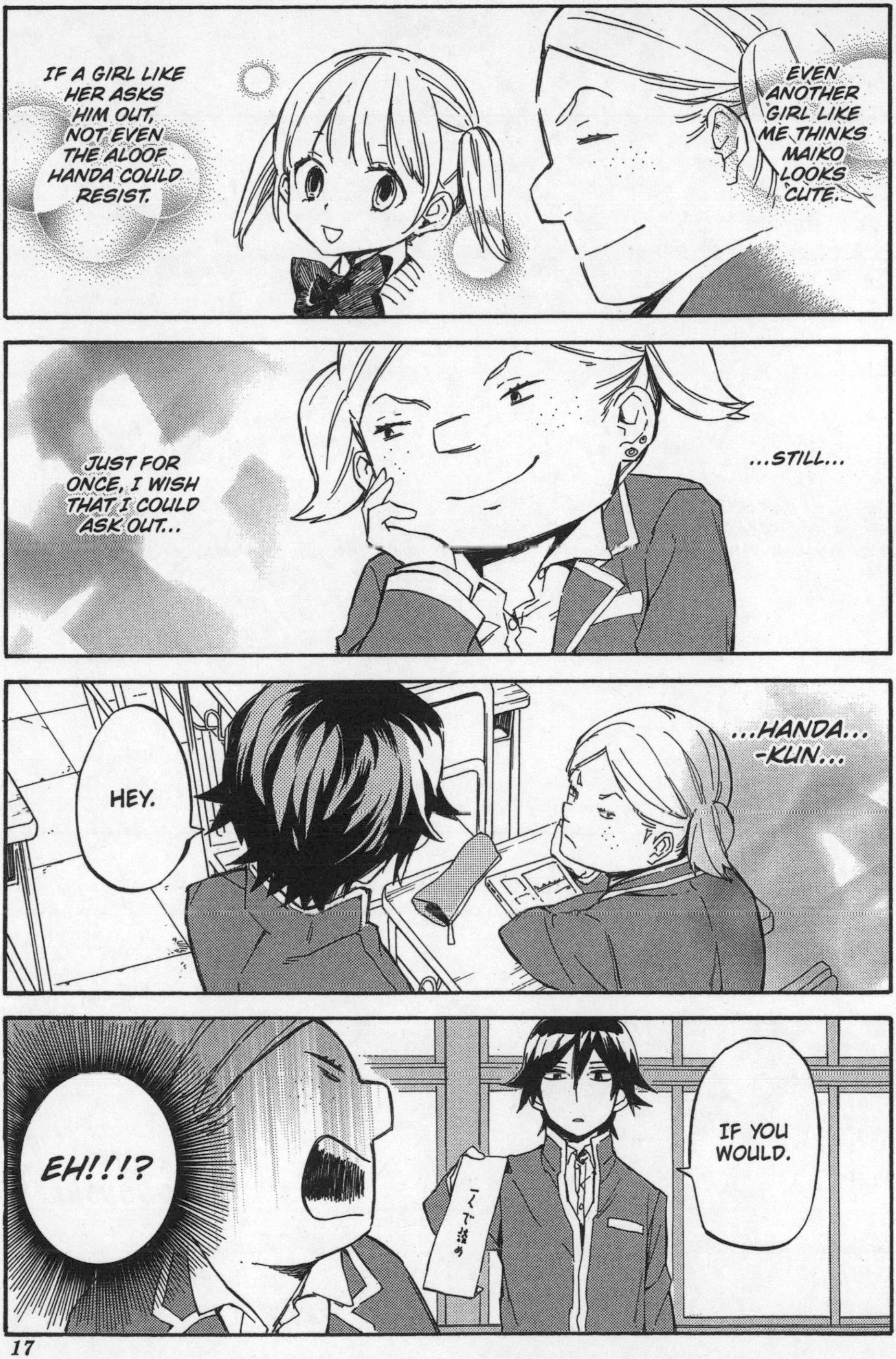
EVEN ANOTHER GIRL LIKE ME THINKS MAIKO LOOKS CUTE.
IF A GIRL LIKE HER ASKS HIM OUT, NOT EVEN THE ALOOF HANDA COULD RESIST.
...STILL...
JUST FOR ONCE, I WISH THAT I COULD ASK OUT...
...HANDA... -KUN...
HEY.
IF YOU WOULD.
一人で読め
EH!!!?

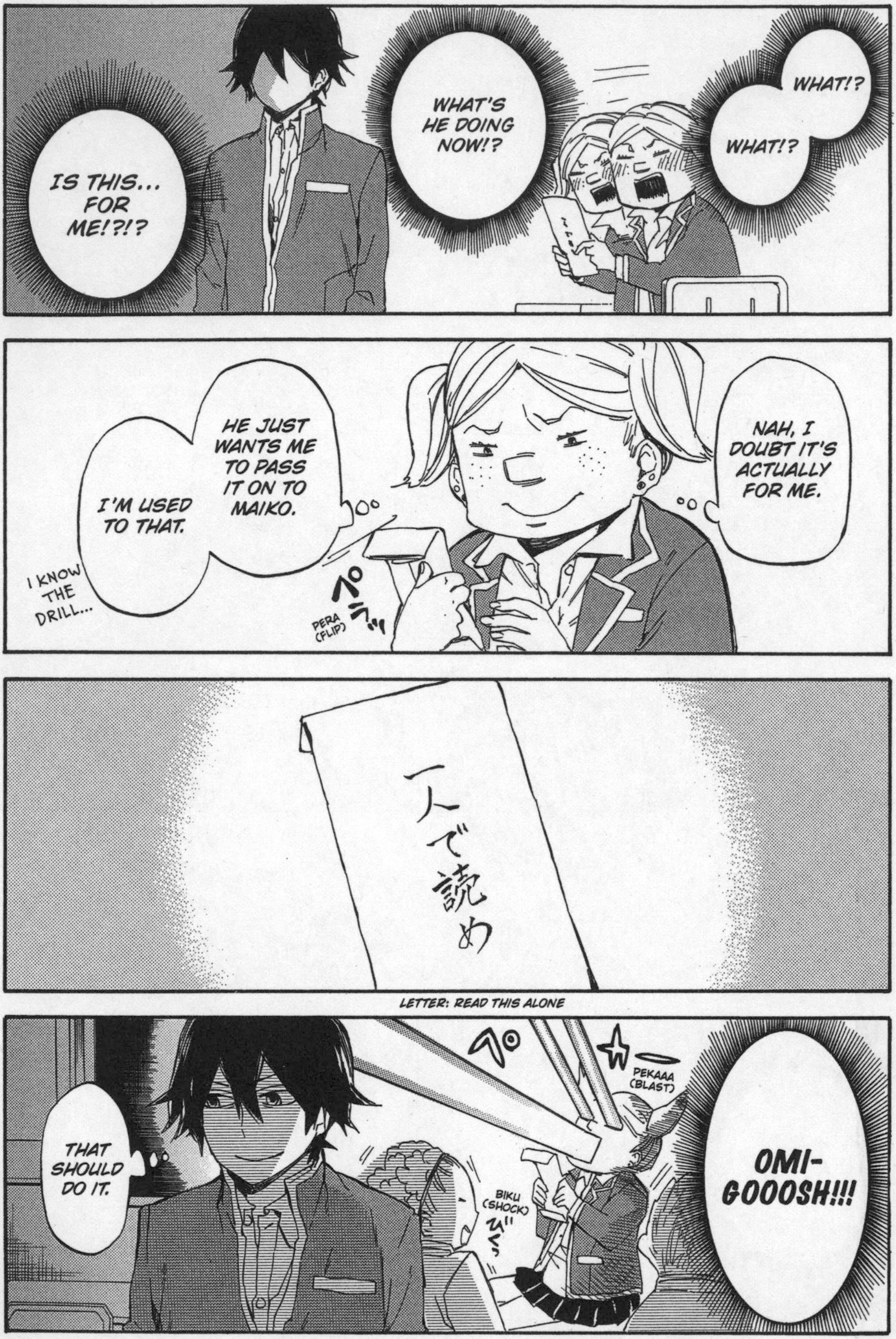
WHAT!?
WHAT!?
WHAT'S HE DOING NOW!?
IS THIS... FOR ME!?!?
NAH, I DOUBT IT'S ACTUALLY FOR ME.
HE JUST WANTS ME TO PASS IT ON TO MAIKO.
I'M USED TO THAT.
I KNOW THE DRILL...
PERA (FLIP)
一人で読め
LETTER: READ THIS ALONE
OMI-GOOOSH!!!
PEKAAA (BLAST)
BIKU (SHOCK)
THAT SHOULD DO IT.

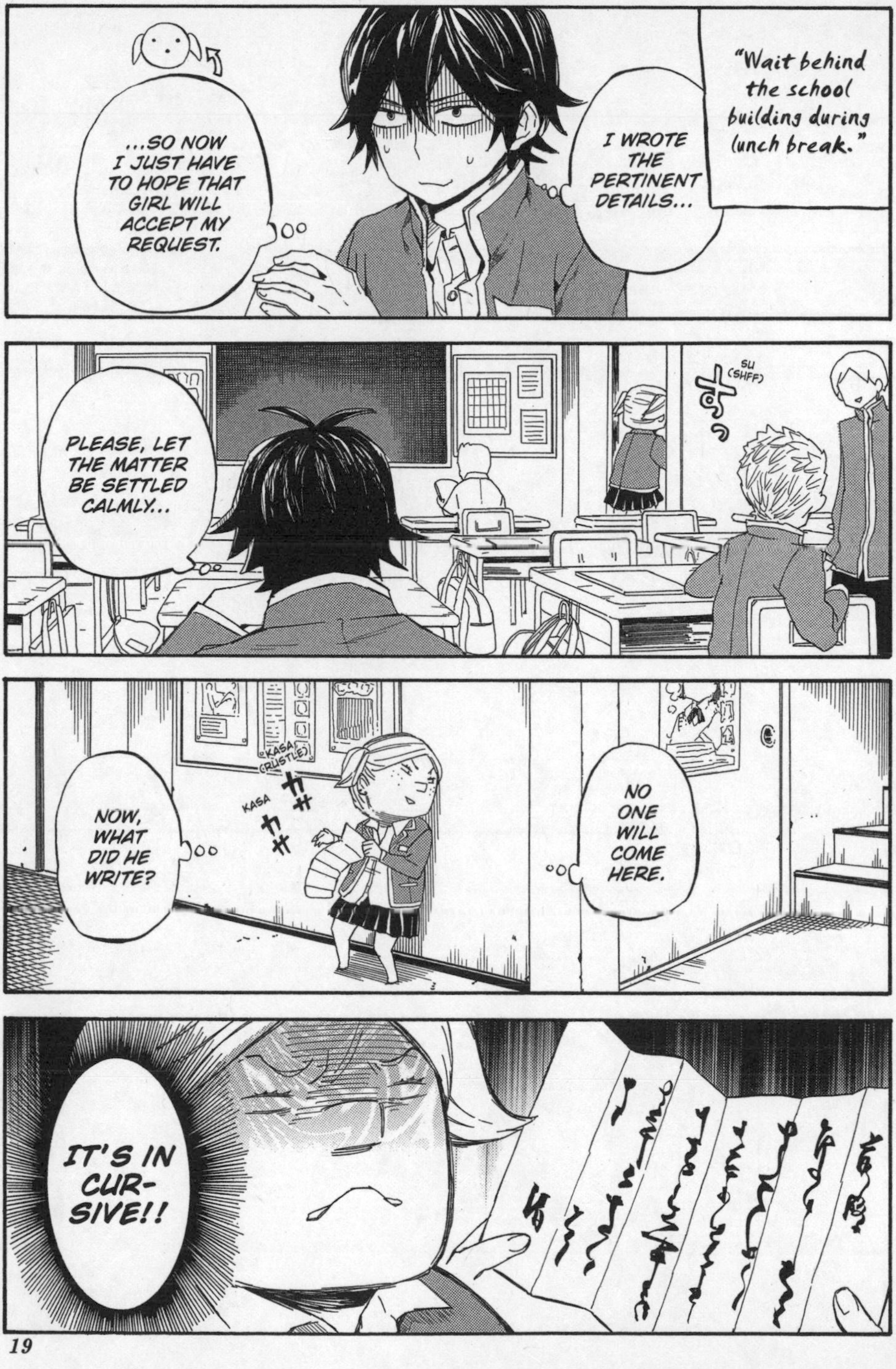
"Wait behind the school building during lunch break."
I WROTE THE PERTINENT DETAILS...
...SO NOW I JUST HAVE TO HOPE THAT GIRL WILL ACCEPT MY REQUEST.
SU (SHFF)
PLEASE, LET THE MATTER BE SETTLED CALMLY...
NO ONE WILL COME HERE.
KASA (RUSTLE)
KASA
NOW, WHAT DID HE WRITE?
IT'S IN CUR-SIVE!!

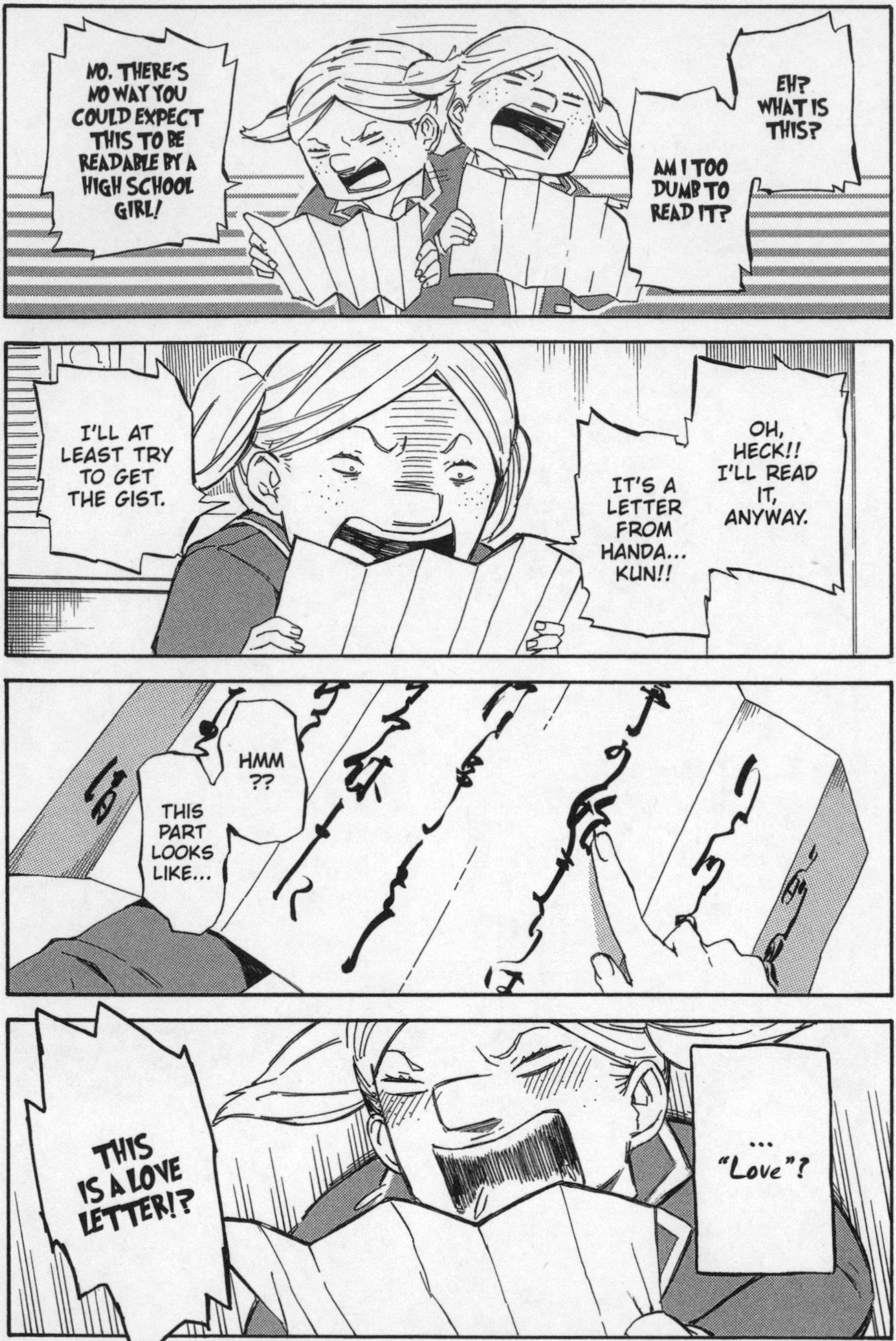
EH? WHAT IS THIS?
AM I TOO DUMB TO READ IT?
NO. THERE'S NO WAY YOU COULD EXPECT THIS TO BE READABLE BY A HIGH SCHOOL GIRL!
OH, HECK!! I'LL READ IT, ANYWAY.
IT'S A LETTER FROM HANDA... KUN!!
I'LL AT LEAST TRY TO GET THE GIST.
HMM ??
THIS PART LOOKS LIKE...
... "Love"?
THIS IS A LOVE LETTER!?

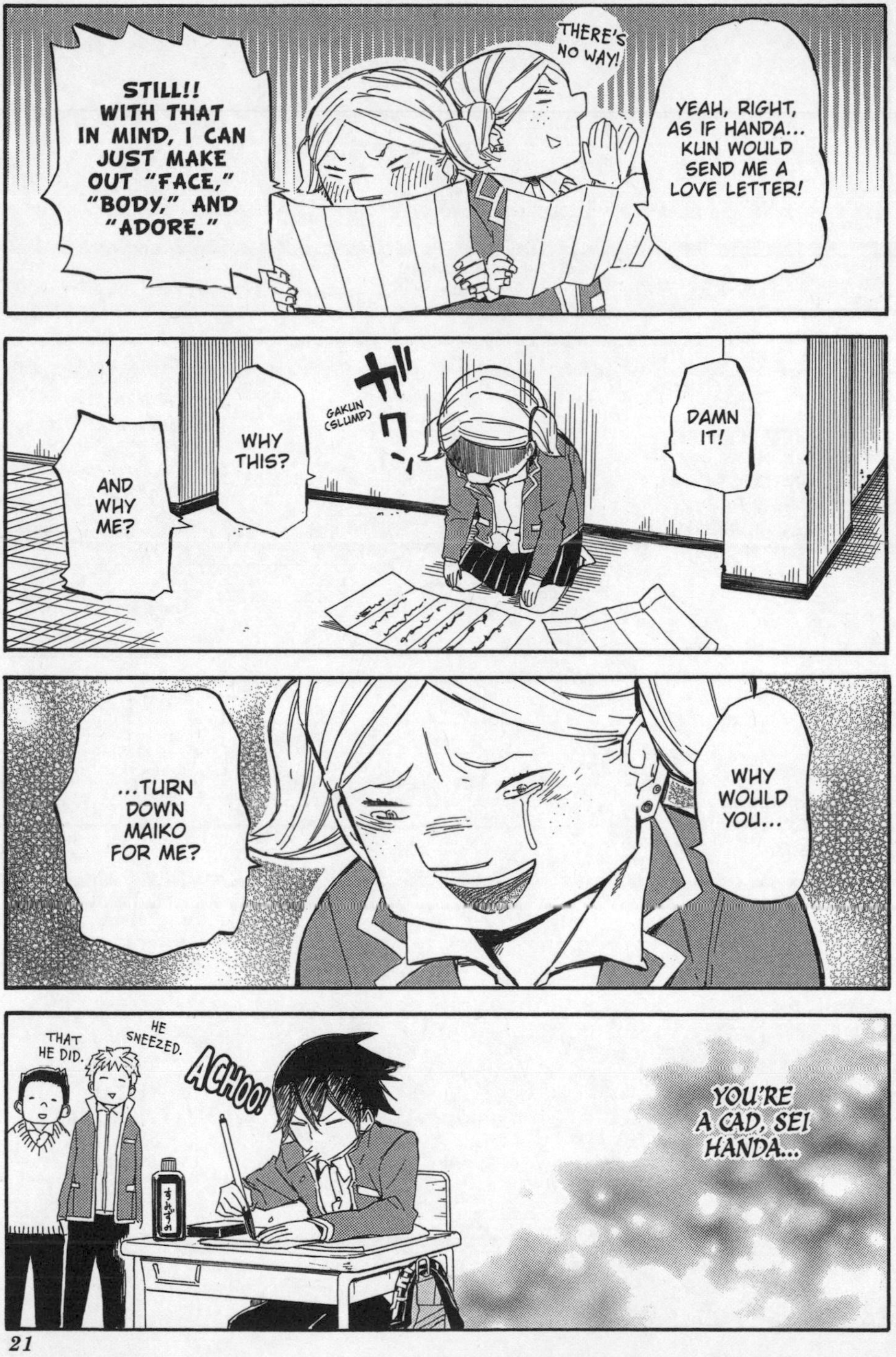
YEAH, RIGHT, AS IF HANDA... KUN WOULD SEND ME A LOVE LETTER!
THERE'S NO WAY!
STILL!! WITH THAT IN MIND, I CAN JUST MAKE OUT "FACE," "BODY," AND "ADORE."
DAMN IT!
GAKUN (SLUMP)
WHY THIS?
AND WHY ME?
WHY WOULD YOU...
...TURN DOWN MAIKO FOR ME?
YOU'RE A CAD, SEI HANDA...
ACHOO!
HE SNEEZED.
THAT HE DID.

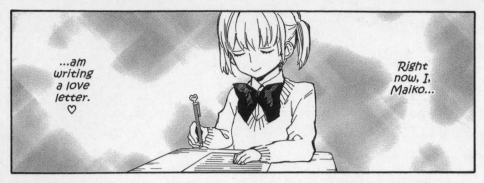

Right now, I, Maiko...
...am writing a love letter. ♡
I fell in love with Handa-kun at first sight at the entrance ceremony...
To my best-best-best-loved Handa-kun,
When I saw you at the entrance ceremony,
I fell in love with you
Handa-kun.♡
...and while we have never been in the same class, I have always, always loved him.
Let my love bear fruit.
Let it reach across the sky.
LET IT CROSS THE OCEAN ON A DOLPHIN'S BACK.
MORI'S CUTE, BUT THIS MUCH IS JUST LETHAL.
SHUBA (LUNGE)
YOU IDIOT! THAT'S THE WHOLE APPEAL!
SHE'S PUTTING HER ALL INTO IT!

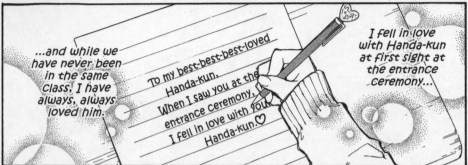

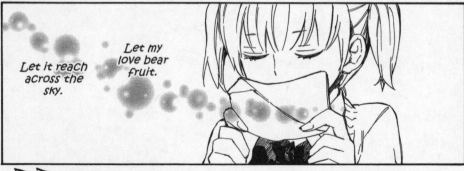

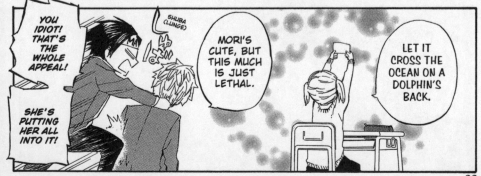

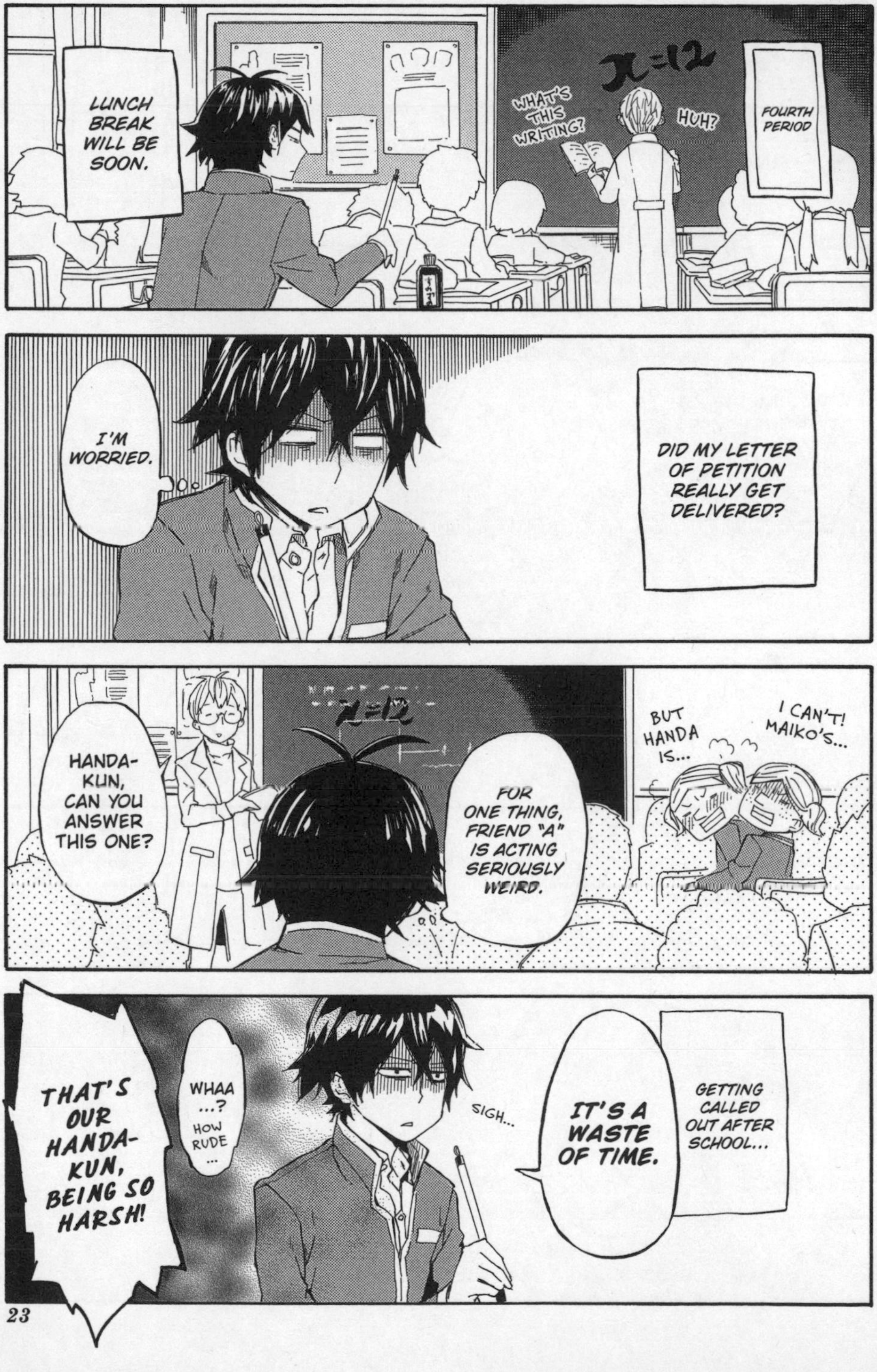
FOURTH PERIOD
HUH?
WHAT'S THIS WRITING?
LUNCH BREAK WILL BE SOON.
DID MY LETTER OF PETITION REALLY GET DELIVERED?
I'M WORRIED.
I CAN'T! MAIKO'S...
BUT HANDA IS...
FOR ONE THING, FRIEND "A" IS ACTING SERIOUSLY WEIRD.
HANDA-KUN, CAN YOU ANSWER THIS ONE?
GETTING CALLED OUT AFTER SCHOOL...
IT'S A WASTE OF TIME.
SIGH...
WHAA ...? HOW RUDE ...
THAT'S OUR HANDA-KUN, BEING SO HARSH!

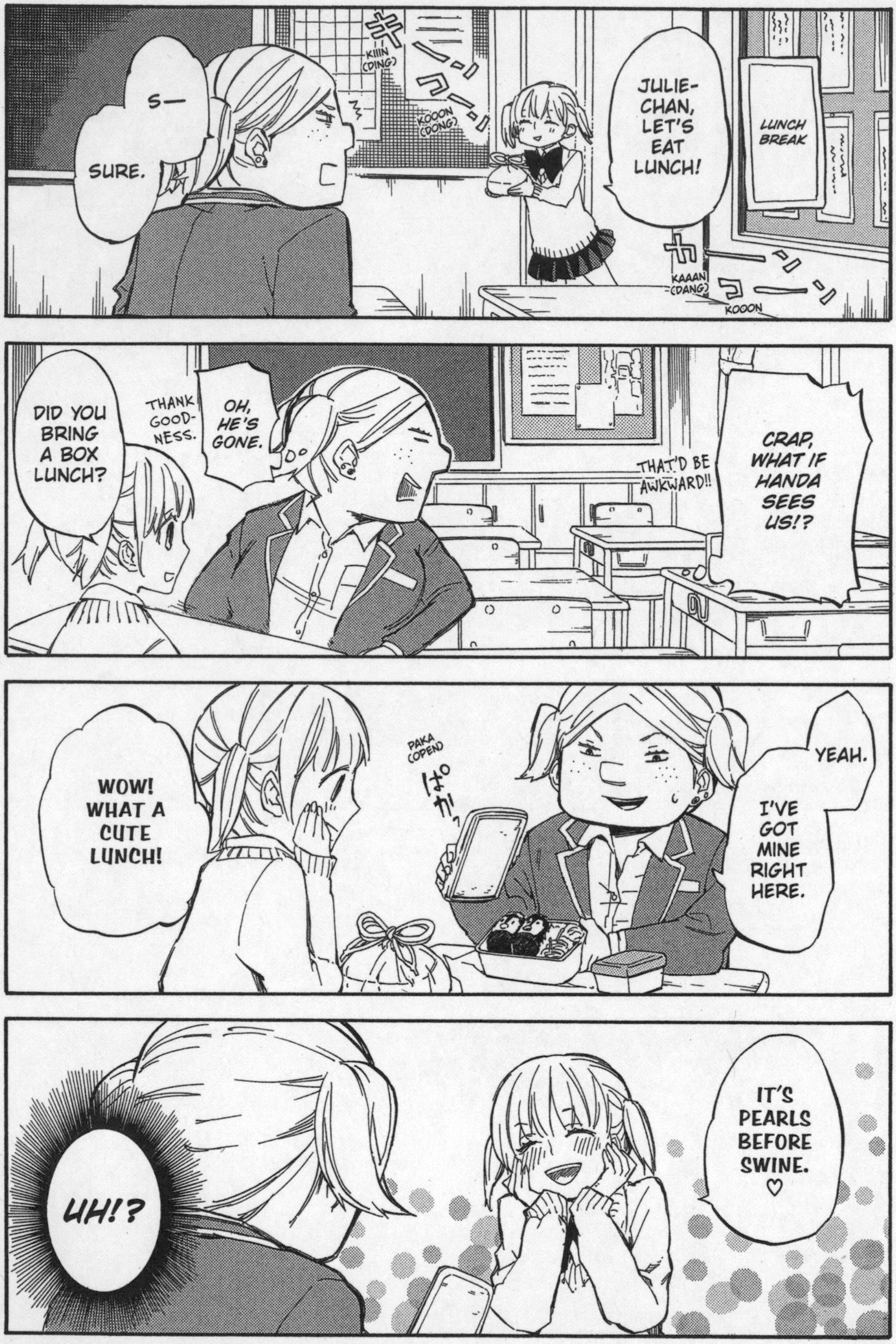
LUNCH BREAK
JULIE-CHAN, LET'S EAT LUNCH!
KAAAN (DANG)
KOOON
KIIIN (DING)
KOOON (DONG)
S— SURE.
CRAP, WHAT IF HANDA SEES US!?
THAT'D BE AWKWARD!!
OH, HE'S GONE.
THANK GOODNESS.
DID YOU BRING A BOX LUNCH?
YEAH.
I'VE GOT MINE RIGHT HERE.
PAKA (OPEN)
WOW! WHAT A CUTE LUNCH!
IT'S PEARLS BEFORE SWINE. ♡
UH!?

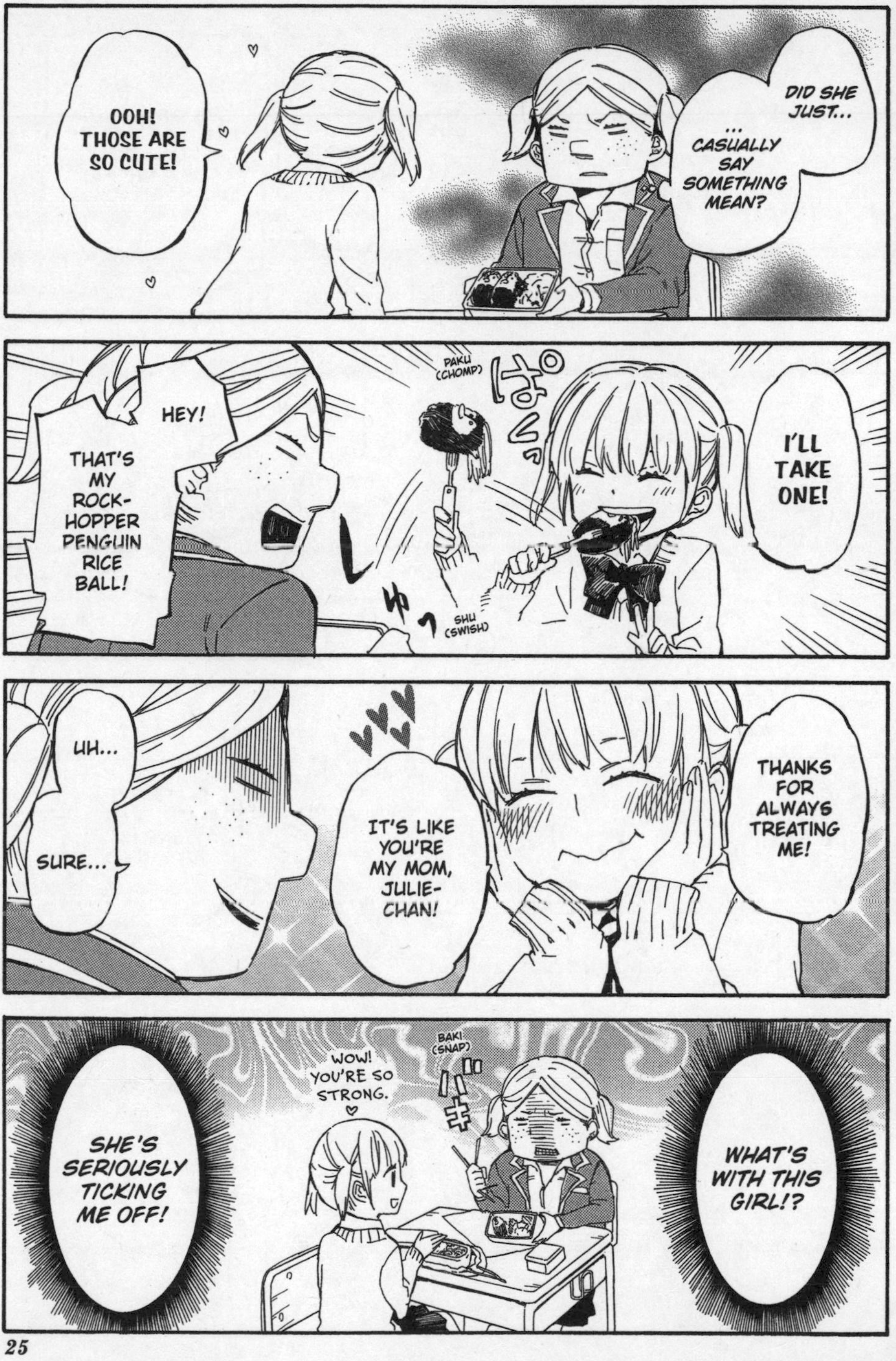
DID SHE JUST... ...CASUALLY SAY SOMETHING MEAN?
OOH! THOSE ARE SO CUTE!
I'LL TAKE ONE!
PAKU (CHOMP)
SHU (SWISH)
HEY!
THAT'S MY ROCK-HOPPER PENGUIN RICE BALL!
THANKS FOR ALWAYS TREATING ME!
IT'S LIKE YOU'RE MY MOM, JULIE-CHAN!
UH...
SURE...
WHAT'S WITH THIS GIRL!?
BAKI (SNAP)
WOW! YOU'RE SO STRONG.
SHE'S SERIOUSLY TICKING ME OFF!

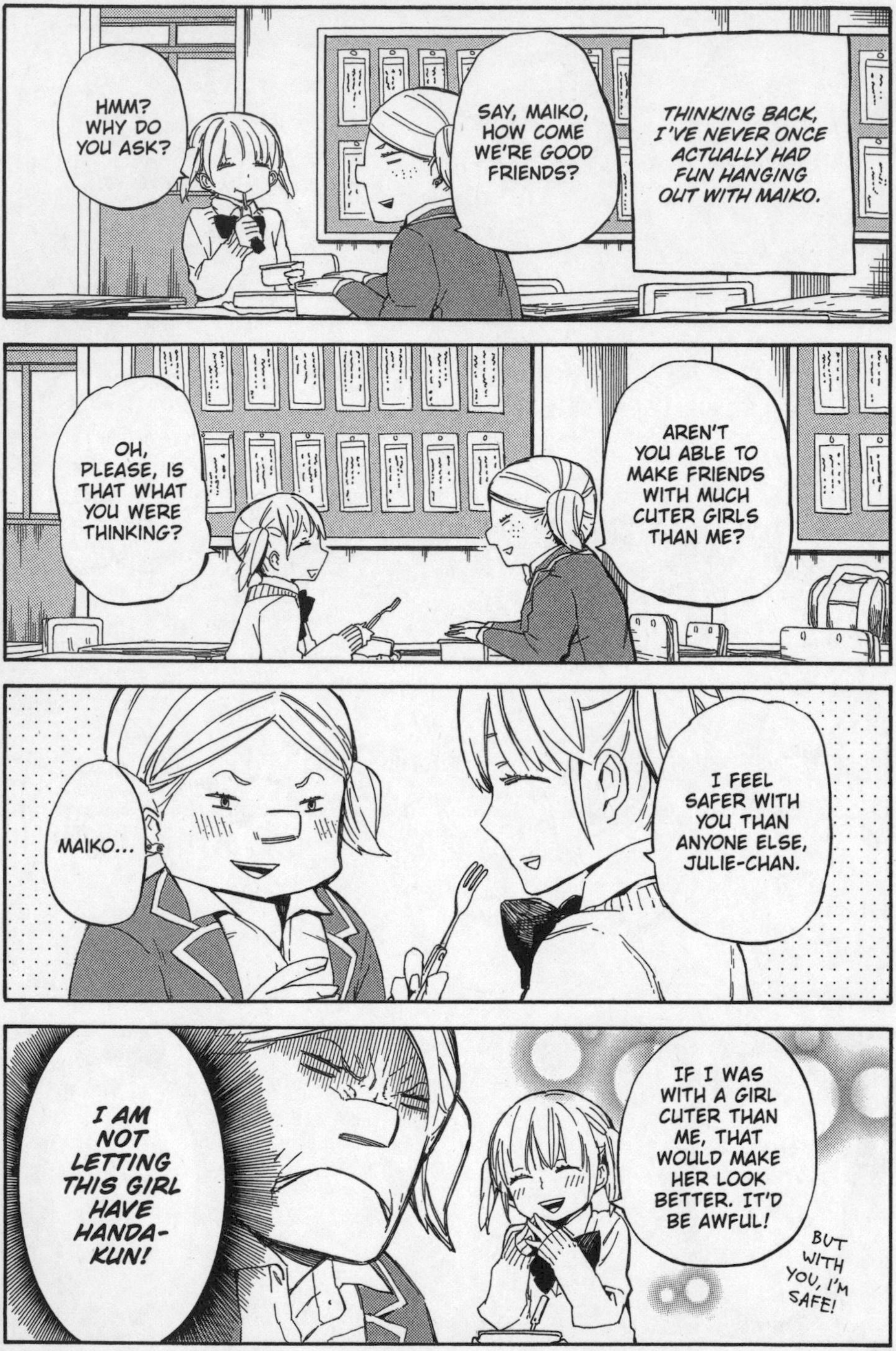
THINKING BACK, I'VE NEVER ONCE ACTUALLY HAD FUN HANGING OUT WITH MAIKO.
SAY, MAIKO, HOW COME WE'RE GOOD FRIENDS?
HMM? WHY DO YOU ASK?
AREN'T YOU ABLE TO MAKE FRIENDS WITH MUCH CUTER GIRLS THAN ME?
OH, PLEASE, IS THAT WHAT YOU WERE THINKING?
I FEEL SAFER WITH YOU THAN ANYONE ELSE, JULIE-CHAN.
MAIKO...
IF I WAS WITH A GIRL CUTER THAN ME, THAT WOULD MAKE HER LOOK BETTER. IT'D BE AWFUL!
BUT WITH YOU, I'M SAFE!
I AM NOT LETTING THIS GIRL HAVE HANDA-KUN!

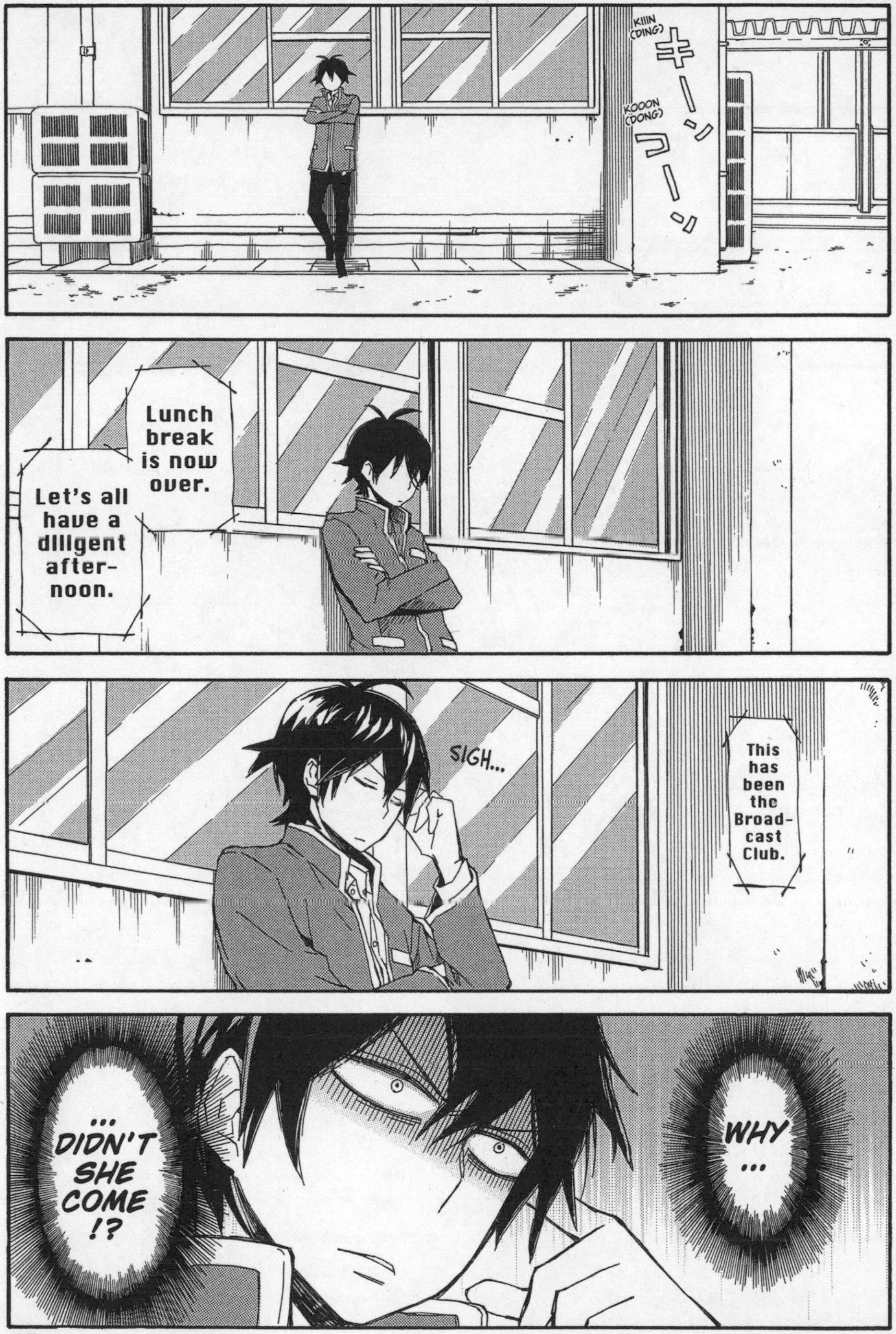
KIIIN (DING)
キーン
KOOON (DONG)
コーン
Lunch break is now over.
Let's all have a diligent after-noon.
This has been the Broad-cast Club.
SIGH...
WHY ...
... DIDN'T SHE COME !?

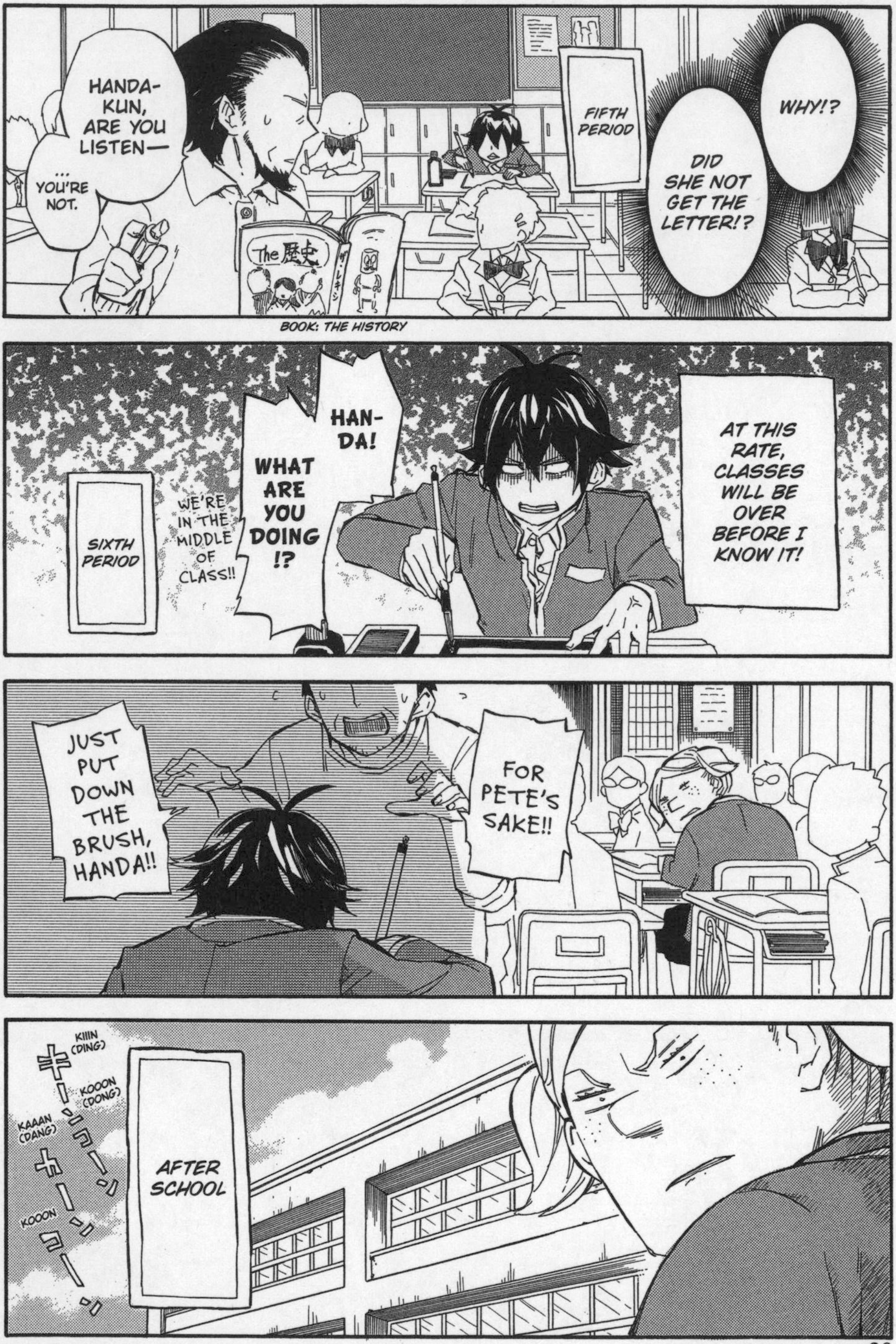
WHY!?
DID SHE NOT GET THE LETTER!?
FIFTH PERIOD
HANDA-KUN, ARE YOU LISTEN—
... YOU'RE NOT.
The 歴史
BOOK: THE HISTORY
AT THIS RATE, CLASSES WILL BE OVER BEFORE I KNOW IT!
HANDA! WHAT ARE YOU DOING!?
WE'RE IN THE MIDDLE OF CLASS!!
SIXTH PERIOD
FOR PETE'S SAKE!!
JUST PUT DOWN THE BRUSH, HANDA!!
AFTER SCHOOL
KIIIN (DING)
KOOON (DONG)
KAAAN (DANG)
KOOON

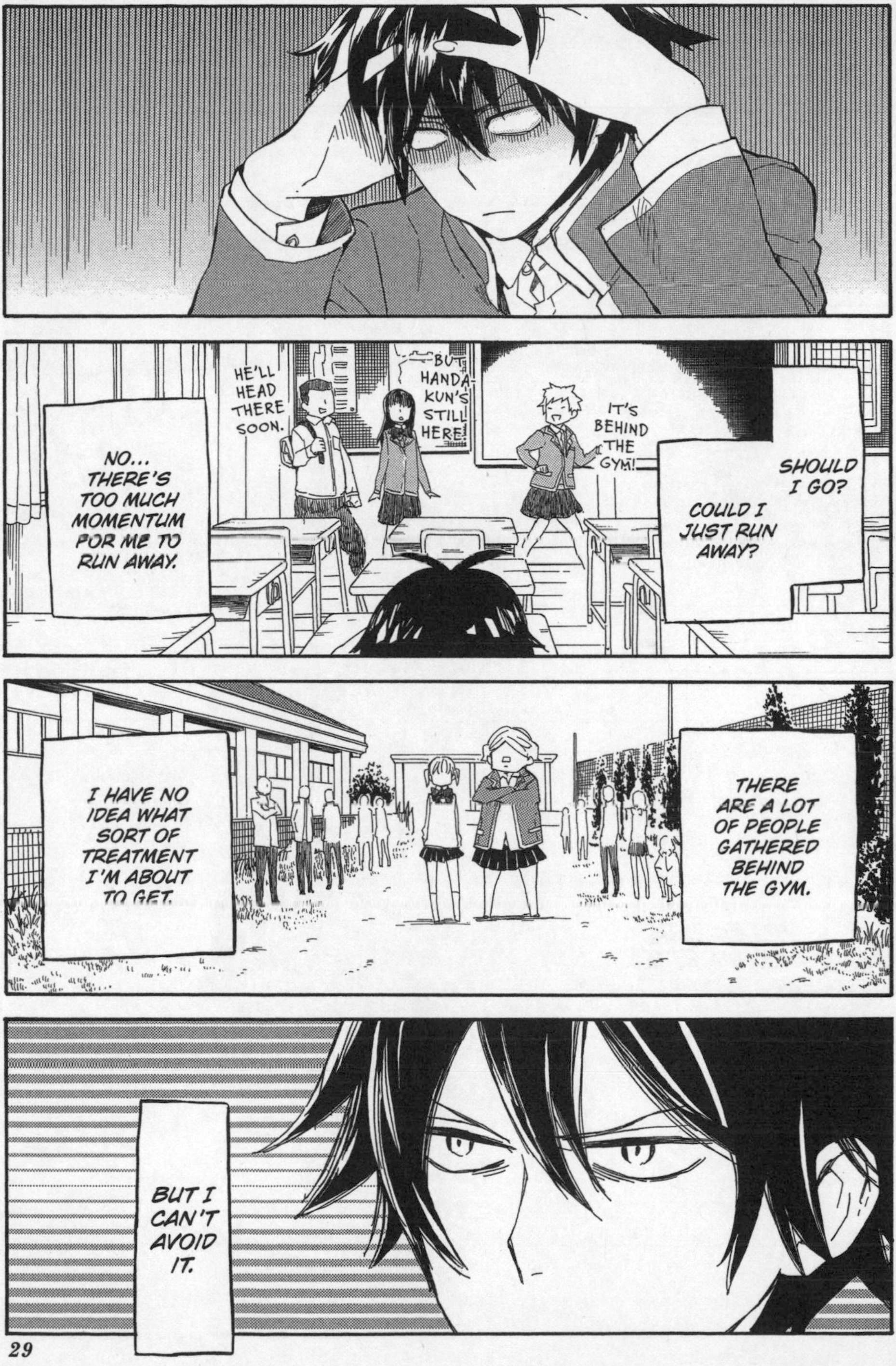
SHOULD I GO?
COULD I JUST RUN AWAY?
IT'S BEHIND THE GYM!
BUT HANDA-KUN'S STILL HERE!
HE'LL HEAD THERE SOON.
NO... THERE'S TOO MUCH MOMENTUM FOR ME TO RUN AWAY.
THERE ARE A LOT OF PEOPLE GATHERED BEHIND THE GYM.
I HAVE NO IDEA WHAT SORT OF TREATMENT I'M ABOUT TO GET.
BUT I CAN'T AVOID IT.

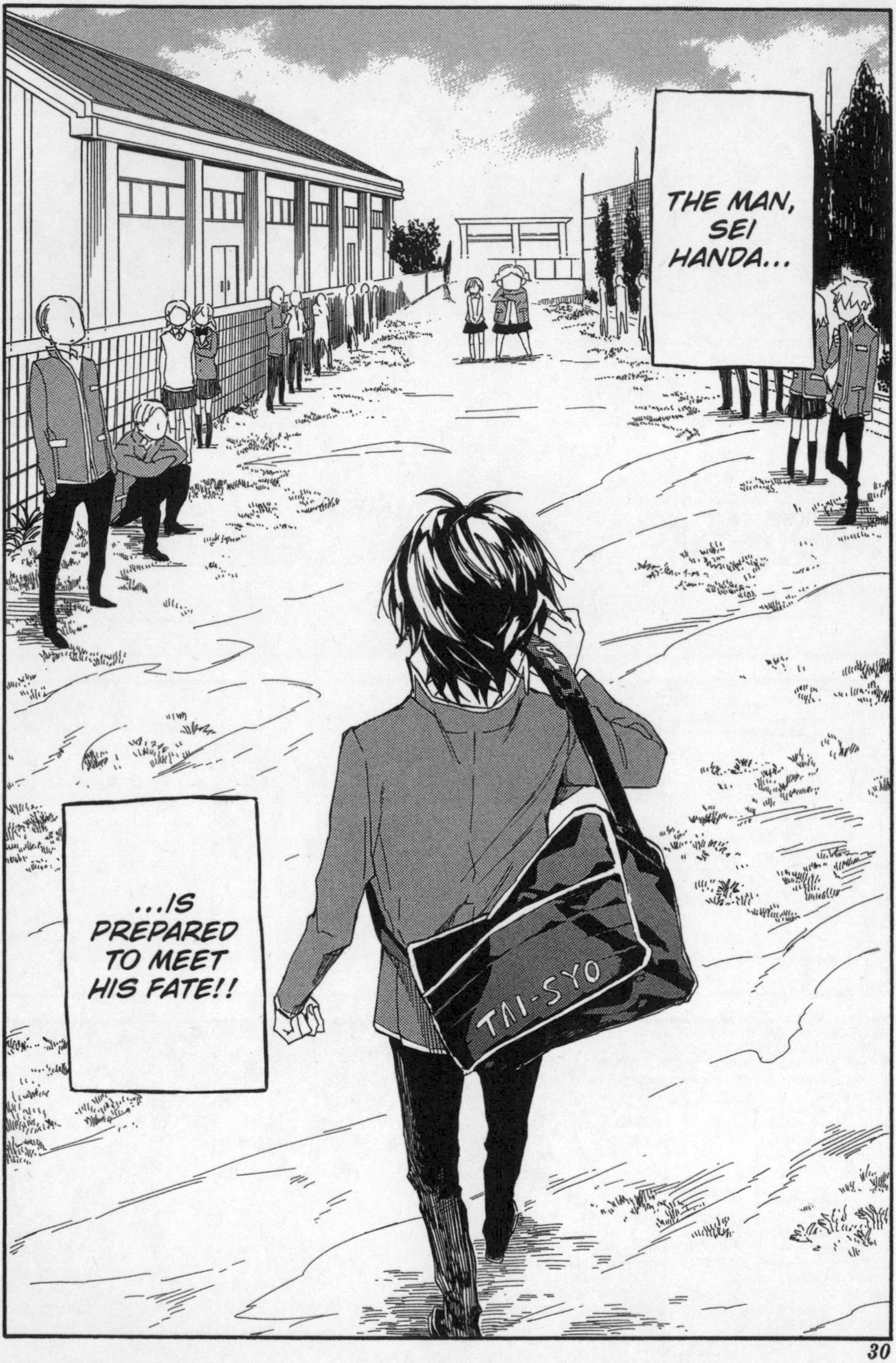
THE MAN, SEI HANDA...
...IS PREPARED TO MEET HIS FATE!!
TAI-SYO

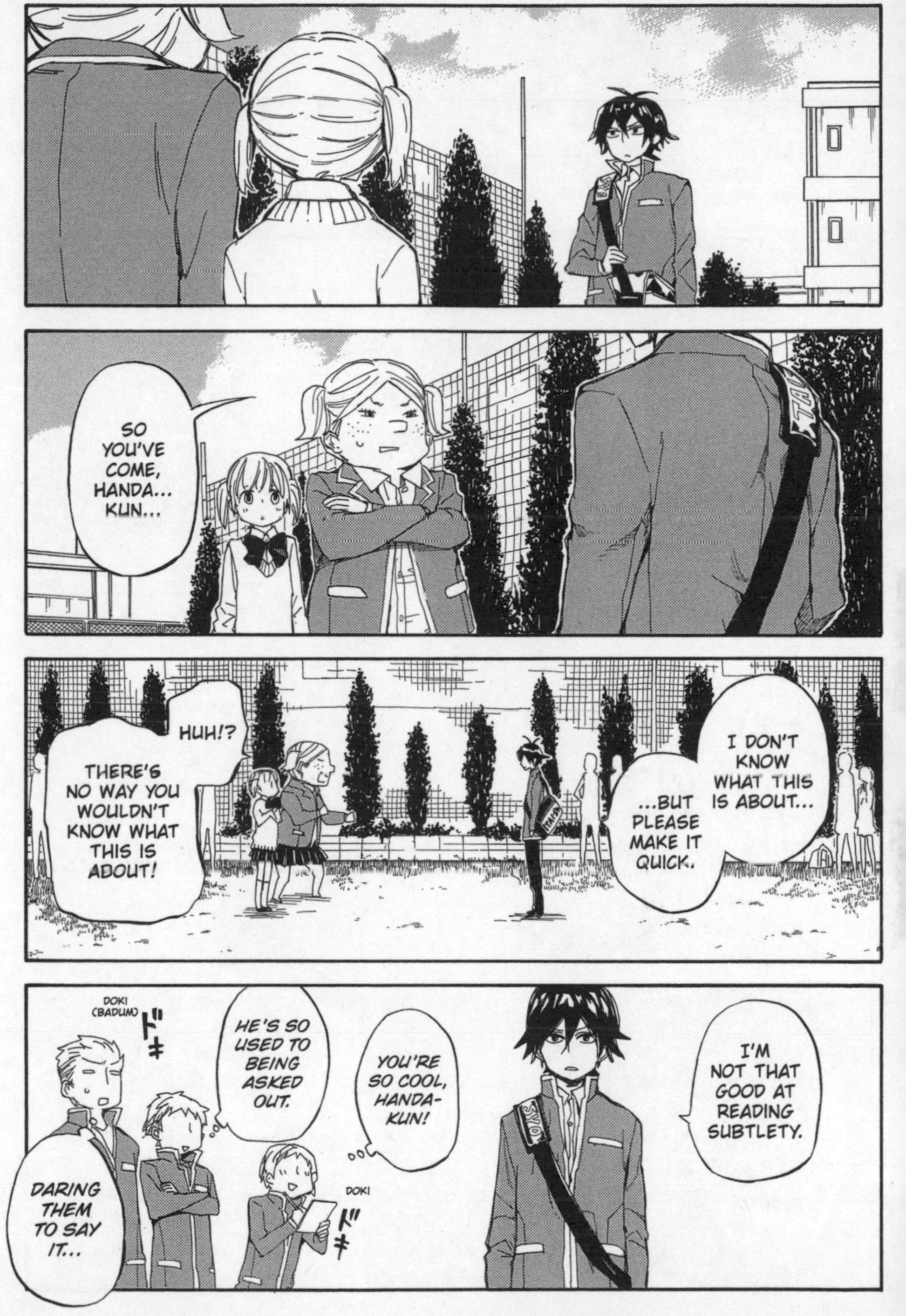
SO YOU'VE COME, HANDA... KUN...
I DON'T KNOW WHAT THIS IS ABOUT...
...BUT PLEASE MAKE IT QUICK.
HUH!?
THERE'S NO WAY YOU WOULDN'T KNOW WHAT THIS IS ABOUT!
I'M NOT THAT GOOD AT READING SUBTLETY.
YOU'RE SO COOL, HANDA-KUN!
HE'S SO USED TO BEING ASKED OUT.
DOKI (BADUM)
ドキ
DOKI
ドキ
DARING THEM TO SAY IT...

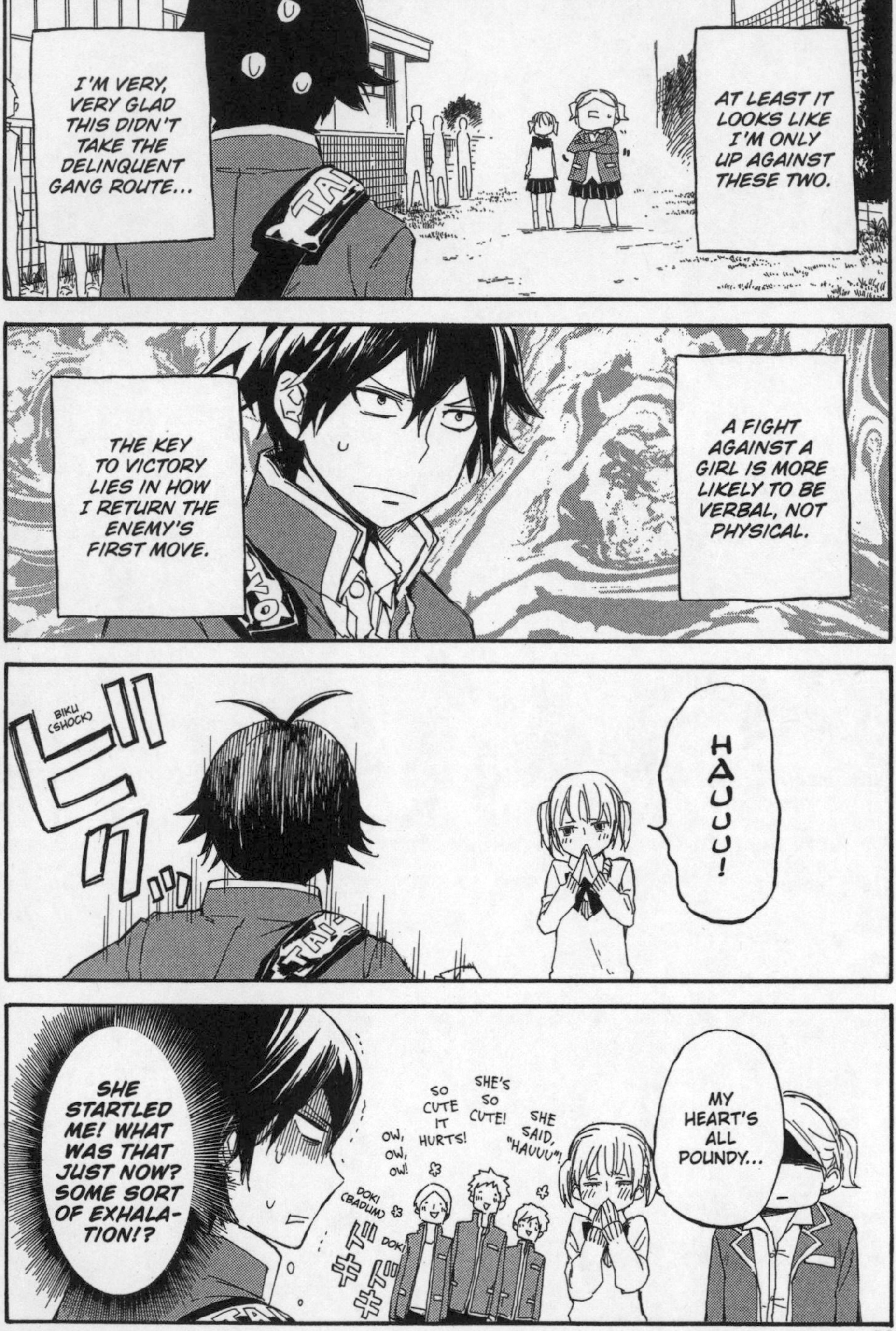
AT LEAST IT LOOKS LIKE I'M ONLY UP AGAINST THESE TWO.
I'M VERY, VERY GLAD THIS DIDN'T TAKE THE DELINQUENT GANG ROUTE...
A FIGHT AGAINST A GIRL IS MORE LIKELY TO BE VERBAL, NOT PHYSICAL.
THE KEY TO VICTORY LIES IN HOW I RETURN THE ENEMY'S FIRST MOVE.
HAUUU!
BIKU (SHOCK)
MY HEART'S ALL POUNDY...
SHE SAID, "HAUUU"!
SHE'S SO CUTE!
SO CUTE IT HURTS!
OW, OW, OW!
DOKI (BADUM)
SHE STARTLED ME! WHAT WAS THAT JUST NOW? SOME SORT OF EXHALA-TION!?

I'M TOO NERVOUS TO SAY IT...
...SO I BROUGHT A LETTER.
DOKI
ドキ
DOKI
ドキ
PLEASE ACCEPT TH—
BASUN (TWHACK)
ばすん
SORRY. MY HAND SLIPPED.
!?

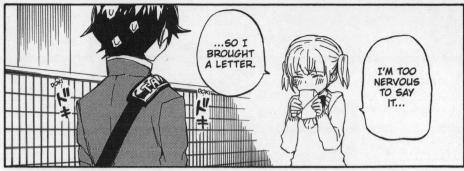

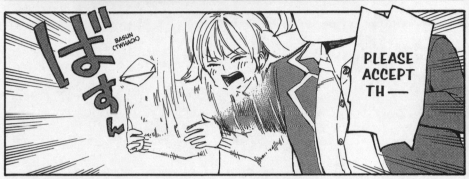

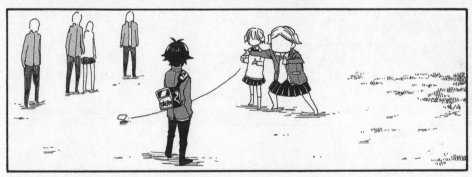

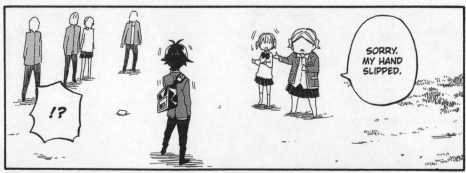

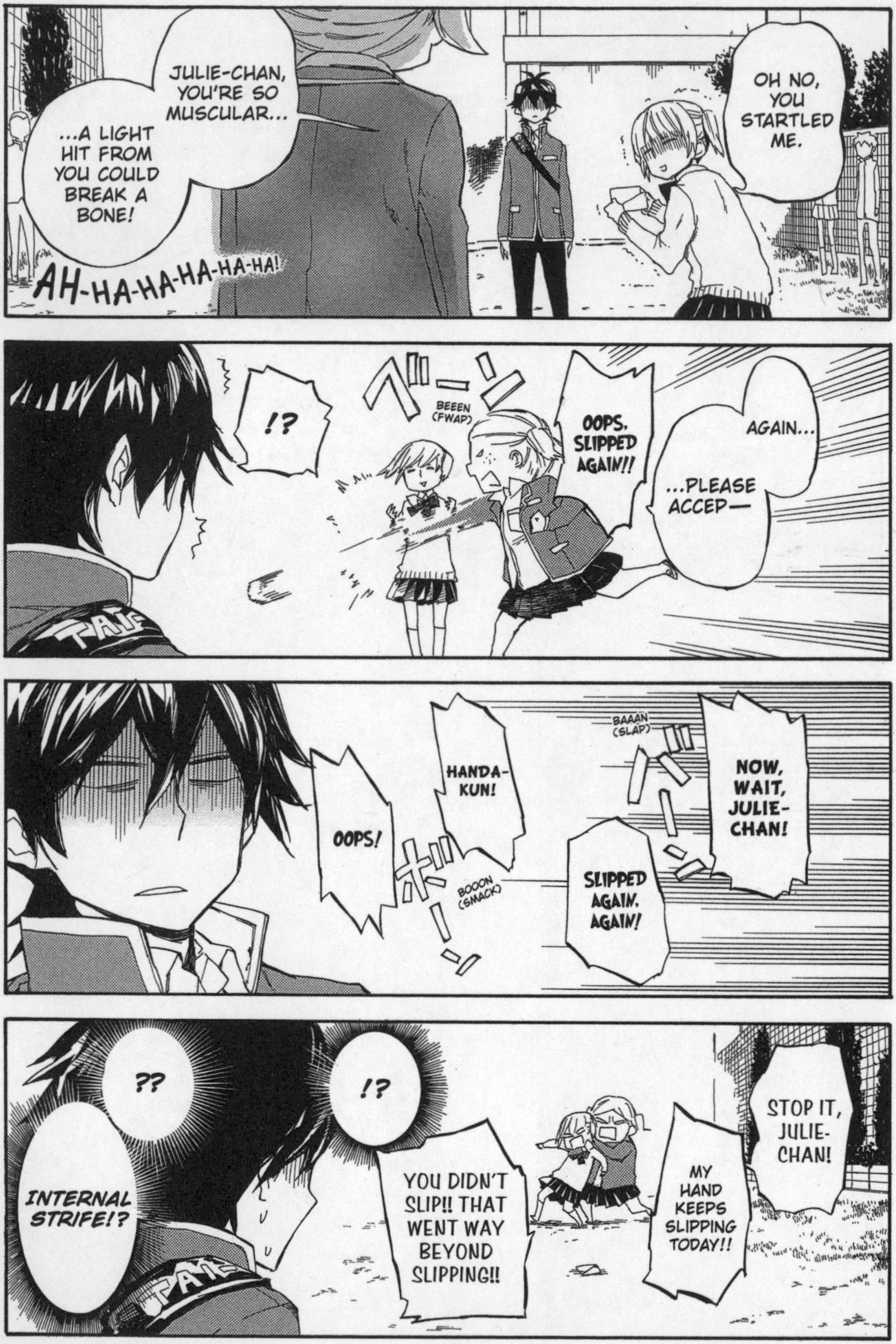
OH NO, YOU STARTLED ME.
JULIE-CHAN, YOU'RE SO MUSCULAR...
...A LIGHT HIT FROM YOU COULD BREAK A BONE!
AH-HA-HA-HA-HA-HA!
AGAIN... ...PLEASE ACCEP—
OOPS, SLIPPED AGAIN!!
BEEEN (FWAP)
!?
NOW, WAIT, JULIE-CHAN!
BAAAN (SLAP)
SLIPPED AGAIN, AGAIN!
HANDA-KUN!
BOOON (SMACK)
OOPS!
STOP IT, JULIE-CHAN!
MY HAND KEEPS SLIPPING TODAY!!
YOU DIDN'T SLIP!! THAT WENT WAY BEYOND SLIPPING!!
!?
??
INTERNAL STRIFE!?

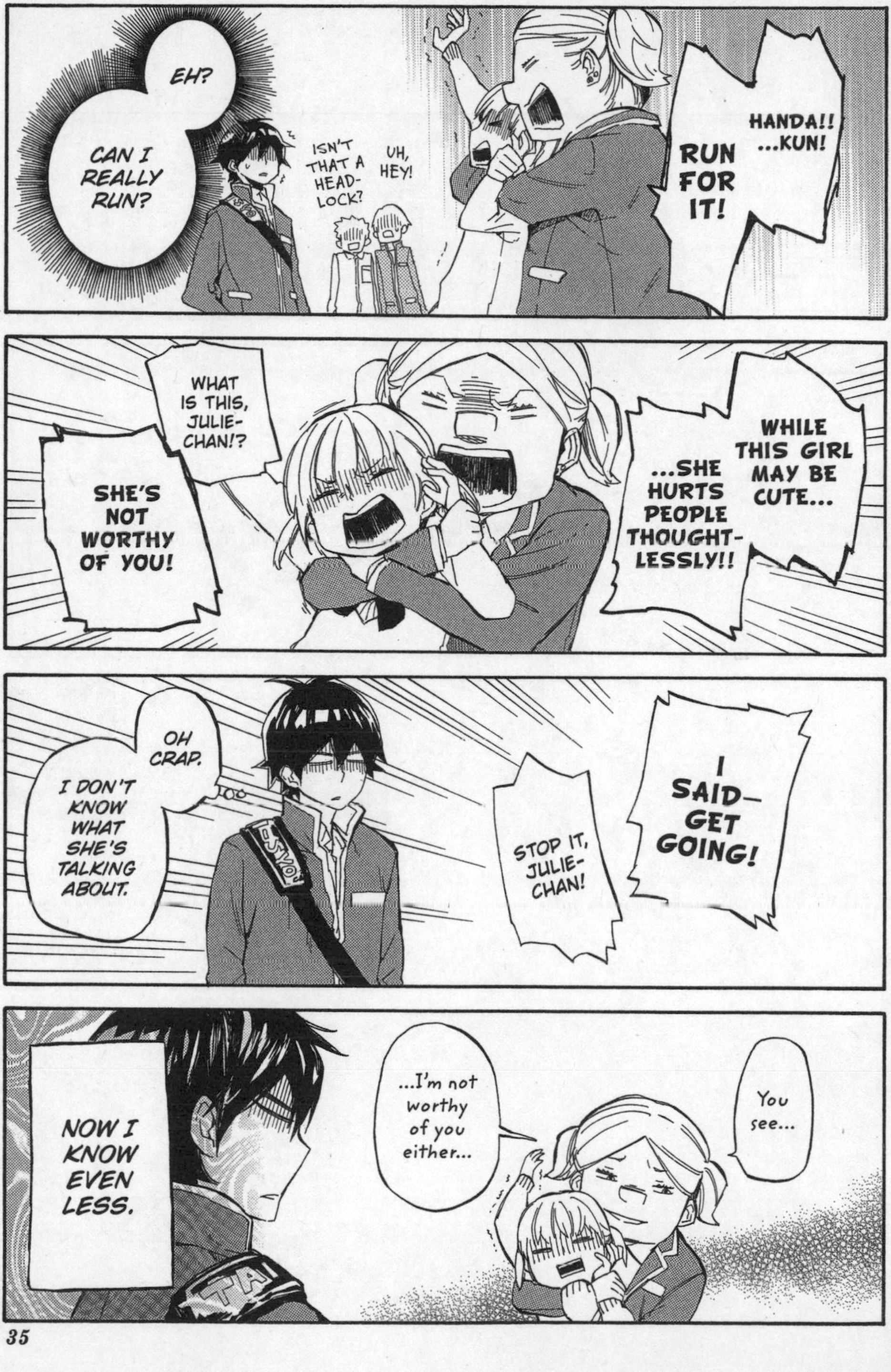
HANDA!! ...KUN!
RUN FOR IT!
UH, HEY!
ISN'T THAT A HEAD-LOCK?
EH?
CAN I REALLY RUN?
WHILE THIS GIRL MAY BE CUTE...
...SHE HURTS PEOPLE THOUGHT-LESSLY!!
WHAT IS THIS, JULIE-CHAN!?
SHE'S NOT WORTHY OF YOU!
I SAID—GET GOING!
STOP IT, JULIE-CHAN!
OH CRAP.
I DON'T KNOW WHAT SHE'S TALKING ABOUT.
You see...
...I'm not worthy of you either...
NOW I KNOW EVEN LESS.

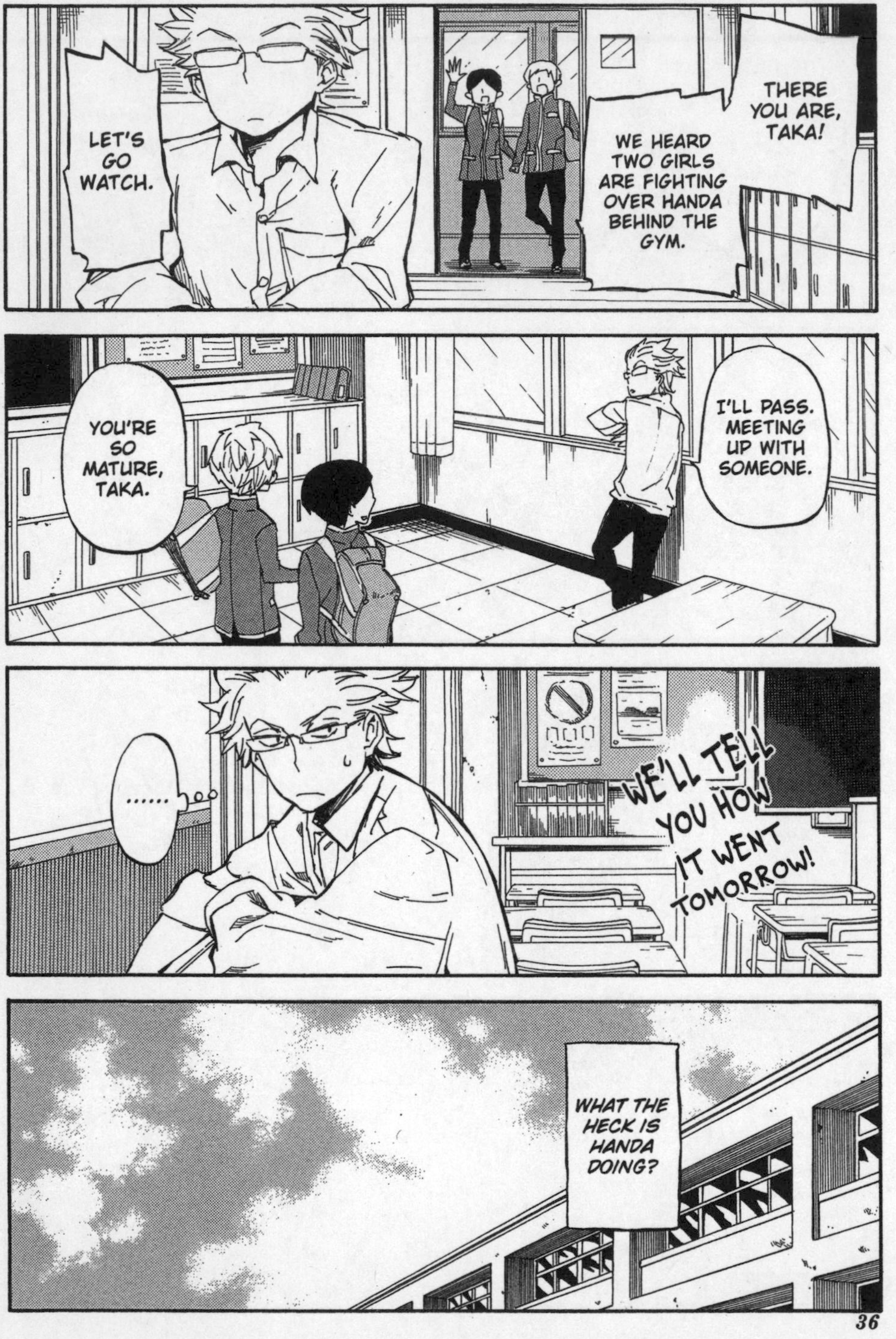
THERE YOU ARE, TAKA!
WE HEARD TWO GIRLS ARE FIGHTING OVER HANDA BEHIND THE GYM.
LET'S GO WATCH.
I'LL PASS. MEETING UP WITH SOMEONE.
YOU'RE SO MATURE, TAKA.
WE'LL TELL YOU HOW IT WENT TOMORROW!
......
WHAT THE HECK IS HANDA DOING?

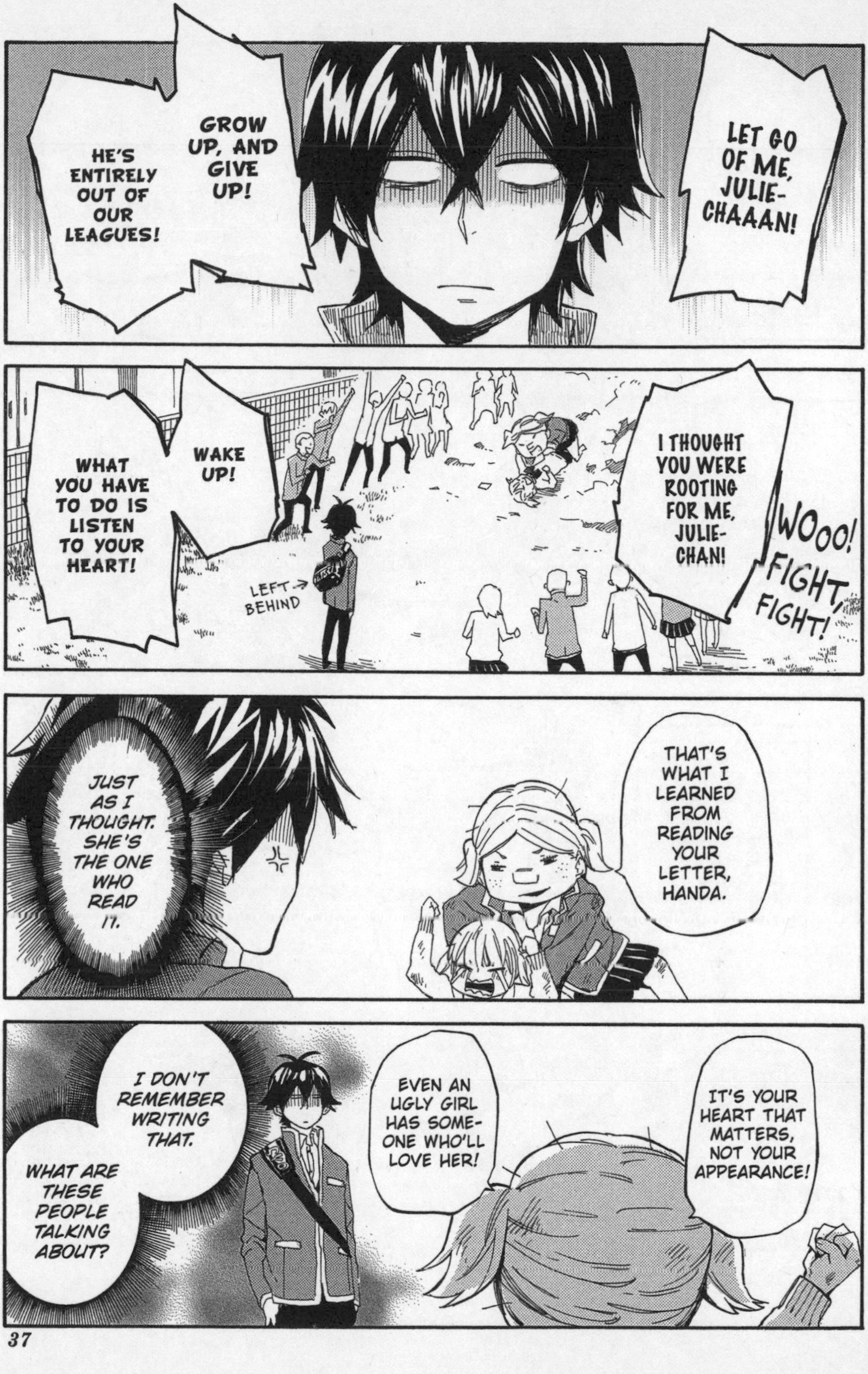
LET GO OF ME, JULIE-CHAAAN!
GROW UP, AND GIVE UP!
HE'S ENTIRELY OUT OF OUR LEAGUES!
WOOO! FIGHT, FIGHT!
I THOUGHT YOU WERE ROOTING FOR ME, JULIE-CHAN!
WAKE UP!
WHAT YOU HAVE TO DO IS LISTEN TO YOUR HEART!
LEFT BEHIND
THAT'S WHAT I LEARNED FROM READING YOUR LETTER, HANDA.
JUST AS I THOUGHT. SHE'S THE ONE WHO READ IT.
IT'S YOUR HEART THAT MATTERS, NOT YOUR APPEARANCE!
EVEN AN UGLY GIRL HAS SOME-ONE WHO'LL LOVE HER!
I DON'T REMEMBER WRITING THAT.
WHAT ARE THESE PEOPLE TALKING ABOUT?

YOU SAW ME THERE IN MAIKO'S SHADOW AND PITIED ME, DIDN'T YOU?
I CAN TELL THAT MUCH.
I CAN'T TELL ANYTHING.
WHEN I WAS JEALOUS OF THIS GIRL...
...MY HEART WAS UGLY TOO.
DON'T SAY A WORD. JUST LEAVE.
STOP IT!
FORGET ABOUT US BOTH.
I'M NOT GOING TO BE ABLE TO FORGET HAVING THIS IMPACTFUL PERSON IN MY CLASS, NO MATTER HOW HARD I TRY.
STILL, I'M GLAD.
IT LOOKS LIKE I CAN ESCAPE.
OKAY.
I'LL BE GOING NOW...
WHOA! HANDA-KUN'S JUST UP AND LEAVING!

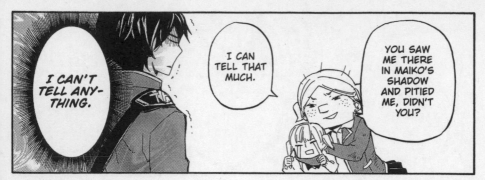

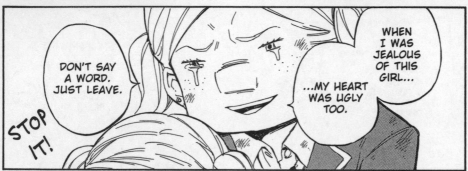

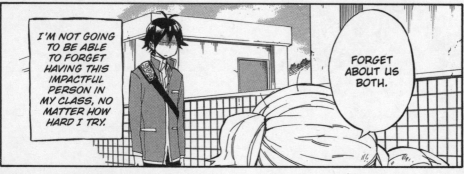

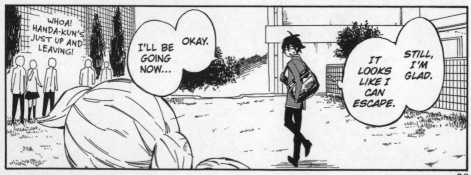

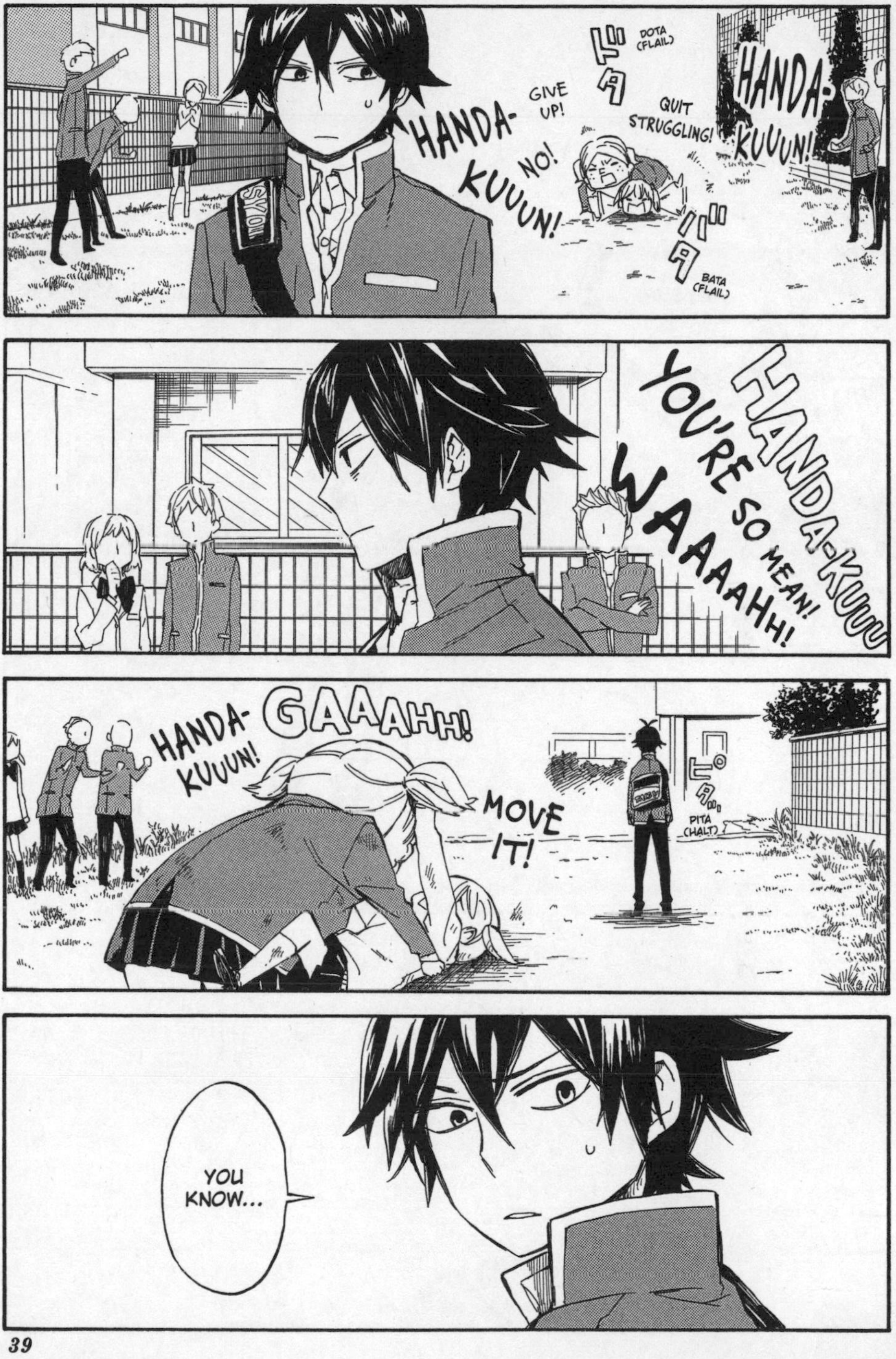
HANDA-KUUUN!
QUIT STRUGGLING!
ドタ
DOTA (FLAIL)
バタ
BATA (FLAIL)
GIVE UP!
NO!
HANDA-KUUUN!
HANDA-KUUU
YOU'RE SO MEAN!
WAAAAAHH!
ピタ
PITA (HALT)
MOVE IT!
GAAAHH!
HANDA-KUUUN!
YOU KNOW...

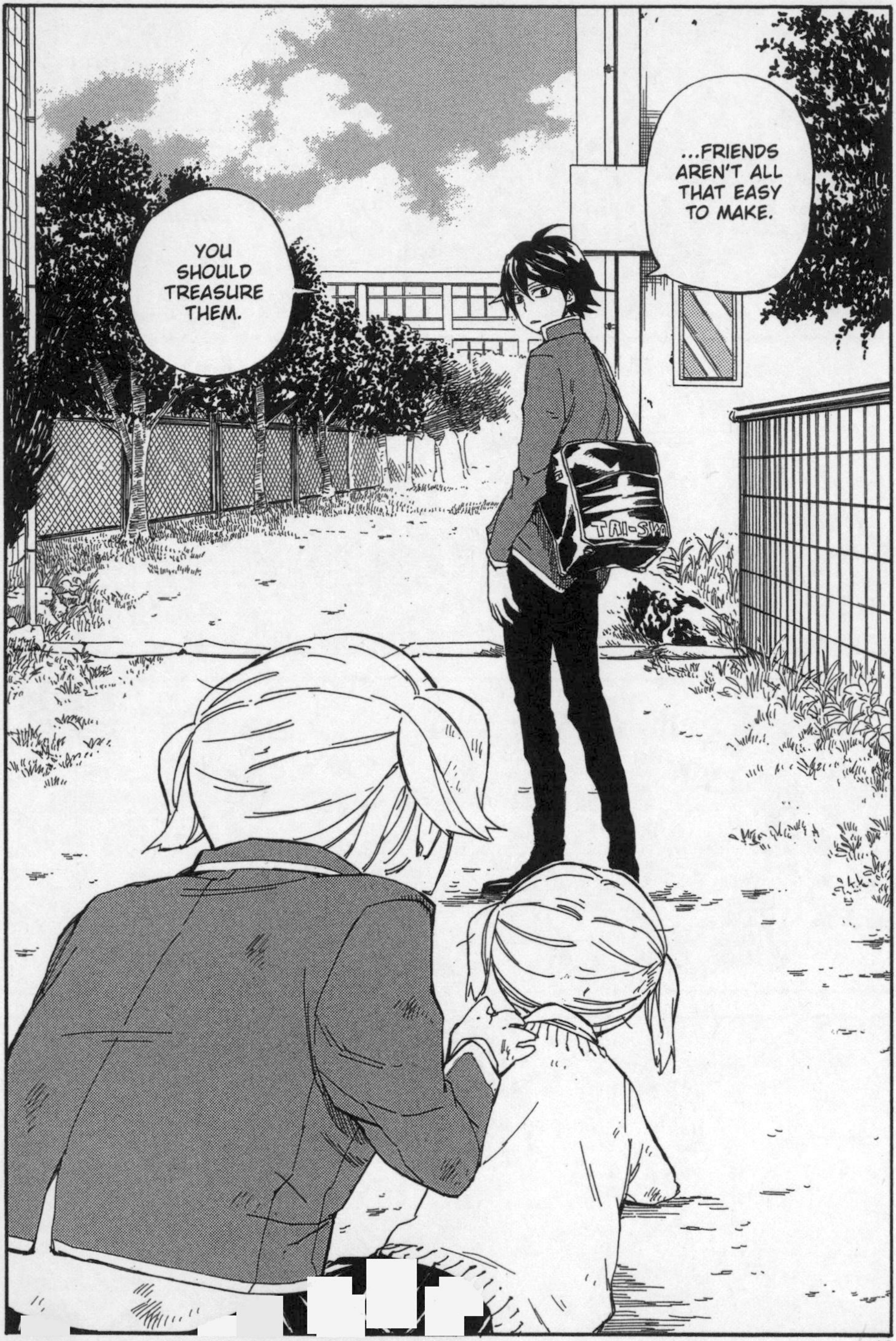
...FRIENDS AREN'T ALL THAT EASY TO MAKE.
YOU SHOULD TREASURE THEM.

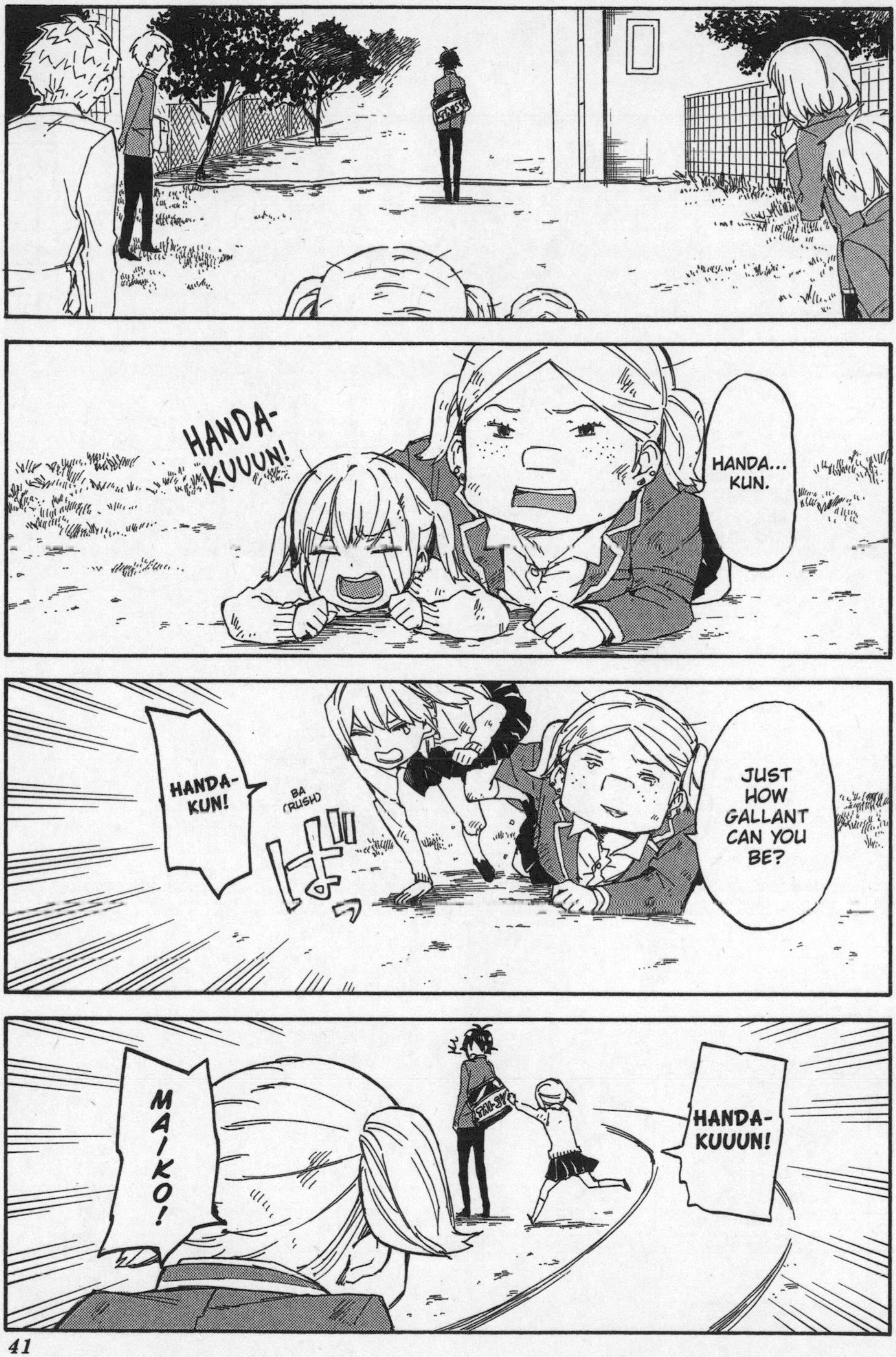
HANDA... KUN.
HANDA-KUUUN!
JUST HOW GALLANT CAN YOU BE?
BA (RUSH)
ばっ
HANDA-KUN!
HANDA-KUUUN!
MAIKO!

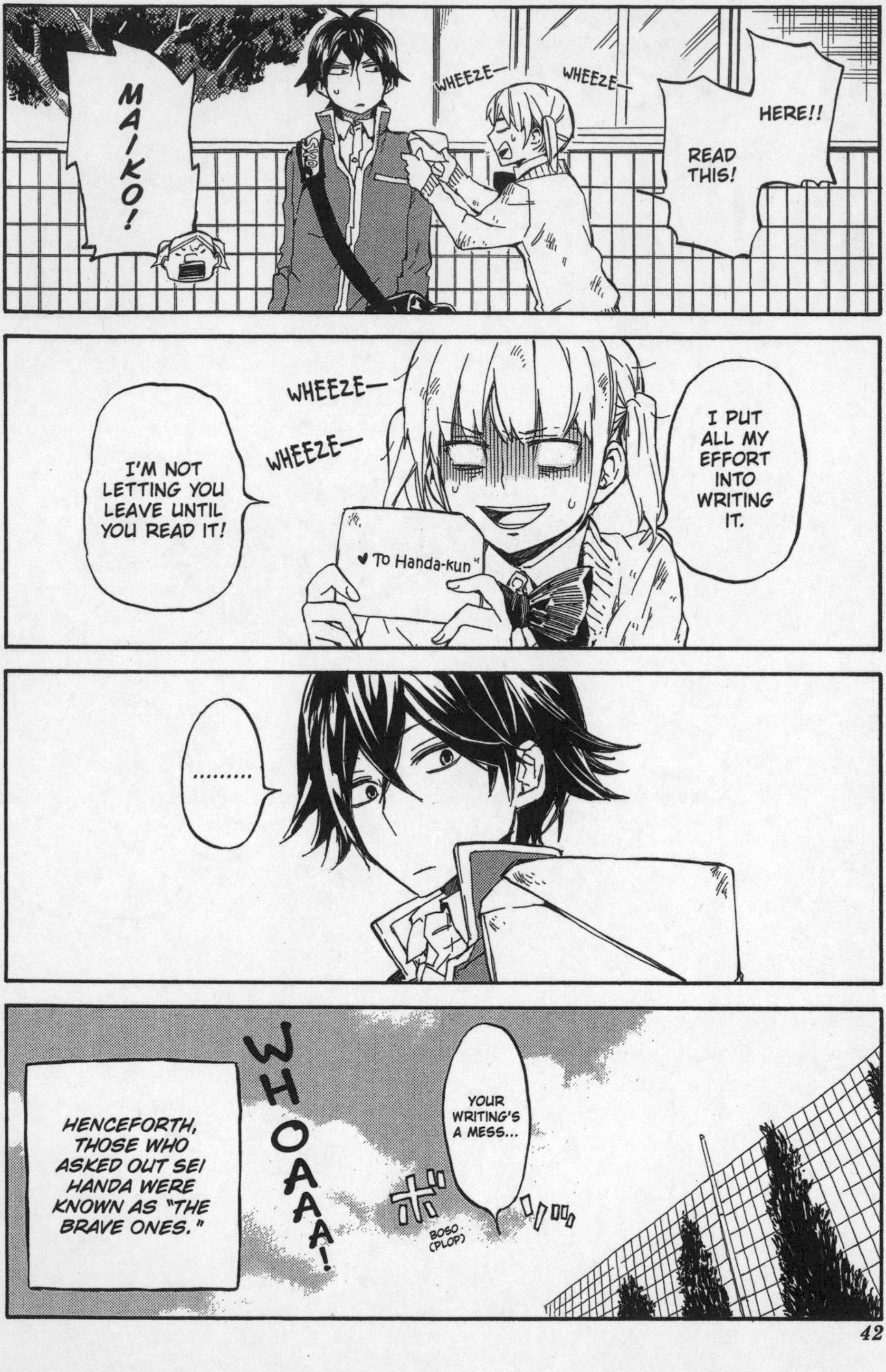
HERE!! READ THIS!
WHEEZE—
WHEEZE—
MAIKO!
I PUT ALL MY EFFORT INTO WRITING IT.
WHEEZE—
WHEEZE—
♥ To Handa-kun
I'M NOT LETTING YOU LEAVE UNTIL YOU READ IT!
....
YOUR WRITING'S A MESS...
WHOAAA!
BOSO (PLOP)
HENCEFORTH, THOSE WHO ASKED OUT SEI HANDA WERE KNOWN AS "THE BRAVE ONES."

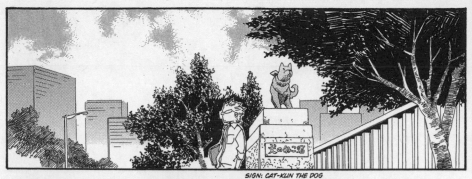

犬のねこ君
SIGN: CAT-KUN THE DOG
WAIT LONG, KAWA-FUJI?
YOU'RE LATE.
GET CALLED OUT AND THEN BEAT UP?
YOU'RE WELL IN-FORMED.
YEAH, SINCE IT'S ABOUT YOU.
......
MAYBE SOMEDAY YOU'LL THROW A PUNCH AT ME TOO.
HUH!?

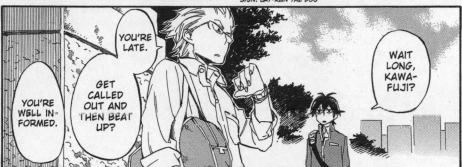

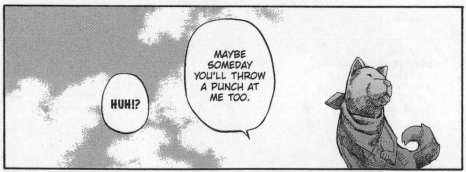

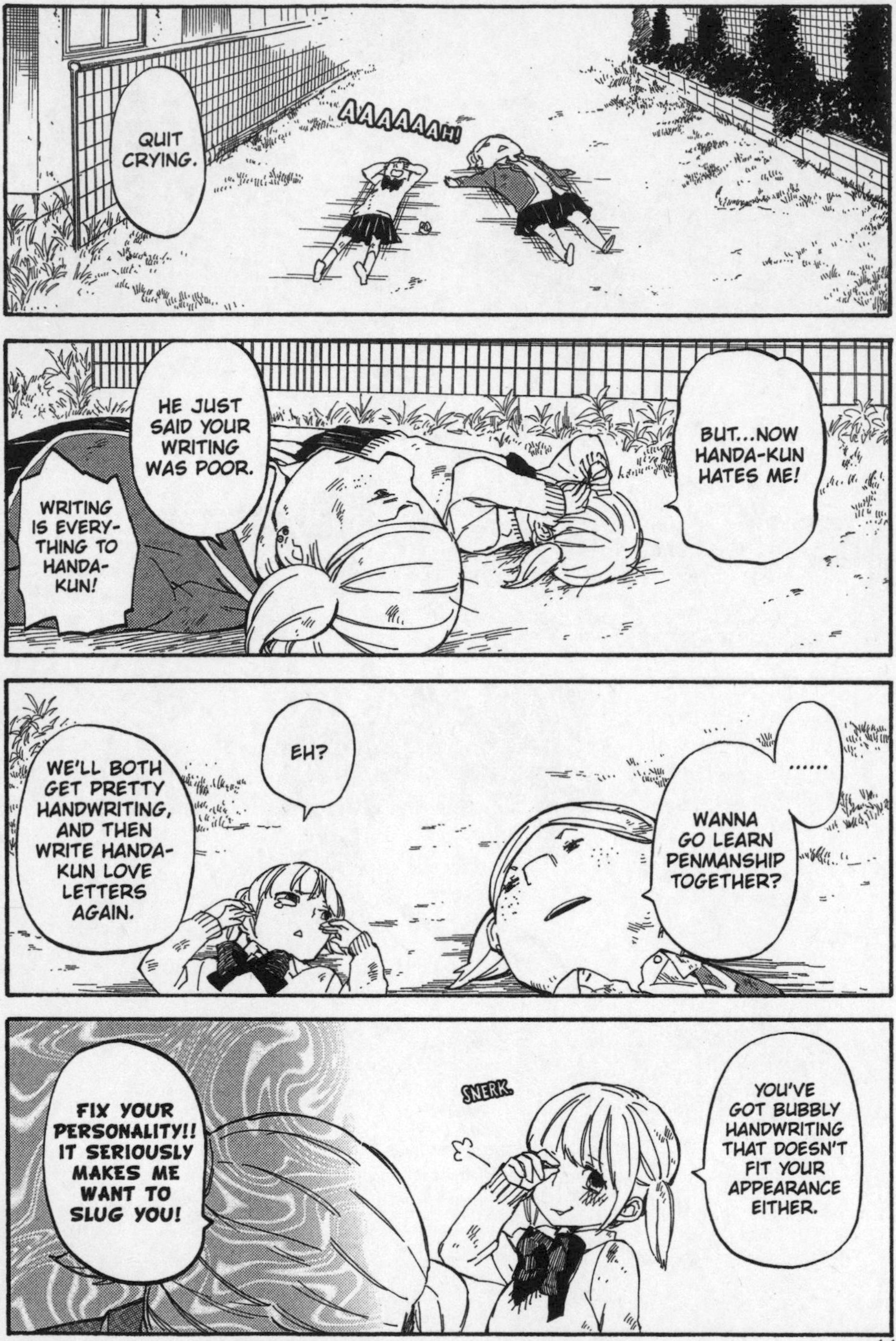
AAAAAAH!
QUIT CRYING.
BUT...NOW HANDA-KUN HATES ME!
HE JUST SAID YOUR WRITING WAS POOR.
WRITING IS EVERYTHING TO HANDA-KUN!
......
WANNA GO LEARN PENMANSHIP TOGETHER?
EH?
WE'LL BOTH GET PRETTY HANDWRITING, AND THEN WRITE HANDA-KUN LOVE LETTERS AGAIN.
YOU'VE GOT BUBBLY HANDWRITING THAT DOESN'T FIT YOUR APPEARANCE EITHER.
SNERK.
FIX YOUR PERSONALITY!! IT SERIOUSLY MAKES ME WANT TO SLUG YOU!

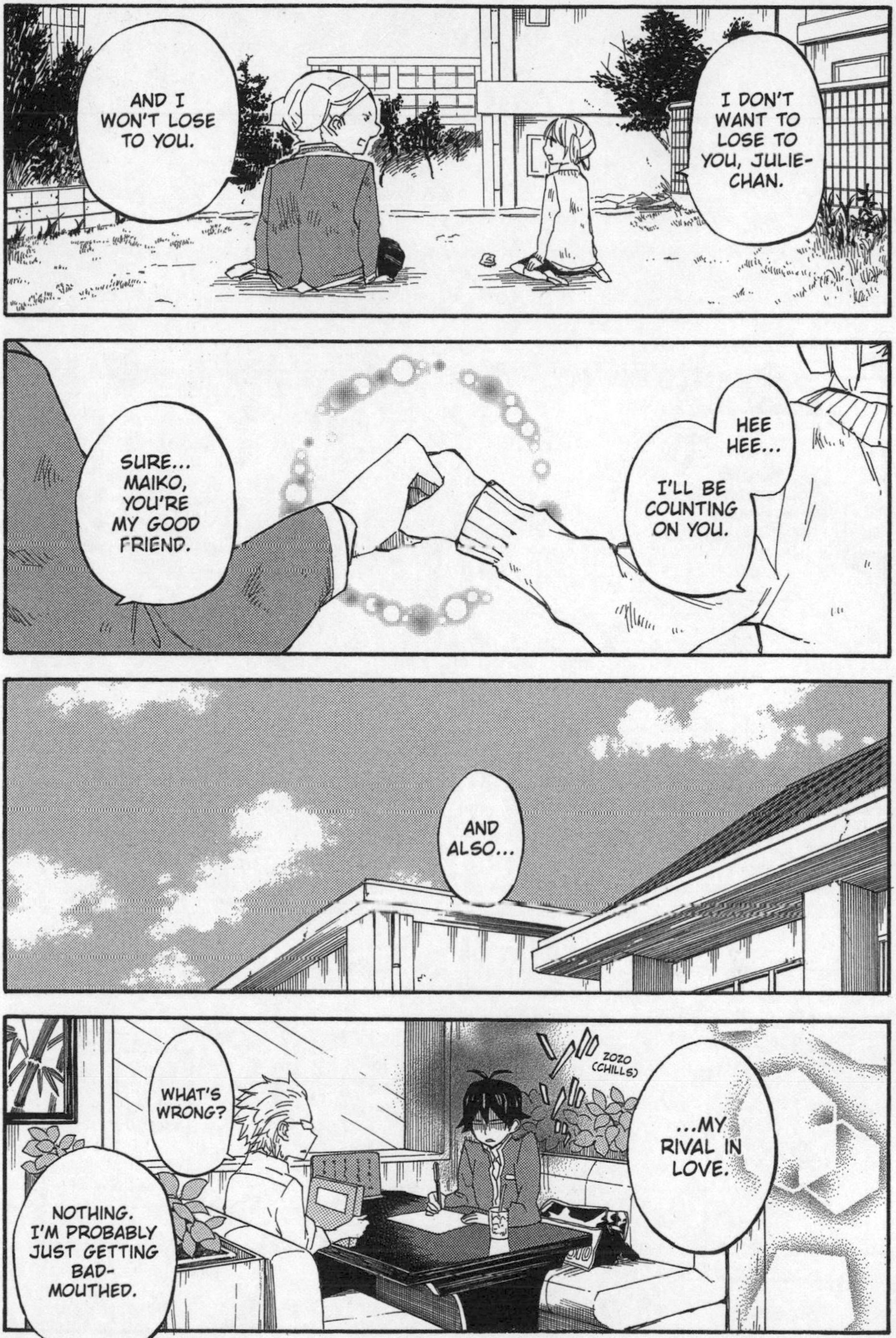
I DON'T WANT TO LOSE TO YOU, JULIE-CHAN.
AND I WON'T LOSE TO YOU.
HEE HEE... I'LL BE COUNTING ON YOU.
SURE... MAIKO, YOU'RE MY GOOD FRIEND.
AND ALSO...
...MY RIVAL IN LOVE.
ZOZO (CHILLS)
WHAT'S WRONG?
NOTHING. I'M PROBABLY JUST GETTING BAD-MOUTHED.

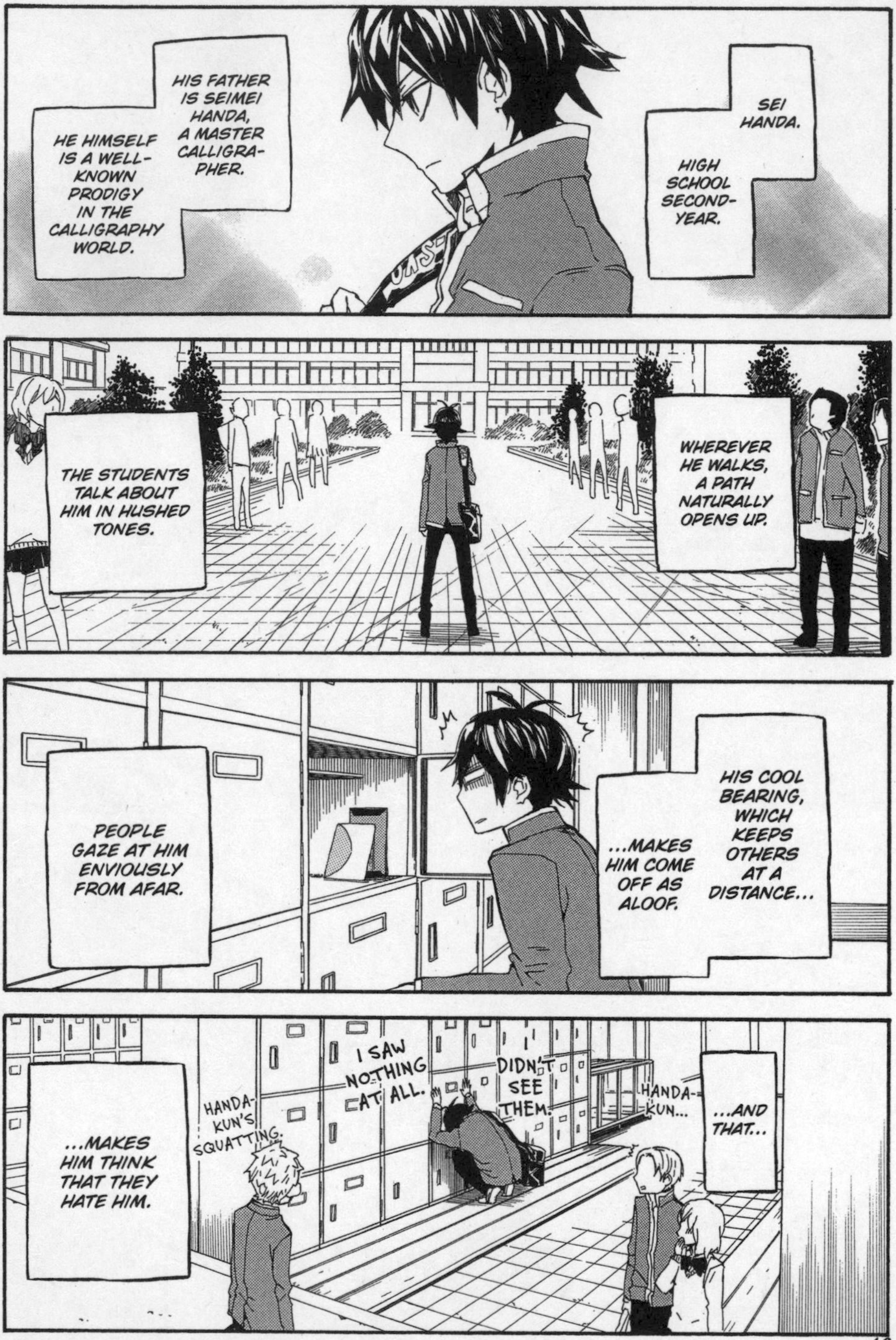
SEI HANDA.
HIGH SCHOOL SECOND-YEAR.
HIS FATHER IS SEIMEI HANDA, A MASTER CALLIGRAPHER.
HE HIMSELF IS A WELL-KNOWN PRODIGY IN THE CALLIGRAPHY WORLD.
WHEREVER HE WALKS, A PATH NATURALLY OPENS UP.
THE STUDENTS TALK ABOUT HIM IN HUSHED TONES.
HIS COOL BEARING, WHICH KEEPS OTHERS AT A DISTANCE...
...MAKES HIM COME OFF AS ALOOF.
PEOPLE GAZE AT HIM ENVIOUSLY FROM AFAR.
...AND THAT...
HANDA-KUN...
DIDN'T SEE THEM.
I SAW NOTHING AT ALL.
HANDA-KUN'S SQUATTING.
...MAKES HIM THINK THAT THEY HATE HIM.

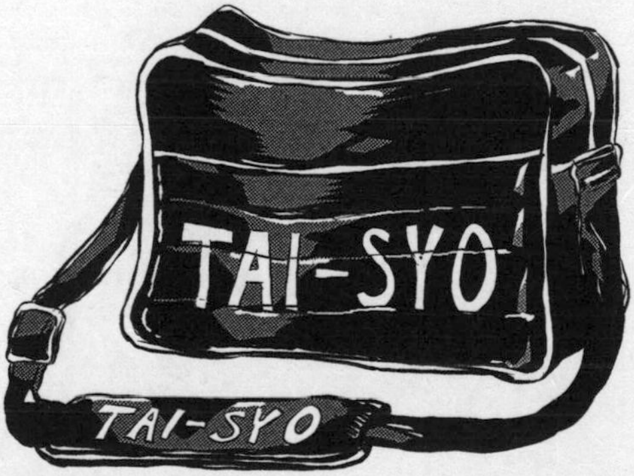
TAI-SYO
TAI-SYO

Handa-
kun

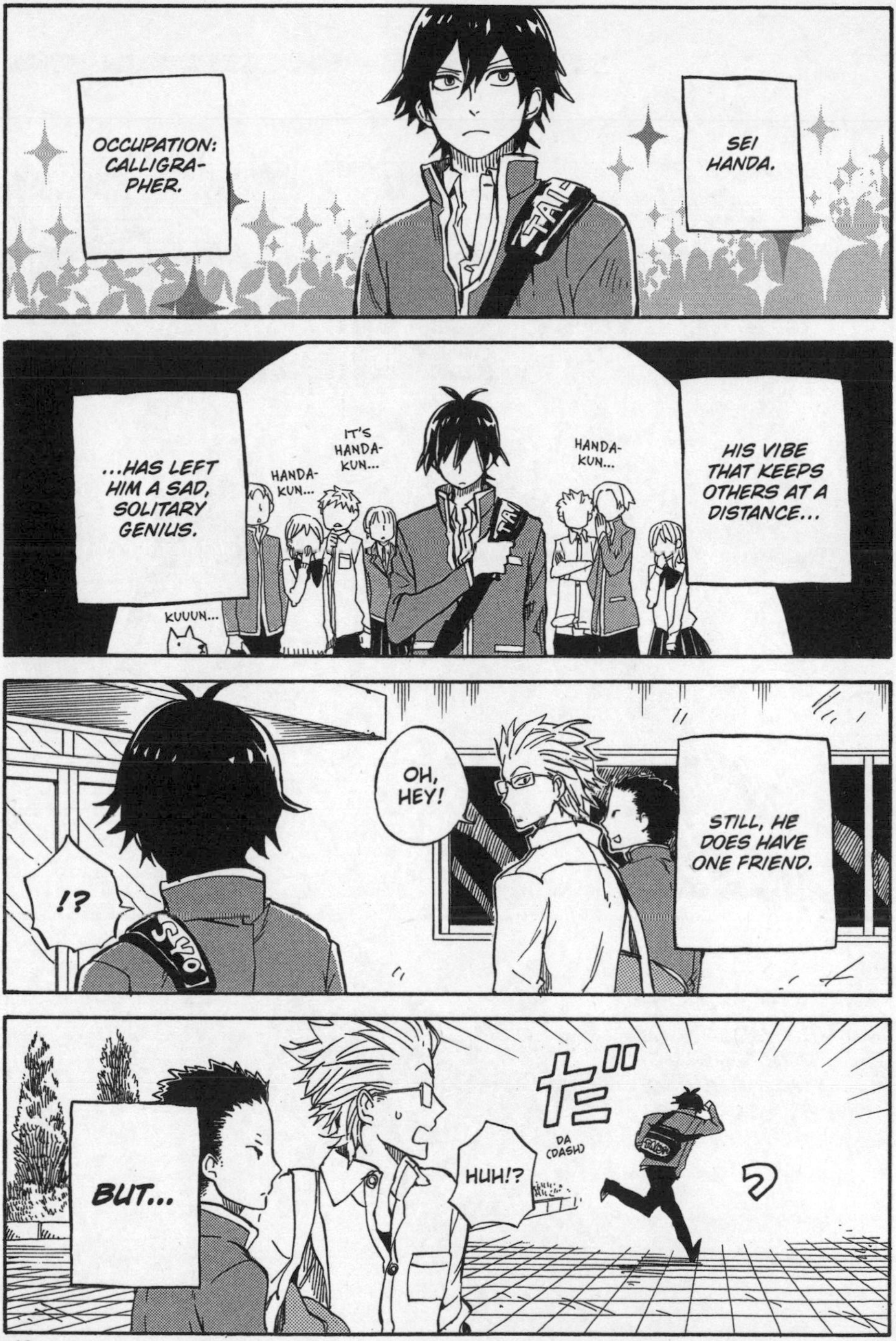
SEI HANDA.
OCCUPATION: CALLIGRAPHER.
HIS VIBE THAT KEEPS OTHERS AT A DISTANCE...
HANDA-KUN...
IT'S HANDA-KUN...
HANDA-KUN...
...HAS LEFT HIM A SAD, SOLITARY GENIUS.
KUUUN...
STILL, HE DOES HAVE ONE FRIEND.
OH, HEY!
!?
DA (DASH)
HUH!?
BUT...

Chapter 2: Handa-kun & His Good Friend

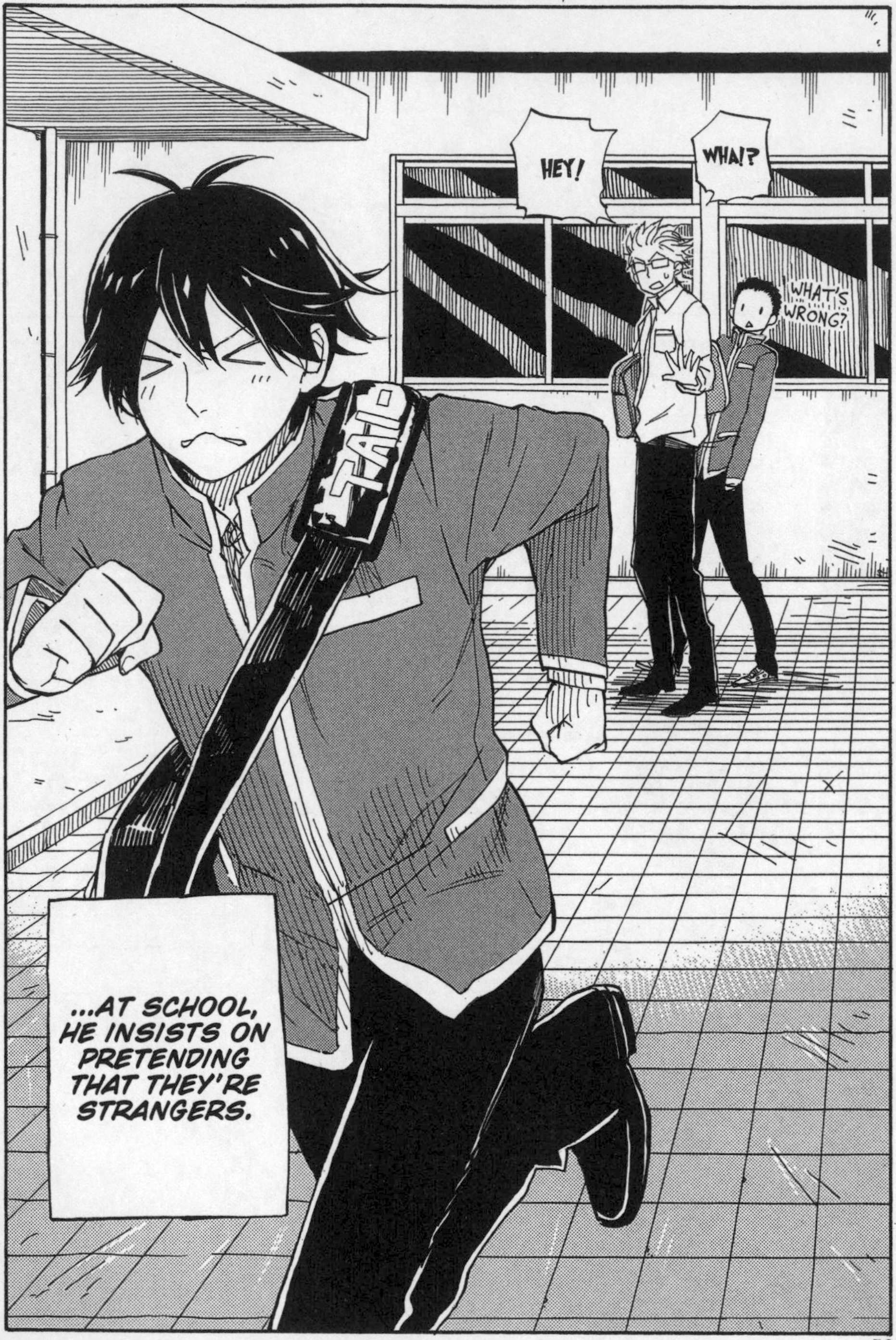
WHA!?
HEY!
WHAT'S WRONG?
...AT SCHOOL, HE INSISTS ON PRETENDING THAT THEY'RE STRANGERS.

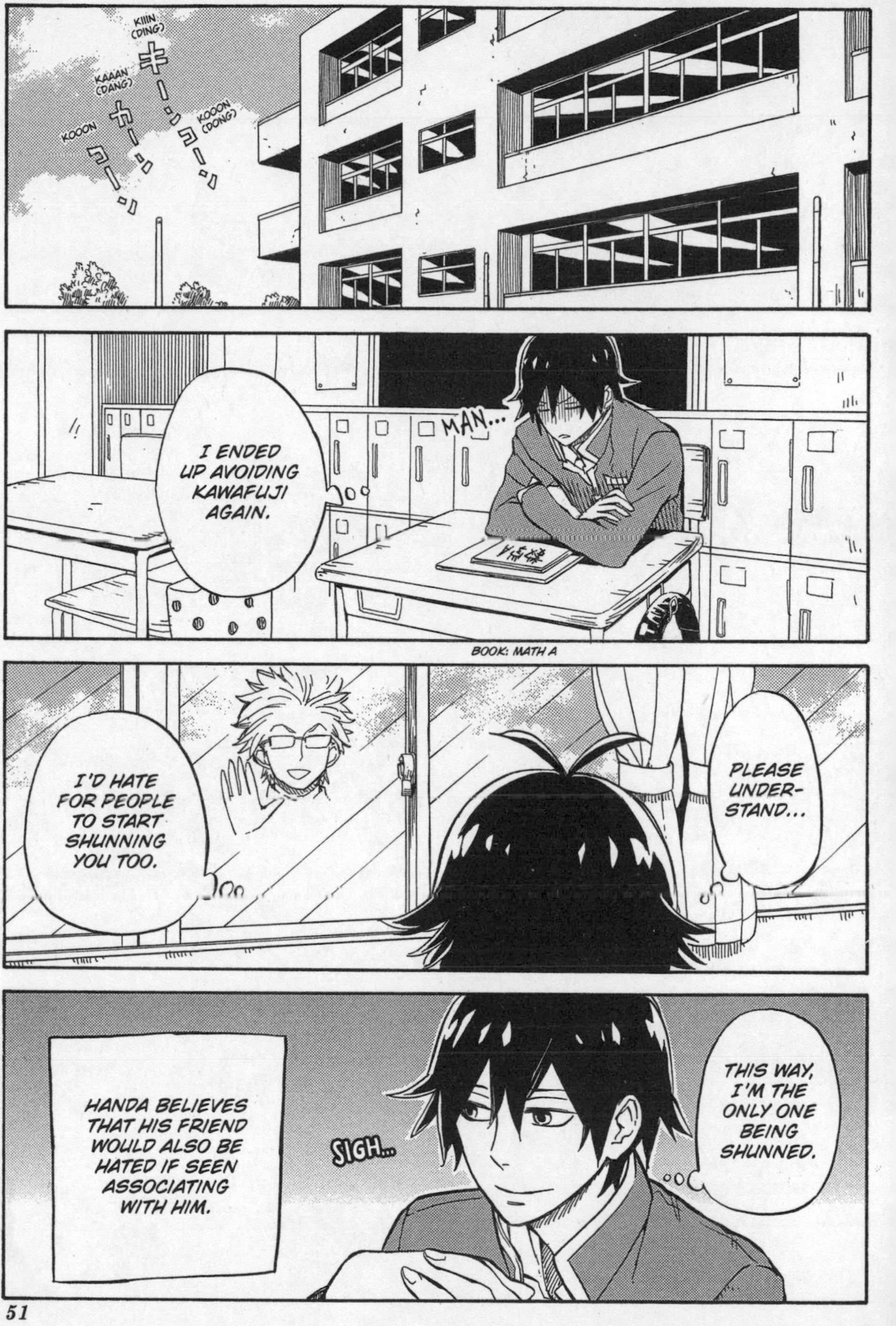
KIIIN (DING)
KOOON (DONG)
KAAAN (DANG)
KOOON
MAN...
I ENDED UP AVOIDING KAWAFUJI AGAIN.
BOOK: MATH A
PLEASE UNDER-STAND...
I'D HATE FOR PEOPLE TO START SHUNNING YOU TOO.
THIS WAY, I'M THE ONLY ONE BEING SHUNNED.
SIGH...
HANDA BELIEVES THAT HIS FRIEND WOULD ALSO BE HATED IF SEEN ASSOCIATING WITH HIM.

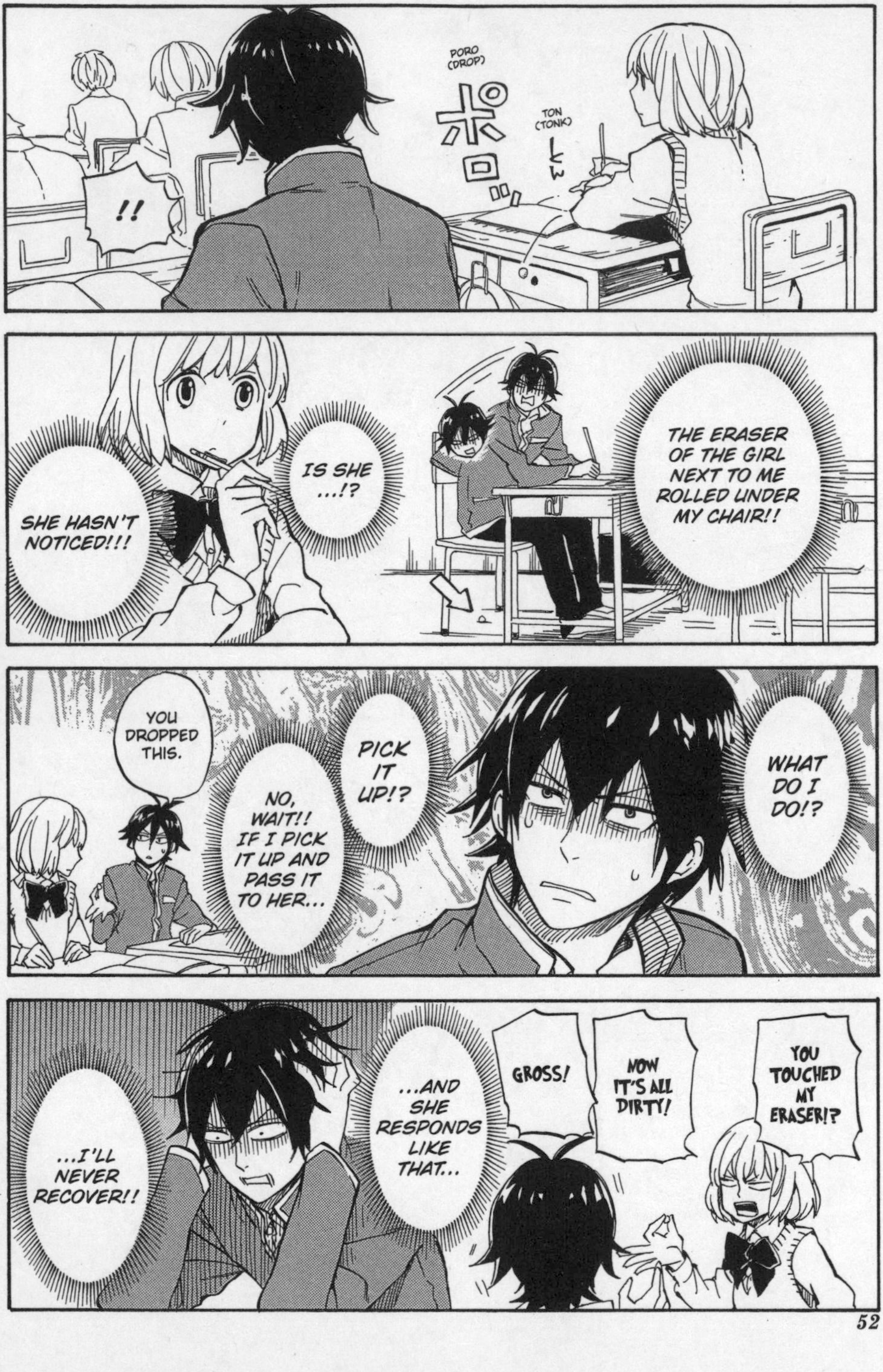
TON (TONK)
とん
PORO (DROP)
ポロ
!!
THE ERASER OF THE GIRL NEXT TO ME ROLLED UNDER MY CHAIR!!
IS SHE ...!?
SHE HASN'T NOTICED!!!
WHAT DO I DO!?
PICK IT UP!?
NO, WAIT!! IF I PICK IT UP AND PASS IT TO HER...
YOU DROPPED THIS.
YOU TOUCHED MY ERASER!?
NOW IT'S ALL DIRTY!
GROSS!
...AND SHE RESPONDS LIKE THAT...
...I'LL NEVER RECOVER!!

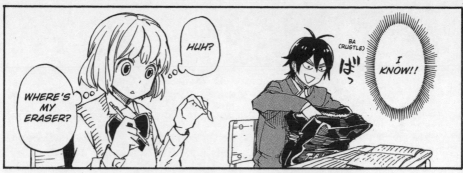

I KNOW!!
BA (RUSTLE)
ばっ
HUH?
WHERE'S MY ERASER?
TON
トン
USE THAT.
EH?
OH NO!
COULD IT BE...
...HE SAW THAT MY ERASER WAS ALMOST OUT...
...AND REPLACED IT WITH A NEW ONE?
THANK GOODNESS I HAD A BRAND-NEW ERASER.
MY HUNCH THAT A NEW ONE WOULD PLACATE HER WAS CORRECT!!

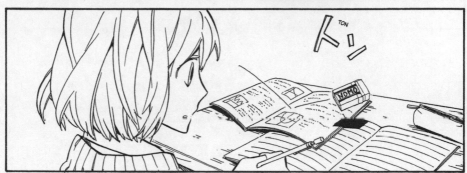

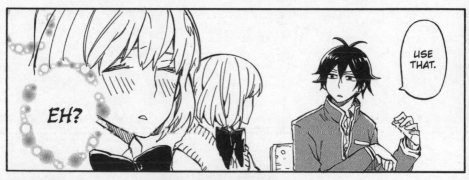

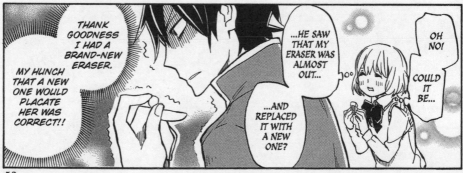

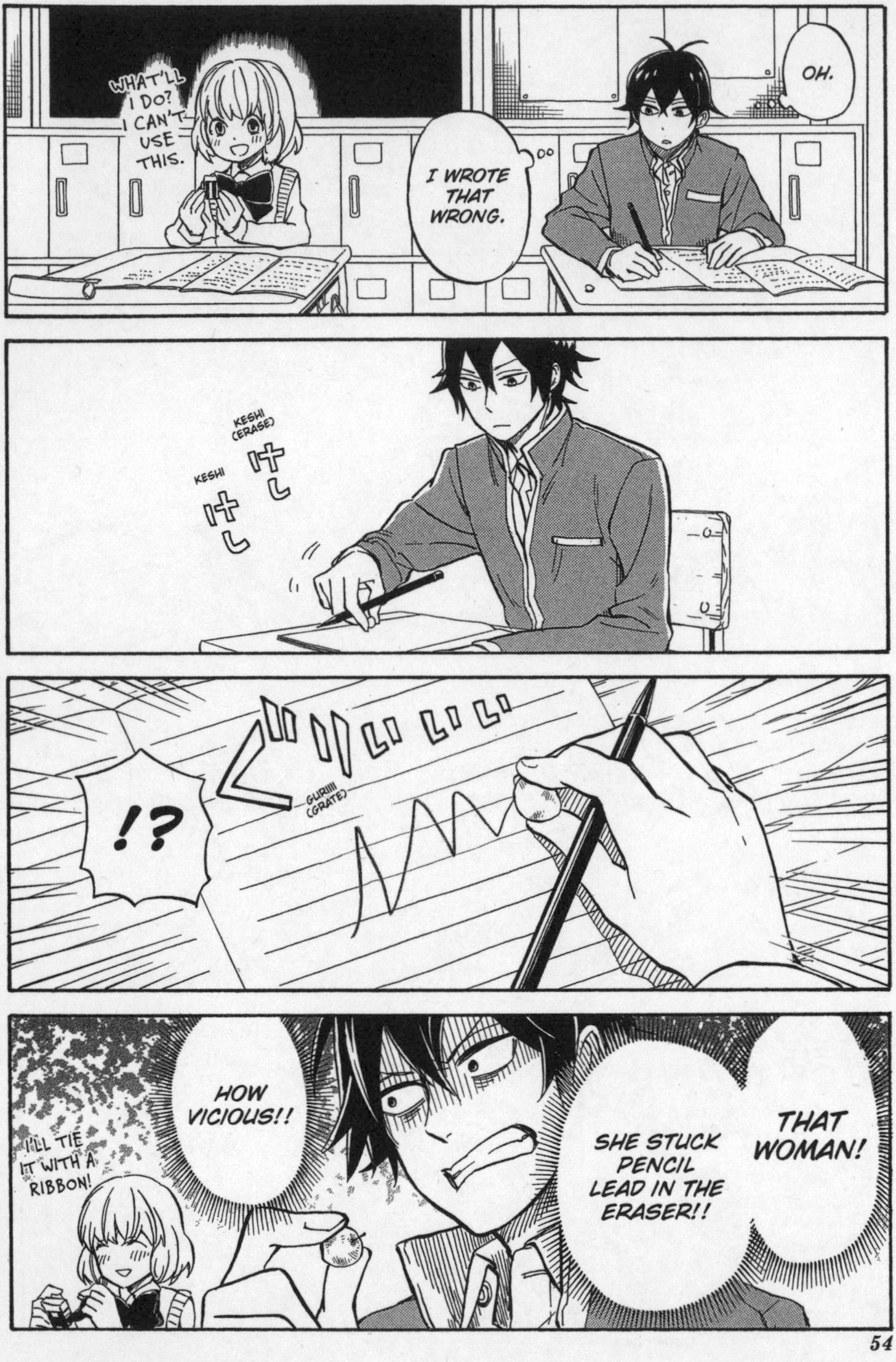
OH.
I WROTE THAT WRONG.
WHAT'LL I DO? I CAN'T USE THIS.
KESHI (ERASE)
けし
KESHI
けし
GURIIII (GRATE)
!?
THAT WOMAN!
SHE STUCK PENCIL LEAD IN THE ERASER!!
HOW VICIOUS!!
I'LL TIE IT WITH A RIBBON!

HANDA-KUN'S AURA IS GOING FULL BLAST AGAIN TODAY.
NEGATIVE AURA
NOT MANY CAN PULL OFF LOOKING THAT COOL STANDING BY THE WINDOW.
MOVED BY THE WINDOW TO AVOID BEING TREATED AS AN INTRUDER
YOU'RE SO LUCKY YOU SIT NEXT TO HIM, MIYOKO!
I'M NOT LUCKY AT ALL!
I CAN'T LOOK HIS WAY!
I GET NERVOUS!
YOU COULD "TRIP AND FALL"...
...AND GIVE HIM A HUG!
ACK! NO WAY, NO WAY!
TAKE ADVANTAGE OF BEING NEXT TO HIM!
OH GOD, NO!
YOU TRY SITTING NEXT TO HIM INSTEAD!!
DON'T CRY. DON'T CRY.

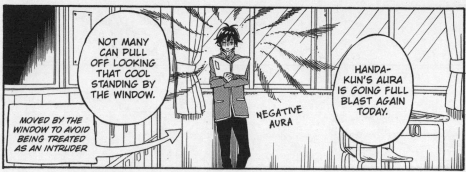

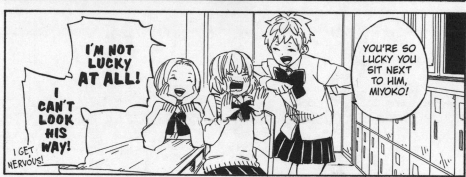

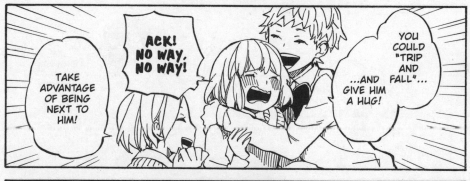

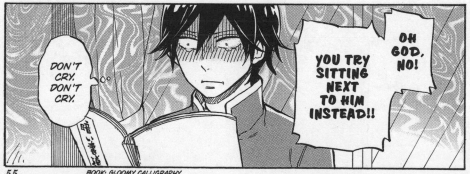

BOOK: GLOOMY CALLIGRAPHY

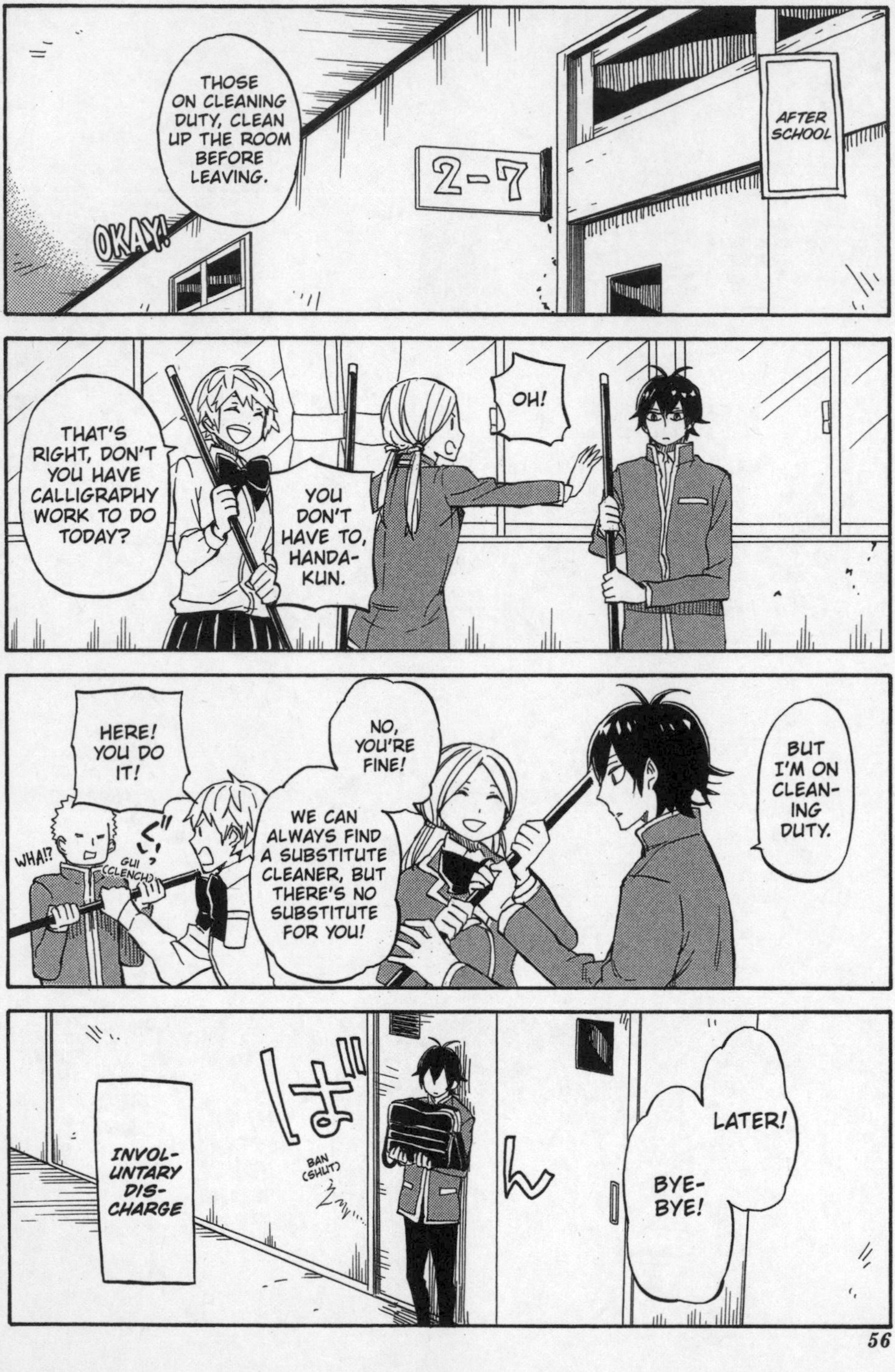
AFTER SCHOOL
2-7
THOSE ON CLEANING DUTY, CLEAN UP THE ROOM BEFORE LEAVING.
OKAY!
OH!
YOU DON'T HAVE TO, HANDA-KUN.
THAT'S RIGHT, DON'T YOU HAVE CALLIGRAPHY WORK TO DO TODAY?
BUT I'M ON CLEANING-ING DUTY.
NO, YOU'RE FINE!
WE CAN ALWAYS FIND A SUBSTITUTE CLEANER, BUT THERE'S NO SUBSTITUTE FOR YOU!
HERE! YOU DO IT!
GUI (CLENCH)
WHA!?
LATER!
BYE-BYE!
BAN (SHUT)
INVOLUNTARY DIS-CHARGE

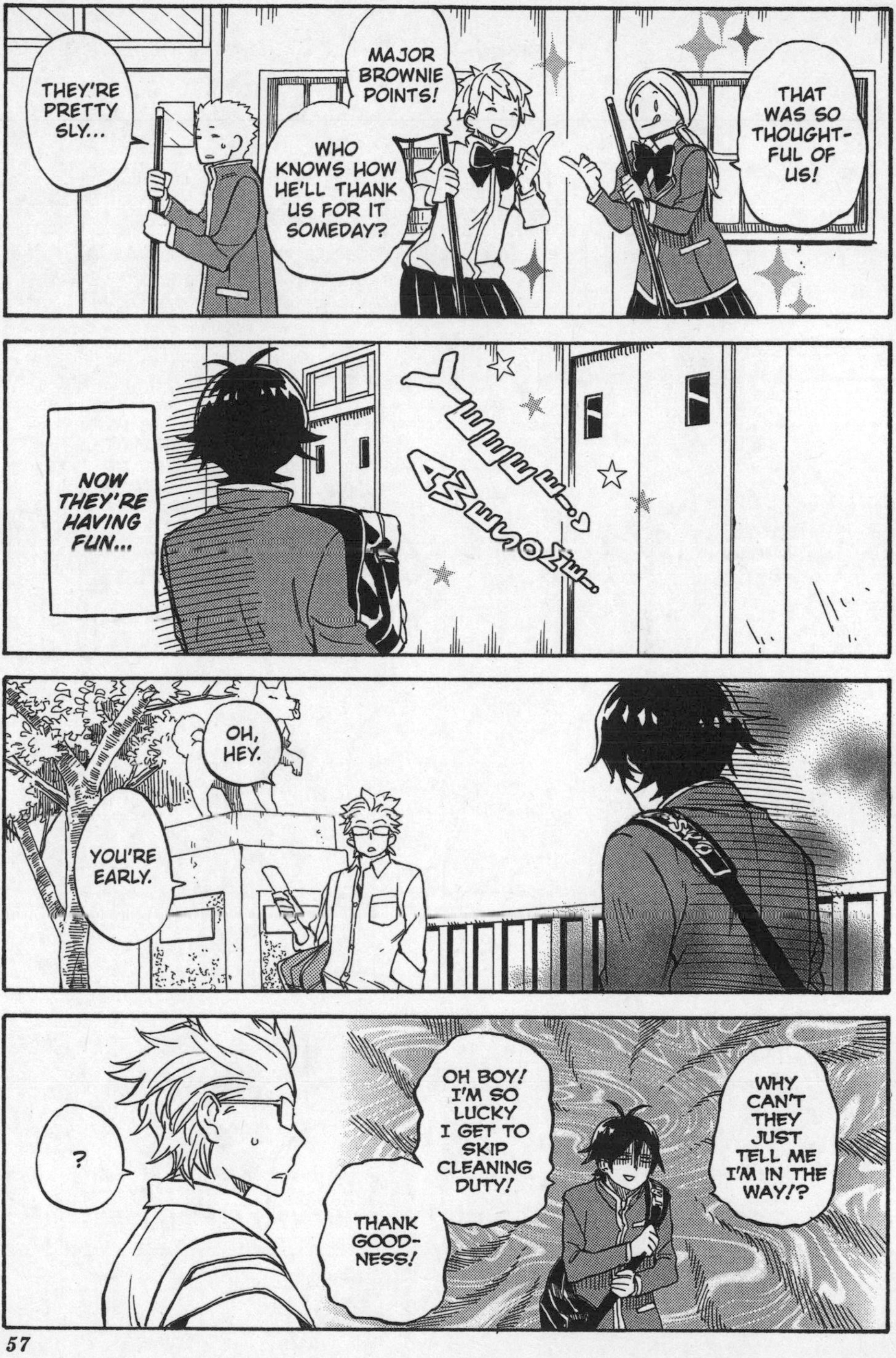
THAT WAS SO THOUGHTFUL OF US!
MAJOR BROWNIE POINTS!
WHO KNOWS HOW HE'LL THANK US FOR IT SOMEDAY?
THEY'RE PRETTY SLY...
YEEEEE--♡
AWESOME--
NOW THEY'RE HAVING FUN...
OH, HEY.
YOU'RE EARLY.
WHY CAN'T THEY JUST TELL ME I'M IN THE WAY!?
OH BOY! I'M SO LUCKY I GET TO SKIP CLEANING DUTY!
THANK GOOD-NESS!
?

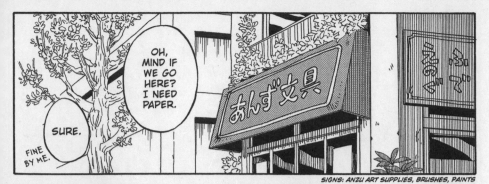

あんず文具
ふで
えのぐ
OH, MIND IF WE GO HERE? I NEED PAPER.
SURE.
FINE BY ME.
IT'S FOR PRACTICE, SO I'D BETTER BUY A LOT.
WON'T THAT BE A LOT TO CARRY?
EXCUSE US!
OH, IT'S KAWA-FUJI!
OH, HEY! YOU'RE FROM THE ART CLUB.
SHOP-PING BY YOUR-SELF?
THAT'S PRETTY SAD.
I'M NOT BY MY-SELF!
I'M WITH...
!?
SIGNS: ANZU ART SUPPLIES, BRUSHES, PAINTS

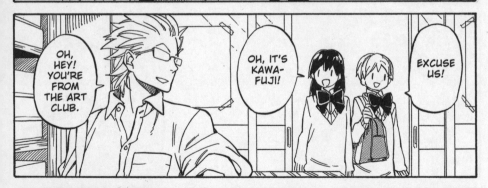

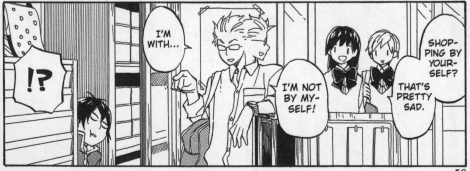

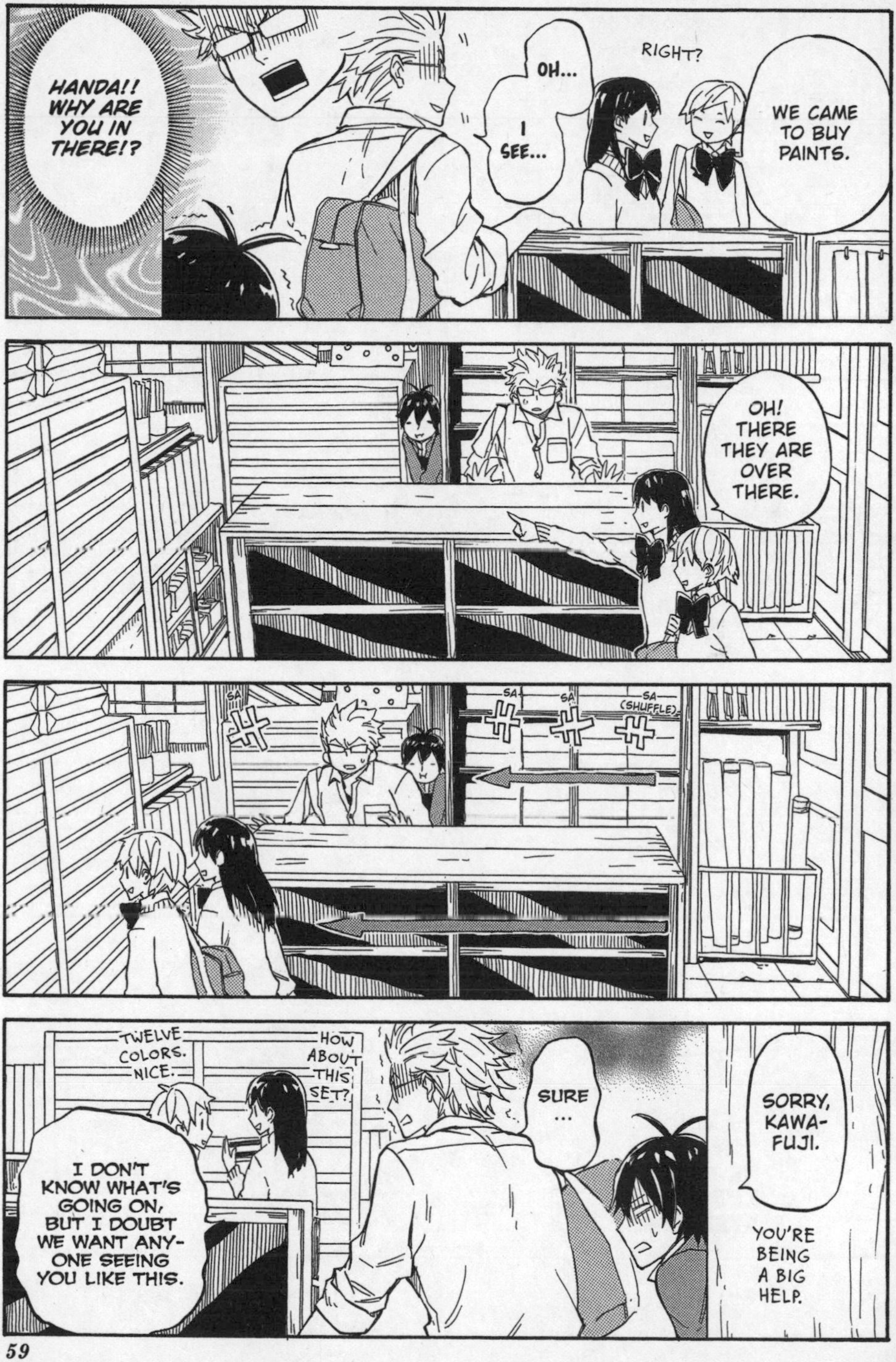
WE CAME TO BUY PAINTS.
RIGHT?
OH... I SEE...
HANDA!! WHY ARE YOU IN THERE!?
OH! THERE THEY ARE OVER THERE.
SA (SHUFFLE)
SA
SA
SA
SORRY, KAWAFUJI.
YOU'RE BEING A BIG HELP.
SURE...
HOW ABOUT THIS SET?
TWELVE COLORS. NICE.
I DON'T KNOW WHAT'S GOING ON, BUT I DOUBT WE WANT ANYONE SEEING YOU LIKE THIS.

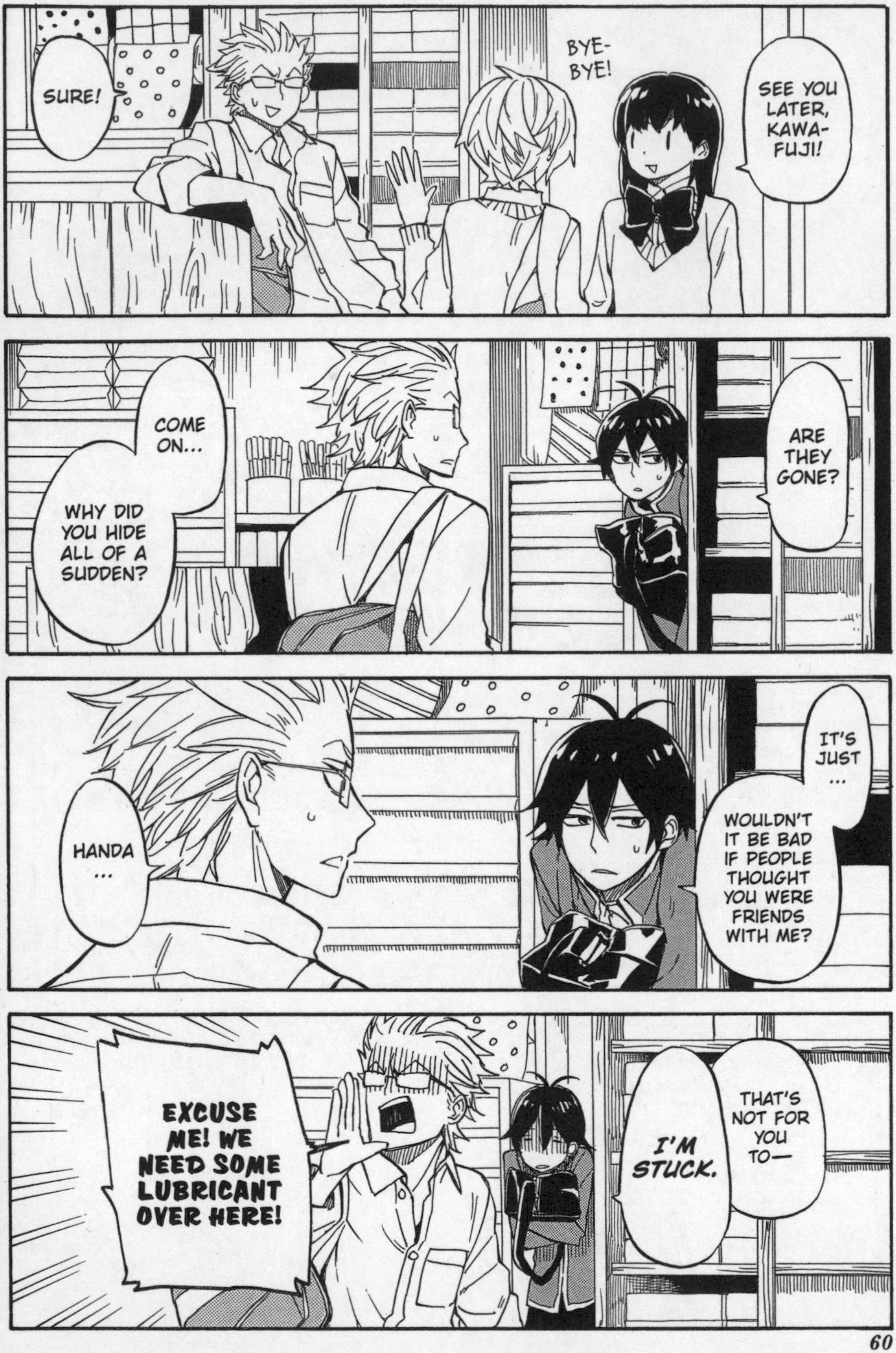
SEE YOU LATER, KAWA-FUJI!
BYE-BYE!
SURE!
ARE THEY GONE?
COME ON...
WHY DID YOU HIDE ALL OF A SUDDEN?
IT'S JUST ...
WOULDN'T IT BE BAD IF PEOPLE THOUGHT YOU WERE FRIENDS WITH ME?
HANDA ...
THAT'S NOT FOR YOU TO—
I'M STUCK.
EXCUSE ME! WE NEED SOME LUBRICANT OVER HERE!

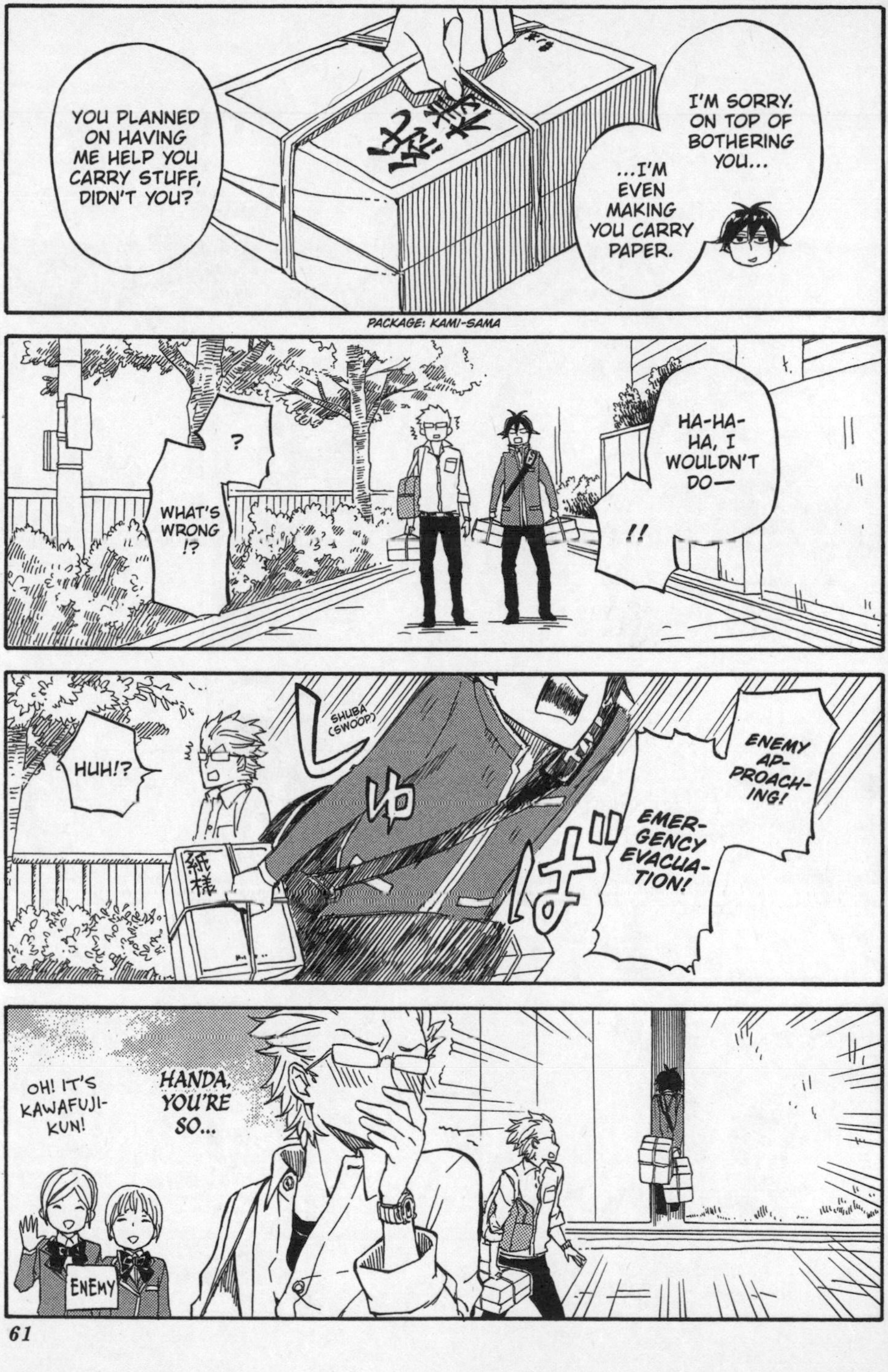
I'M SORRY. ON TOP OF BOTHERING YOU...
...I'M EVEN MAKING YOU CARRY PAPER.
YOU PLANNED ON HAVING ME HELP YOU CARRY STUFF, DIDN'T YOU?
PACKAGE: KAMI-SAMA
HA-HA-HA, I WOULDN'T DO—
!!
?
WHAT'S WRONG !?
ENEMY AP-PROACH-ING!
EMER-GENCY EVACUA-TION!
SHUBA (SWOOP)
HUH!?
HANDA, YOU'RE SO...
OH! IT'S KAWAFUJI-KUN!
ENEMY

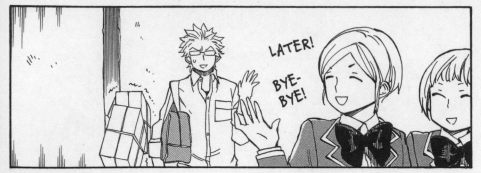

LATER!
BYE-BYE!
ARE THEY GONE?
NU (POP)
DO YOU ALWAYS HIDE THIS MUCH?
I DON'T HIDE WHEN I'M ALONE.
I JUST DON'T WANT TO CAUSE YOU ANY TROUBLE.
OH, HANDA...
OH, HERE COME SOME MORE.
GA (WHAP)
DAMN. THERE'RE A LOT OF PEDESTRIANS HERE!

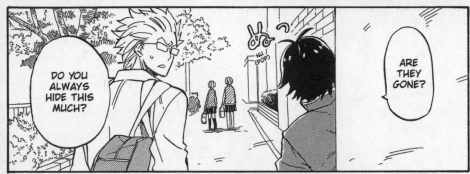

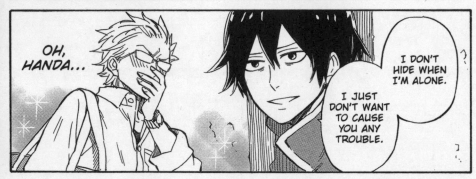

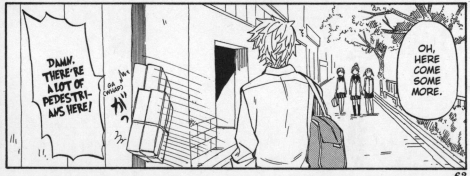

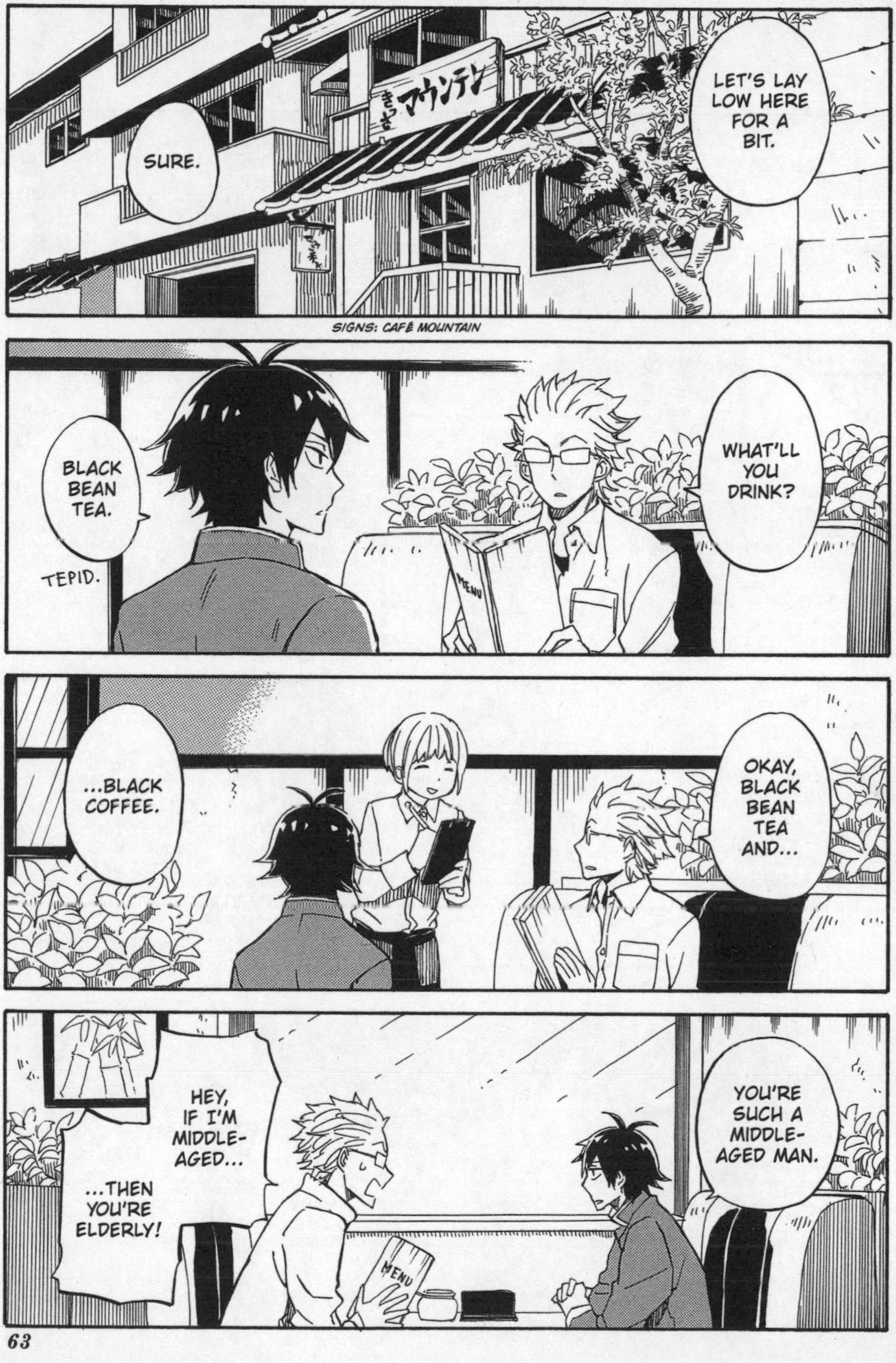
LET'S LAY LOW HERE FOR A BIT.
SURE.
きっさ マウンテン
SIGNS: CAFÉ MOUNTAIN
WHAT'LL YOU DRINK?
BLACK BEAN TEA.
TEPID.
OKAY, BLACK BEAN TEA AND...
...BLACK COFFEE.
YOU'RE SUCH A MIDDLE-AGED MAN.
HEY, IF I'M MIDDLE-AGED...
...THEN YOU'RE ELDERLY!

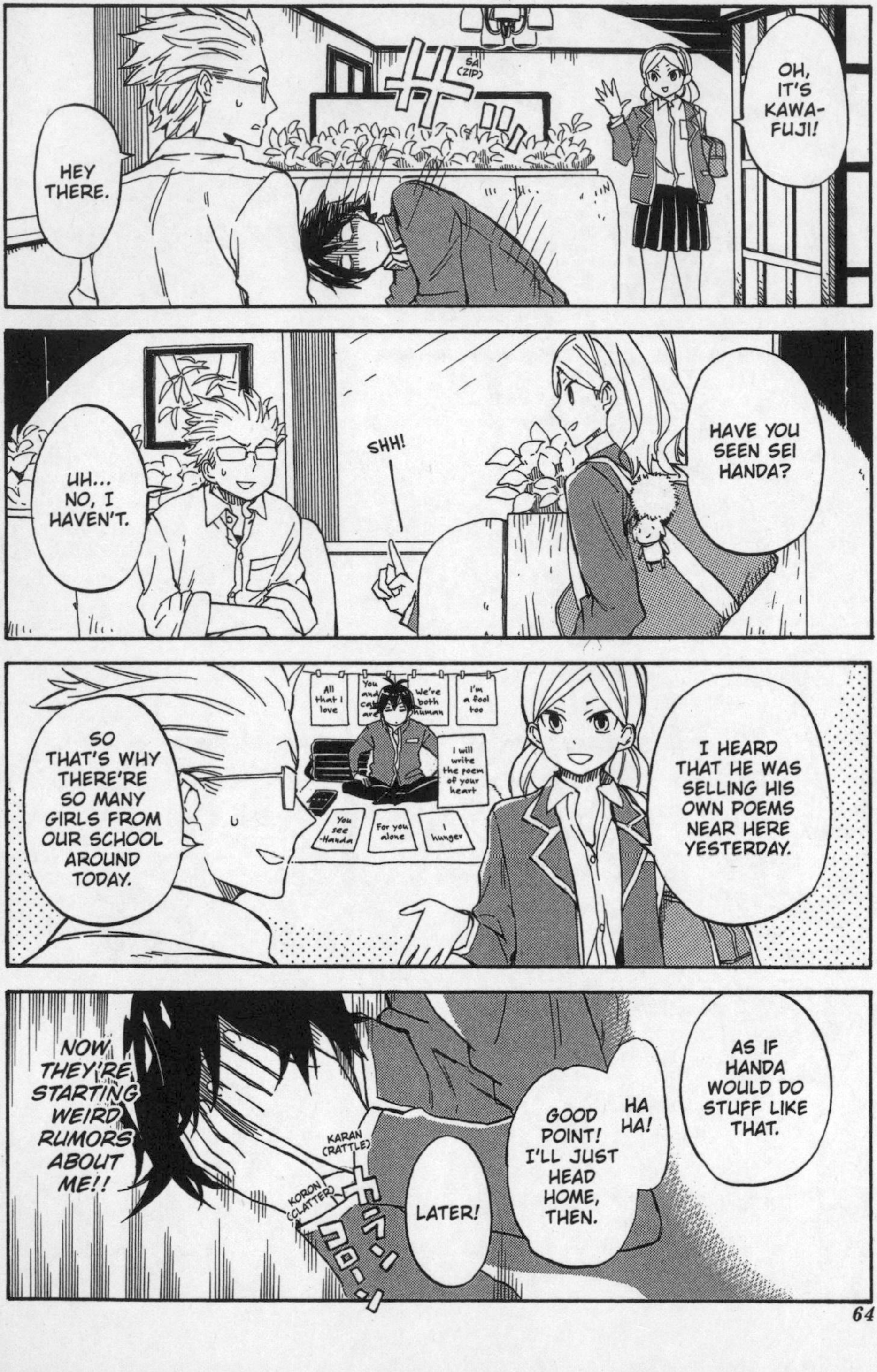
OH, IT'S KAWA-FUJI!
SA (ZIP)
HEY THERE.
HAVE YOU SEEN SEI HANDA?
SHH!
UH... NO, I HAVEN'T.
I HEARD THAT HE WAS SELLING HIS OWN POEMS NEAR HERE YESTERDAY.
All that I love
We're both human
I'm a fool too
I will write the poem of your heart
You see -Handa
For you alone
I hunger
SO THAT'S WHY THERE'RE SO MANY GIRLS FROM OUR SCHOOL AROUND TODAY.
AS IF HANDA WOULD DO STUFF LIKE THAT.
HA HA!
GOOD POINT! I'LL JUST HEAD HOME, THEN.
LATER!
KARAN (RATTLE)
KORON (CLATTER)
NOW THEY'RE STARTING WEIRD RUMORS ABOUT ME!!

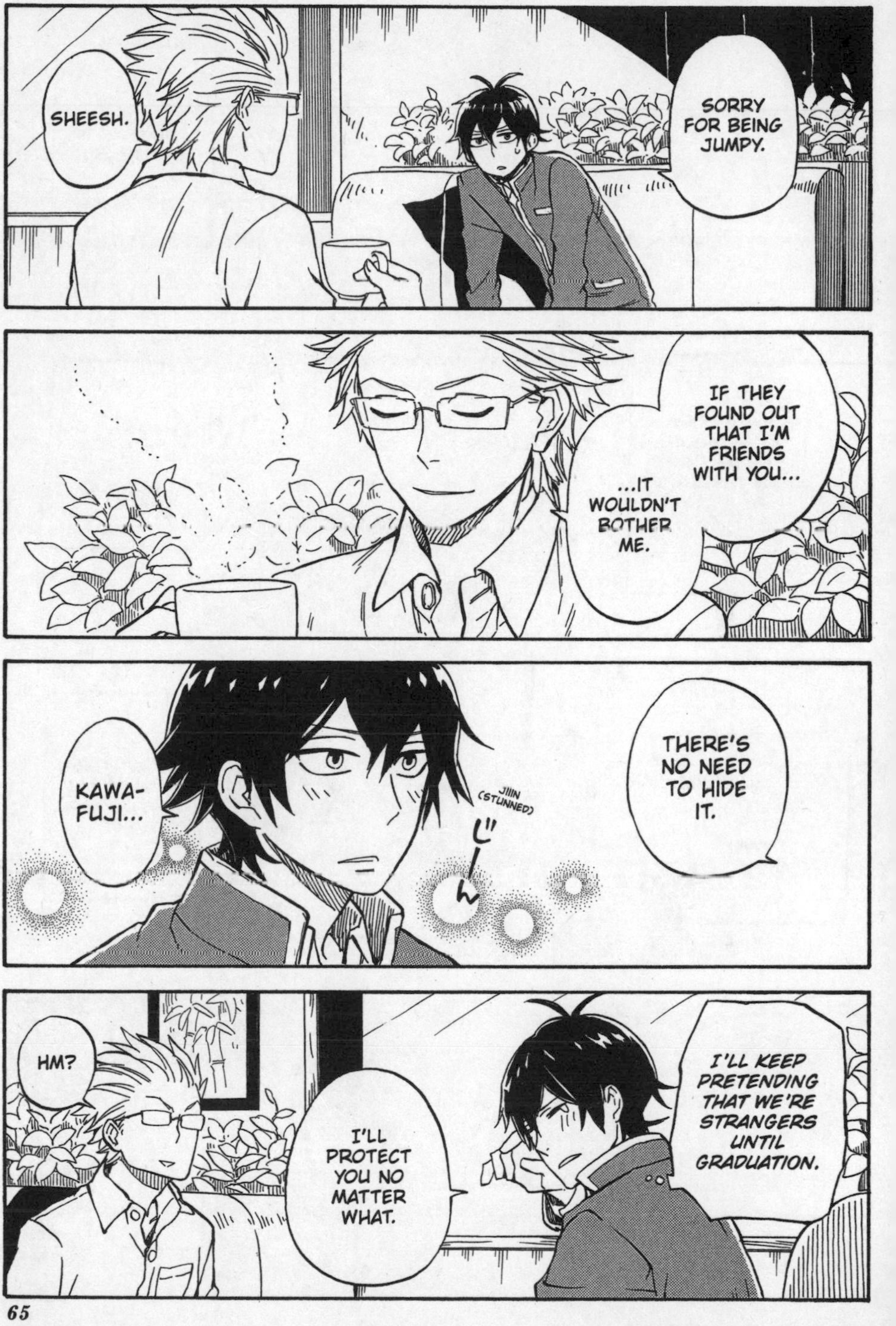
SORRY FOR BEING JUMPY.
SHEESH.
IF THEY FOUND OUT THAT I'M FRIENDS WITH YOU...
...IT WOULDN'T BOTHER ME.
THERE'S NO NEED TO HIDE IT.
JIIIN (STUNNED)
じ～ん
KAWA-FUJI...
I'LL KEEP PRETENDING THAT WE'RE STRANGERS UNTIL GRADUATION.
I'LL PROTECT YOU NO MATTER WHAT.
HM?

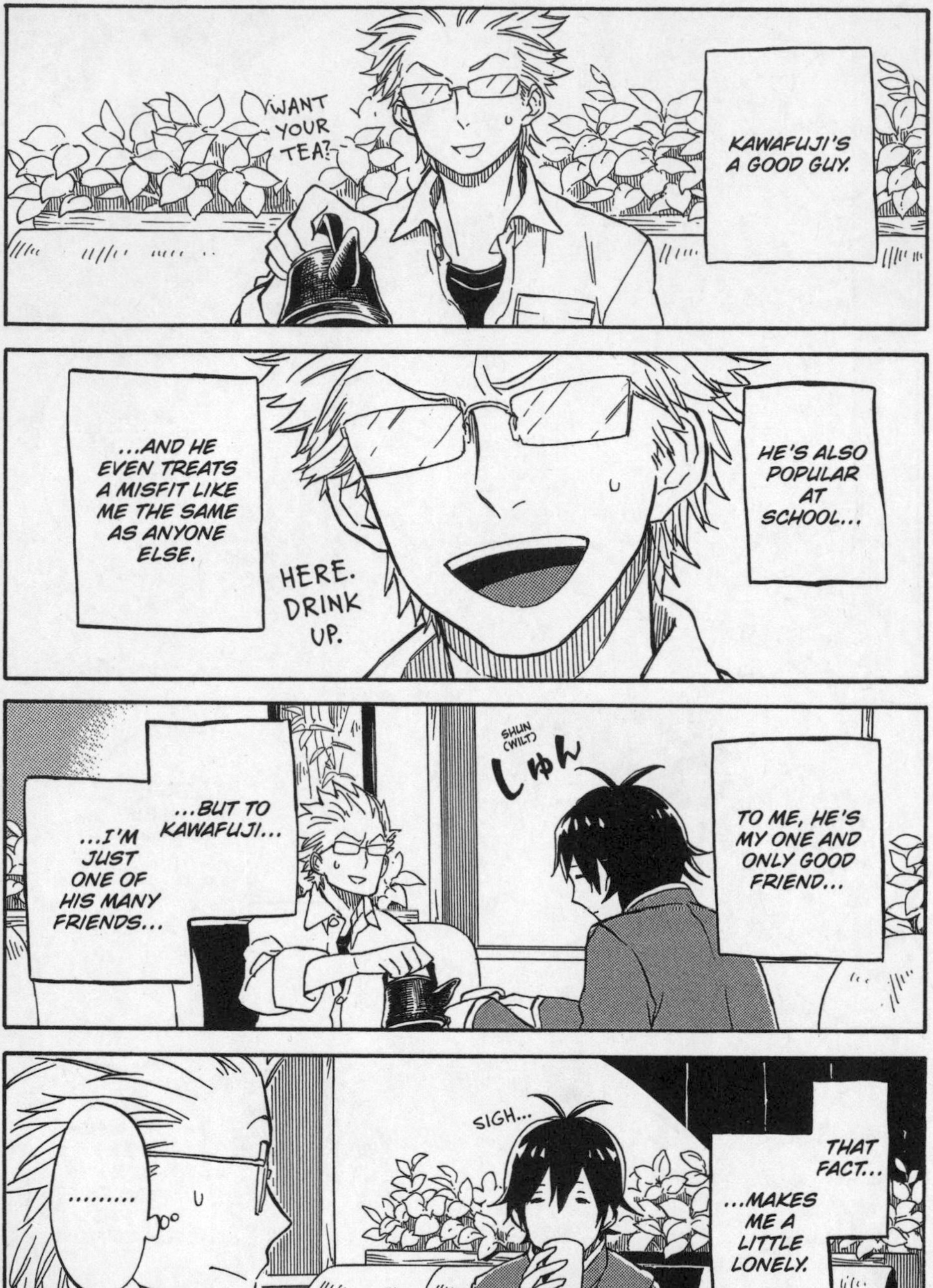
KAWAFUJI'S A GOOD GUY.
WANT YOUR TEA?
HE'S ALSO POPULAR AT SCHOOL...
...AND HE EVEN TREATS A MISFIT LIKE ME THE SAME AS ANYONE ELSE.
HERE. DRINK UP.
TO ME, HE'S MY ONE AND ONLY GOOD FRIEND...
SHUN (WILT)
しゅん
...BUT TO KAWAFUJI...
...I'M JUST ONE OF HIS MANY FRIENDS...
THAT FACT...
...MAKES ME A LITTLE LONELY.
SIGH...
....

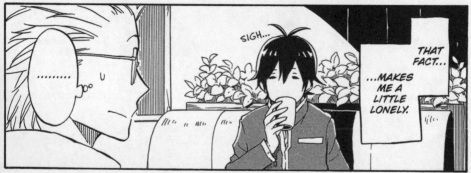

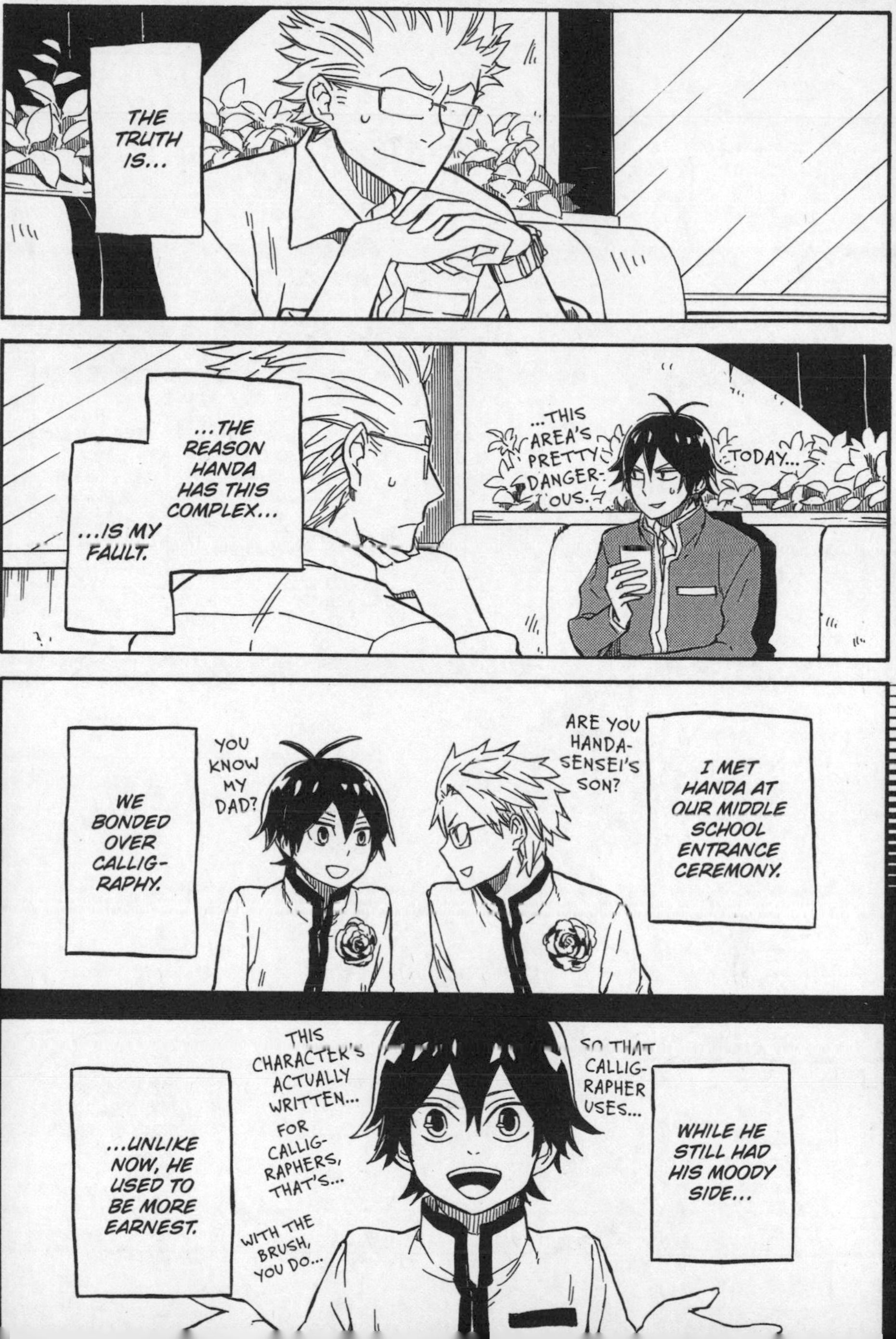
THE TRUTH IS...
TODAY...
...THIS AREA'S PRETTY DANGER-OUS.
...THE REASON HANDA HAS THIS COMPLEX...
...IS MY FAULT.
I MET HANDA AT OUR MIDDLE SCHOOL ENTRANCE CEREMONY.
ARE YOU HANDA-SENSEI'S SON?
YOU KNOW MY DAD?
WE BONDED OVER CALLIG-RAPHY.
WHILE HE STILL HAD HIS MOODY SIDE...
SO THAT CALLIG-RAPHER USES...
THIS CHARACTER'S ACTUALLY WRITTEN...
FOR CALLIG-RAPHERS, THAT'S...
WITH THE BRUSH, YOU DO...
...UNLIKE NOW, HE USED TO BE MORE EARNEST.

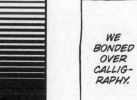

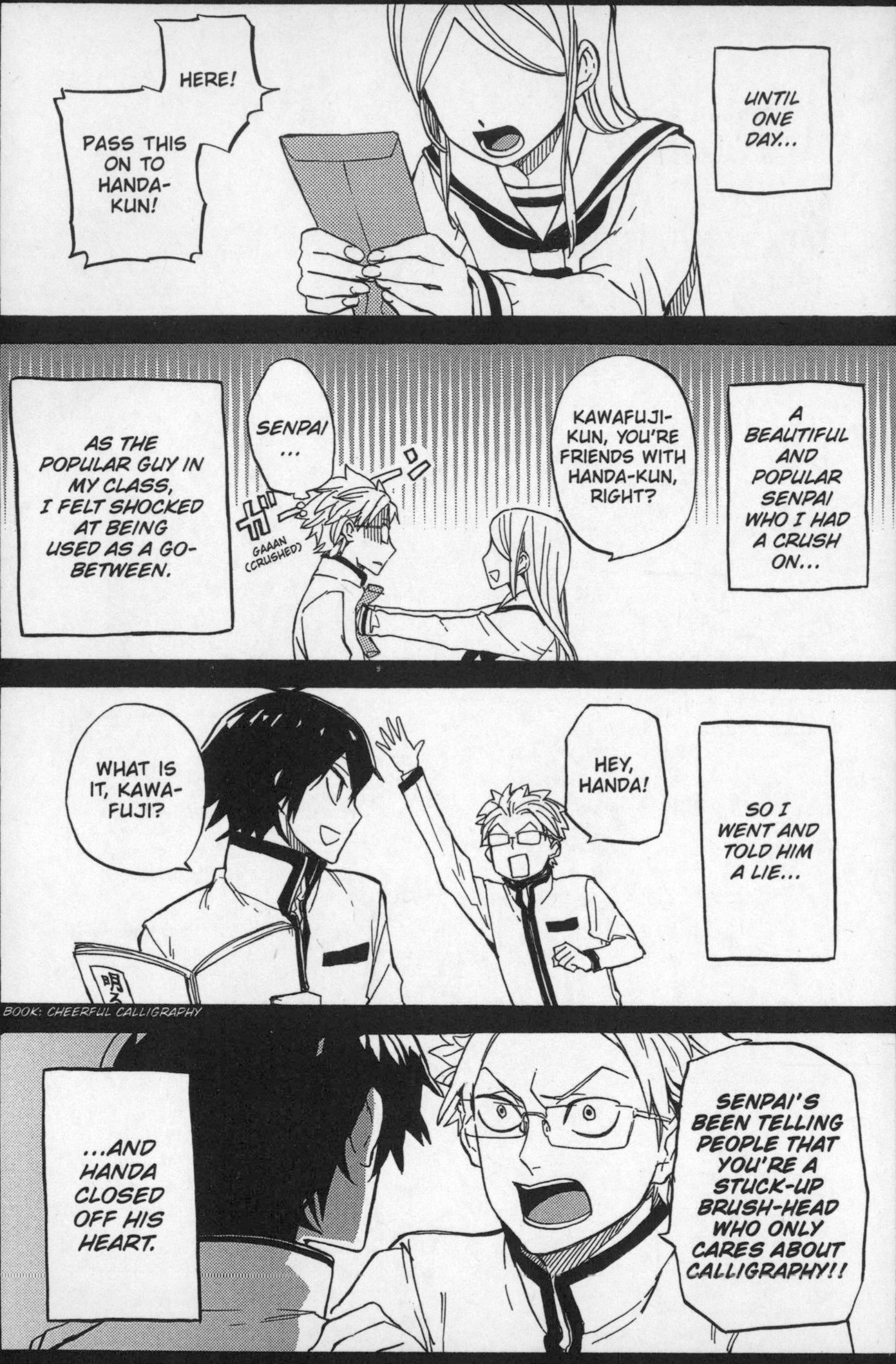
UNTIL ONE DAY...
HERE!
PASS THIS ON TO HANDA-KUN!
A BEAUTIFUL AND POPULAR SENPAI WHO I HAD A CRUSH ON...
KAWAFUJI-KUN, YOU'RE FRIENDS WITH HANDA-KUN, RIGHT?
SENPAI ...
GAAAN (CRUSHED)
AS THE POPULAR GUY IN MY CLASS, I FELT SHOCKED AT BEING USED AS A GO-BETWEEN.
SO I WENT AND TOLD HIM A LIE...
HEY, HANDA!
WHAT IS IT, KAWAFUJI?
BOOK: CHEERFUL CALLIGRAPHY
SENPAI'S BEEN TELLING PEOPLE THAT YOU'RE A STUCK-UP BRUSH-HEAD WHO ONLY CARES ABOUT CALLIGRAPHY!!
...AND HANDA CLOSED OFF HIS HEART.

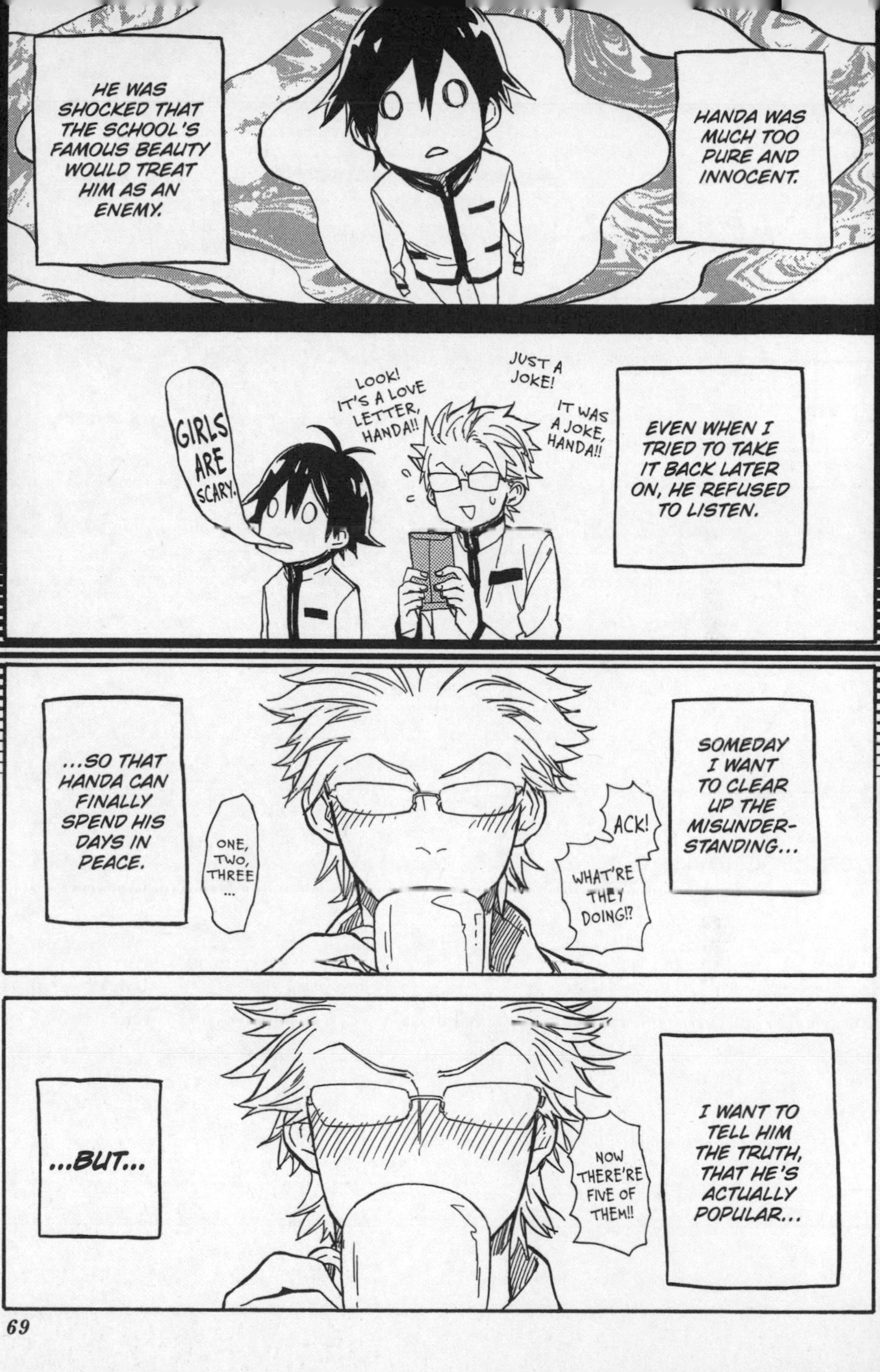
HANDA WAS MUCH TOO PURE AND INNOCENT.
HE WAS SHOCKED THAT THE SCHOOL'S FAMOUS BEAUTY WOULD TREAT HIM AS AN ENEMY.
EVEN WHEN I TRIED TO TAKE IT BACK LATER ON, HE REFUSED TO LISTEN.
IT WAS A JOKE, HANDA!!
JUST A JOKE!
LOOK! IT'S A LOVE LETTER, HANDA!!
GIRLS ARE SCARY.
SOMEDAY I WANT TO CLEAR UP THE MISUNDER-STANDING...
ACK!
WHAT'RE THEY DOING!?
ONE, TWO, THREE...
...SO THAT HANDA CAN FINALLY SPEND HIS DAYS IN PEACE.
I WANT TO TELL HIM THE TRUTH, THAT HE'S ACTUALLY POPULAR...
NOW THERE'RE FIVE OF THEM!!
...BUT...

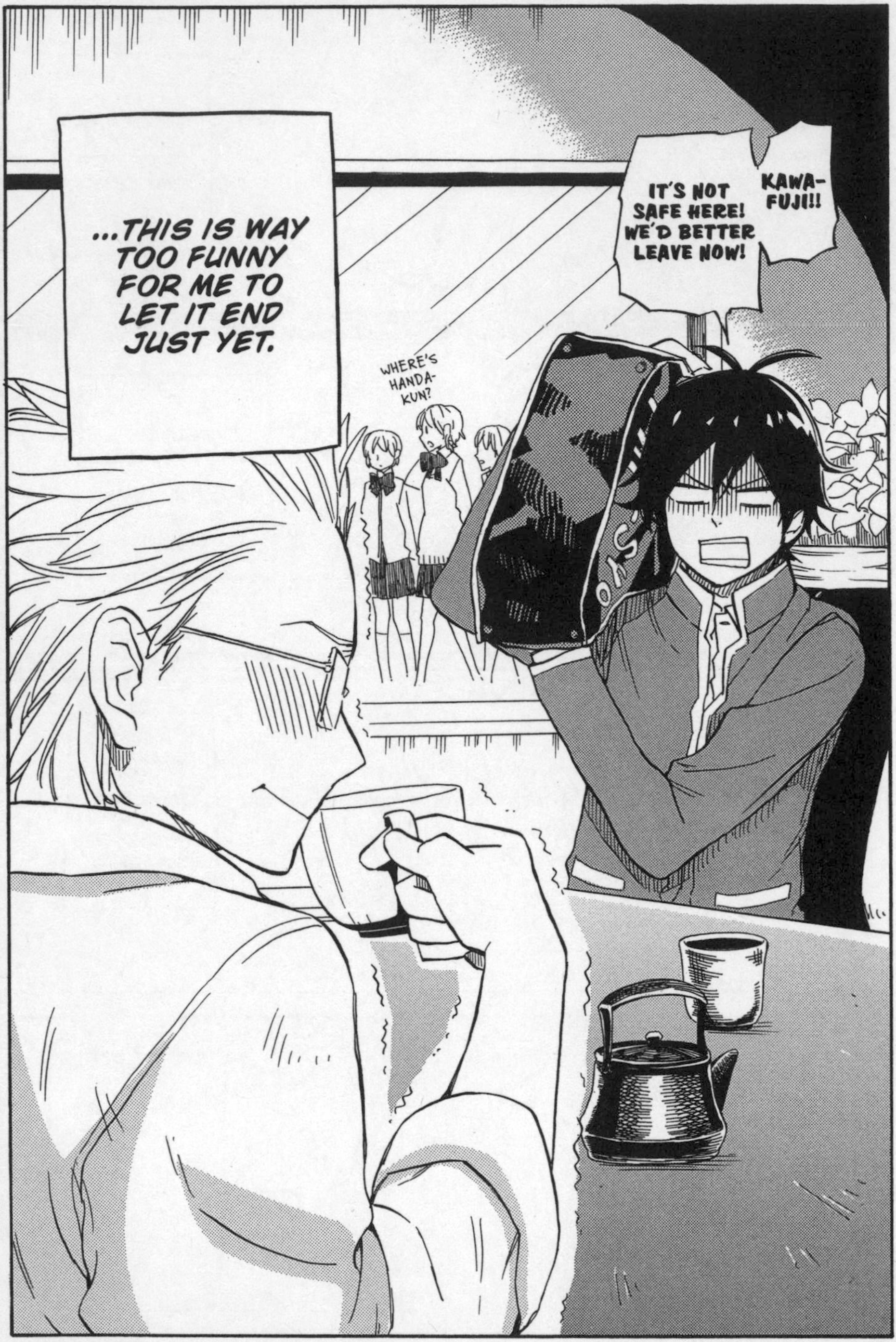
KAWA-FUJI!!
IT'S NOT SAFE HERE! WE'D BETTER LEAVE NOW!
WHERE'S HANDA-KUN?
...THIS IS WAY TOO FUNNY FOR ME TO LET IT END JUST YET.

Handa-
Kun

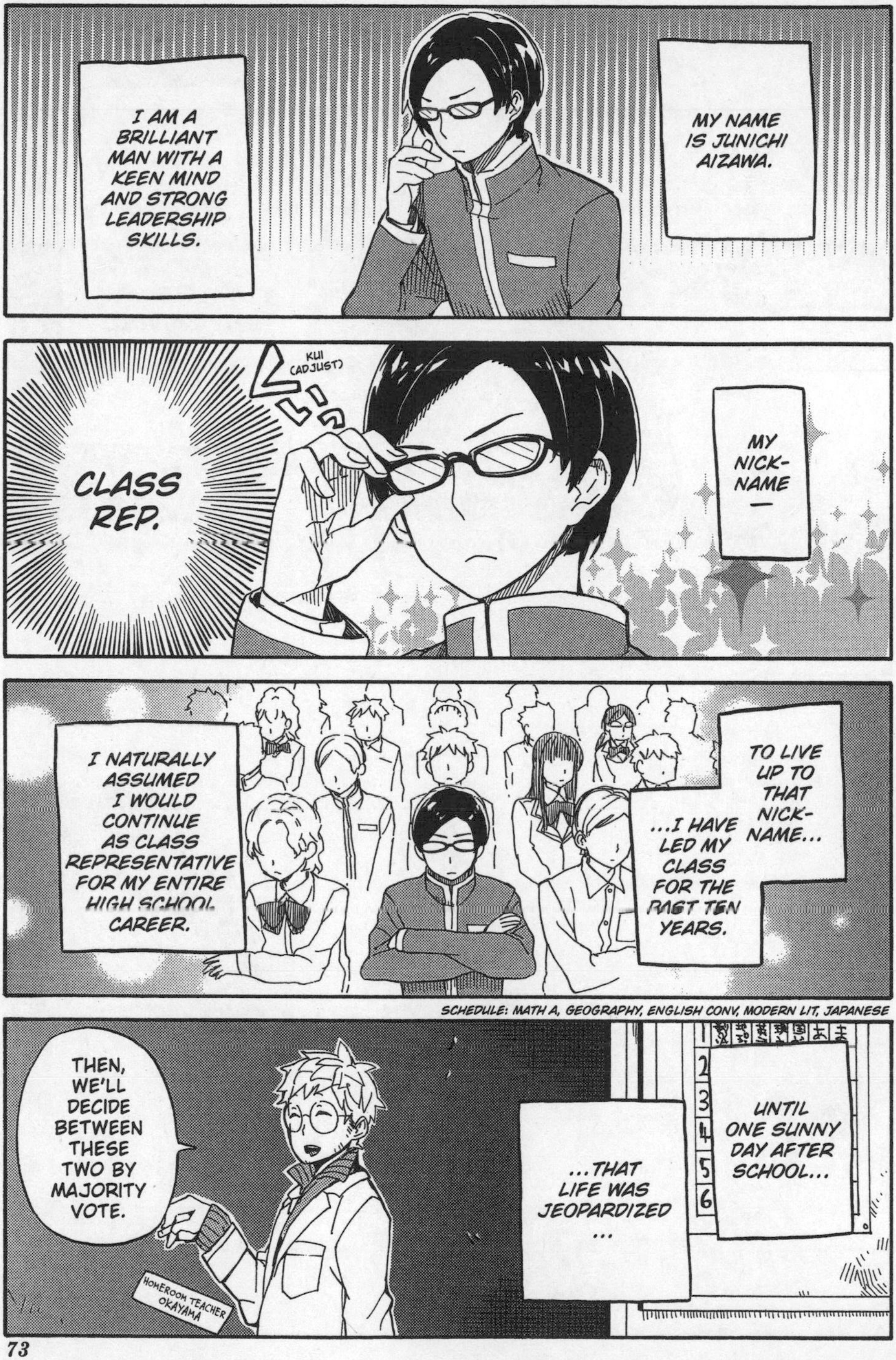
MY NAME IS JUNICHI AIZAWA.
I AM A BRILLIANT MAN WITH A KEEN MIND AND STRONG LEADERSHIP SKILLS.
MY NICK-NAME —
KUI (ADJUST)
CLASS REP.
TO LIVE UP TO THAT NICK-NAME…
…I HAVE LED MY CLASS FOR THE PAST TEN YEARS.
I NATURALLY ASSUMED I WOULD CONTINUE AS CLASS REPRESENTATIVE FOR MY ENTIRE HIGH SCHOOL CAREER.
SCHEDULE: MATH A, GEOGRAPHY, ENGLISH CONV, MODERN LIT, JAPANESE
UNTIL ONE SUNNY DAY AFTER SCHOOL…
…THAT LIFE WAS JEOPARDIZED…
THEN, WE'LL DECIDE BETWEEN THESE TWO BY MAJORITY VOTE.
HOMEROOM TEACHER OKAYAMA

Chapter 3: Handa-kun & the Class Rep

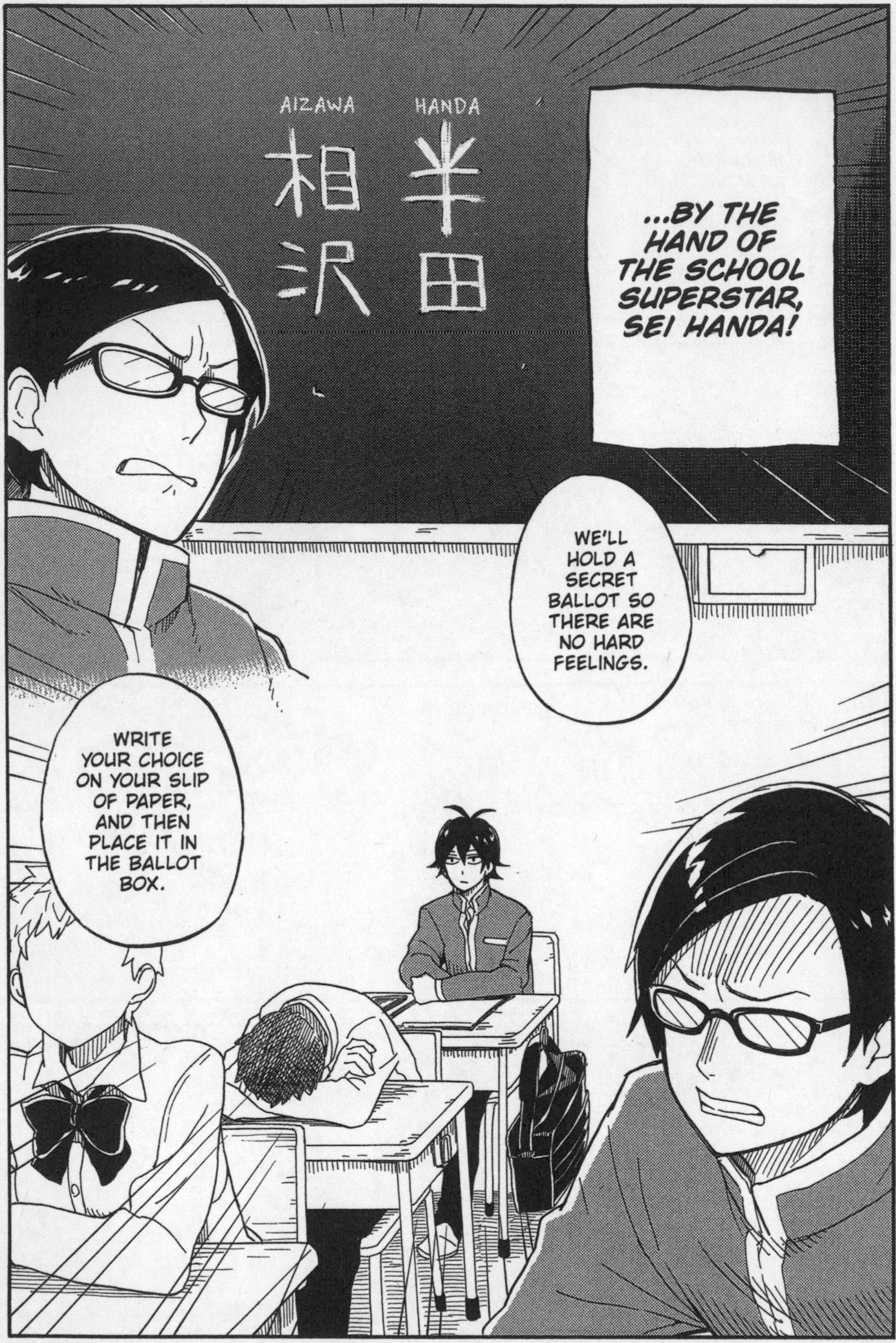
...BY THE HAND OF THE SCHOOL SUPERSTAR, SEI HANDA!
HANDA
半田
AIZAWA
相沢
WE'LL HOLD A SECRET BALLOT SO THERE ARE NO HARD FEELINGS.
WRITE YOUR CHOICE ON YOUR SLIP OF PAPER, AND THEN PLACE IT IN THE BALLOT BOX.

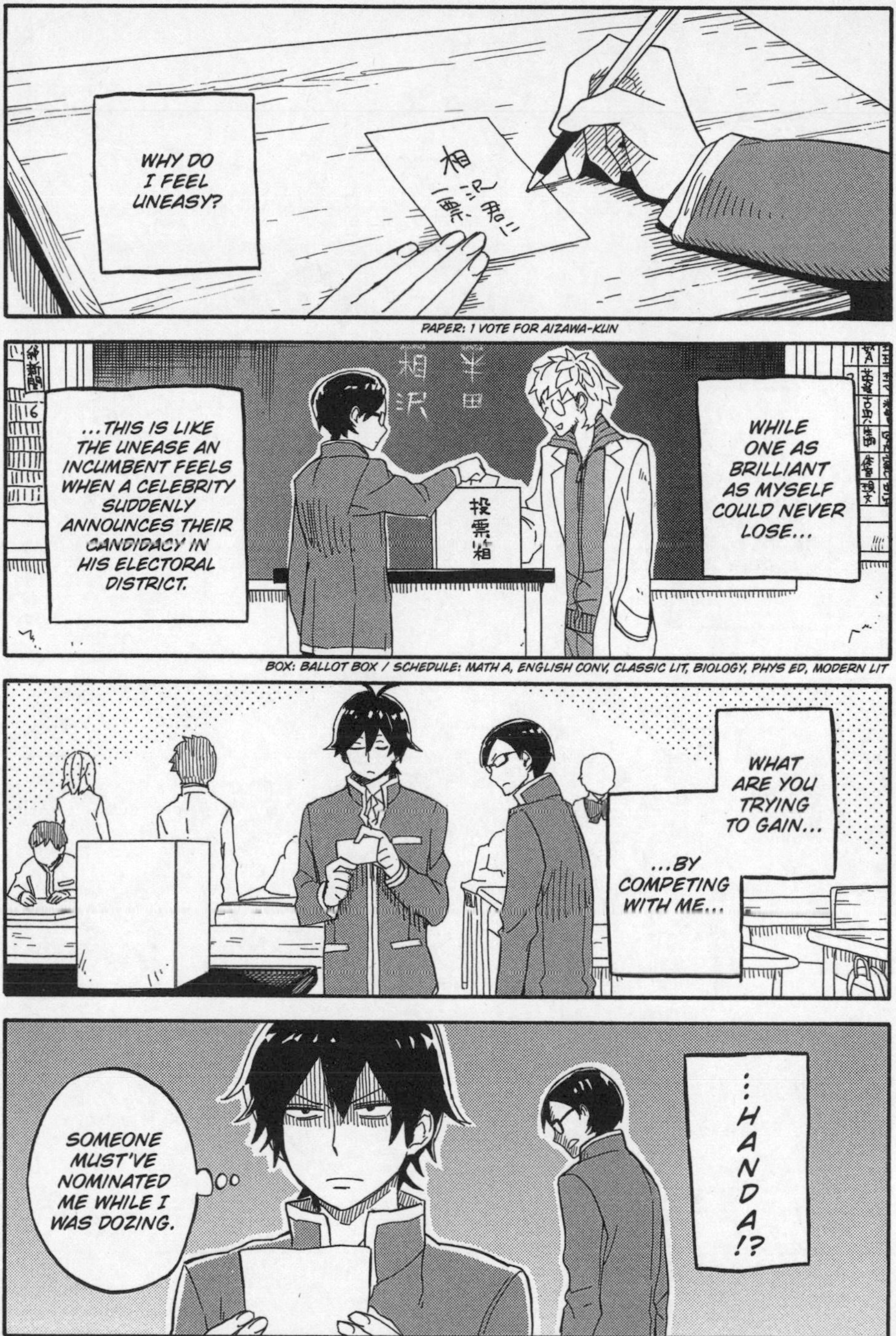
WHY DO I FEEL UNEASY?
相沢君に一票
PAPER: 1 VOTE FOR AIZAWA-KUN
WHILE ONE AS BRILLIANT AS MYSELF COULD NEVER LOSE...
...THIS IS LIKE THE UNEASE AN INCUMBENT FEELS WHEN A CELEBRITY SUDDENLY ANNOUNCES THEIR CANDIDACY IN HIS ELECTORAL DISTRICT.
半田
相沢
投票箱
BOX: BALLOT BOX / SCHEDULE: MATH A, ENGLISH CONV, CLASSIC LIT, BIOLOGY, PHYS ED, MODERN LIT
WHAT ARE YOU TRYING TO GAIN...
...BY COMPETING WITH ME...
...HANDA!?
SOMEONE MUST'VE NOMINATED ME WHILE I WAS DOZING.

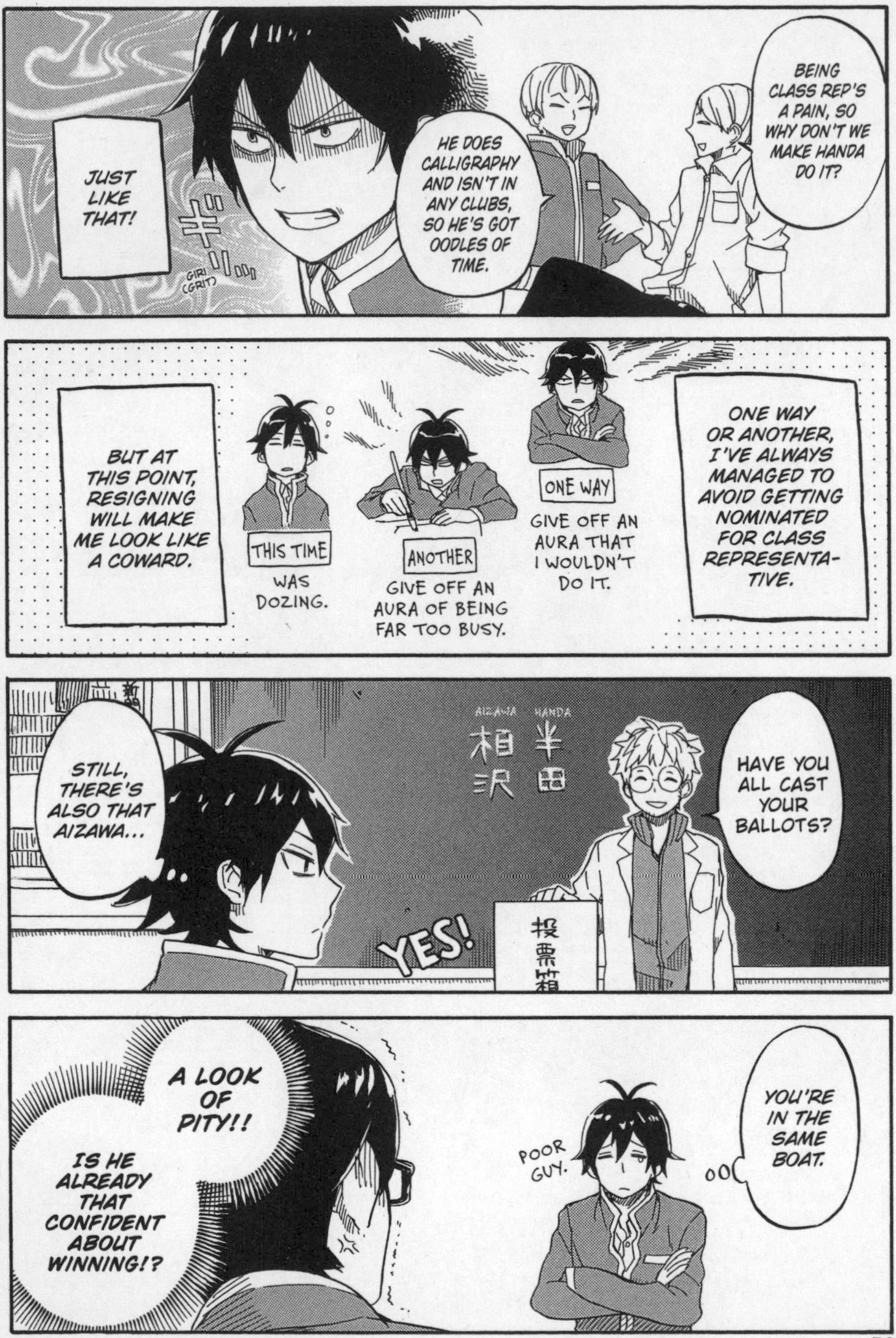
BEING CLASS REP'S A PAIN, SO WHY DON'T WE MAKE HANDA DO IT?
HE DOES CALLIGRAPHY AND ISN'T IN ANY CLUBS, SO HE'S GOT OODLES OF TIME.
GIRI (GRIT)
JUST LIKE THAT!
ONE WAY OR ANOTHER, I'VE ALWAYS MANAGED TO AVOID GETTING NOMINATED FOR CLASS REPRESENTATIVE.
ONE WAY
GIVE OFF AN AURA THAT I WOULDN'T DO IT.
ANOTHER
GIVE OFF AN AURA OF BEING FAR TOO BUSY.
THIS TIME
WAS DOZING.
BUT AT THIS POINT, RESIGNING WILL MAKE ME LOOK LIKE A COWARD.
HAVE YOU ALL CAST YOUR BALLOTS?
HANDA 半田
AIZAWA 相沢
投票箱
YES!
STILL, THERE'S ALSO THAT AIZAWA...
YOU'RE IN THE SAME BOAT.
POOR GUY.
A LOOK OF PITY!!
IS HE ALREADY THAT CONFIDENT ABOUT WINNING!?

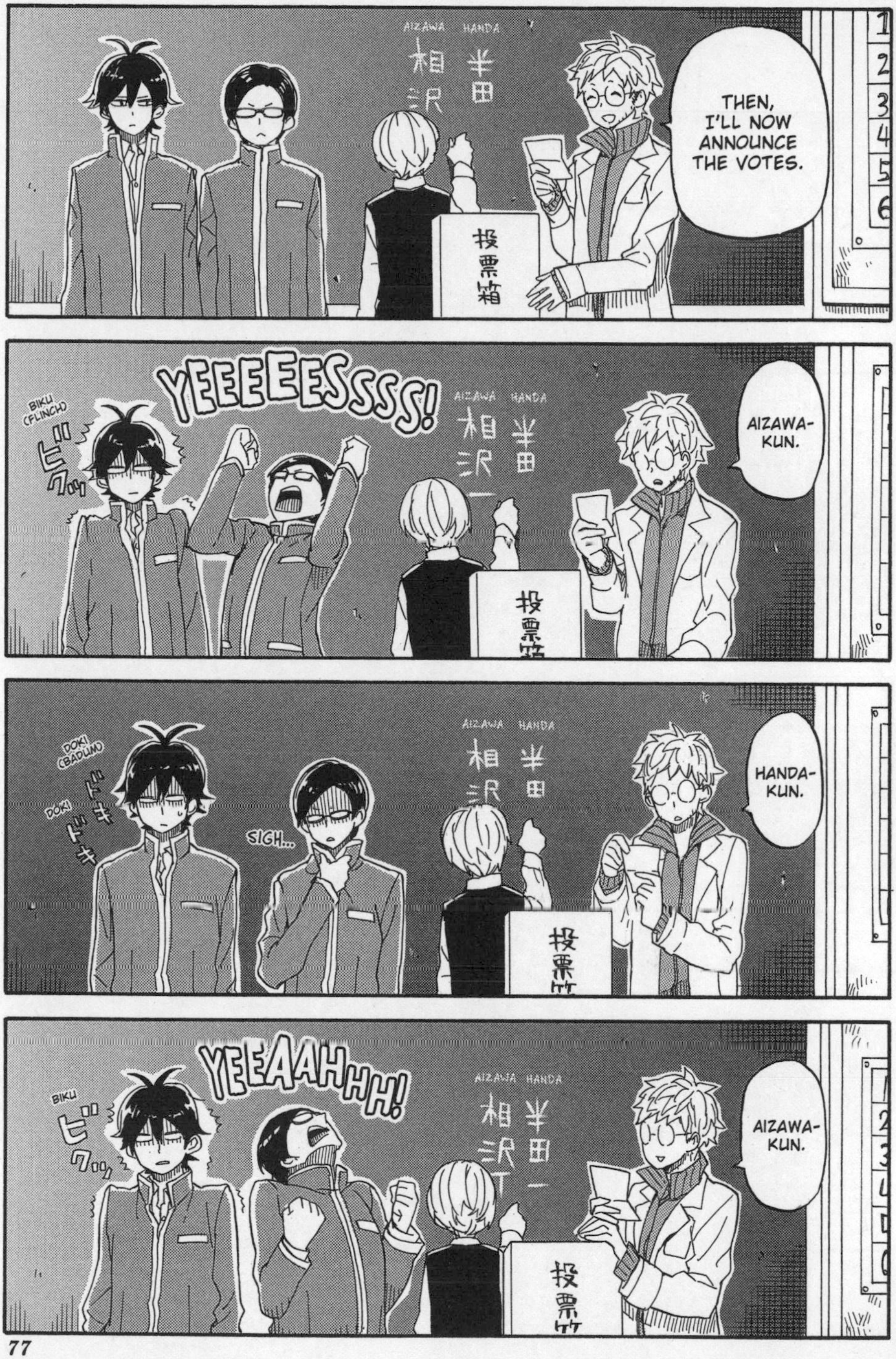
THEN, I'LL NOW ANNOUNCE THE VOTES.
AIZAWA HANDA
相沢 半田
投票箱
AIZAWA-KUN.
AIZAWA HANDA
YEEEEESSSSS!
BIKU (FLINCH)
ビクッ
HANDA-KUN.
AIZAWA HANDA
SIGH...
DOKI (BADUM)
ドキ
DOKI
ドキ
AIZAWA-KUN.
AIZAWA HANDA
YEEAAHHH!
BIKU
ビクッ

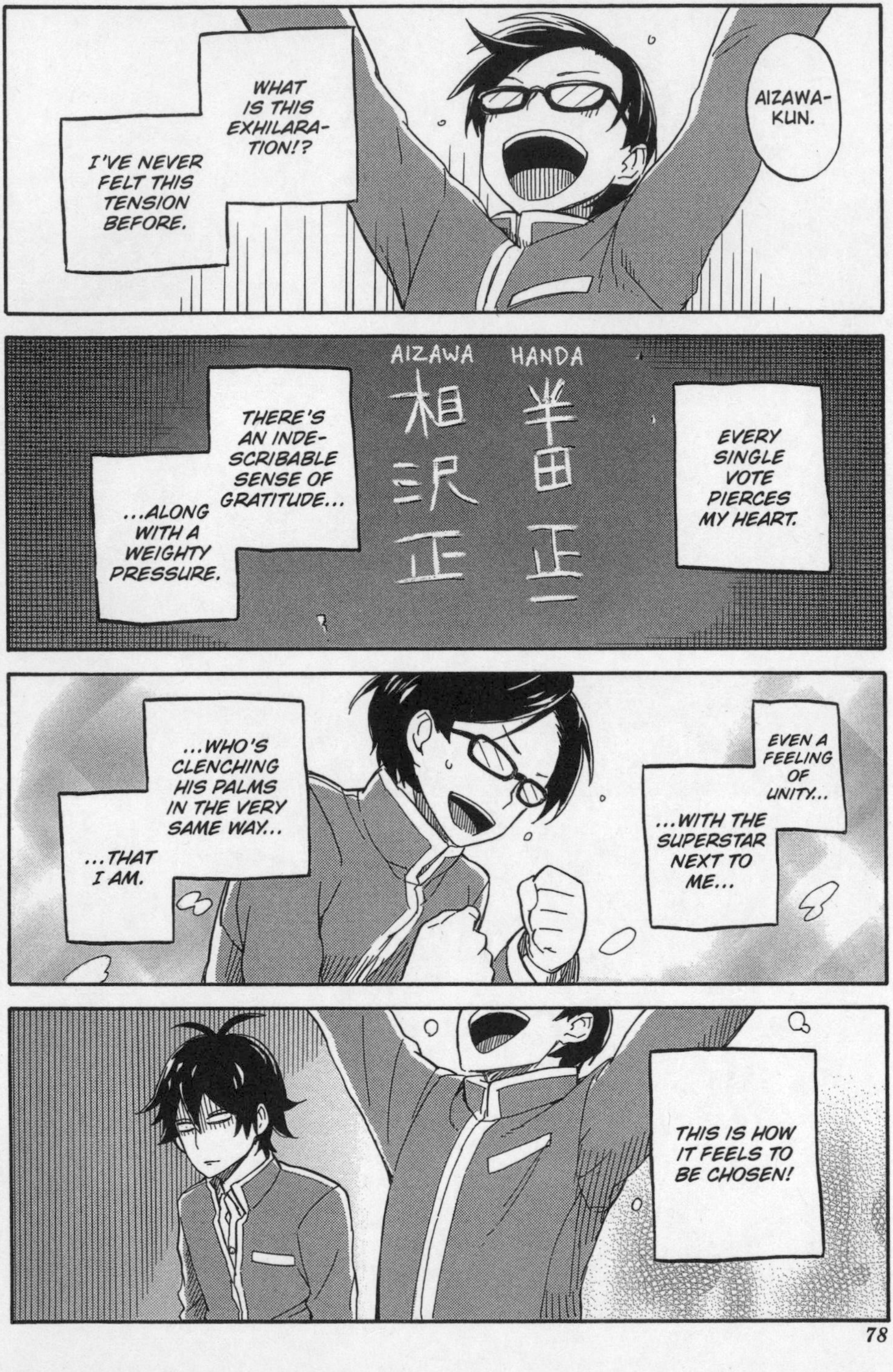
AIZAWA-KUN.
WHAT IS THIS EXHILARATION!?
I'VE NEVER FELT THIS TENSION BEFORE.
EVERY SINGLE VOTE PIERCES MY HEART.
HANDA
半田 正正
AIZAWA
相沢 正
THERE'S AN INDESCRIBABLE SENSE OF GRATITUDE...
...ALONG WITH A WEIGHTY PRESSURE.
EVEN A FEELING OF UNITY...
...WITH THE SUPERSTAR NEXT TO ME...
...WHO'S CLENCHING HIS PALMS IN THE VERY SAME WAY...
...THAT I AM.
THIS IS HOW IT FEELS TO BE CHOSEN!

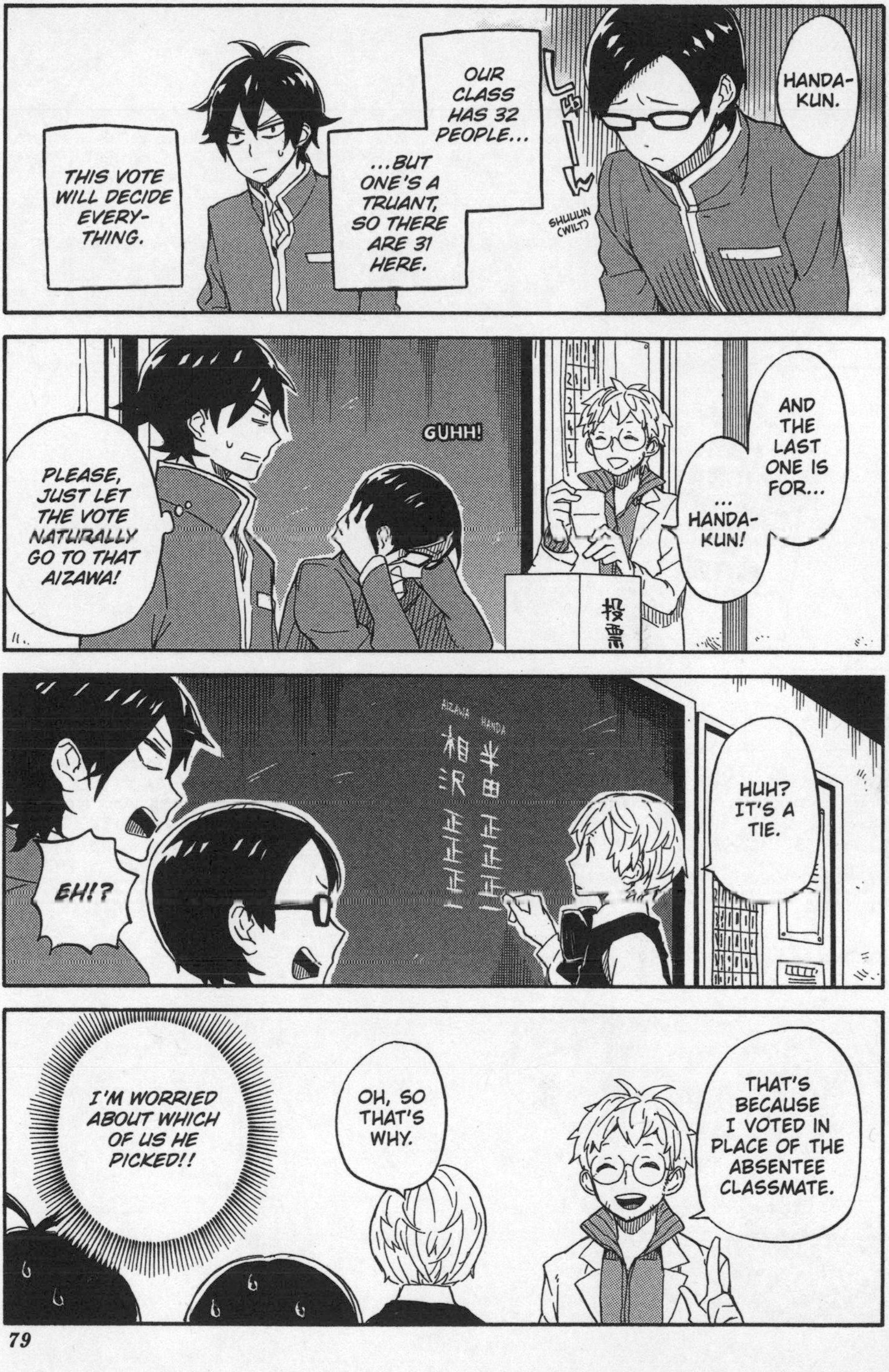
HANDA-KUN.
SHUUUN (WILT)
OUR CLASS HAS 32 PEOPLE...
...BUT ONE'S A TRUANT, SO THERE ARE 31 HERE.
THIS VOTE WILL DECIDE EVERYTHING.
AND THE LAST ONE IS FOR... ...HANDA-KUN!
投票
GUHH!
PLEASE, JUST LET THE VOTE NATURALLY GO TO THAT AIZAWA!
HUH? IT'S A TIE.
HANDA 半田
AIZAWA 相沢
EH!?
THAT'S BECAUSE I VOTED IN PLACE OF THE ABSENTEE CLASSMATE.
OH, SO THAT'S WHY.
I'M WORRIED ABOUT WHICH OF US HE PICKED!!

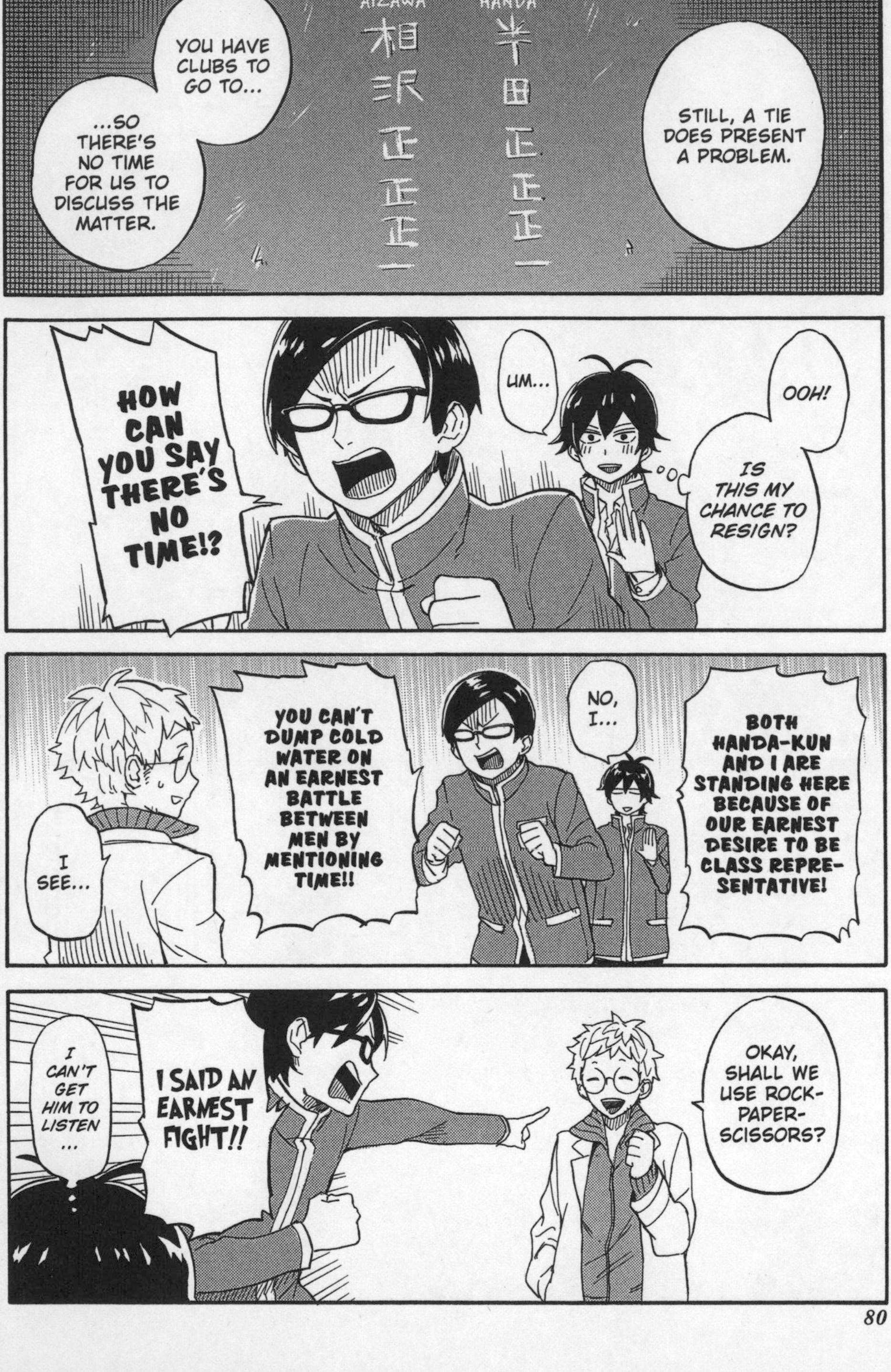
STILL, A TIE DOES PRESENT A PROBLEM.
HANDA
半田
AIZAWA
相沢
YOU HAVE CLUBS TO GO TO...
...SO THERE'S NO TIME FOR US TO DISCUSS THE MATTER.
OOH!
IS THIS MY CHANCE TO RESIGN?
UM...
HOW CAN YOU SAY THERE'S NO TIME!?
BOTH HANDA-KUN AND I ARE STANDING HERE BECAUSE OF OUR EARNEST DESIRE TO BE CLASS REPRESENTATIVE!
NO, I...
YOU CAN'T DUMP COLD WATER ON AN EARNEST BATTLE BETWEEN MEN BY MENTIONING TIME!!
I SEE...
OKAY, SHALL WE USE ROCK-PAPER-SCISSORS?
I SAID AN EARNEST FIGHT!!
I CAN'T GET HIM TO LISTEN...

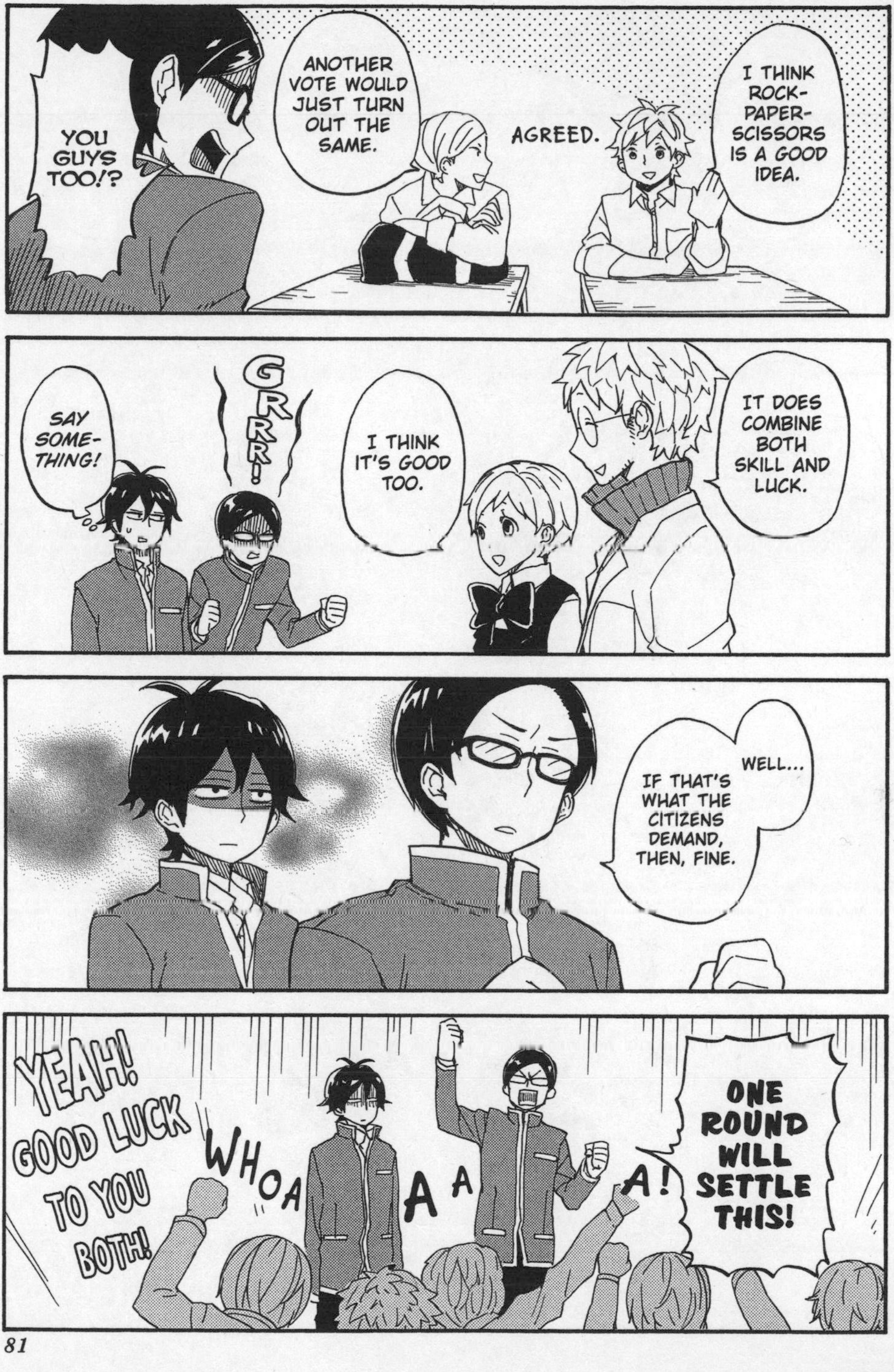
I THINK ROCK-PAPER-SCISSORS IS A GOOD IDEA.
AGREED.
ANOTHER VOTE WOULD JUST TURN OUT THE SAME.
YOU GUYS TOO!?
IT DOES COMBINE BOTH SKILL AND LUCK.
I THINK IT'S GOOD TOO.
GRRR!
SAY SOME-THING!
WELL...
IF THAT'S WHAT THE CITIZENS DEMAND, THEN, FINE.
ONE ROUND WILL SETTLE THIS!
WHOA A A A!
YEAH! GOOD LUCK TO YOU BOTH!

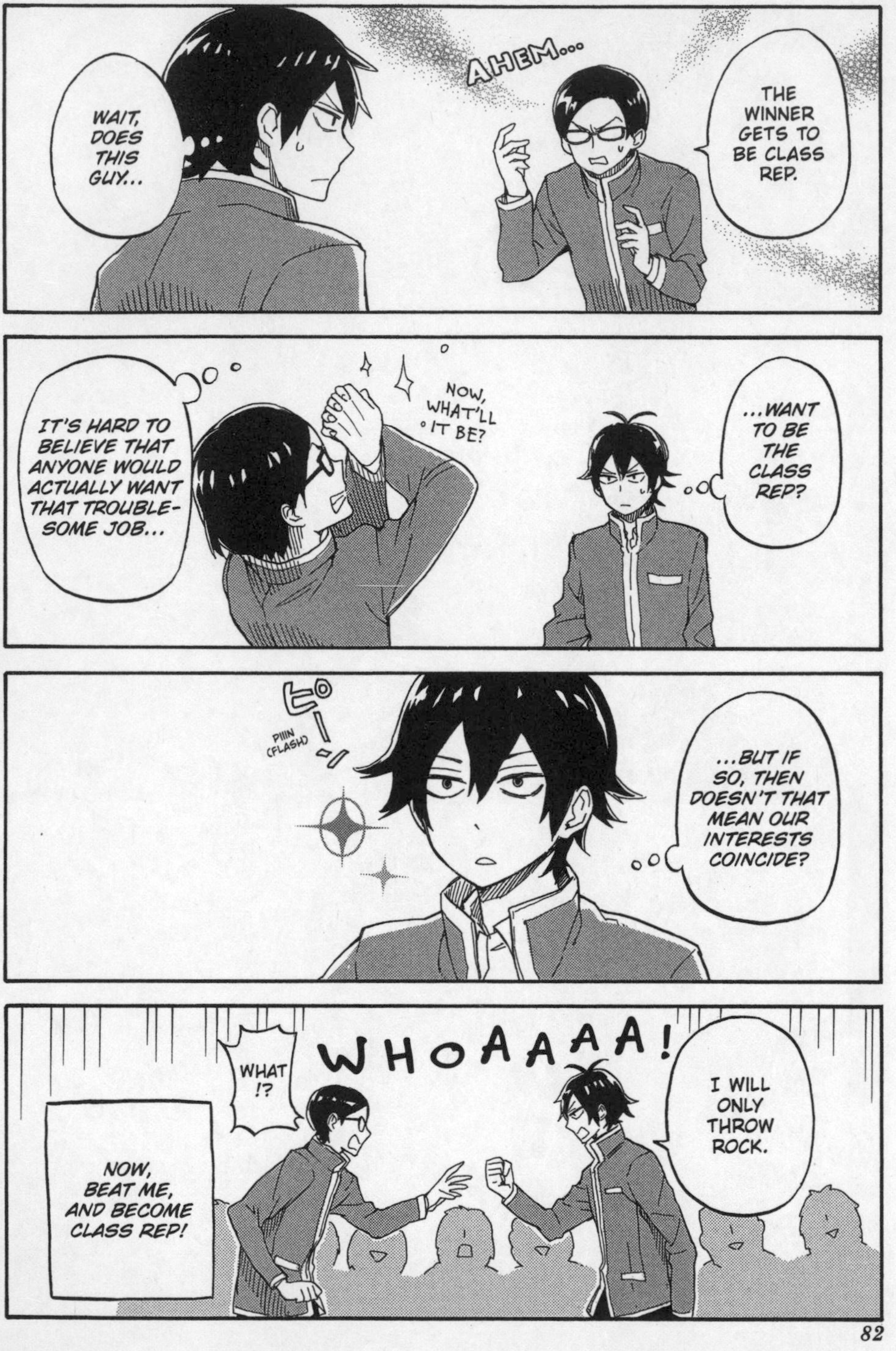
THE WINNER GETS TO BE CLASS REP.
AHEM...
WAIT, DOES THIS GUY...
...WANT TO BE THE CLASS REP?
NOW, WHAT'LL IT BE?
IT'S HARD TO BELIEVE THAT ANYONE WOULD ACTUALLY WANT THAT TROUBLE-SOME JOB...
...BUT IF SO, THEN DOESN'T THAT MEAN OUR INTERESTS COINCIDE?
PIIIN (FLASH)
I WILL ONLY THROW ROCK.
WHOAAAAA!
WHAT!?
NOW, BEAT ME, AND BECOME CLASS REP!

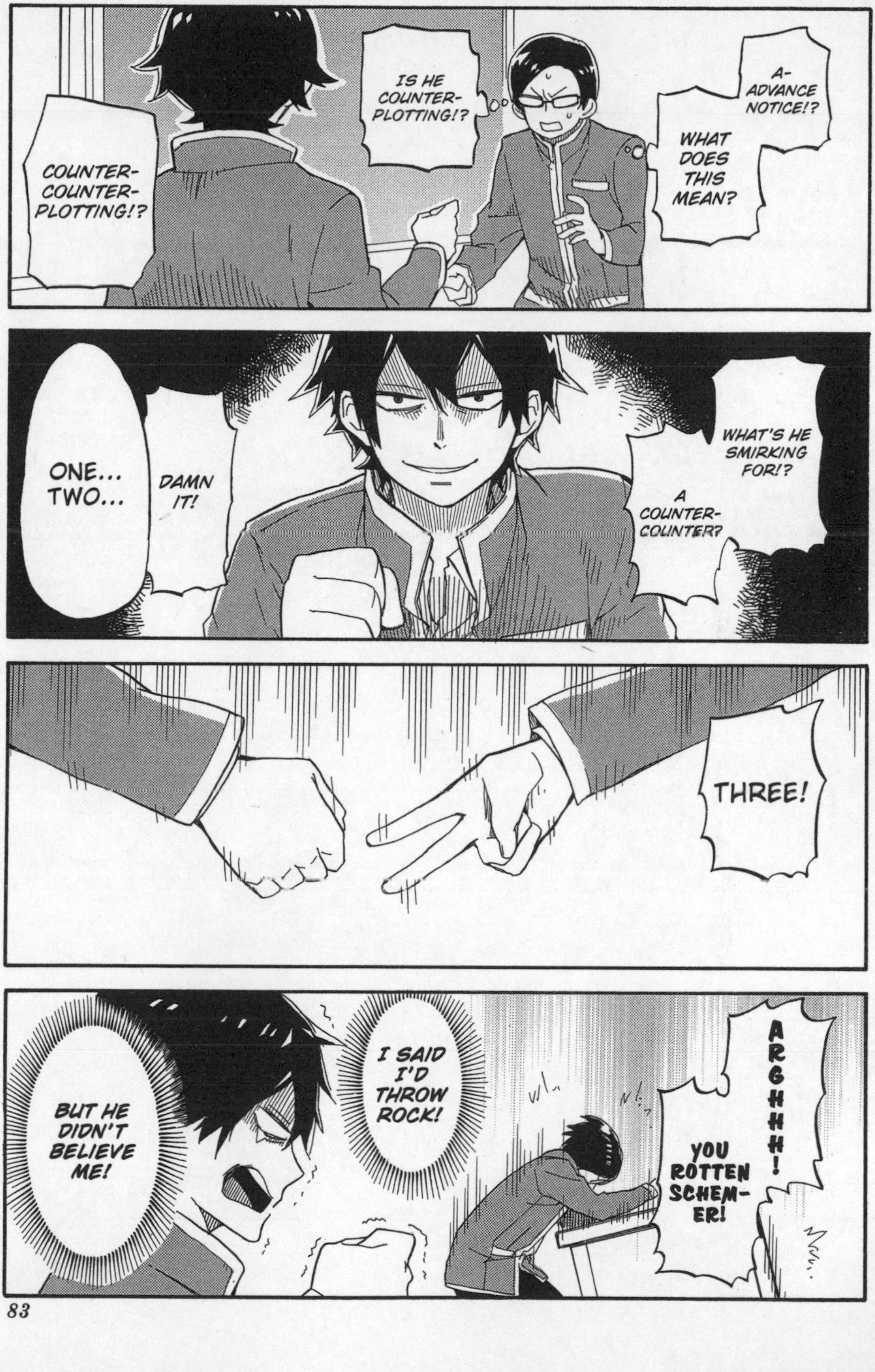
A-ADVANCE NOTICE!?
WHAT DOES THIS MEAN?
IS HE COUNTER-PLOTTING!?
COUNTER-COUNTER-PLOTTING!?
WHAT'S HE SMIRKING FOR!?
A COUNTER-COUNTER?
DAMN IT!
ONE... TWO...
THREE!
ARGHHH!
YOU ROTTEN SCHEM-ER!
I SAID I'D THROW ROCK!
BUT HE DIDN'T BELIEVE ME!

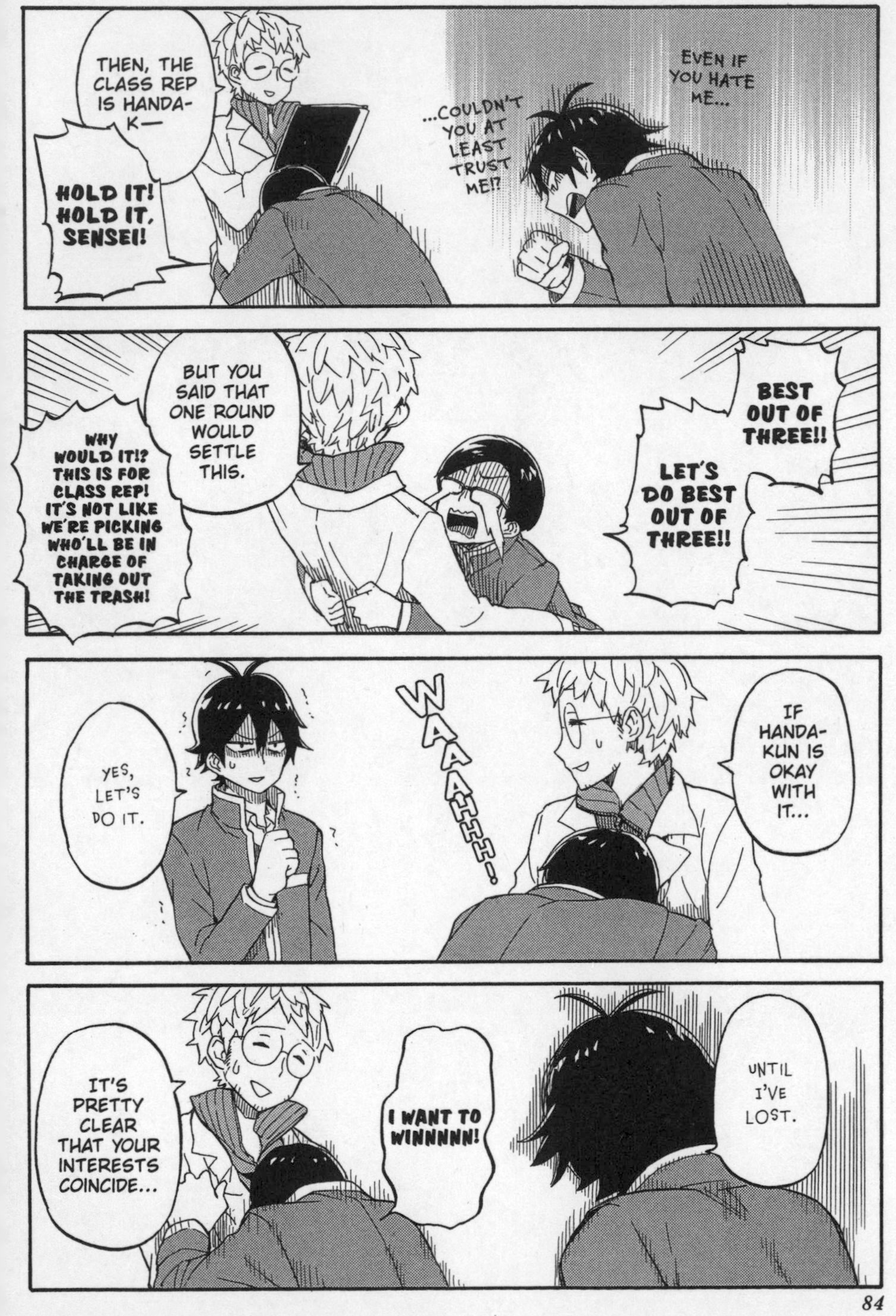
EVEN IF YOU HATE ME...
...COULDN'T YOU AT LEAST TRUST ME!?
THEN, THE CLASS REP IS HANDA-K—
HOLD IT! HOLD IT, SENSEI!
BEST OUT OF THREE!!
LET'S DO BEST OUT OF THREE!!
BUT YOU SAID THAT ONE ROUND WOULD SETTLE THIS.
WHY WOULD IT!? THIS IS FOR CLASS REP! IT'S NOT LIKE WE'RE PICKING WHO'LL BE IN CHARGE OF TAKING OUT THE TRASH!
IF HANDA-KUN IS OKAY WITH IT...
WAAAHHH!
YES, LET'S DO IT.
UNTIL I'VE LOST.
I WANT TO WINNNNN!
IT'S PRETTY CLEAR THAT YOUR INTERESTS COINCIDE...

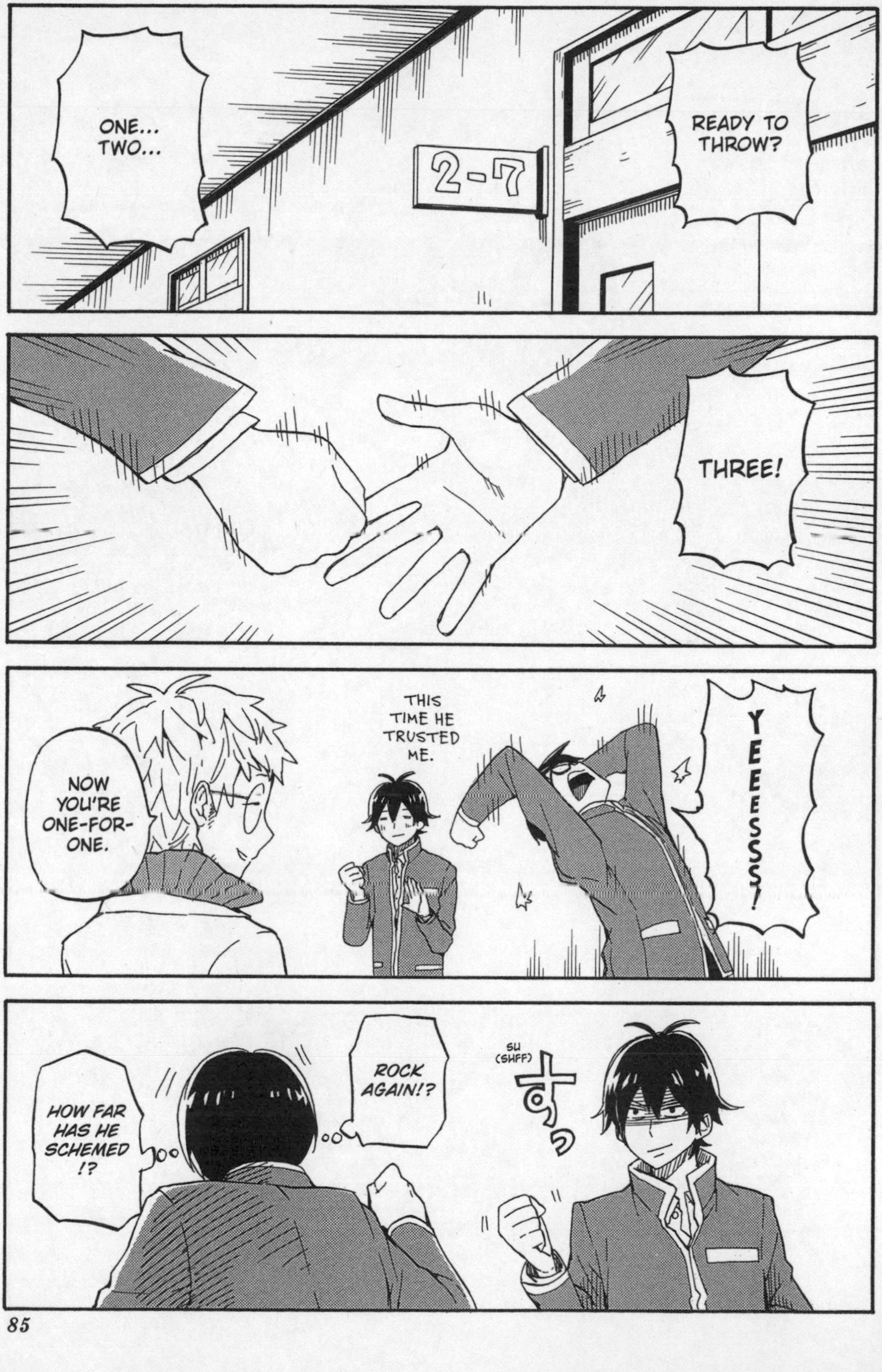
READY TO THROW?
ONE... TWO...
THREE!
YEEESSS!
THIS TIME HE TRUSTED ME.
NOW YOU'RE ONE-FOR-ONE.
すっ
SU (SHFF)
ROCK AGAIN!?
HOW FAR HAS HE SCHEMED!?

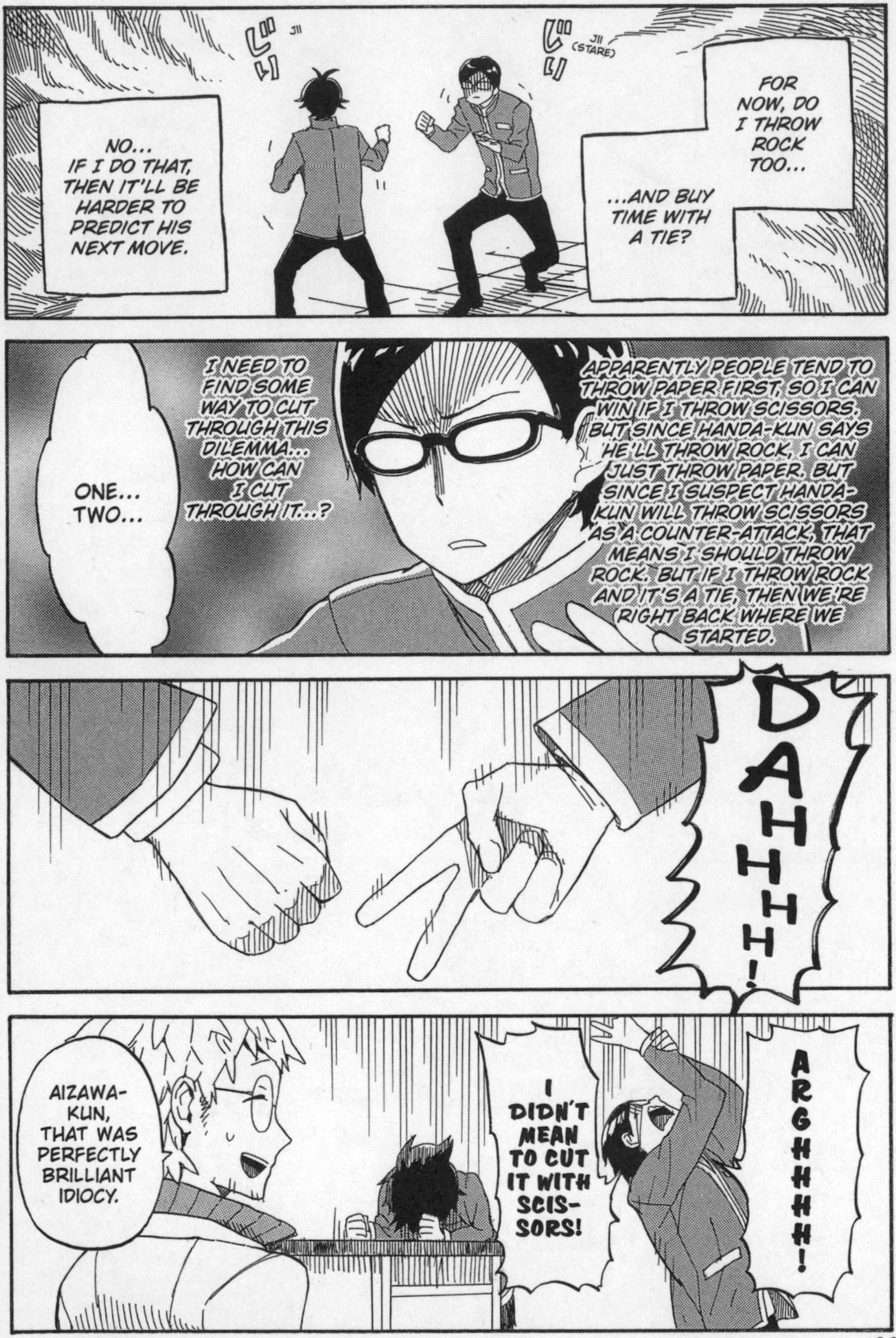
JII (STARE)
FOR NOW, DO I THROW ROCK TOO...
...AND BUY TIME WITH A TIE?
JII
NO... IF I DO THAT, THEN IT'LL BE HARDER TO PREDICT HIS NEXT MOVE.
APPARENTLY PEOPLE TEND TO THROW PAPER FIRST, SO I CAN WIN IF I THROW SCISSORS. BUT SINCE HANDA-KUN SAYS HE'LL THROW ROCK, I CAN JUST THROW PAPER. BUT SINCE I SUSPECT HANDA-KUN WILL THROW SCISSORS AS A COUNTER-ATTACK, THAT MEANS I SHOULD THROW ROCK. BUT IF I THROW ROCK AND IT'S A TIE, THEN WE'RE RIGHT BACK WHERE WE STARTED.
I NEED TO FIND SOME WAY TO CUT THROUGH THIS DILEMMA... HOW CAN I CUT THROUGH IT...?
ONE... TWO...
DAHHHHH!
ARGHHHHH!
I DIDN'T MEAN TO CUT IT WITH SCIS-SORS!
AIZAWA-KUN, THAT WAS PERFECTLY BRILLIANT IDIOCY.

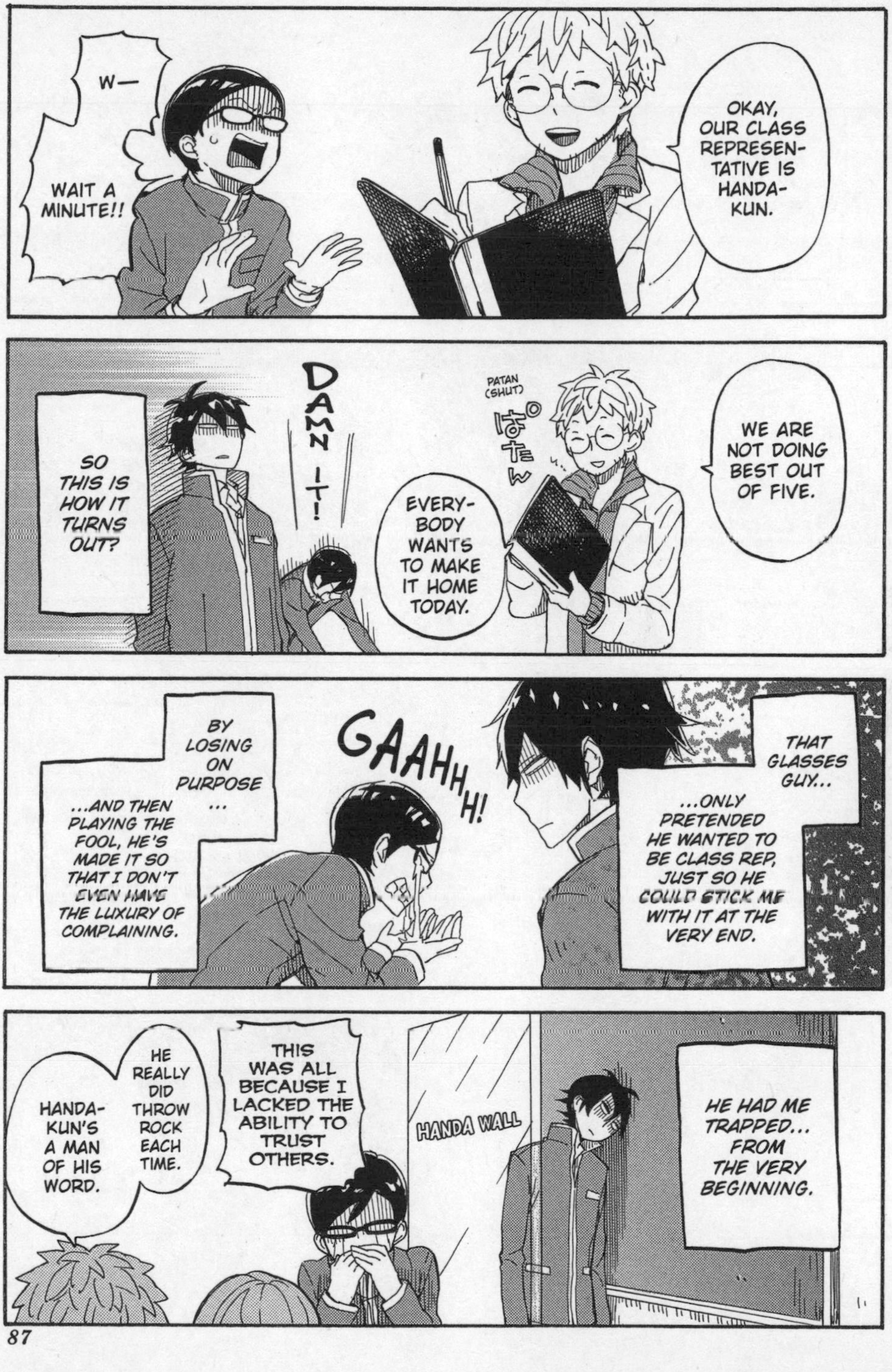
OKAY, OUR CLASS REPRESEN-TATIVE IS HANDA-KUN.
W—
WAIT A MINUTE!!
WE ARE NOT DOING BEST OUT OF FIVE.
PATAN (SHUT)
ぱたん
EVERY-BODY WANTS TO MAKE IT HOME TODAY.
DAMN IT!
SO THIS IS HOW IT TURNS OUT?
THAT GLASSES GUY...
...ONLY PRETENDED HE WANTED TO BE CLASS REP, JUST SO HE COULD STICK ME WITH IT AT THE VERY END.
GAAHHHH!
BY LOSING ON PURPOSE...
...AND THEN PLAYING THE FOOL, HE'S MADE IT SO THAT I DON'T EVEN HAVE THE LUXURY OF COMPLAINING.
HE HAD ME TRAPPED... FROM THE VERY BEGINNING.
HANDA WALL
THIS WAS ALL BECAUSE I LACKED THE ABILITY TO TRUST OTHERS.
HE REALLY DID THROW ROCK EACH TIME.
HANDA-KUN'S A MAN OF HIS WORD.

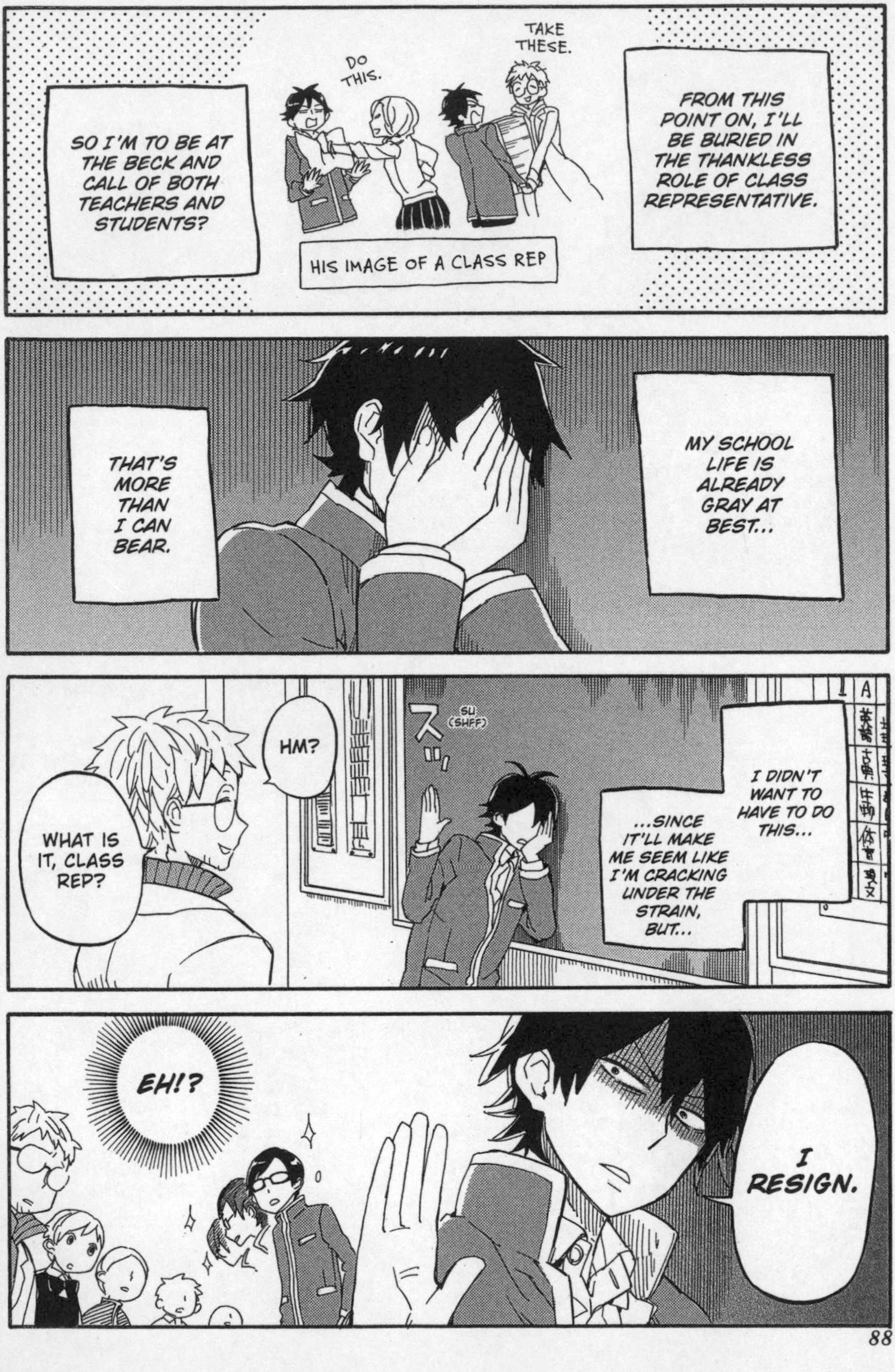
FROM THIS POINT ON, I'LL BE BURIED IN THE THANKLESS ROLE OF CLASS REPRESENTATIVE.
TAKE THESE.
DO THIS.
SO I'M TO BE AT THE BECK AND CALL OF BOTH TEACHERS AND STUDENTS?
HIS IMAGE OF A CLASS REP
MY SCHOOL LIFE IS ALREADY GRAY AT BEST...
THAT'S MORE THAN I CAN BEAR.
I DIDN'T WANT TO HAVE TO DO THIS...
...SINCE IT'LL MAKE ME SEEM LIKE I'M CRACKING UNDER THE STRAIN, BUT...
SU (SHFF)
HM?
WHAT IS IT, CLASS REP?
I RESIGN.
EH!?

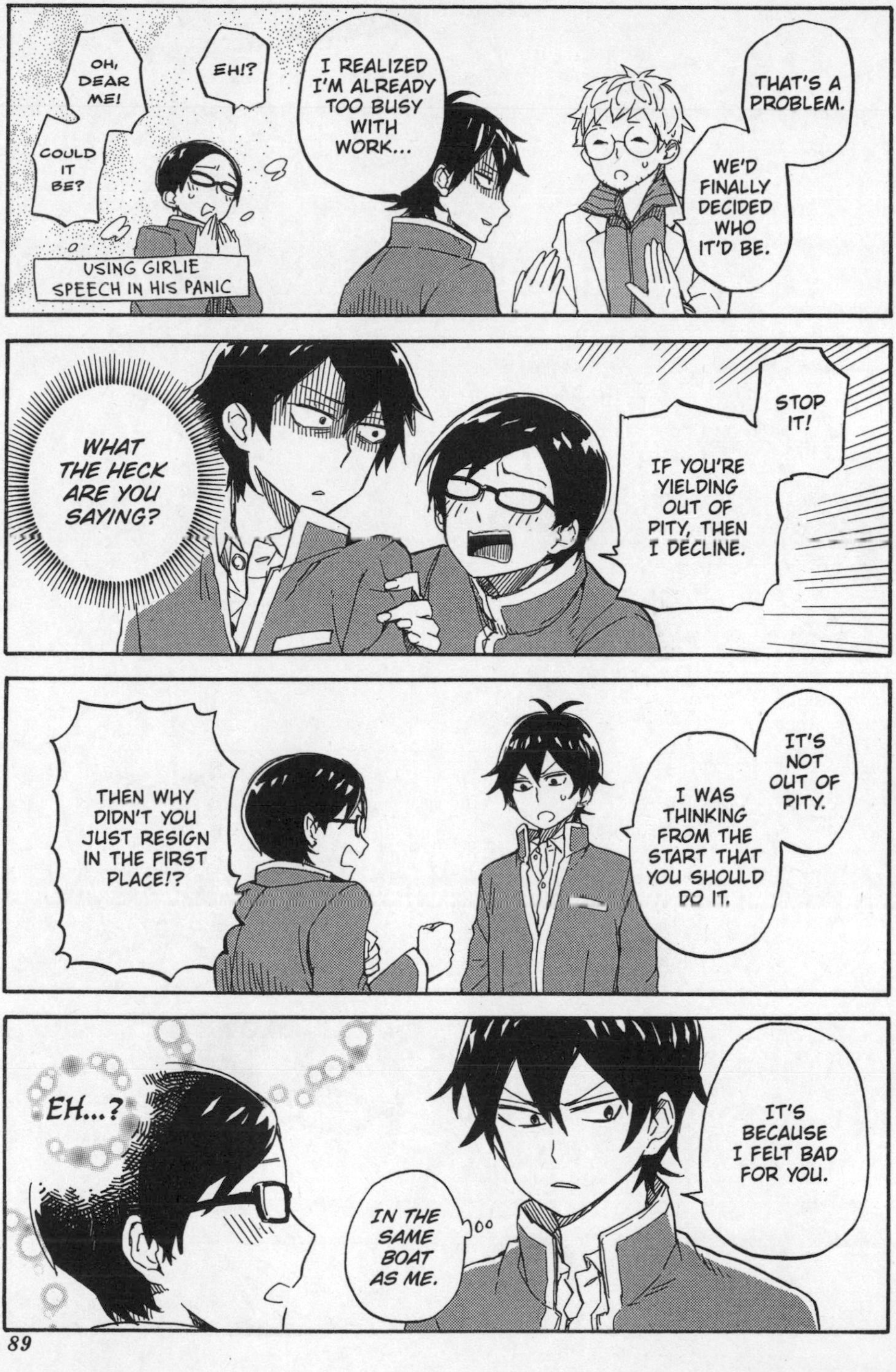
THAT'S A PROBLEM.
WE'D FINALLY DECIDED WHO IT'D BE.
I REALIZED I'M ALREADY TOO BUSY WITH WORK...
EH!?
OH, DEAR ME!
COULD IT BE?
USING GIRLIE SPEECH IN HIS PANIC
STOP IT!
IF YOU'RE YIELDING OUT OF PITY, THEN I DECLINE.
WHAT THE HECK ARE YOU SAYING?
IT'S NOT OUT OF PITY.
I WAS THINKING FROM THE START THAT YOU SHOULD DO IT.
THEN WHY DIDN'T YOU JUST RESIGN IN THE FIRST PLACE!?
IT'S BECAUSE I FELT BAD FOR YOU.
IN THE SAME BOAT AS ME.
EH...?

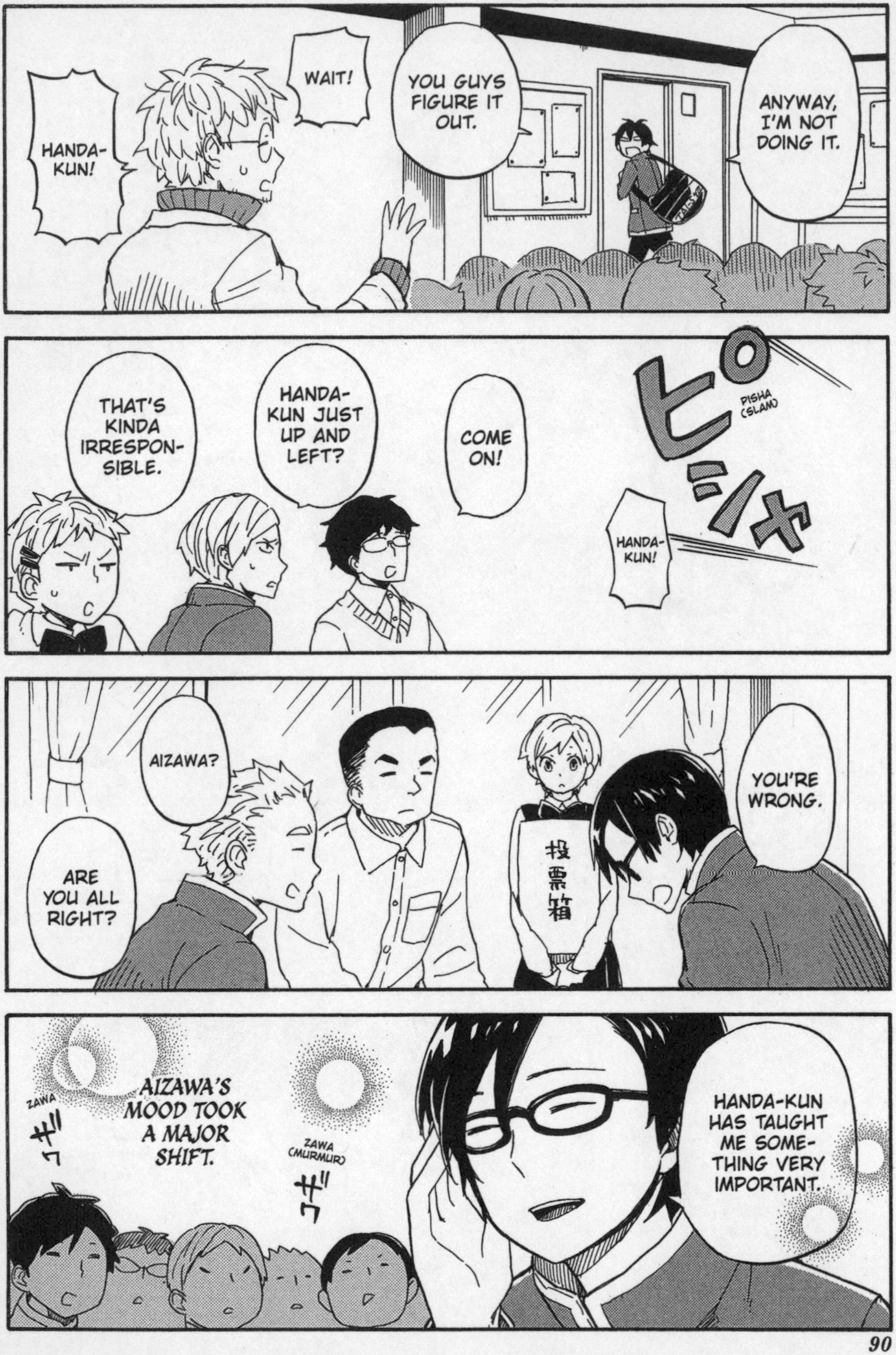
ANYWAY, I'M NOT DOING IT.
YOU GUYS FIGURE IT OUT.
WAIT!
HANDA-KUN!
ピシャ
PISHA (SLAM)
HANDA-KUN!
COME ON!
HANDA-KUN JUST UP AND LEFT?
THAT'S KINDA IRRESPONSIBLE.
YOU'RE WRONG.
投票箱
AIZAWA?
ARE YOU ALL RIGHT?
HANDA-KUN HAS TAUGHT ME SOMETHING VERY IMPORTANT.
ザワ
ZAWA (MURMUR)
AIZAWA'S MOOD TOOK A MAJOR SHIFT.
ザワ
ZAWA

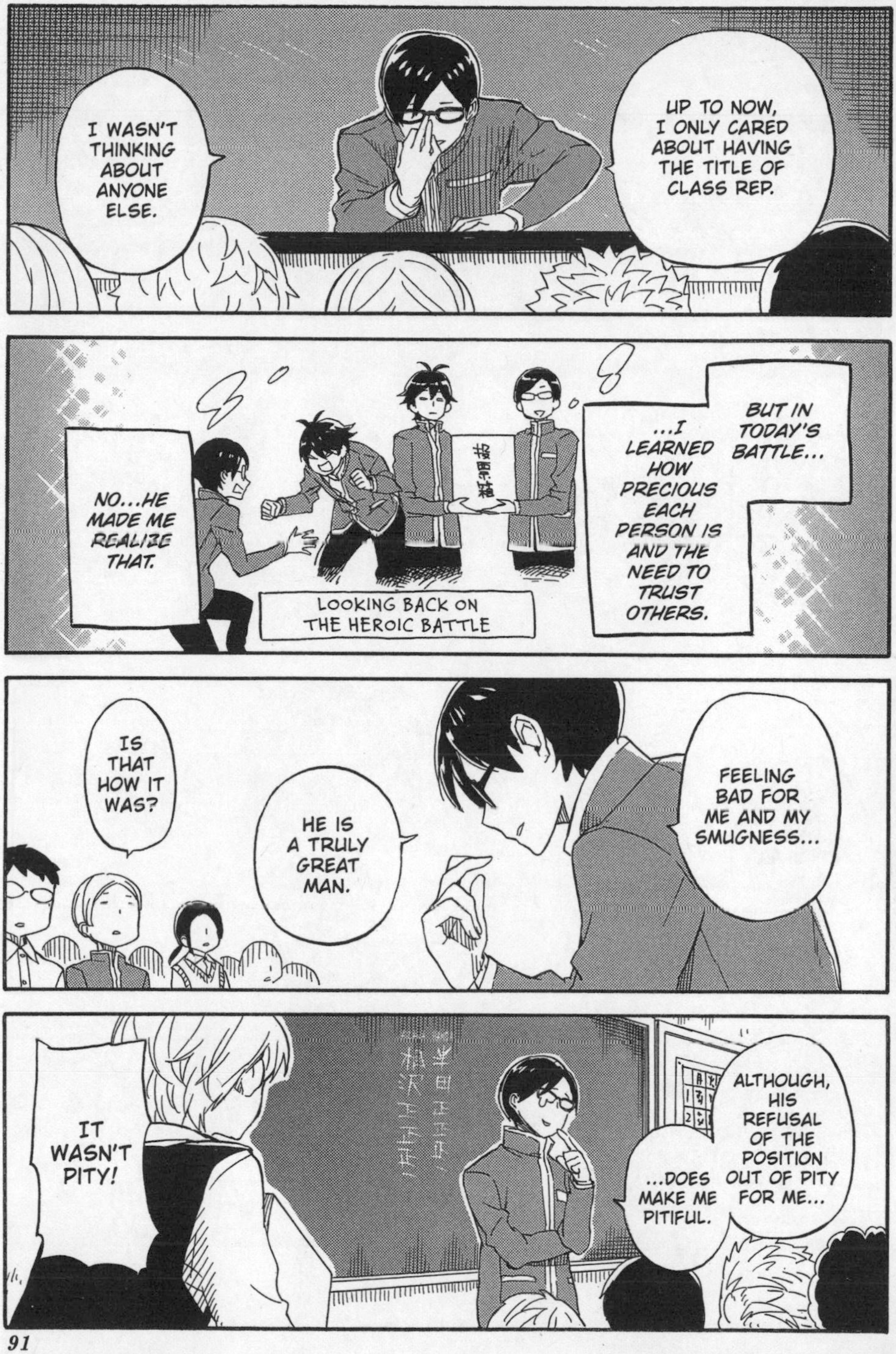
UP TO NOW, I ONLY CARED ABOUT HAVING THE TITLE OF CLASS REP.
I WASN'T THINKING ABOUT ANYONE ELSE.
BUT IN TODAY'S BATTLE...
...I LEARNED HOW PRECIOUS EACH PERSON IS AND THE NEED TO TRUST OTHERS.
投票箱
NO...HE MADE ME REALIZE THAT.
LOOKING BACK ON THE HEROIC BATTLE
FEELING BAD FOR ME AND MY SMUGNESS...
HE IS A TRULY GREAT MAN.
IS THAT HOW IT WAS?
ALTHOUGH, HIS REFUSAL OF THE POSITION OUT OF PITY FOR ME...
...DOES MAKE ME PITIFUL.
IT WASN'T PITY!

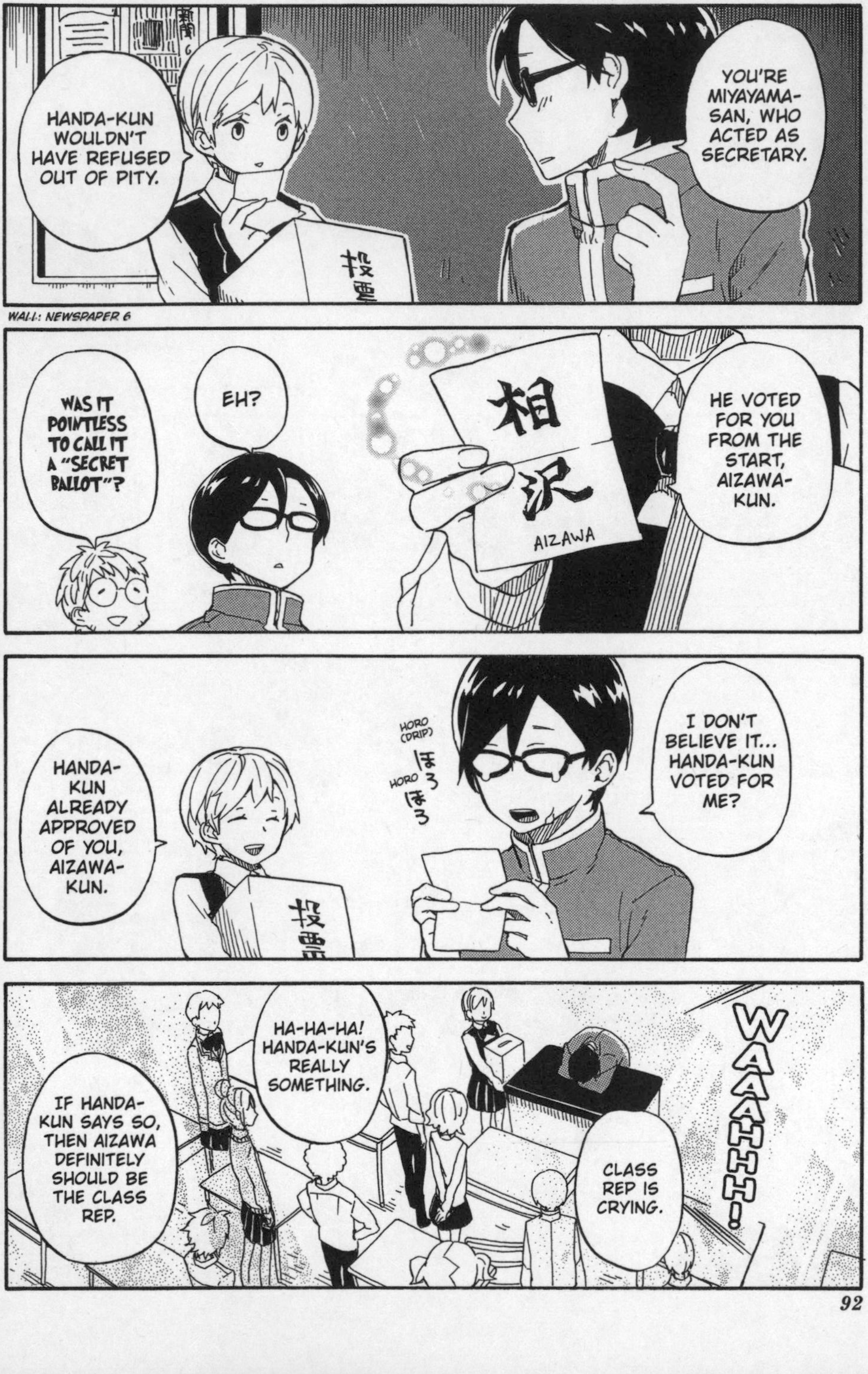
YOU'RE MIYAYAMA-SAN, WHO ACTED AS SECRETARY.
HANDA-KUN WOULDN'T HAVE REFUSED OUT OF PITY.
投票
WALL: NEWSPAPER 6
HE VOTED FOR YOU FROM THE START, AIZAWA-KUN.
相沢
AIZAWA
EH?
WAS IT POINTLESS TO CALL IT A "SECRET BALLOT"?
I DON'T BELIEVE IT... HANDA-KUN VOTED FOR ME?
ほろほろ
HORO (DRIP) HORO
HANDA-KUN ALREADY APPROVED OF YOU, AIZAWA-KUN.
投票
WAAAHHH!
CLASS REP IS CRYING.
HA-HA-HA! HANDA-KUN'S REALLY SOMETHING.
IF HANDA-KUN SAYS SO, THEN AIZAWA DEFINITELY SHOULD BE THE CLASS REP.

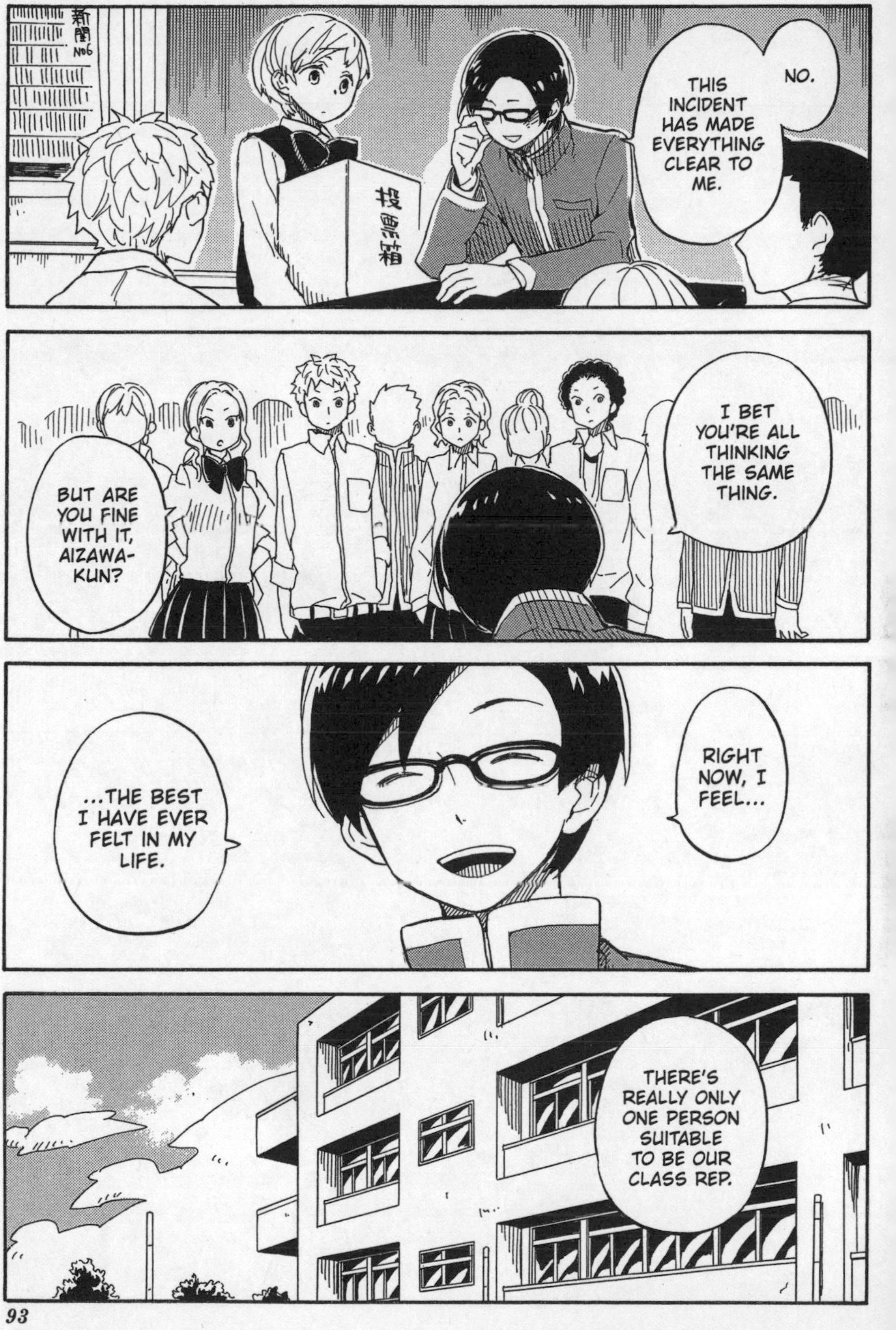
NO.
THIS INCIDENT HAS MADE EVERYTHING CLEAR TO ME.
投票箱
I BET YOU'RE ALL THINKING THE SAME THING.
BUT ARE YOU FINE WITH IT, AIZAWA-KUN?
RIGHT NOW, I FEEL...
...THE BEST I HAVE EVER FELT IN MY LIFE.
THERE'S REALLY ONLY ONE PERSON SUITABLE TO BE OUR CLASS REP.

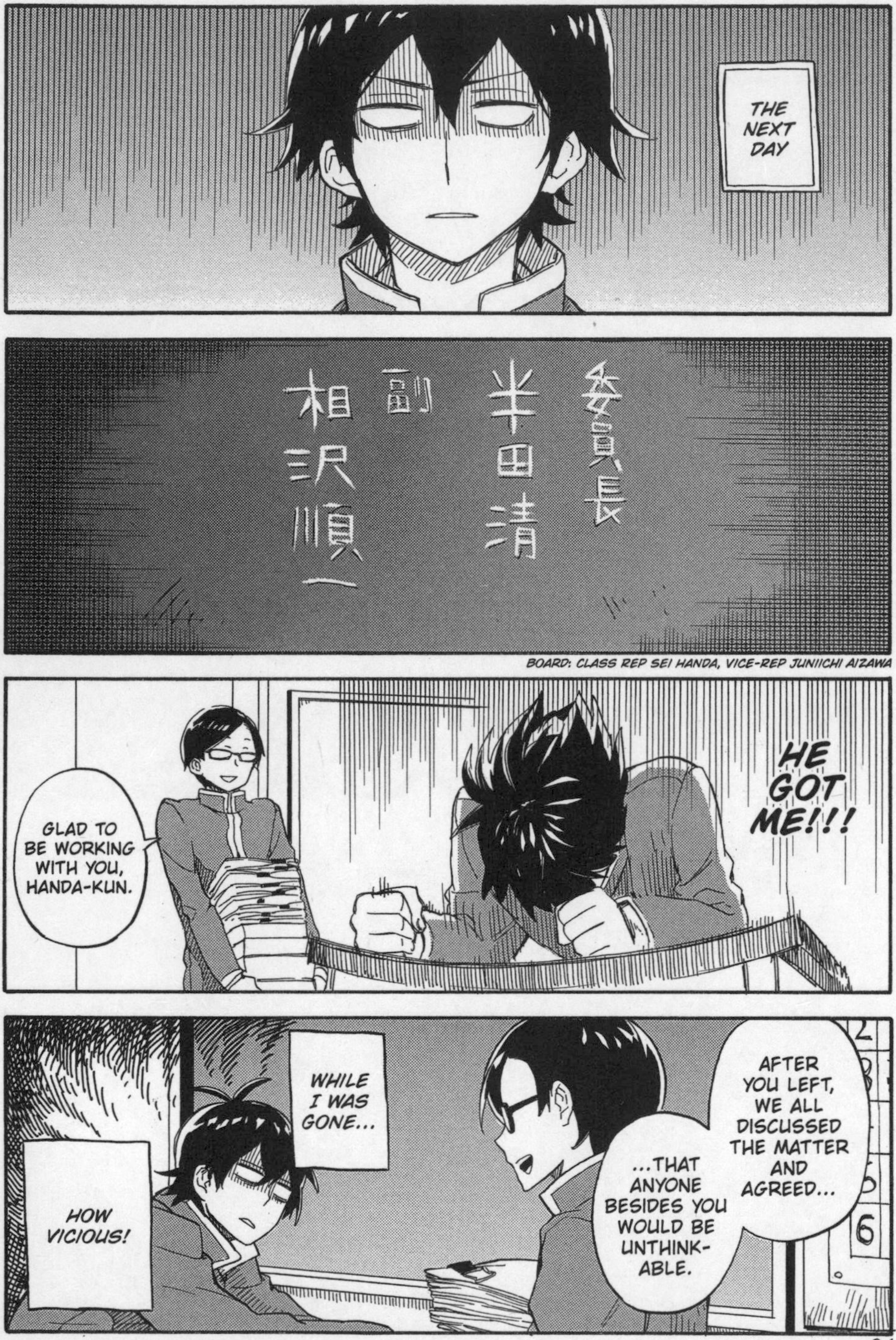
THE NEXT DAY
委員長
半田清
副
相沢順一
BOARD: CLASS REP SEI HANDA, VICE-REP JUNIICHI AIZAWA
HE GOT ME!!!
GLAD TO BE WORKING WITH YOU, HANDA-KUN.
AFTER YOU LEFT, WE ALL DISCUSSED THE MATTER AND AGREED...
...THAT ANYONE BESIDES YOU WOULD BE UNTHINK-ABLE.
WHILE I WAS GONE...
HOW VICIOUS!

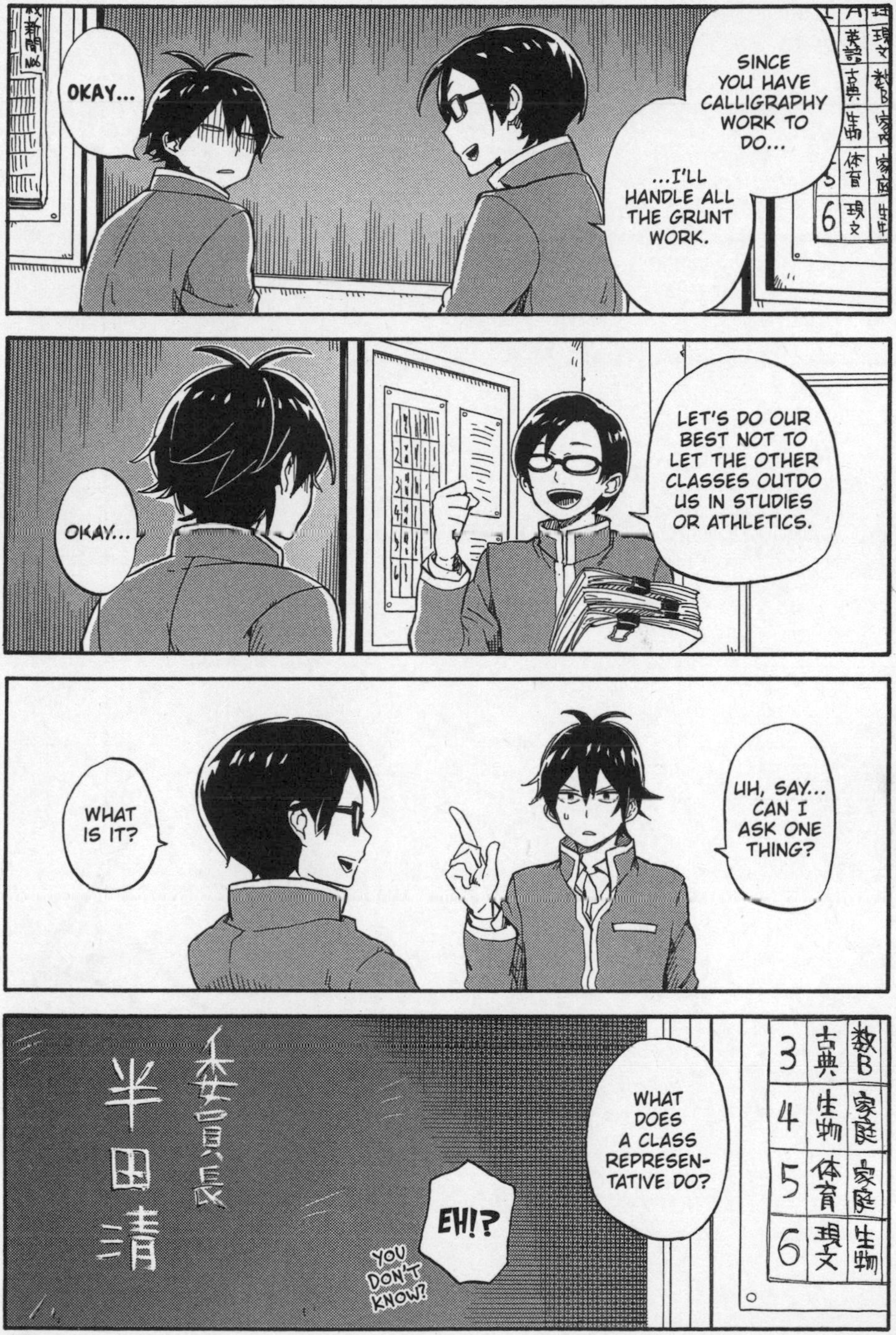
SINCE YOU HAVE CALLIGRAPHY WORK TO DO...
...I'LL HANDLE ALL THE GRUNT WORK.
OKAY...
LET'S DO OUR BEST NOT TO LET THE OTHER CLASSES OUTDO US IN STUDIES OR ATHLETICS.
OKAY...
UH, SAY... CAN I ASK ONE THING?
WHAT IS IT?
WHAT DOES A CLASS REPRESEN-TATIVE DO?
委員長
半田清
EH!?
YOU DON'T KNOW?

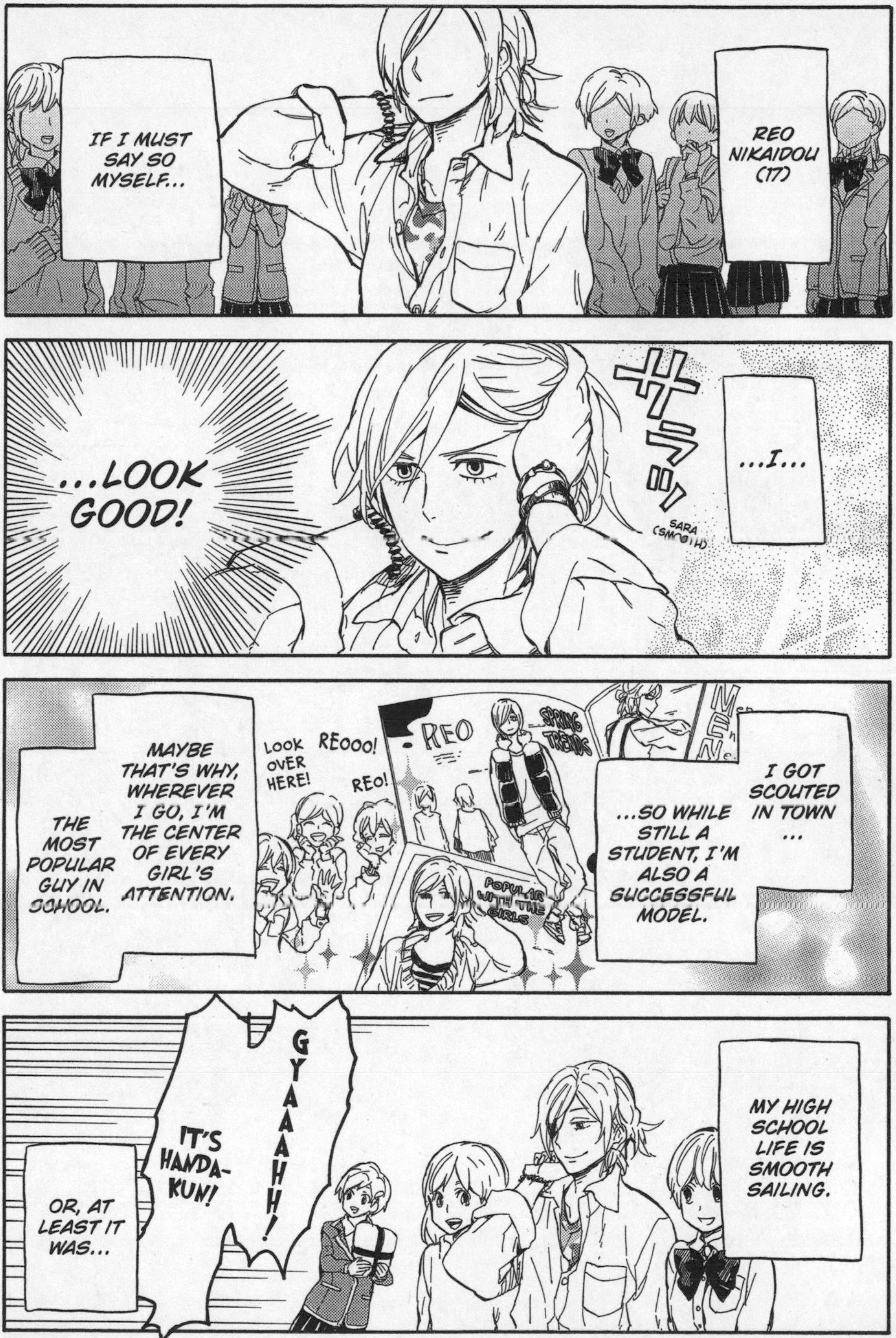
REO NIKAIDOU (17)
IF I MUST SAY SO MYSELF...
...I...
サラッ
SARA (SMOOTH)
...LOOK GOOD!
I GOT SCOUTED IN TOWN ...
...SO WHILE STILL A STUDENT, I'M ALSO A SUCCESSFUL MODEL.
SPRING TRENDS
REO
POPULAR WITH THE GIRLS
REOOO!
LOOK OVER HERE!
REO!
MAYBE THAT'S WHY, WHEREVER I GO, I'M THE CENTER OF EVERY GIRL'S ATTENTION.
THE MOST POPULAR GUY IN SCHOOL.
MY HIGH SCHOOL LIFE IS SMOOTH SAILING.
GYAAAAHH!
IT'S HANDA-KUN!
OR, AT LEAST IT WAS...

Chapter 4: Handa-kun & the Model

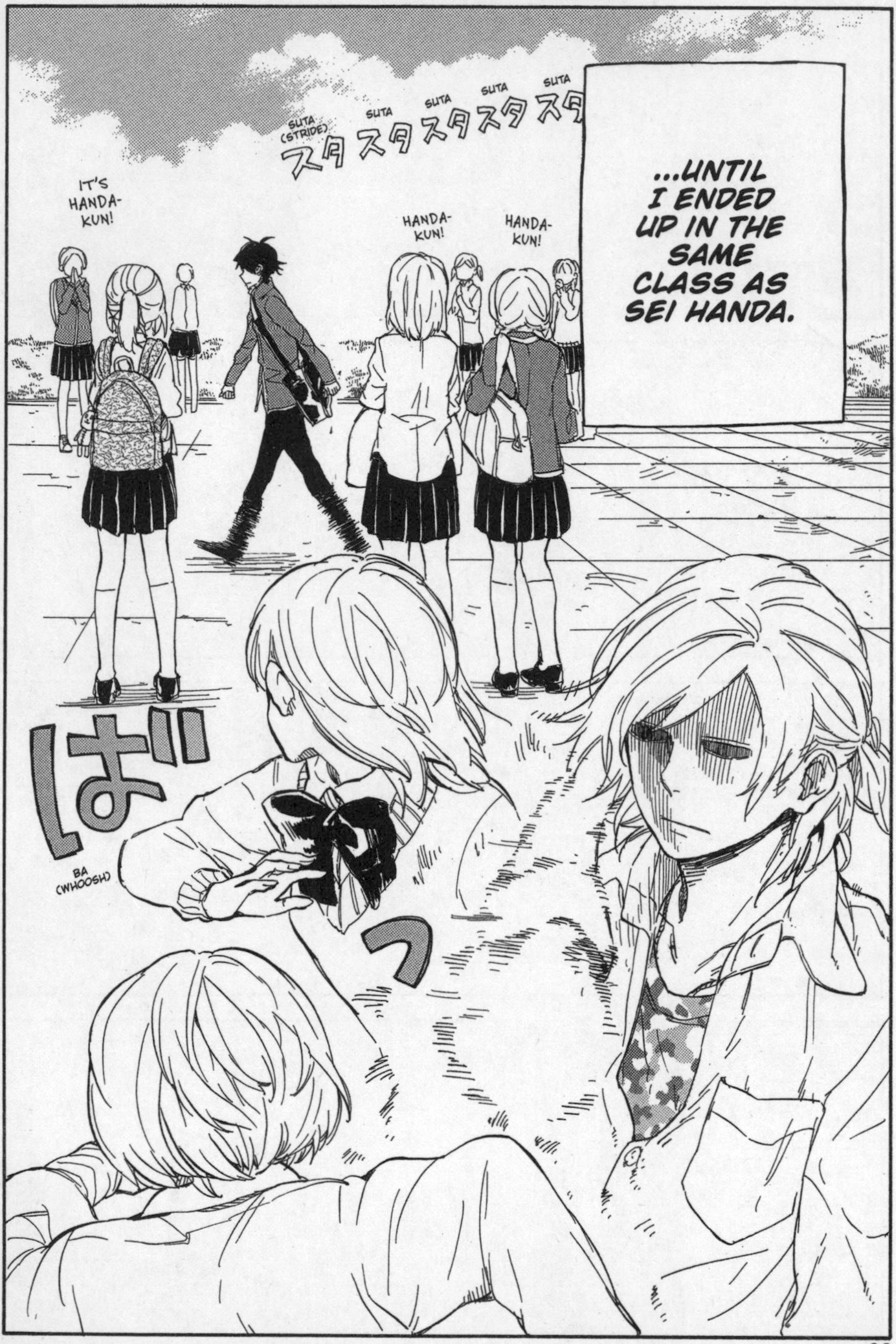
...UNTIL I ENDED UP IN THE SAME CLASS AS SEI HANDA.
SUTA SUTA SUTA SUTA SUTA (STRIDE)
スタスタスタスタ
HANDA-KUN!
HANDA-KUN!
IT'S HANDA-KUN!
ばっ
BA (WHOOSH)

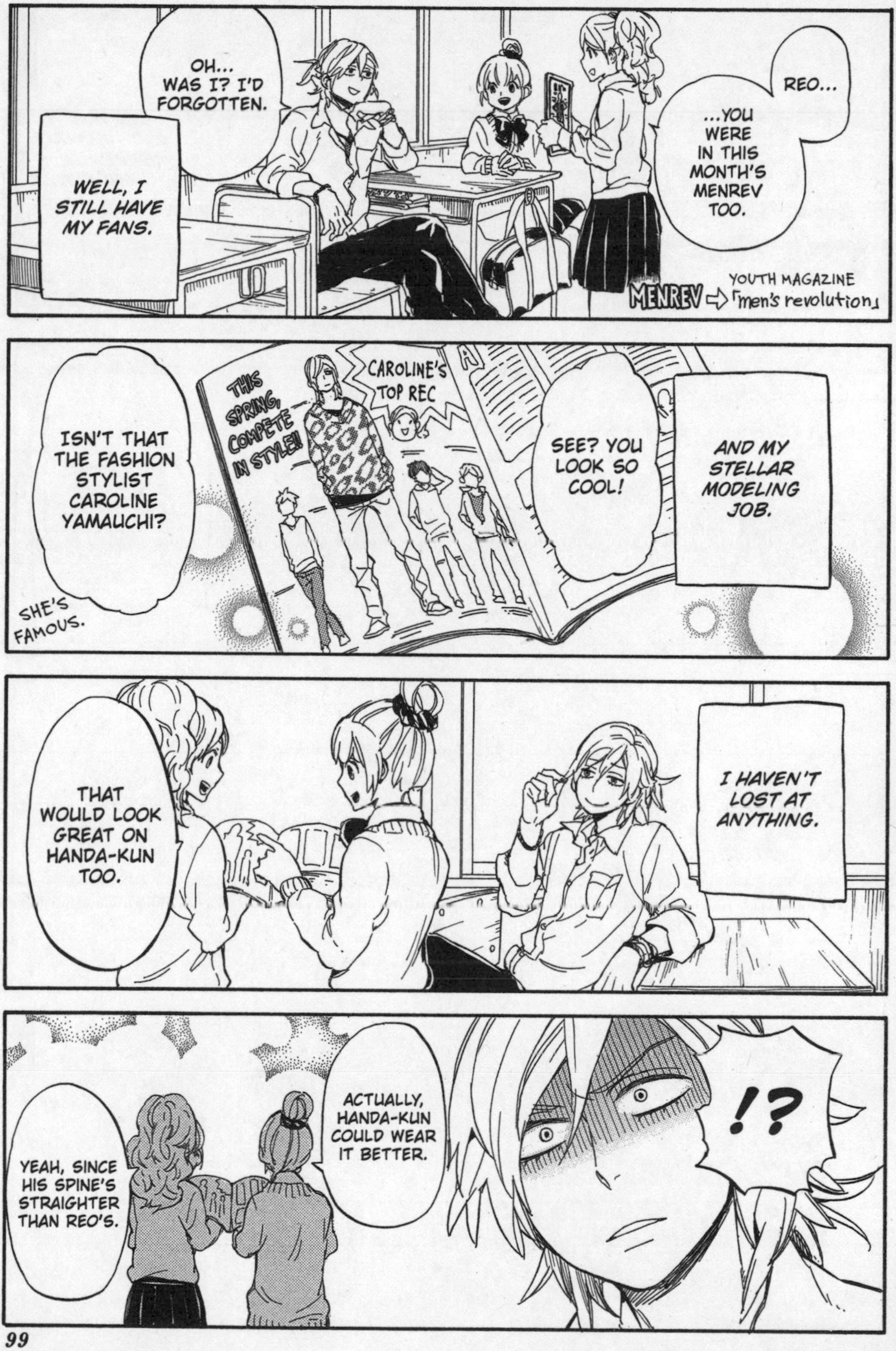
REO...
...YOU WERE IN THIS MONTH'S MENREV TOO.
OH... WAS I? I'D FORGOTTEN.
WELL, I STILL HAVE MY FANS.
MENREV ⇨ YOUTH MAGAZINE 「men's revolution」
AND MY STELLAR MODELING JOB.
SEE? YOU LOOK SO COOL!
CAROLINE'S TOP REC
THIS SPRING, COMPETE IN STYLE!!
ISN'T THAT THE FASHION STYLIST CAROLINE YAMAUCHI?
SHE'S FAMOUS.
I HAVEN'T LOST AT ANYTHING.
THAT WOULD LOOK GREAT ON HANDA-KUN TOO.
!?
ACTUALLY, HANDA-KUN COULD WEAR IT BETTER.
YEAH, SINCE HIS SPINE'S STRAIGHTER THAN REO'S.

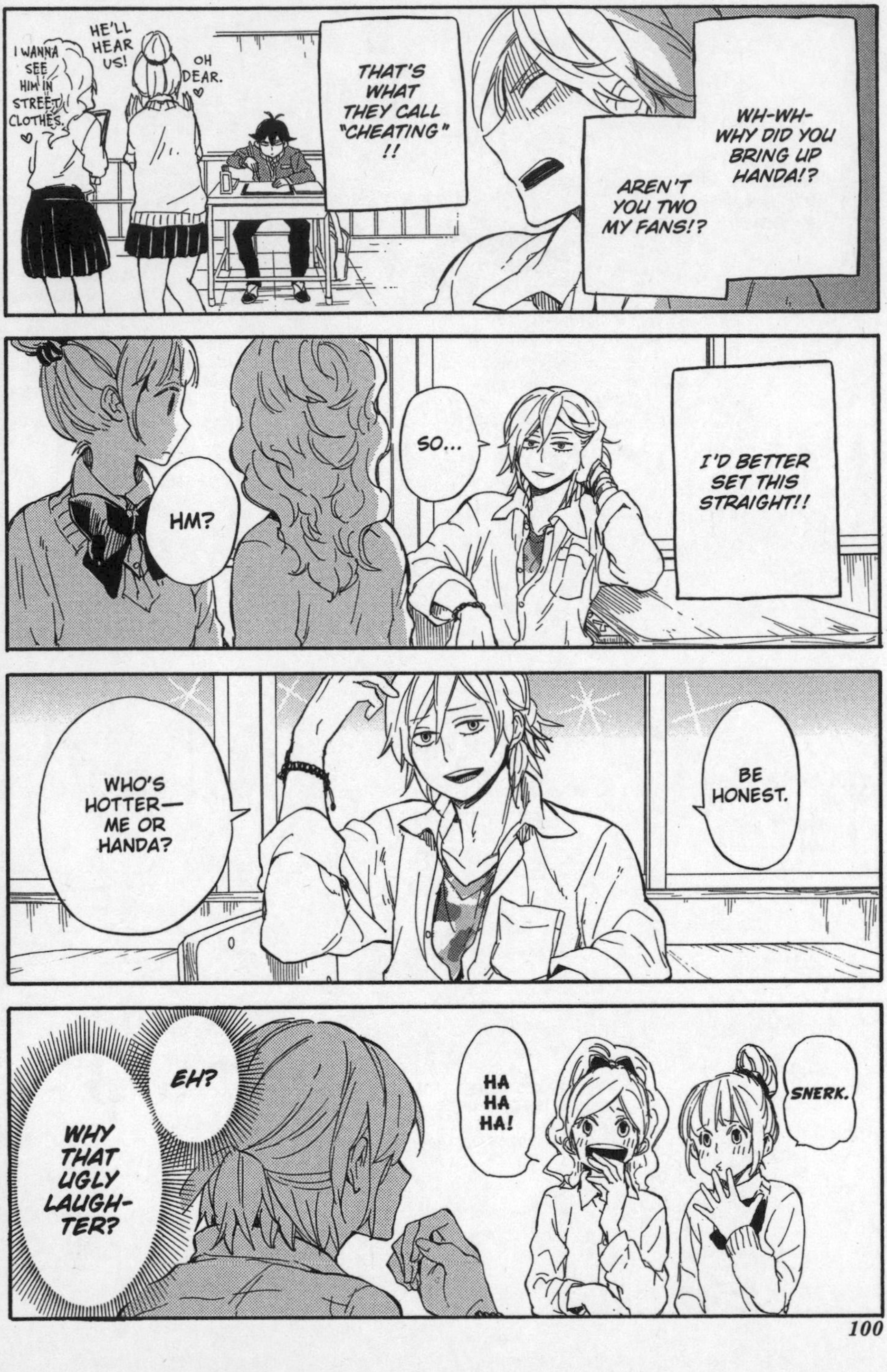
WH-WH-WHY DID YOU BRING UP HANDA!?
AREN'T YOU TWO MY FANS!?
THAT'S WHAT THEY CALL "CHEATING" !!
OH DEAR.
HE'LL HEAR US!
I WANNA SEE HIM IN STREET CLOTHES.
I'D BETTER SET THIS STRAIGHT!!
SO...
HM?
BE HONEST.
WHO'S HOTTER— ME OR HANDA?
SNERK.
HA HA HA!
EH?
WHY THAT UGLY LAUGHTER?

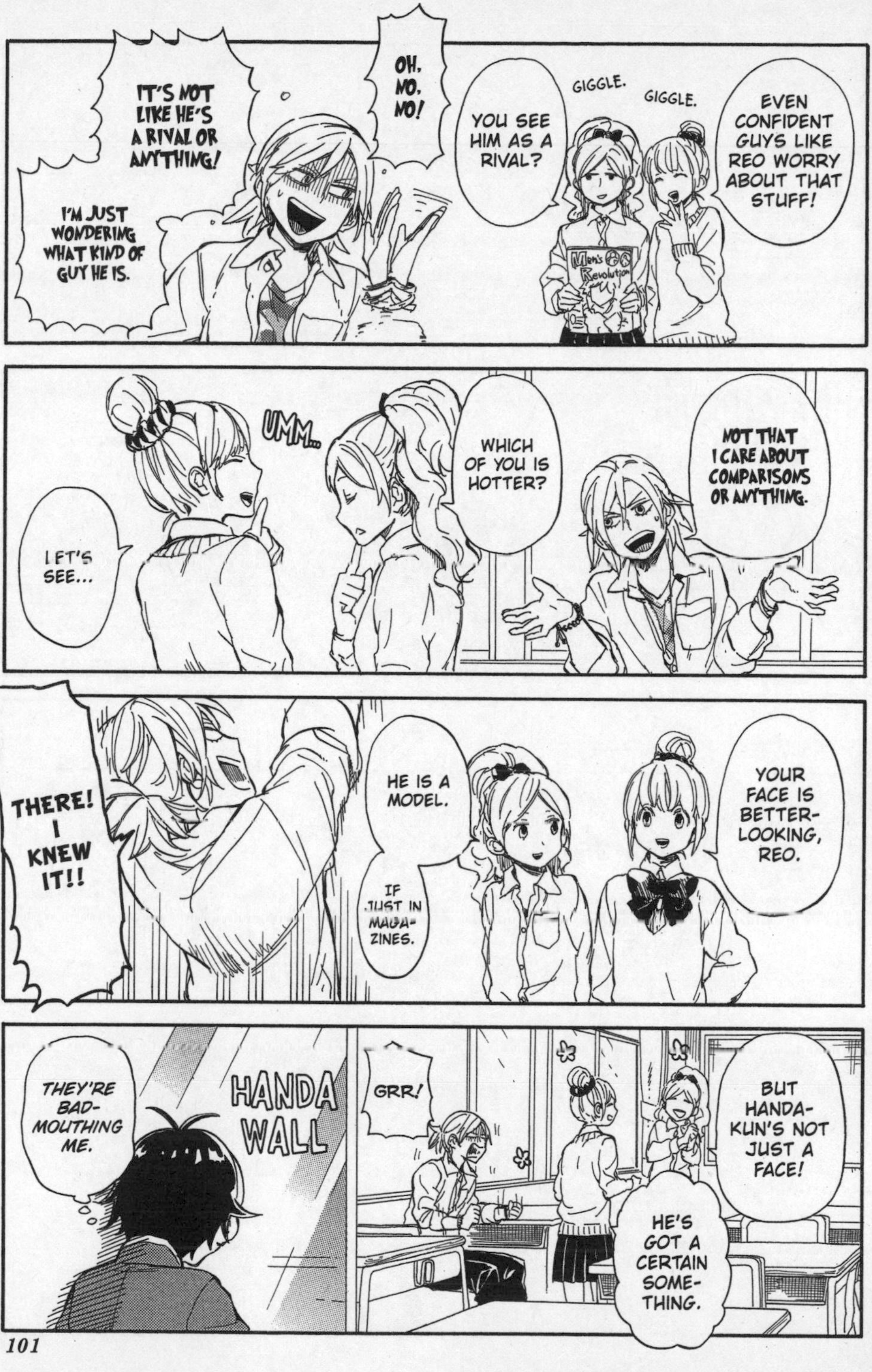
EVEN CONFIDENT GUYS LIKE REO WORRY ABOUT THAT STUFF!
GIGGLE.
GIGGLE.
Men's Revolution
YOU SEE HIM AS A RIVAL?
OH, NO, NO!
IT'S NOT LIKE HE'S A RIVAL OR ANYTHING!
I'M JUST WONDERING WHAT KIND OF GUY HE IS.
NOT THAT I CARE ABOUT COMPARISONS OR ANYTHING.
WHICH OF YOU IS HOTTER?
UMM...
LET'S SEE...
YOUR FACE IS BETTER-LOOKING, REO.
HE IS A MODEL.
IF JUST IN MAGAZINES.
THERE! I KNEW IT!!
BUT HANDA-KUN'S NOT JUST A FACE!
HE'S GOT A CERTAIN SOMETHING.
GRR!
HANDA WALL
THEY'RE BAD-MOUTHING ME.

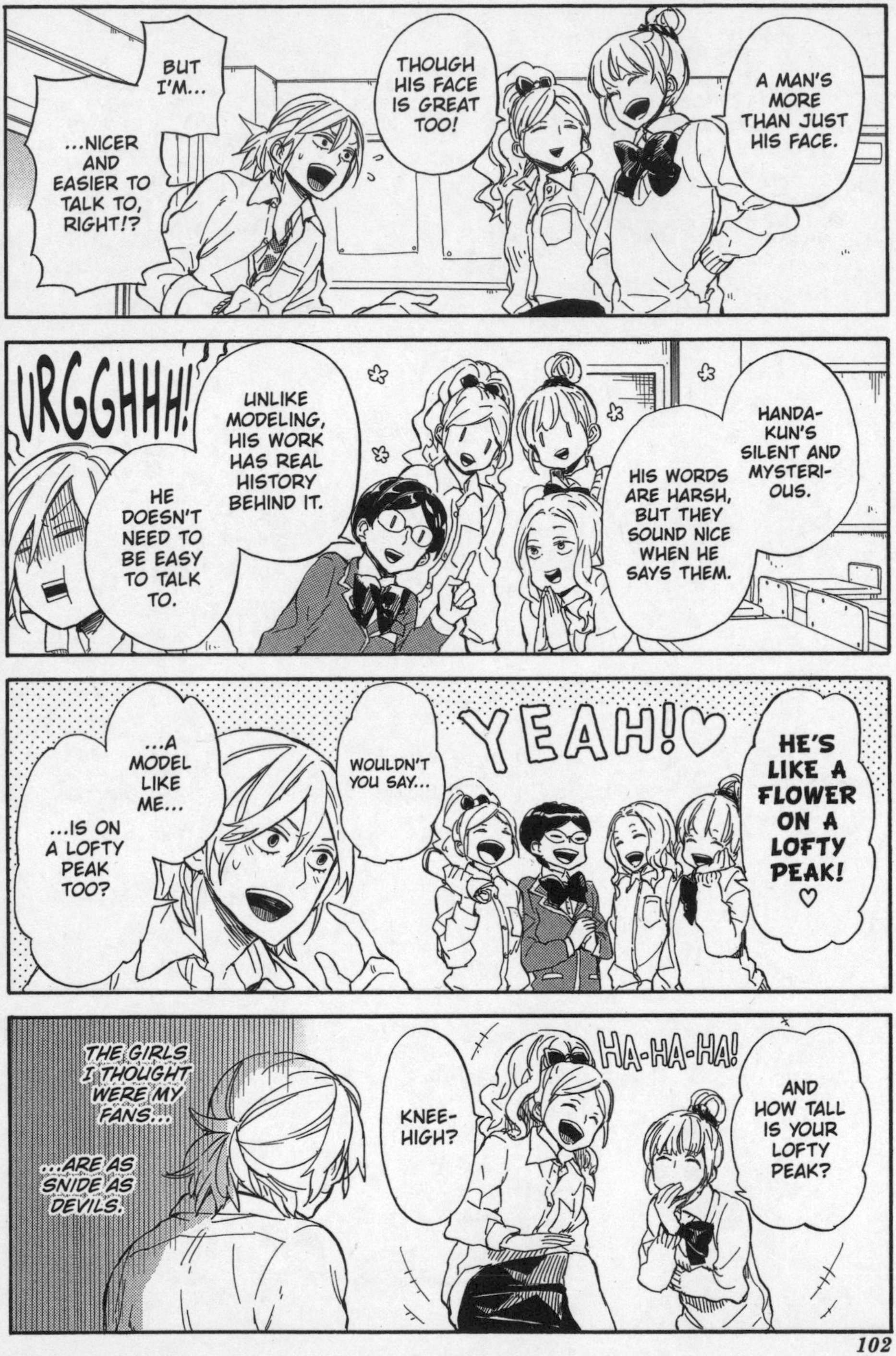
A MAN'S MORE THAN JUST HIS FACE.
THOUGH HIS FACE IS GREAT TOO!
BUT I'M...
...NICER AND EASIER TO TALK TO, RIGHT!?
HANDA-KUN'S SILENT AND MYSTERI-OUS.
HIS WORDS ARE HARSH, BUT THEY SOUND NICE WHEN HE SAYS THEM.
UNLIKE MODELING, HIS WORK HAS REAL HISTORY BEHIND IT.
HE DOESN'T NEED TO BE EASY TO TALK TO.
URGGHHH!
HE'S LIKE A FLOWER ON A LOFTY PEAK! ♡
YEAH!♡
WOULDN'T YOU SAY...
...A MODEL LIKE ME...
...IS ON A LOFTY PEAK TOO?
AND HOW TALL IS YOUR LOFTY PEAK?
HA-HA-HA!
KNEE-HIGH?
THE GIRLS I THOUGHT WERE MY FANS...
...ARE AS SNIDE AS DEVILS.

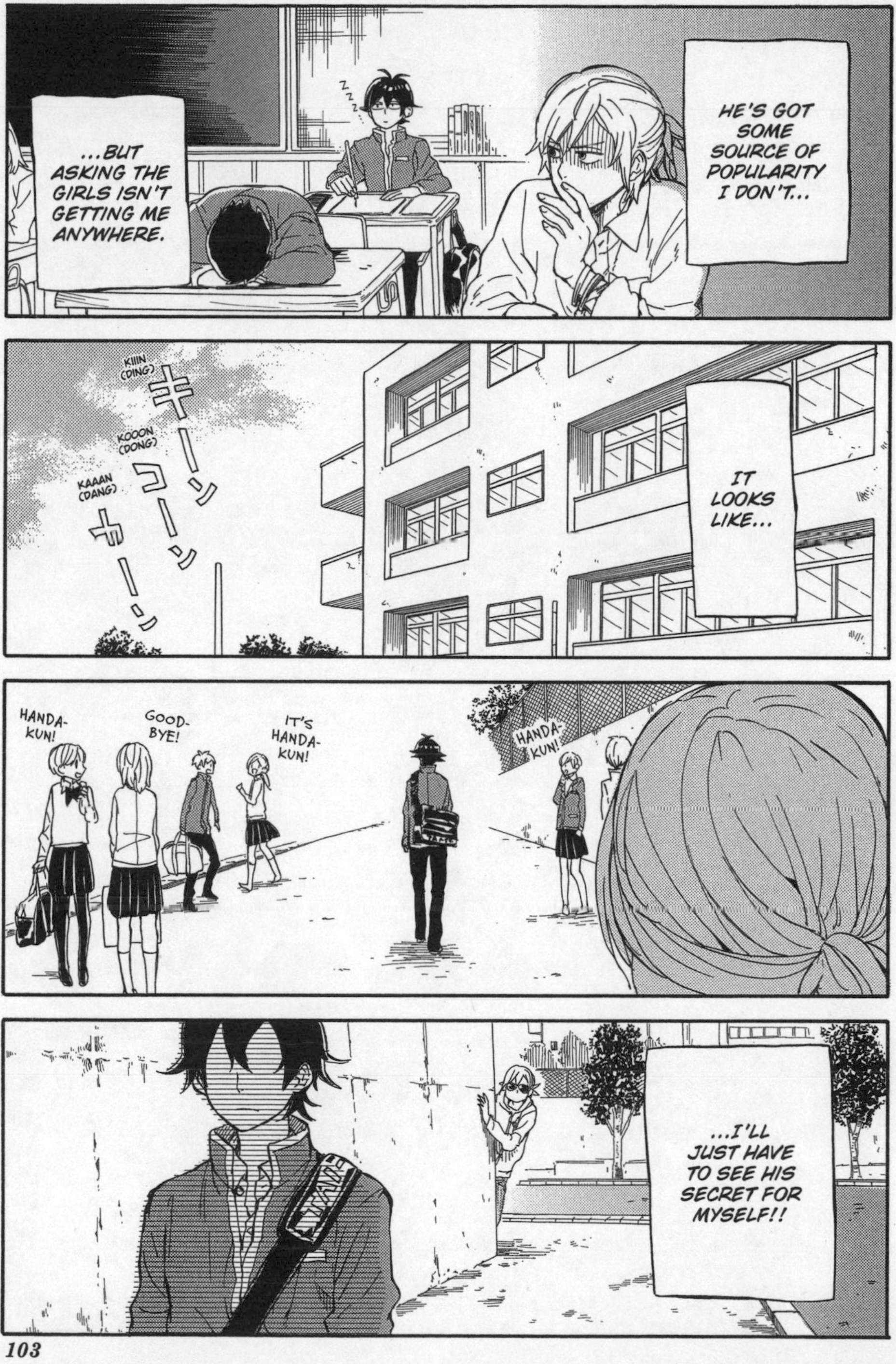
HE'S GOT SOME SOURCE OF POPULARITY I DON'T...
...BUT ASKING THE GIRLS ISN'T GETTING ME ANYWHERE.
IT LOOKS LIKE...
KIIN (DING)
キーンッ
KOOON (DONG)
コーンッ
KAAAN (DANG)
カーンッ
HANDA-KUN!
IT'S HANDA-KUN!
GOOD-BYE!
HANDA-KUN!
...I'LL JUST HAVE TO SEE HIS SECRET FOR MYSELF!!

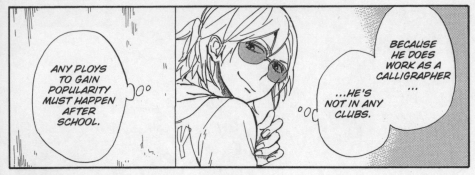

BECAUSE HE DOES WORK AS A CALLIGRAPHER ...
...HE'S NOT IN ANY CLUBS.
ANY PLOYS TO GAIN POPULARITY MUST HAPPEN AFTER SCHOOL.
MAYBE HE'S SECRETLY HITTING ON GIRLS...
...AS A GRASS-ROOTS MOVE-MENT?
DON'T TELL ME...
...HE COULD BE BUYING THEM OFF WITH MONEY!?
HEH HEH HEH...
KOSO
KOSO (SNEAK)
I'M GOING TO EXPOSE...
...YOUR DIRTY LITTLE SECRET...
HANDA...
SOME WEIRDO'S FOLLOWING YOU AROUND...
LET'S GO, KAWA-FUJI!

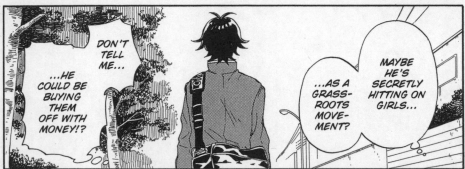

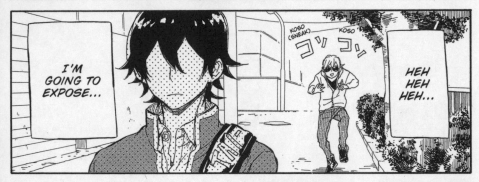

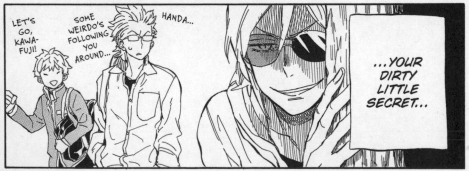

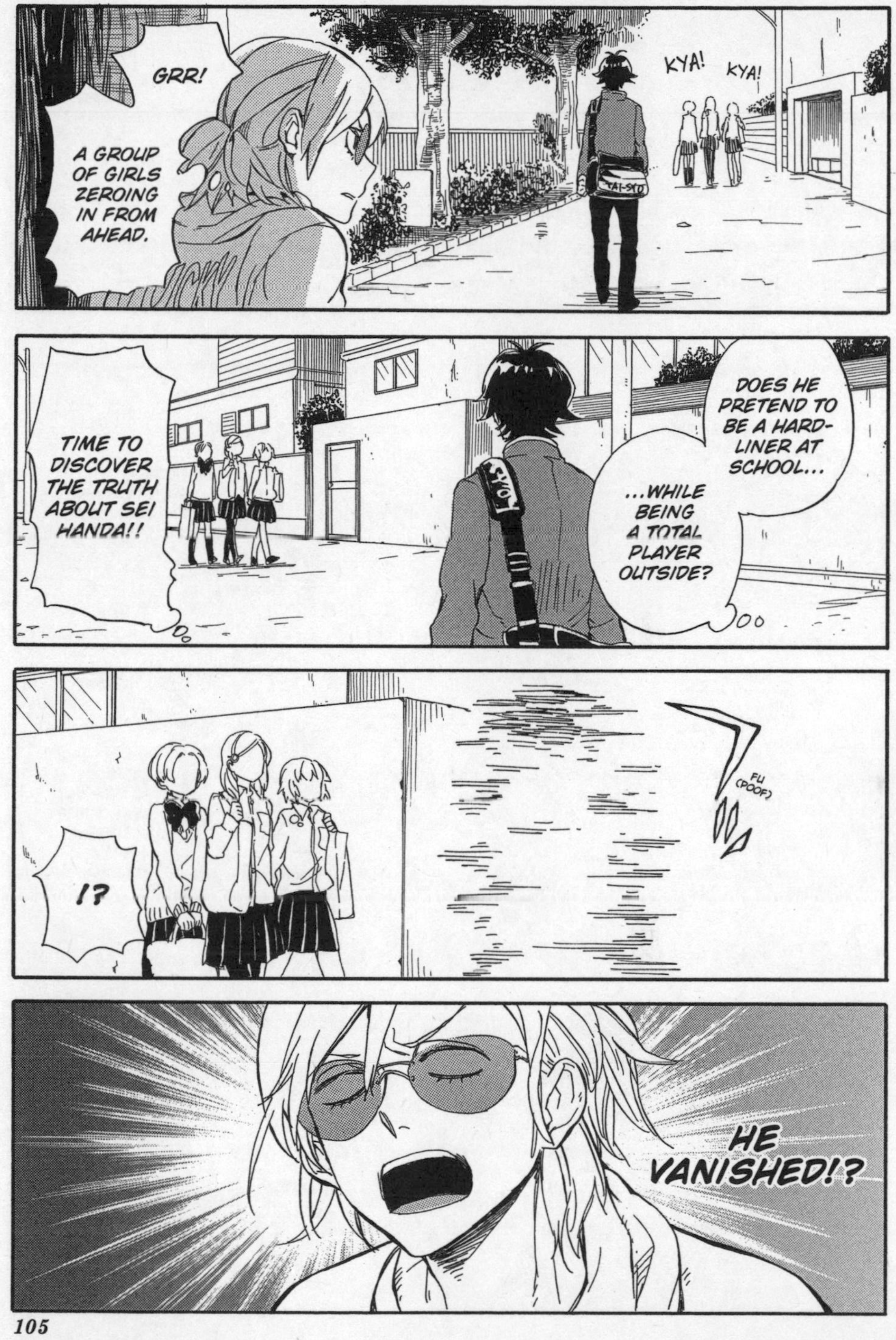
KYA!
KYA!
GRR!
A GROUP OF GIRLS ZEROING IN FROM AHEAD.
DOES HE PRETEND TO BE A HARD-LINER AT SCHOOL...
...WHILE BEING A TOTAL PLAYER OUTSIDE?
TIME TO DISCOVER THE TRUTH ABOUT SEI HANDA!!
FU (POOF)
!?
HE VANISHED!?

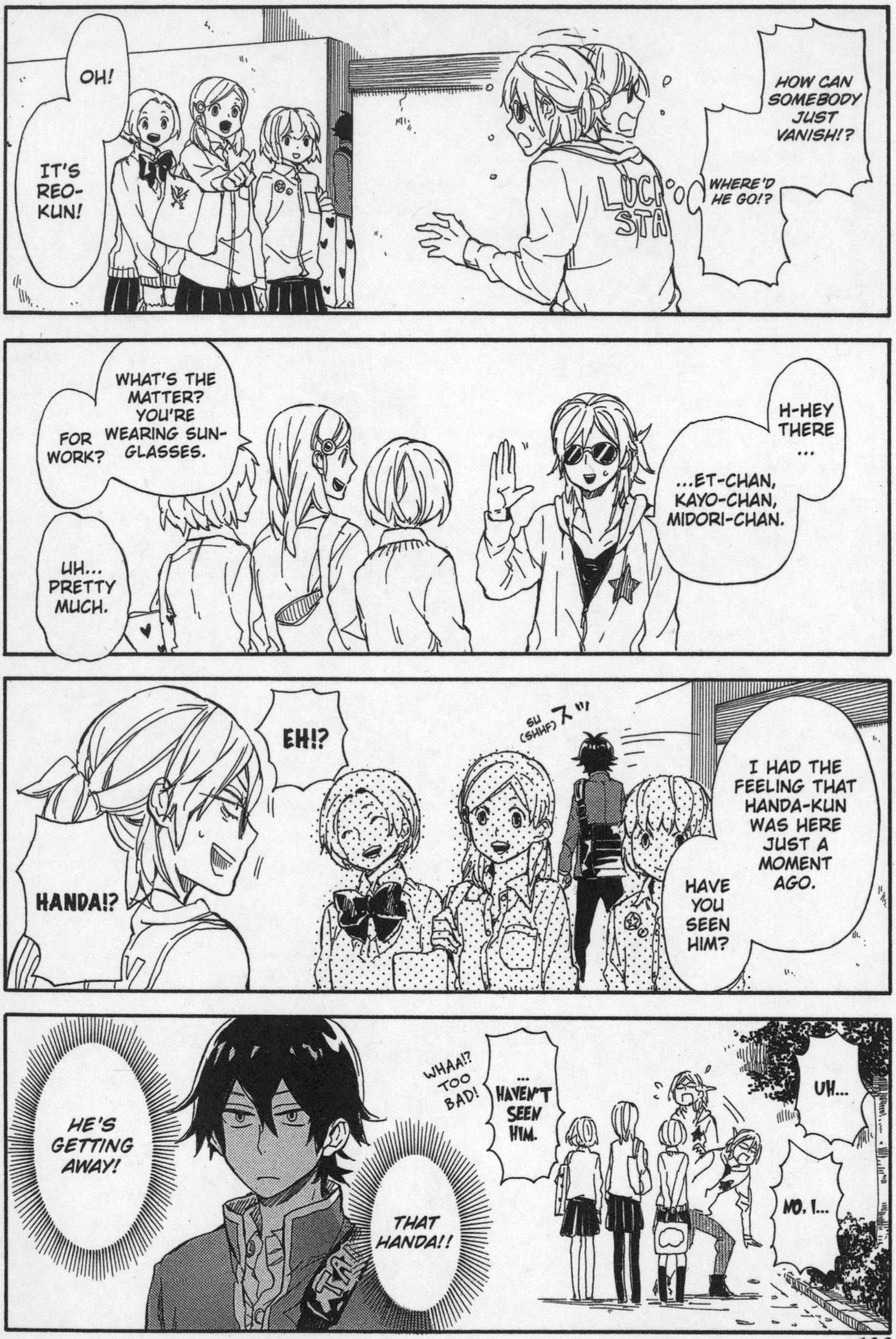
HOW CAN SOMEBODY JUST VANISH!?
WHERE'D HE GO!?
OH!
IT'S REO-KUN!
H-HEY THERE ...
...ET-CHAN, KAYO-CHAN, MIDORI-CHAN.
WHAT'S THE MATTER? YOU'RE WEARING SUN-GLASSES.
FOR WORK?
UH... PRETTY MUCH.
I HAD THE FEELING THAT HANDA-KUN WAS HERE JUST A MOMENT AGO.
HAVE YOU SEEN HIM?
SU (SHHF) スッ
EH!?
HANDA!?
UH...
NO. I...
... HAVEN'T SEEN HIM.
WHAA!? TOO BAD!
HE'S GETTING AWAY!
THAT HANDA!!

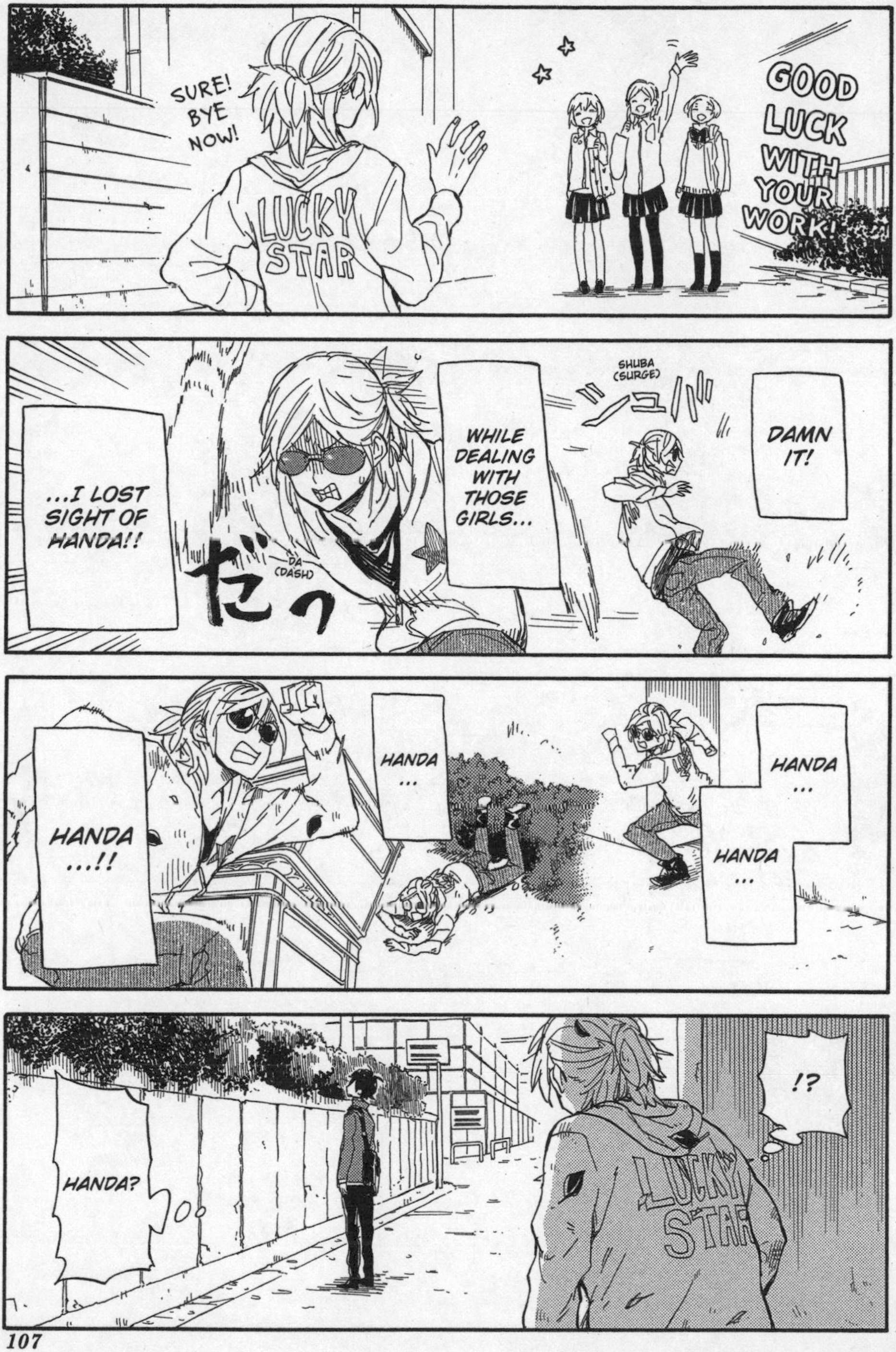
GOOD LUCK WITH YOUR WORK!
SURE! BYE NOW!
DAMN IT!
シュバ
SHUBA (SURGE)
WHILE DEALING WITH THOSE GIRLS...
だっ
DA (DASH)
...I LOST SIGHT OF HANDA!!
HANDA ...
HANDA ...
HANDA ...
HANDA ...!!
!?
HANDA?

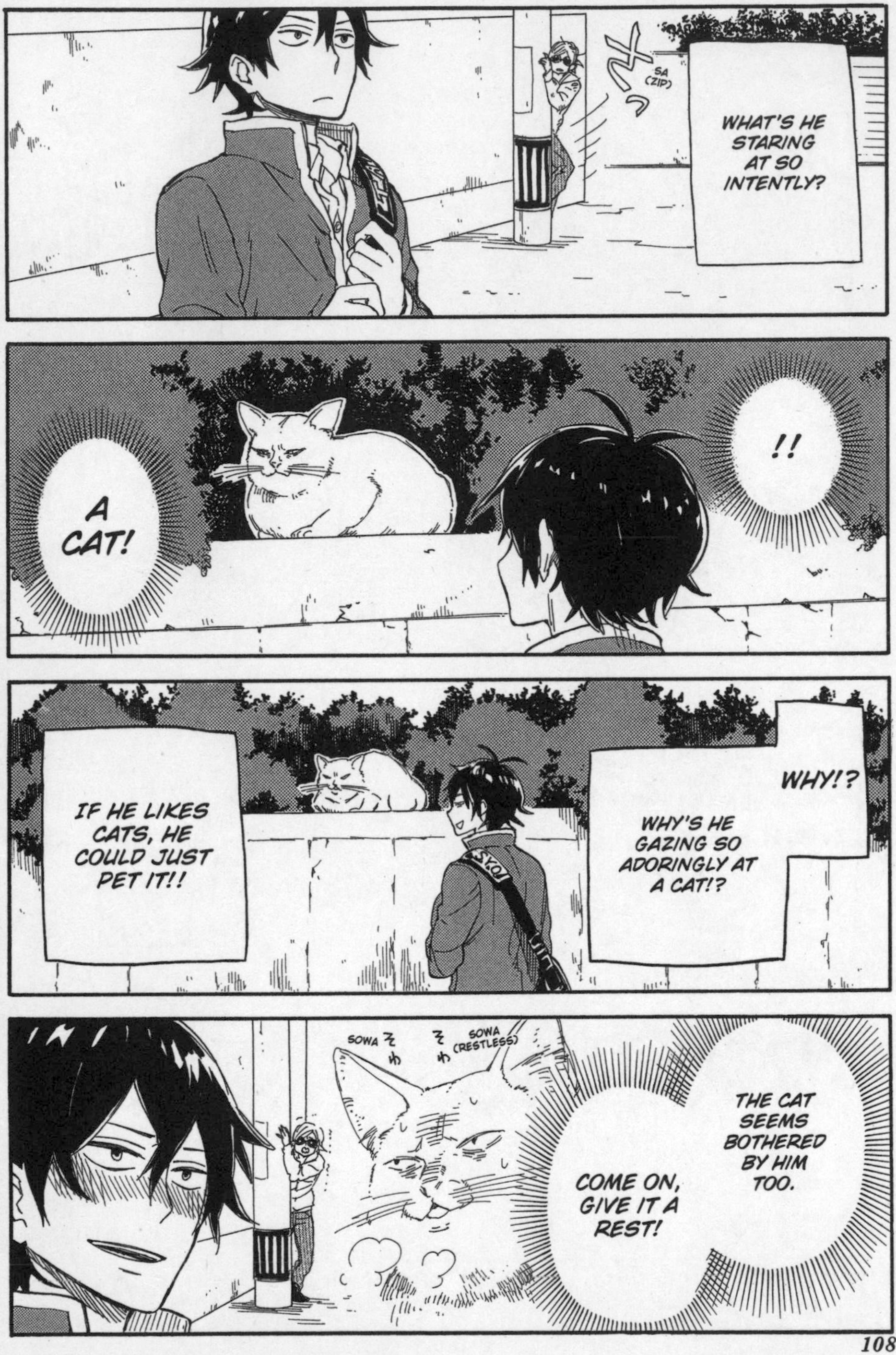
WHAT'S HE STARING AT SO INTENTLY?
SA (ZIP)
!!
A CAT!
WHY!?
WHY'S HE GAZING SO ADORINGLY AT A CAT!?
IF HE LIKES CATS, HE COULD JUST PET IT!!
SOWA (RESTLESS)
SOWA
THE CAT SEEMS BOTHERED BY HIM TOO.
COME ON, GIVE IT A REST!

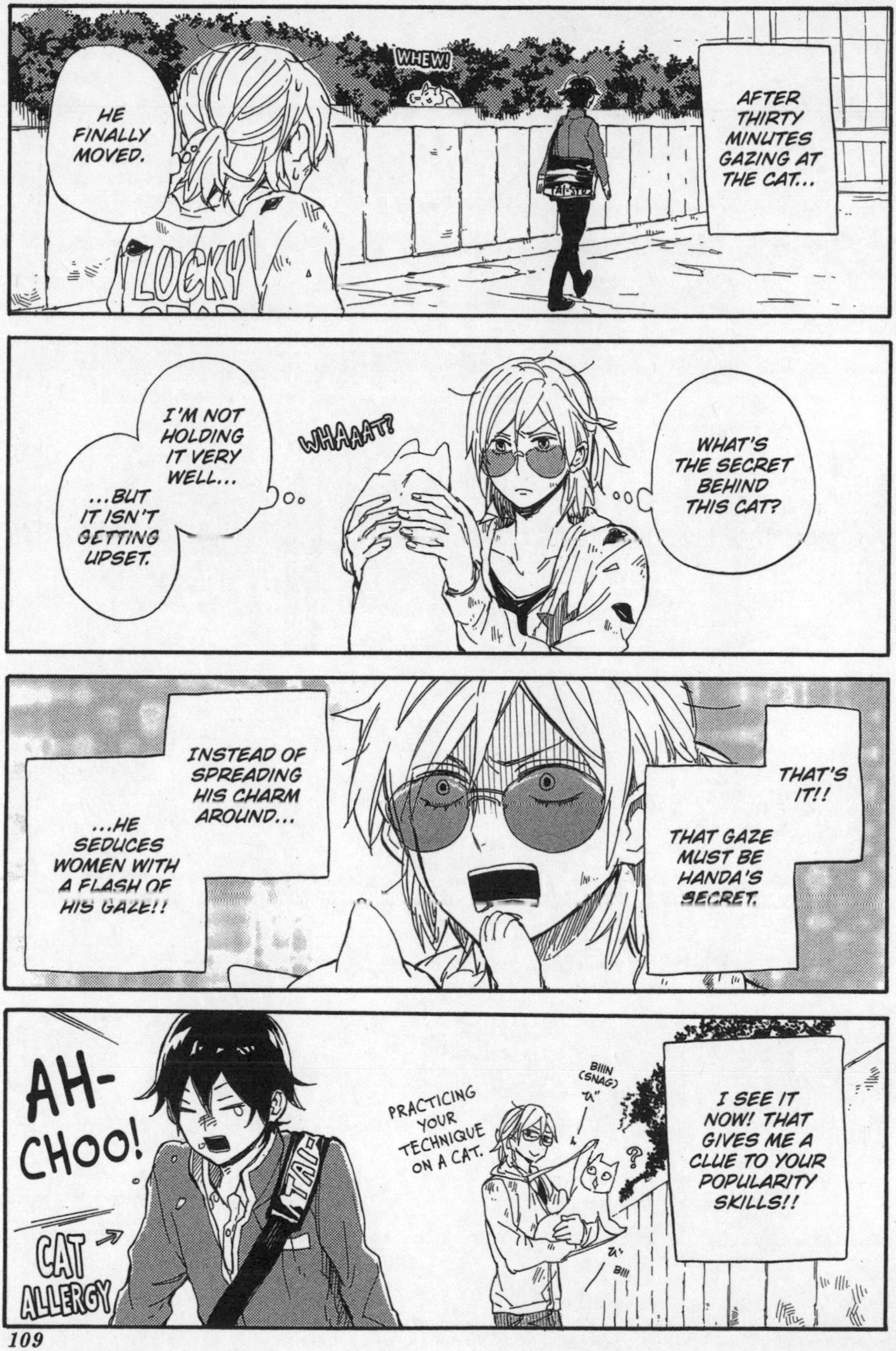
AFTER THIRTY MINUTES GAZING AT THE CAT...
WHEW!
HE FINALLY MOVED.
WHAT'S THE SECRET BEHIND THIS CAT?
WHAAAAT?
I'M NOT HOLDING IT VERY WELL...
...BUT IT ISN'T GETTING UPSET.
THAT'S IT!!
THAT GAZE MUST BE HANDA'S SECRET.
INSTEAD OF SPREADING HIS CHARM AROUND...
...HE SEDUCES WOMEN WITH A FLASH OF HIS GAZE!!
I SEE IT NOW! THAT GIVES ME A CLUE TO YOUR POPULARITY SKILLS!!
BIIIN (SNAG)
PRACTICING YOUR TECHNIQUE ON A CAT.
AH-CHOO!
CAT ALLERGY

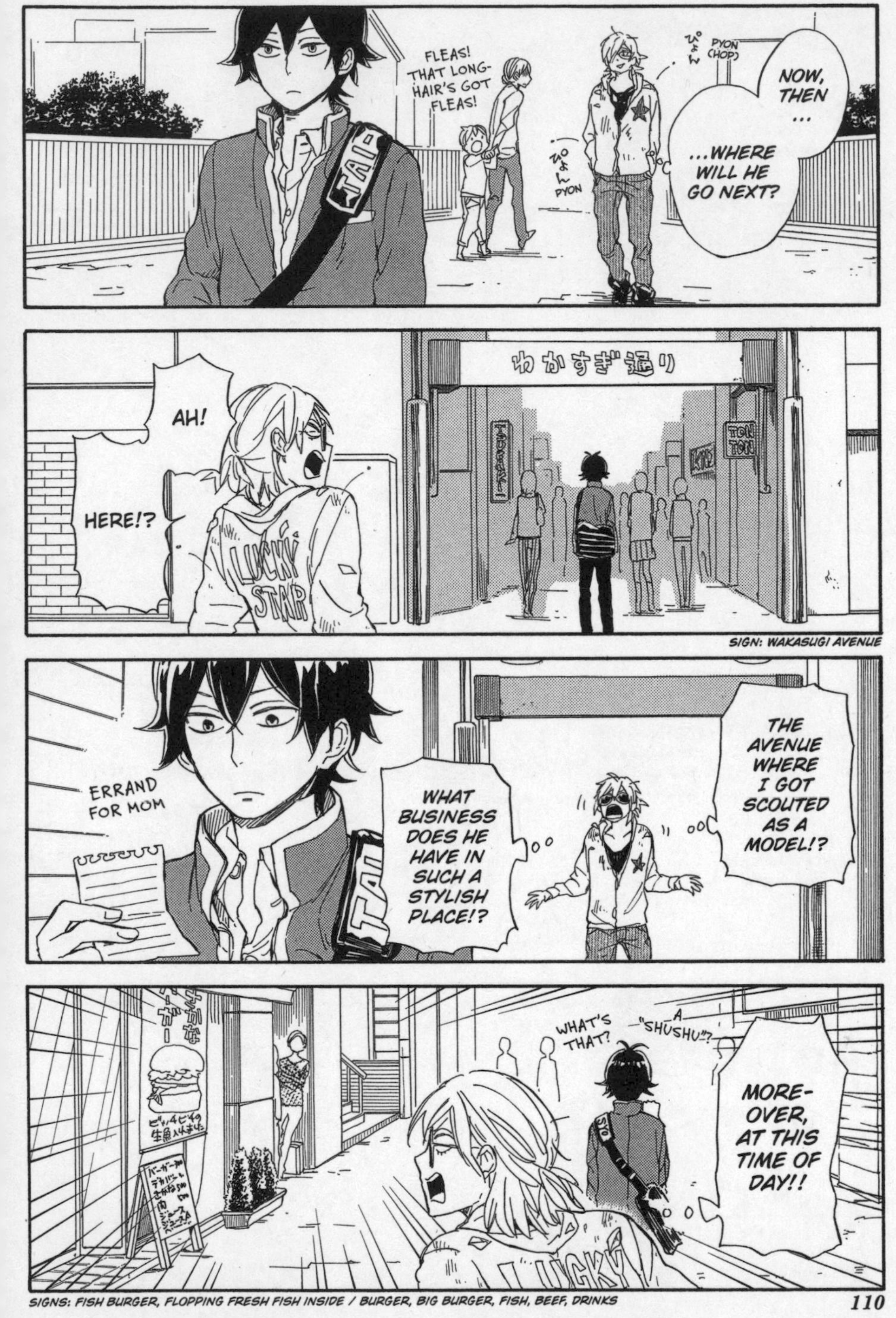
NOW, THEN ...
...WHERE WILL HE GO NEXT?
ぴょん
PYON (HOP)
FLEAS! THAT LONG-HAIR'S GOT FLEAS!
ぴょん
PYON
わかすぎ通り
TON TON
AH!
HERE!?
LUCKY STAR
THE AVENUE WHERE I GOT SCOUTED AS A MODEL!?
WHAT BUSINESS DOES HE HAVE IN SUCH A STYLISH PLACE!?
ERRAND FOR MOM
MORE-OVER, AT THIS TIME OF DAY!!
A "SHUSHU"!?
WHAT'S THAT?

SIGN: WAKASUGI AVENUE

SIGNS: FISH BURGER, FLOPPING FRESH FISH INSIDE / BURGER, BIG BURGER, FISH, BEEF, DRINKS

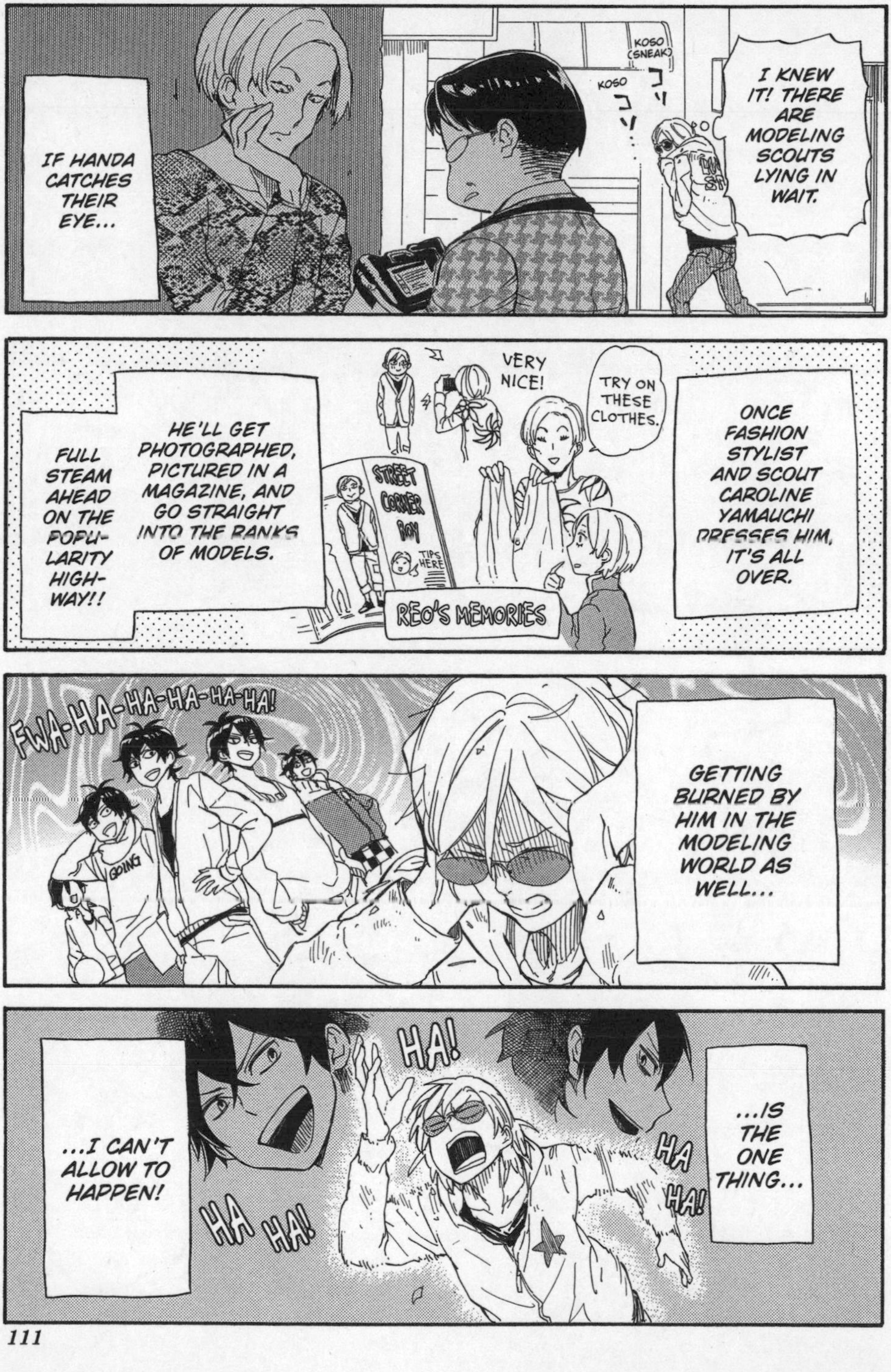
I KNEW IT! THERE ARE MODELING SCOUTS LYING IN WAIT.
KOSO (SNEAK)
KOSO
IF HANDA CATCHES THEIR EYE...
ONCE FASHION STYLIST AND SCOUT CAROLINE YAMAUCHI DRESSES HIM, IT'S ALL OVER.
TRY ON THESE CLOTHES.
VERY NICE!
STREET CORNER BOY
TIPS HERE
REO'S MEMORIES
HE'LL GET PHOTOGRAPHED, PICTURED IN A MAGAZINE, AND GO STRAIGHT INTO THE RANKS OF MODELS.
FULL STEAM AHEAD ON THE POPULARITY HIGHWAY!!
GETTING BURNED BY HIM IN THE MODELING WORLD AS WELL...
FWA-HA-HA-HA-HA-HA!
GOING
...IS THE ONE THING...
HA HA!
HA!
HA HA!
...I CAN'T ALLOW TO HAPPEN!

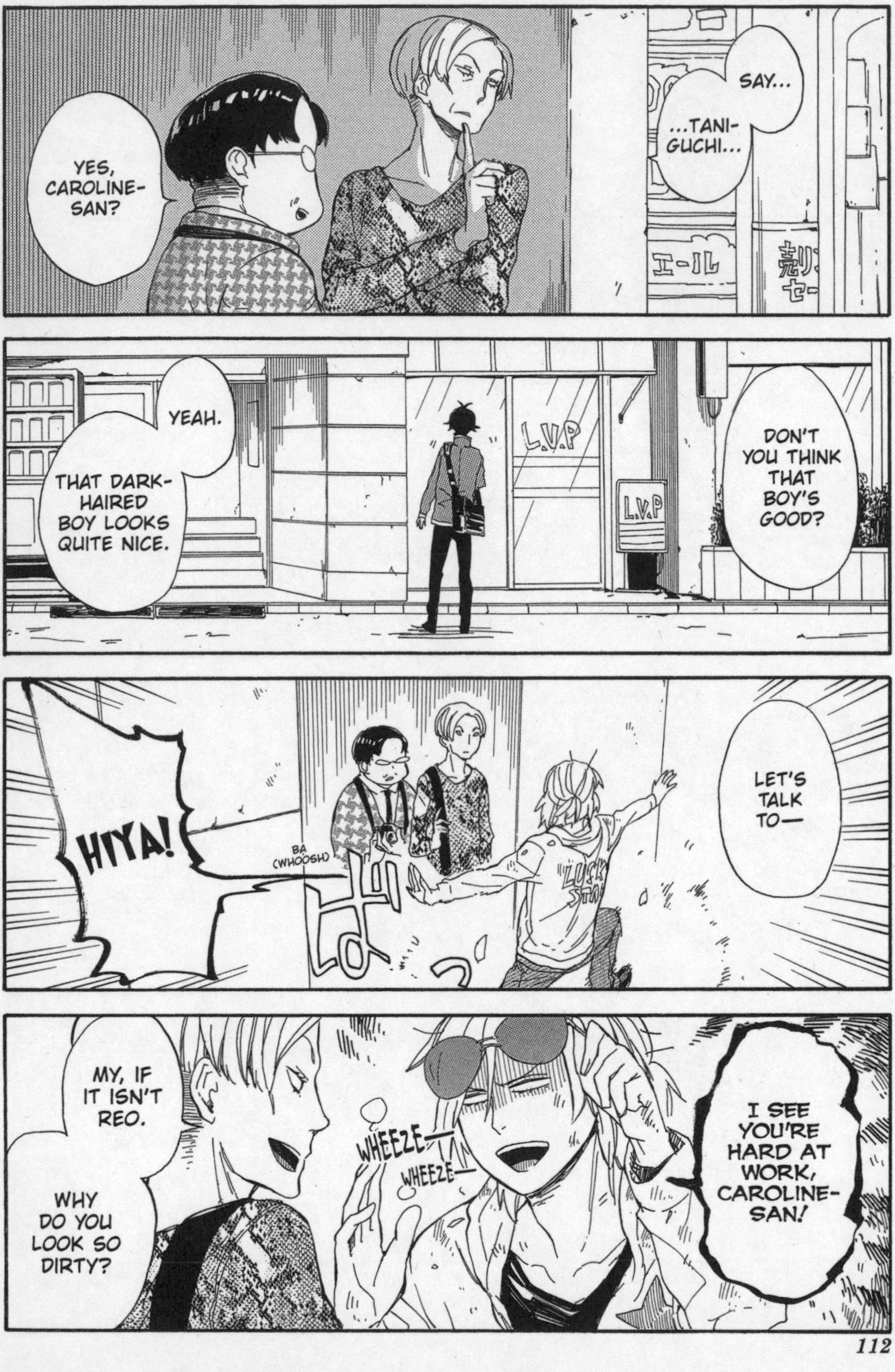
SAY...
...TANI-GUCHI...
YES, CAROLINE-SAN?
DON'T YOU THINK THAT BOY'S GOOD?
L.V.P
L.V.P
YEAH.
THAT DARK-HAIRED BOY LOOKS QUITE NICE.
LET'S TALK TO—
HIYA!
BA (WHOOSH)
I SEE YOU'RE HARD AT WORK, CAROLINE-SAN!
WHEEZE—
WHEEZE—
MY, IF IT ISN'T REO.
WHY DO YOU LOOK SO DIRTY?

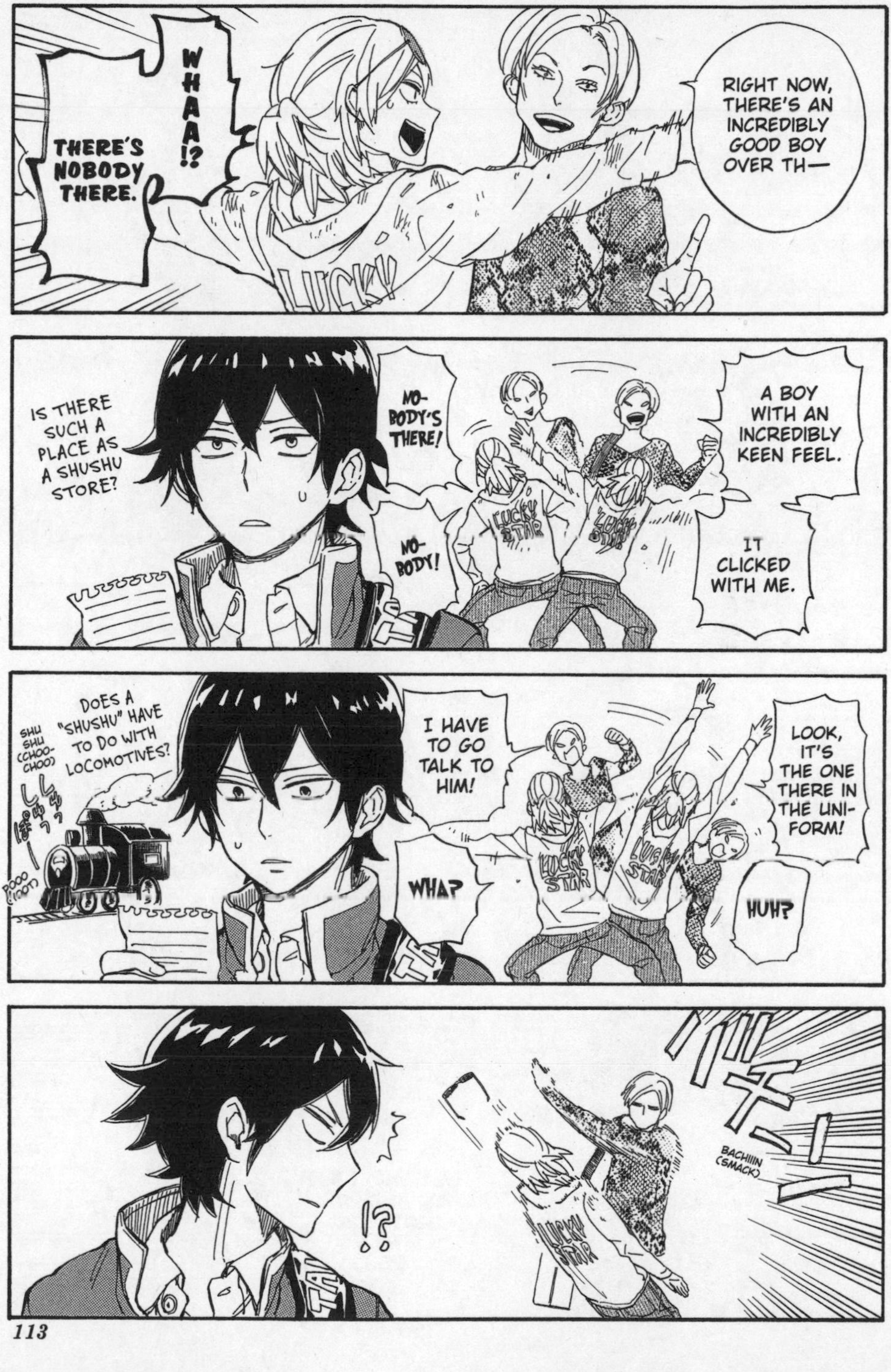
RIGHT NOW, THERE'S AN INCREDIBLY GOOD BOY OVER TH—
WHAAA!?
THERE'S NOBODY THERE.
A BOY WITH AN INCREDIBLY KEEN FEEL.
IT CLICKED WITH ME.
NO-BODY'S THERE!
NO-BODY!
IS THERE SUCH A PLACE AS A SHUSHU STORE?
LOOK, IT'S THE ONE THERE IN THE UNI-FORM!
HUH?
I HAVE TO GO TALK TO HIM!
WHA?
DOES A "SHUSHU" HAVE TO DO WITH LOCOMOTIVES?
SHU SHU (CHOO-CHOO)
POOO (TOOT)
バチーン
BACHIIIN (SMACK)
!?

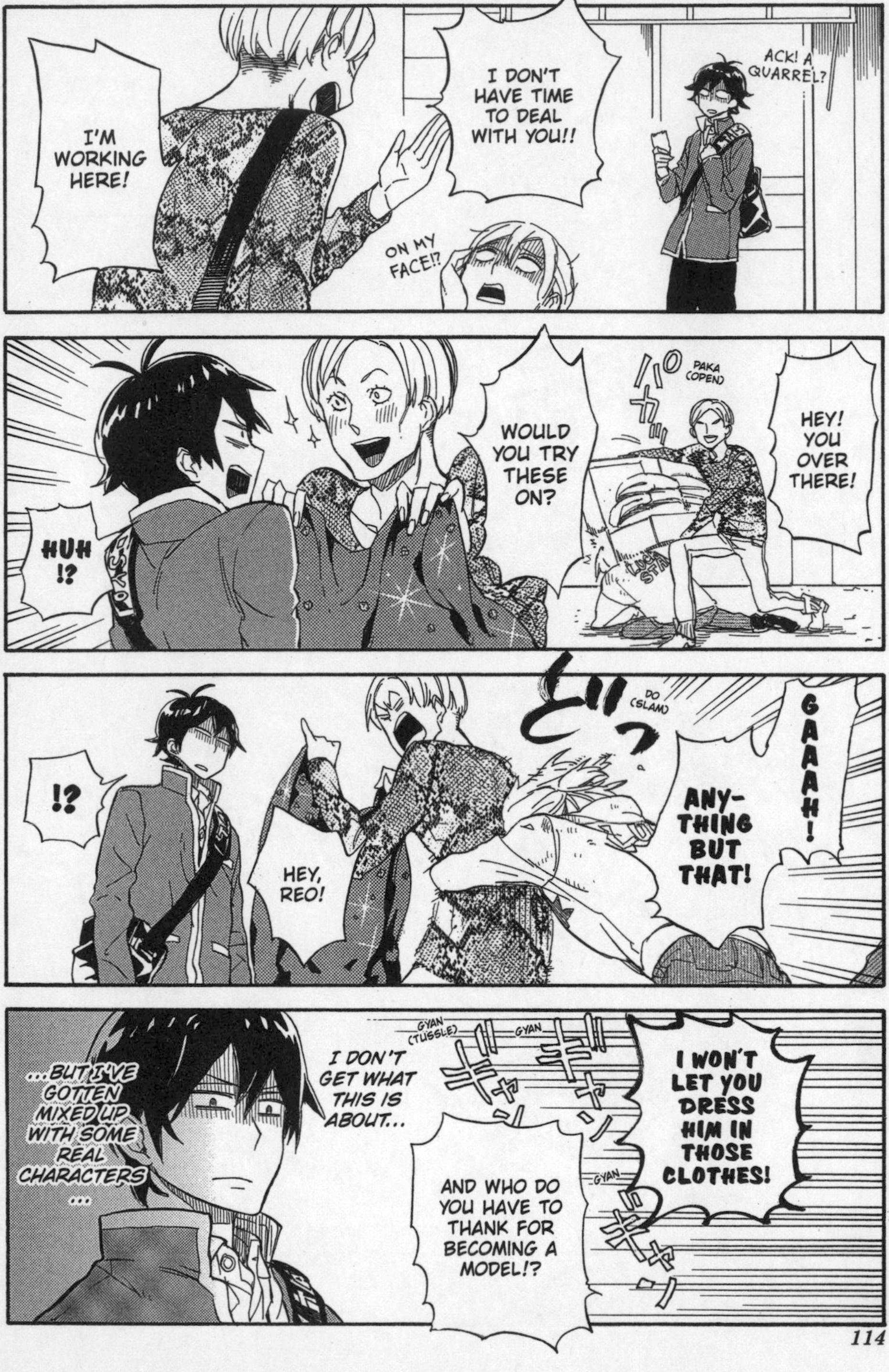
ACK! A QUARREL?
I DON'T HAVE TIME TO DEAL WITH YOU!!
I'M WORKING HERE!
ON MY FACE!?
HEY! YOU OVER THERE!
PAKA (OPEN)
WOULD YOU TRY THESE ON?
HUH!?
GAAAH!
ANYTHING BUT THAT!
DO (SLAM)
HEY, REO!
!?
I WON'T LET YOU DRESS HIM IN THOSE CLOTHES!
GYAN (TUSSLE)
GYAN
GYAN
I DON'T GET WHAT THIS IS ABOUT...
AND WHO DO YOU HAVE TO THANK FOR BECOMING A MODEL!?
...BUT I'VE GOTTEN MIXED UP WITH SOME REAL CHARACTERS...

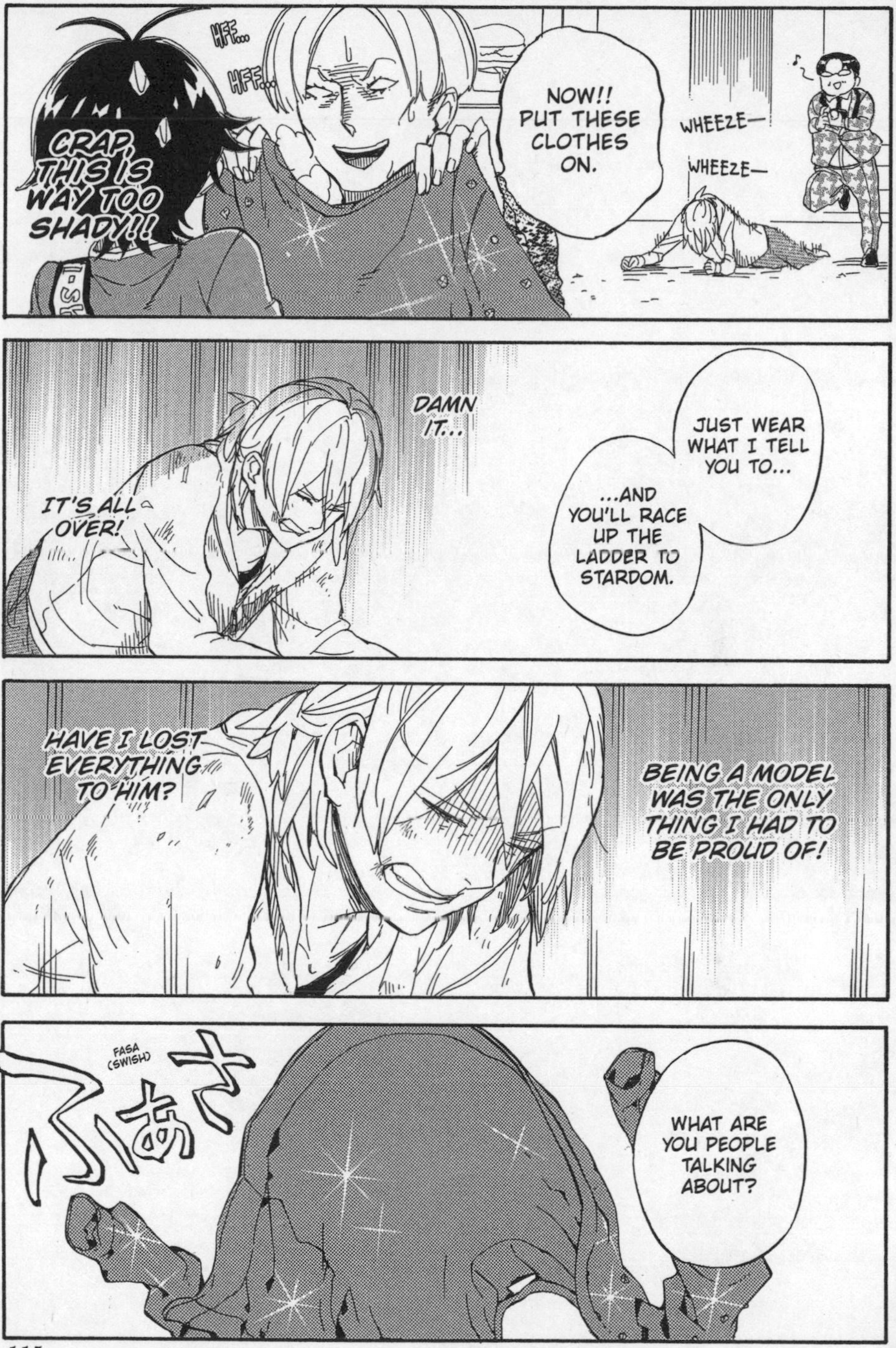
WHEEZE—
WHEEZE—
NOW!! PUT THESE CLOTHES ON.
HFF...
HFF...
CRAP, THIS IS WAY TOO SHADY!!
JUST WEAR WHAT I TELL YOU TO...
...AND YOU'LL RACE UP THE LADDER TO STARDOM.
DAMN IT...
IT'S ALL OVER!
BEING A MODEL WAS THE ONLY THING I HAD TO BE PROUD OF!
HAVE I LOST EVERYTHING TO HIM?
WHAT ARE YOU PEOPLE TALKING ABOUT?
ふぁさ
FASA (SWISH)

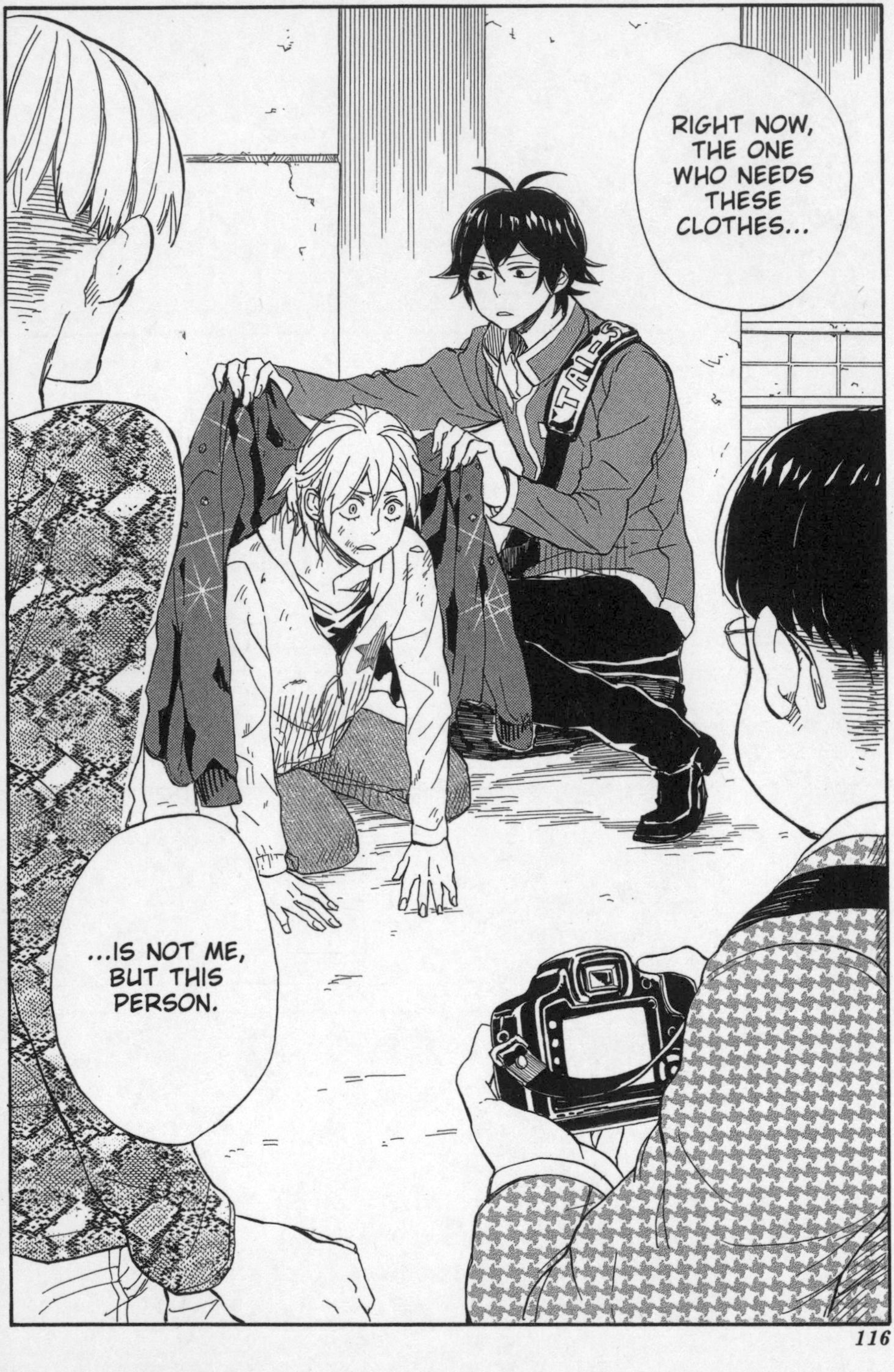
RIGHT NOW, THE ONE WHO NEEDS THESE CLOTHES...
...IS NOT ME, BUT THIS PERSON.

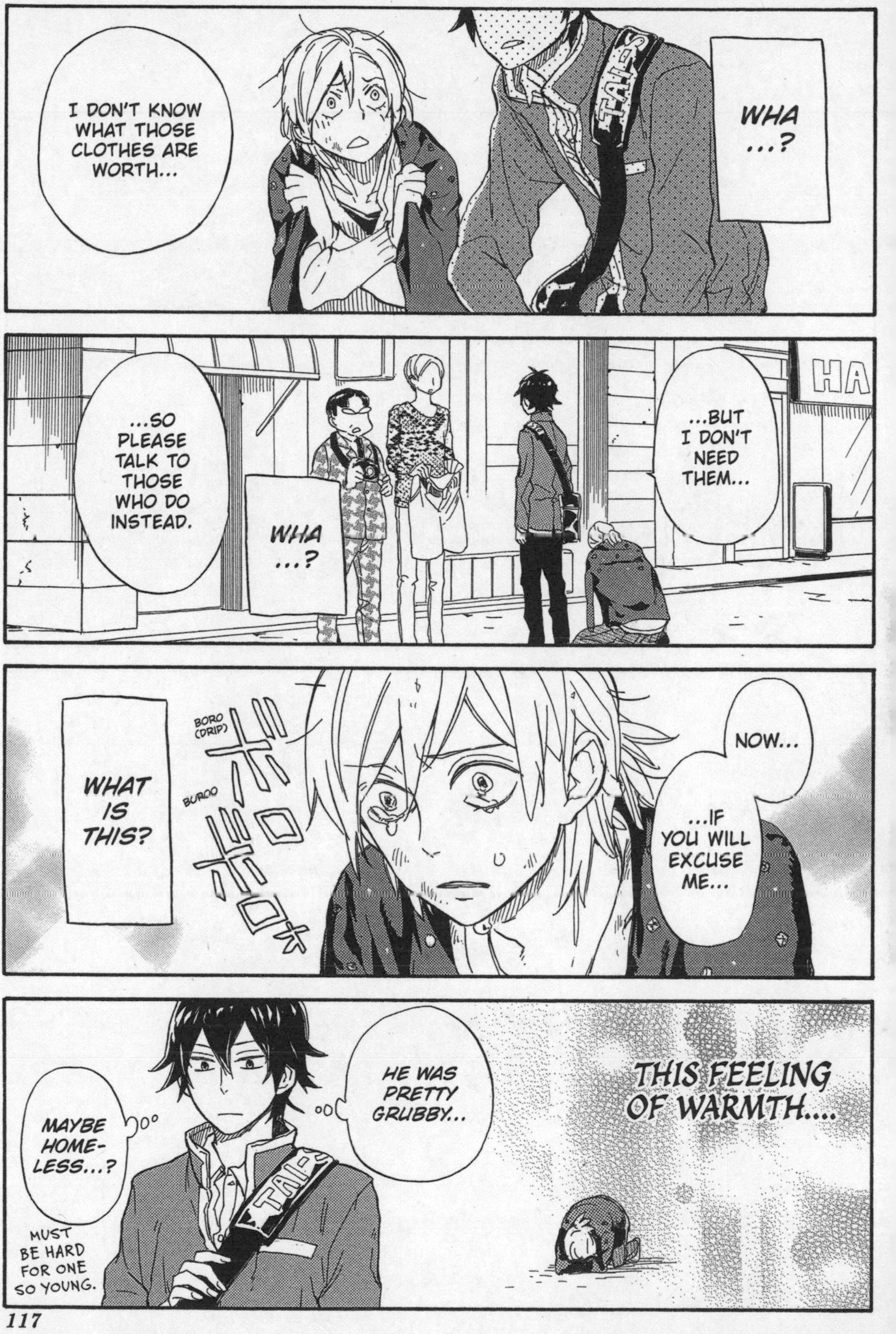

WHA ...?
I DON'T KNOW WHAT THOSE CLOTHES ARE WORTH...
...BUT I DON'T NEED THEM...
HA
...SO PLEASE TALK TO THOSE WHO DO INSTEAD.
WHA ...?
NOW...
...IF YOU WILL EXCUSE ME...
BORO (DRIP)
BUROO
WHAT IS THIS?
THIS FEELING OF WARMTH....
HE WAS PRETTY GRUBBY...
MAYBE HOME-LESS...?
MUST BE HARD FOR ONE SO YOUNG.

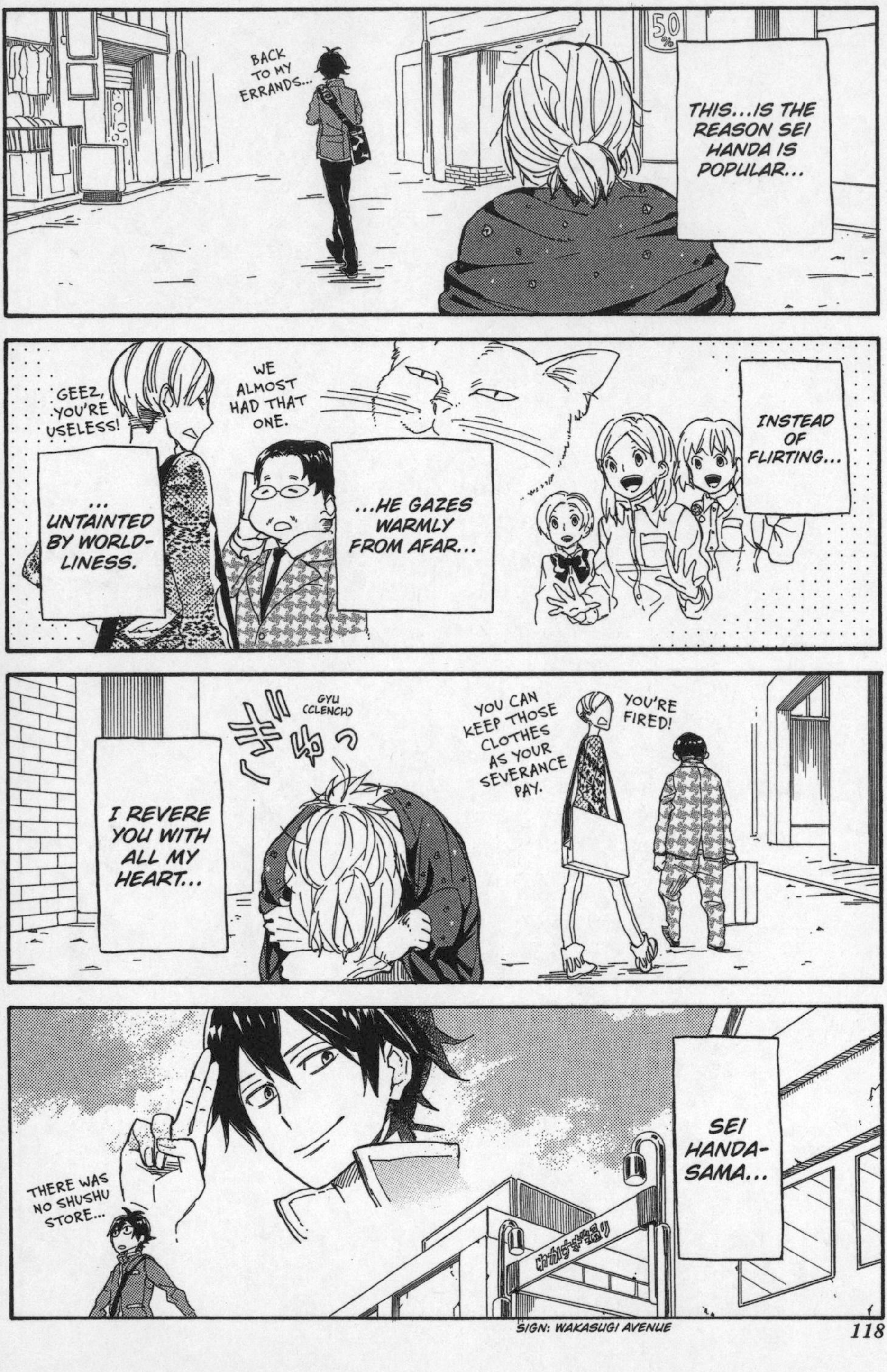
THIS...IS THE REASON SEI HANDA IS POPULAR...
BACK TO MY ERRANDS...
INSTEAD OF FLIRTING...
...HE GAZES WARMLY FROM AFAR...
WE ALMOST HAD THAT ONE.
GEEZ, YOU'RE USELESS!
...UNTAINTED BY WORLDLINESS.
YOU'RE FIRED!
YOU CAN KEEP THOSE CLOTHES AS YOUR SEVERANCE PAY.
GYU (CLENCH)
I REVERE YOU WITH ALL MY HEART...
SEI HANDA-SAMA...
THERE WAS NO SHUSHU STORE...
SIGN: WAKASUGI AVENUE

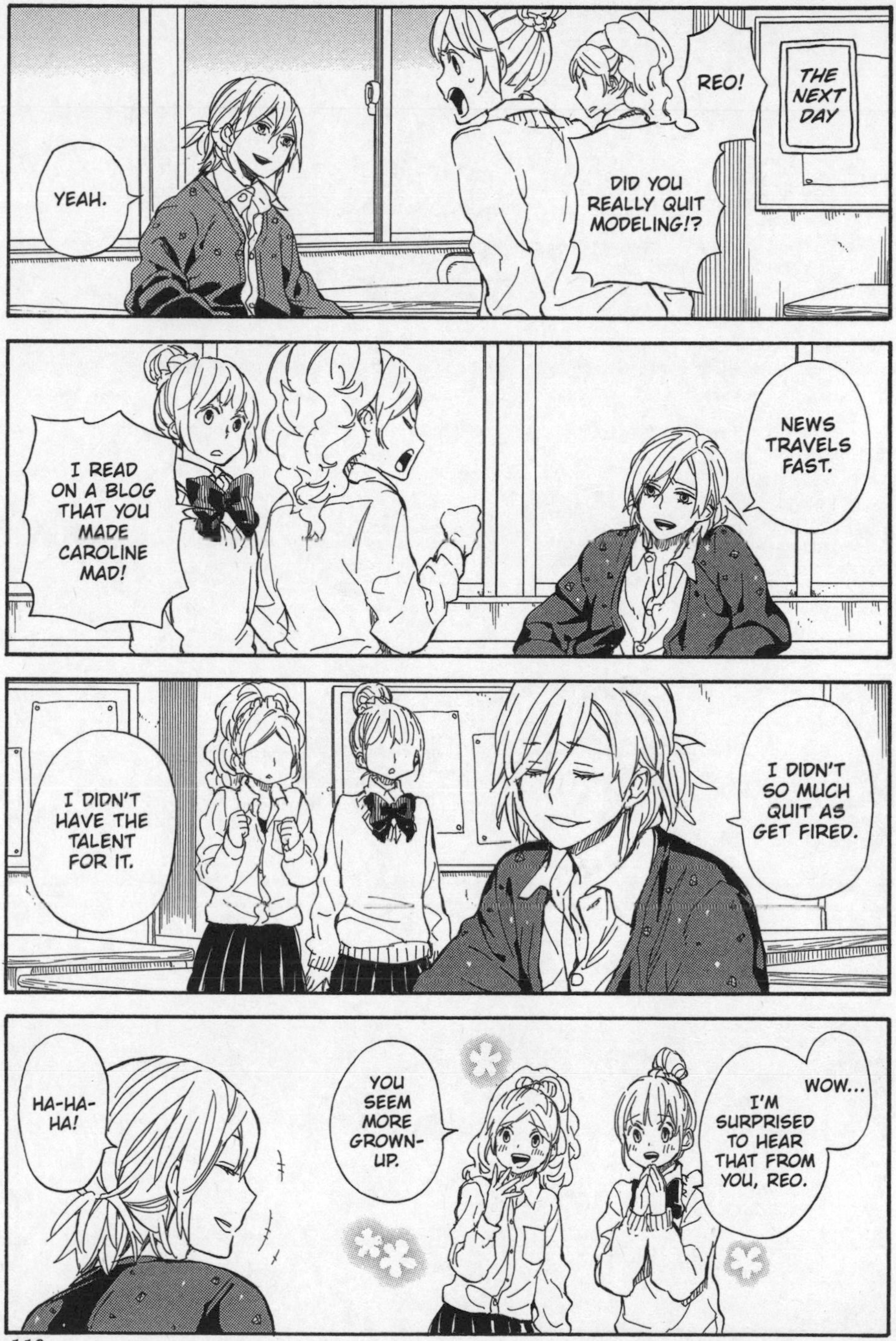
THE NEXT DAY
REO!
DID YOU REALLY QUIT MODELING!?
YEAH.
NEWS TRAVELS FAST.
I READ ON A BLOG THAT YOU MADE CAROLINE MAD!
I DIDN'T SO MUCH QUIT AS GET FIRED.
I DIDN'T HAVE THE TALENT FOR IT.
WOW... I'M SURPRISED TO HEAR THAT FROM YOU, REO.
YOU SEEM MORE GROWN-UP.
HA-HA-HA!

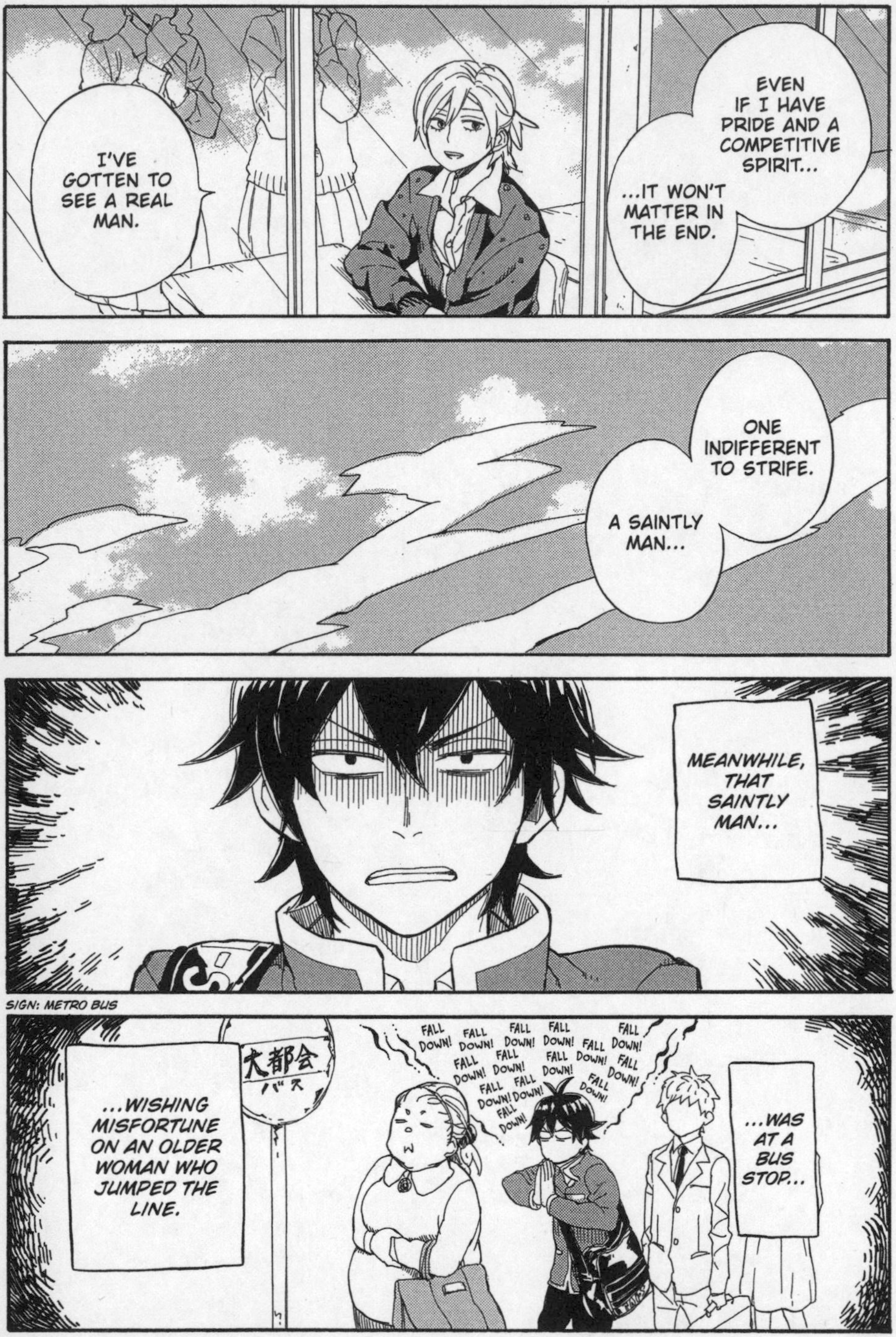
EVEN IF I HAVE PRIDE AND A COMPETITIVE SPIRIT...
...IT WON'T MATTER IN THE END.
I'VE GOTTEN TO SEE A REAL MAN.
ONE INDIFFERENT TO STRIFE.
A SAINTLY MAN...
MEANWHILE, THAT SAINTLY MAN...
SIGN: METRO BUS
...WAS AT A BUS STOP...
FALL DOWN! FALL DOWN! FALL DOWN! FALL DOWN! FALL DOWN! FALL DOWN! FALL DOWN! FALL DOWN! FALL DOWN! FALL DOWN! FALL DOWN! FALL DOWN! FALL DOWN! FALL DOWN!
大都会
バス
...WISHING MISFORTUNE ON AN OLDER WOMAN WHO JUMPED THE LINE.

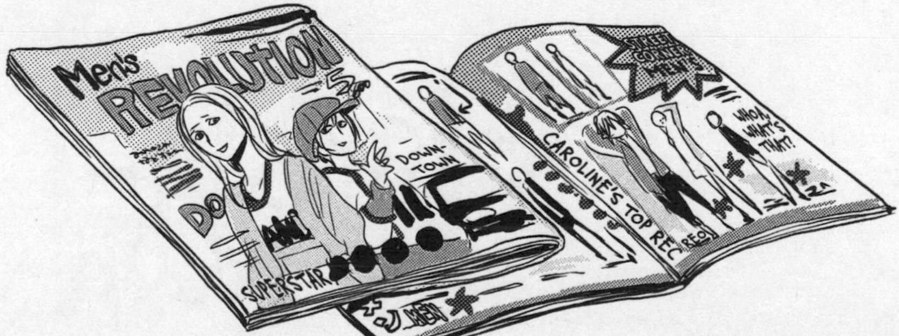
Men's
REVOLUTION
DOWN-
TOWN
SUPERSTAR
CAROLINE'S TOP REC
WHOA, WHAT'S THAT?

Handa-
Kun

Chapter 5: Handa-kun & the Truant

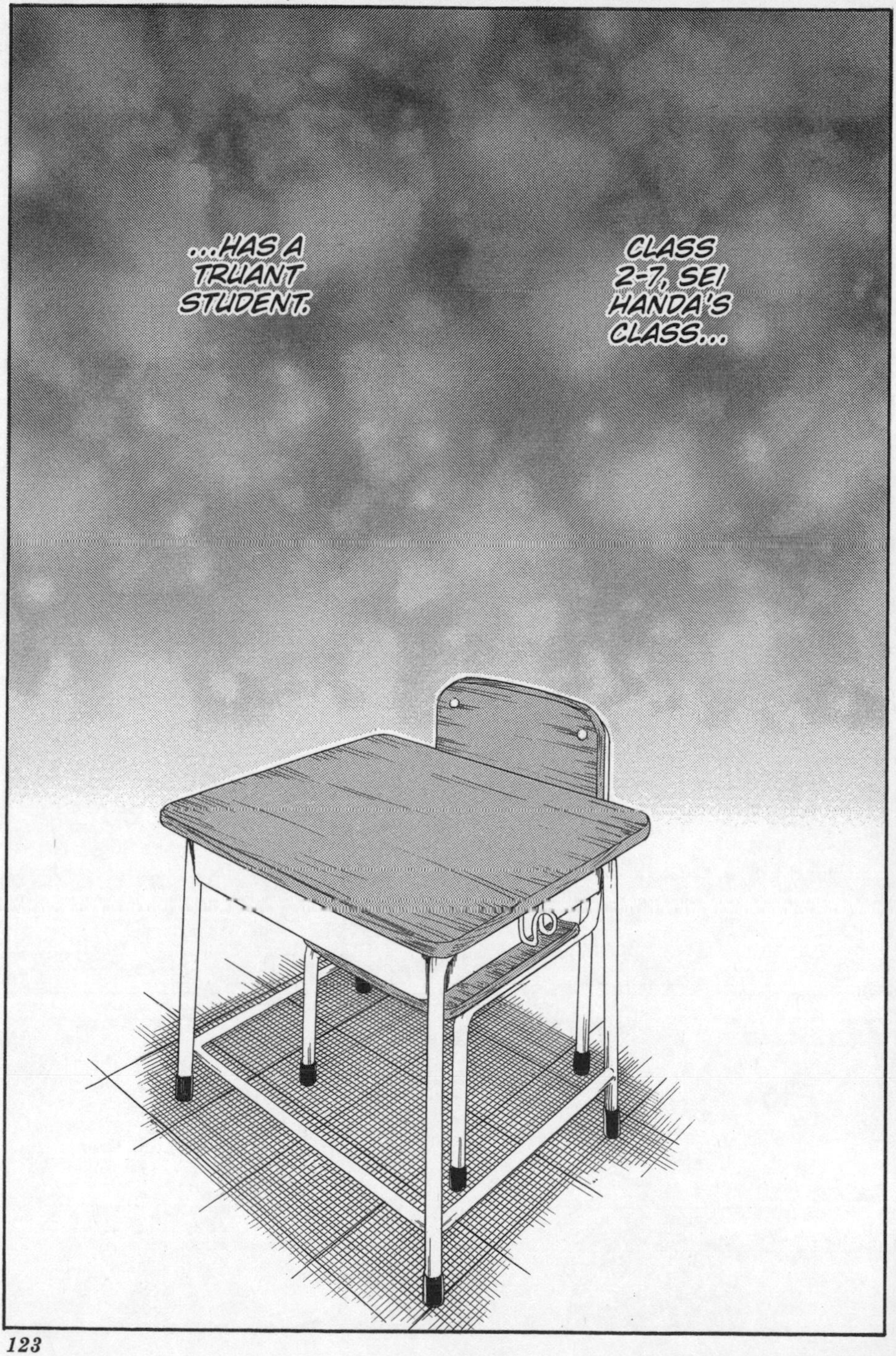
CLASS 2-7, SEI HANDA'S CLASS...
...HAS A TRUANT STUDENT.

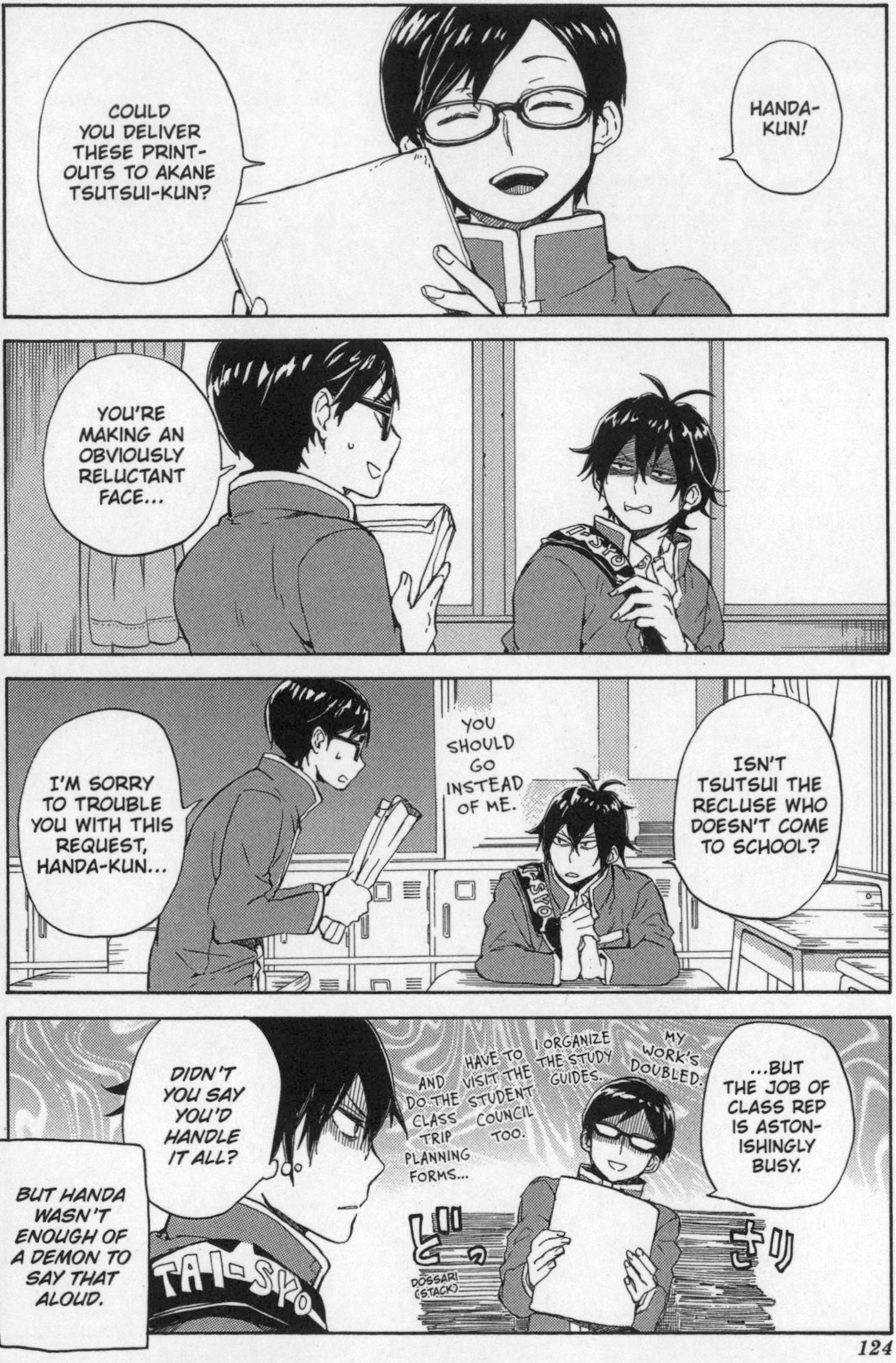
HANDA-KUN!
COULD YOU DELIVER THESE PRINT-OUTS TO AKANE TSUTSUI-KUN?
YOU'RE MAKING AN OBVIOUSLY RELUCTANT FACE...
ISN'T TSUTSUI THE RECLUSE WHO DOESN'T COME TO SCHOOL?
YOU SHOULD GO INSTEAD OF ME.
I'M SORRY TO TROUBLE YOU WITH THIS REQUEST, HANDA-KUN...
...BUT THE JOB OF CLASS REP IS ASTON-ISHINGLY BUSY.
MY WORK'S DOUBLED.
I ORGANIZE THE STUDY GUIDES.
HAVE TO VISIT THE STUDENT COUNCIL TOO.
AND DO THE CLASS TRIP PLANNING FORMS...
どっさり
DOSSARI (STACK)
DIDN'T YOU SAY YOU'D HANDLE IT ALL?
BUT HANDA WASN'T ENOUGH OF A DEMON TO SAY THAT ALOUD.

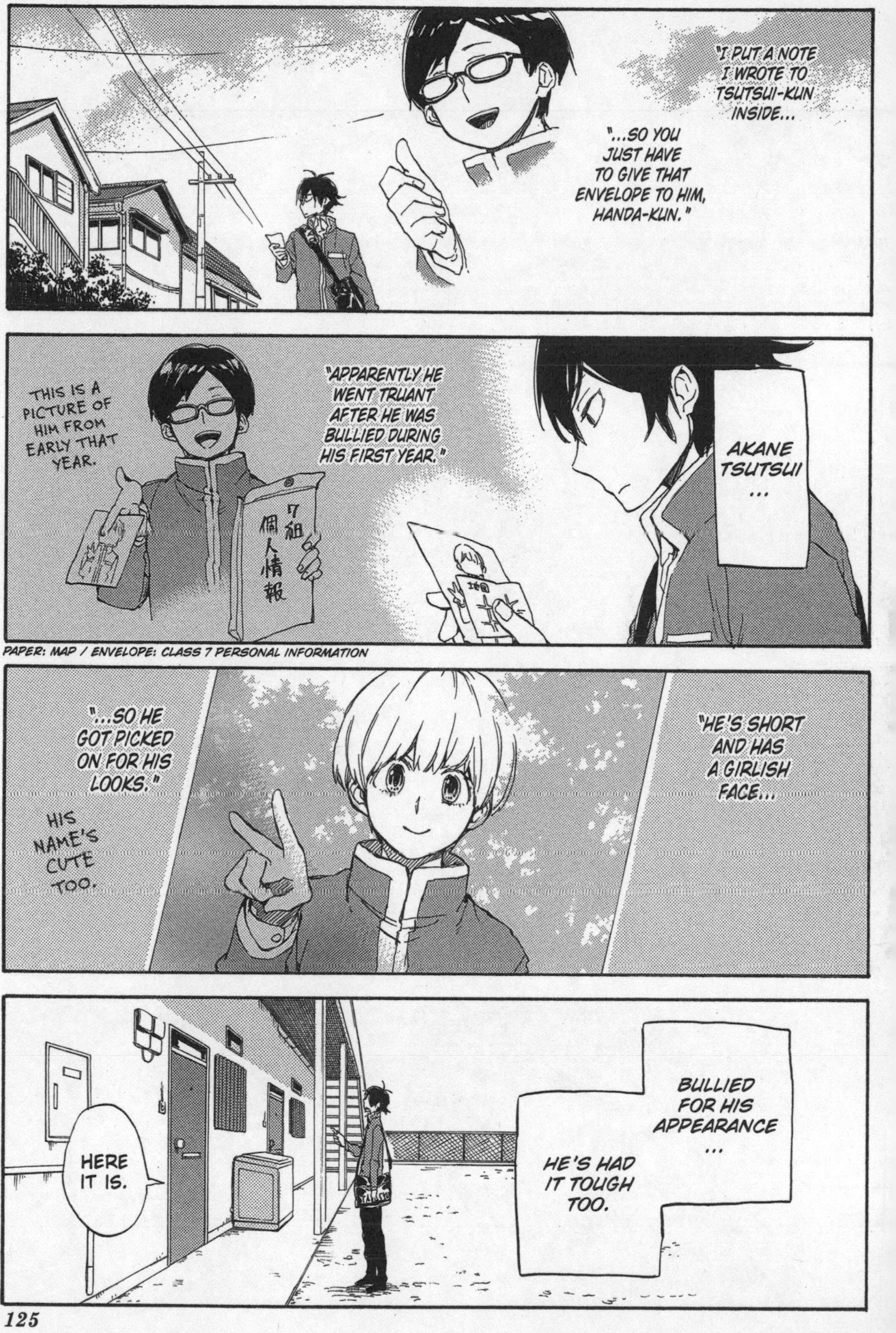
"I PUT A NOTE I WROTE TO TSUTSUI-KUN INSIDE...
"...SO YOU JUST HAVE TO GIVE THAT ENVELOPE TO HIM, HANDA-KUN."
AKANE TSUTSUI...
"APPARENTLY HE WENT TRUANT AFTER HE WAS BULLIED DURING HIS FIRST YEAR."
THIS IS A PICTURE OF HIM FROM EARLY THAT YEAR.
PAPER: MAP / ENVELOPE: CLASS 7 PERSONAL INFORMATION
"HE'S SHORT AND HAS A GIRLISH FACE...
"...SO HE GOT PICKED ON FOR HIS LOOKS."
HIS NAME'S CUTE TOO.
BULLIED FOR HIS APPEARANCE...
HE'S HAD IT TOUGH TOO.
HERE IT IS.

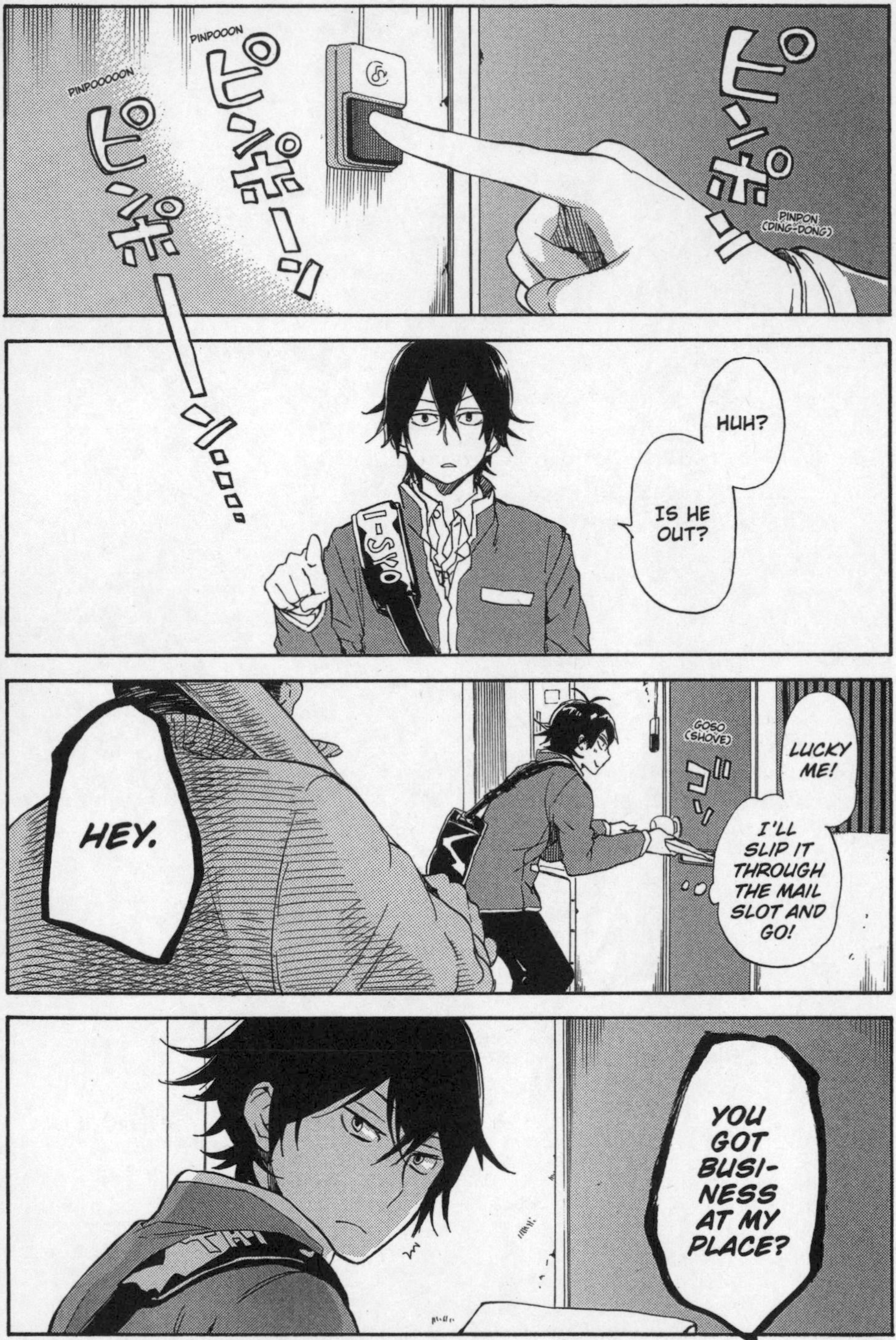
ピンポーン
PINPON (DING-DONG)
ピンポーン
PINPOOON
ピンポーーーン
PINPOOOOON
HUH?
IS HE OUT?
GOSO (SHOVE)
ゴソ
LUCKY ME!
I'LL SLIP IT THROUGH THE MAIL SLOT AND GO!
HEY.
YOU GOT BUSI-NESS AT MY PLACE?

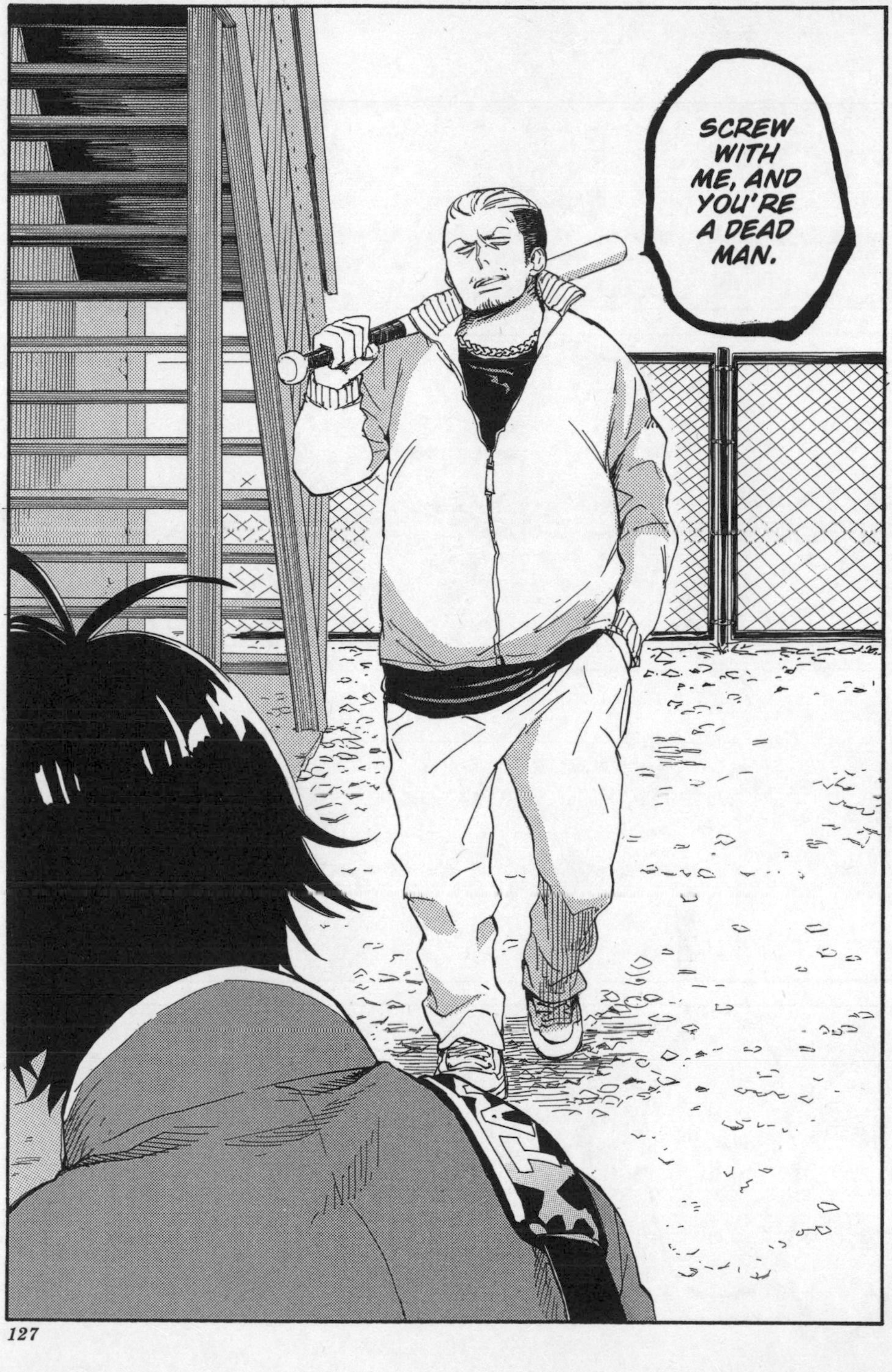
SCREW WITH ME, AND YOU'RE A DEAD MAN.

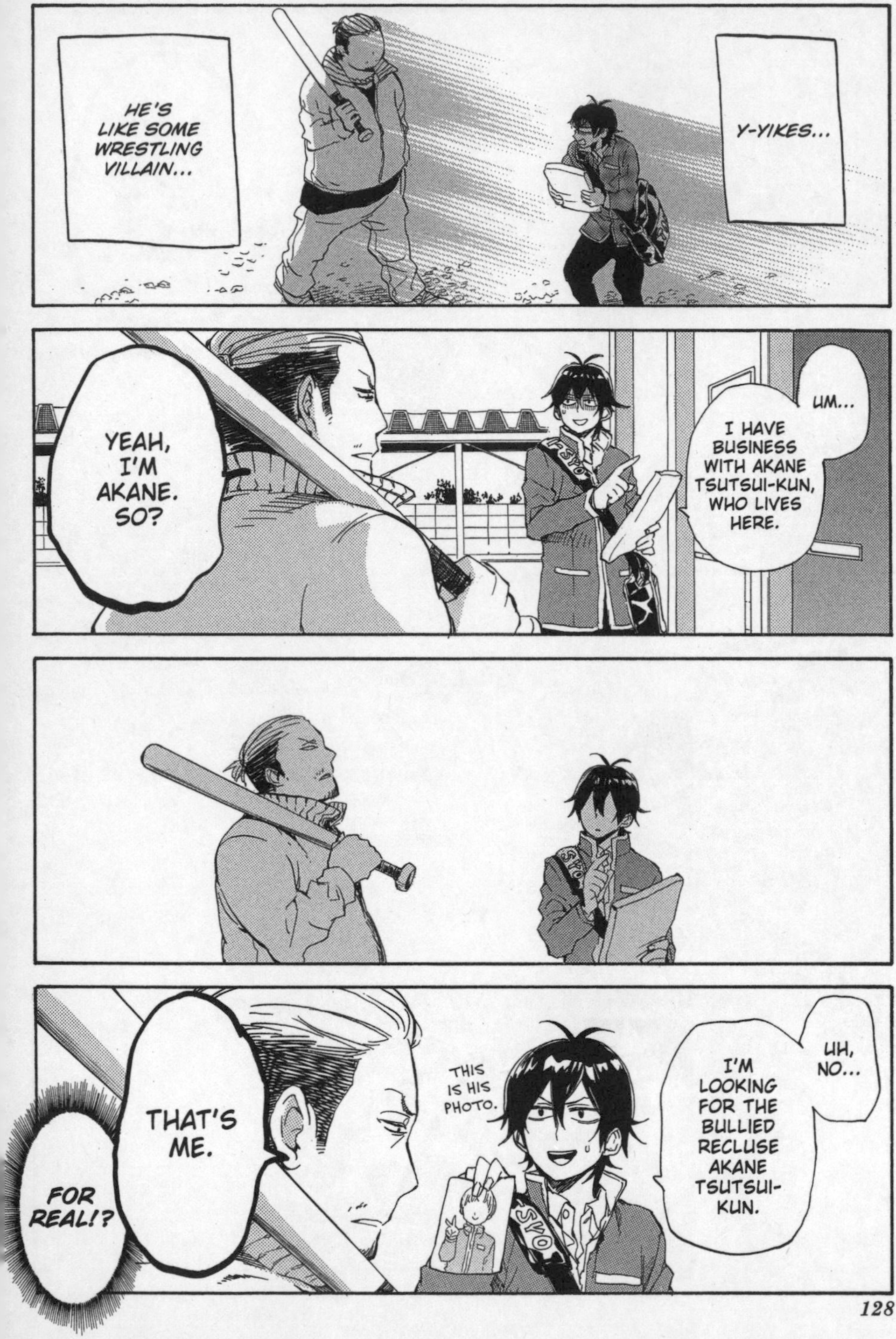
Y-YIKES...
HE'S LIKE SOME WRESTLING VILLAIN...
UM... I HAVE BUSINESS WITH AKANE TSUTSUI-KUN, WHO LIVES HERE.
YEAH, I'M AKANE. SO?
UH, NO... I'M LOOKING FOR THE BULLIED RECLUSE AKANE TSUTSUI-KUN.
THIS IS HIS PHOTO.
THAT'S ME.
FOR REAL!?

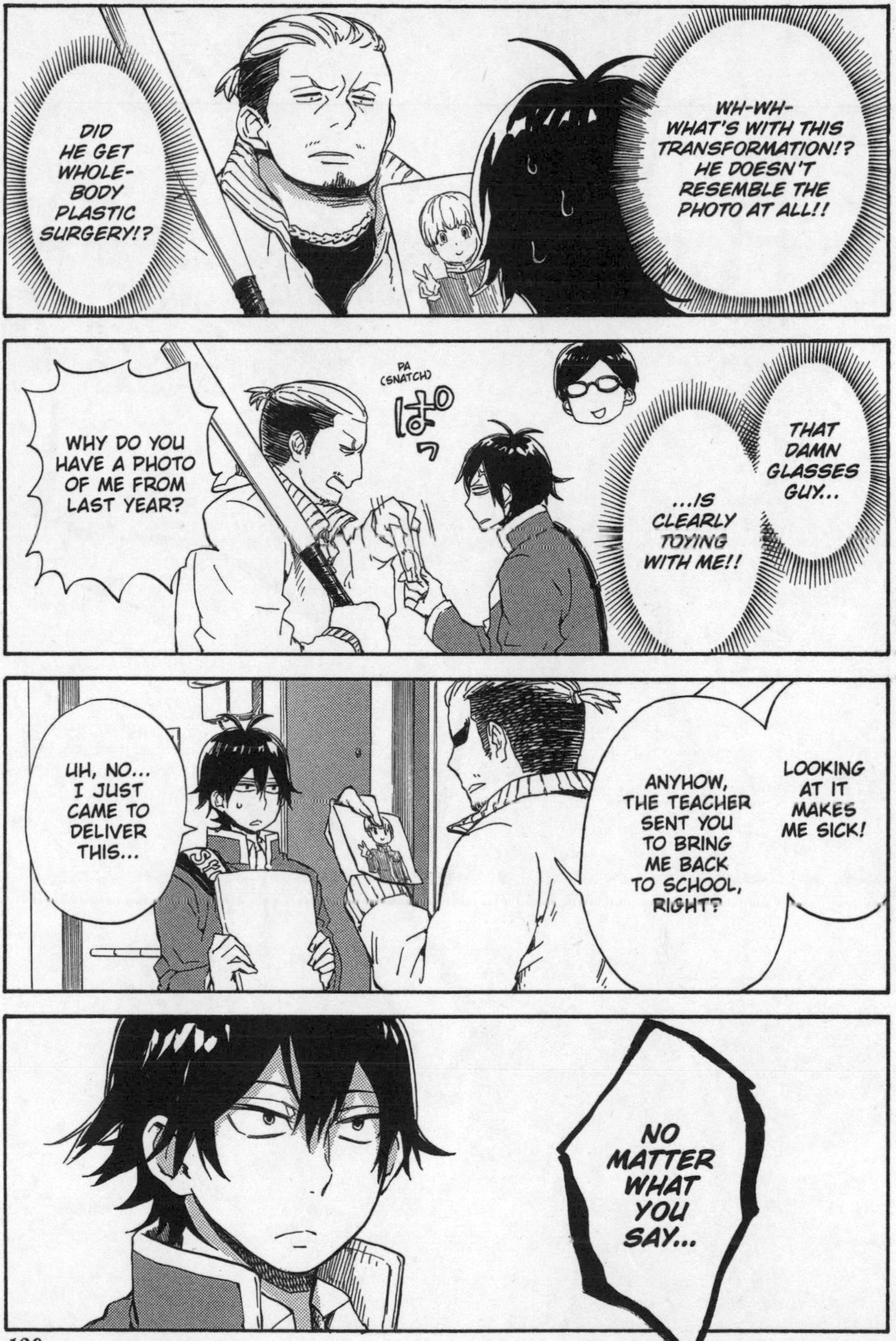
WH-WH- WHAT'S WITH THIS TRANSFORMATION!? HE DOESN'T RESEMBLE THE PHOTO AT ALL!!
DID HE GET WHOLE-BODY PLASTIC SURGERY!?
THAT DAMN GLASSES GUY...
...IS CLEARLY TOYING WITH ME!!
PA (SNATCH)
ぱっ
WHY DO YOU HAVE A PHOTO OF ME FROM LAST YEAR?
LOOKING AT IT MAKES ME SICK!
ANYHOW, THE TEACHER SENT YOU TO BRING ME BACK TO SCHOOL, RIGHT?
UH, NO... I JUST CAME TO DELIVER THIS...
NO MATTER WHAT YOU SAY...

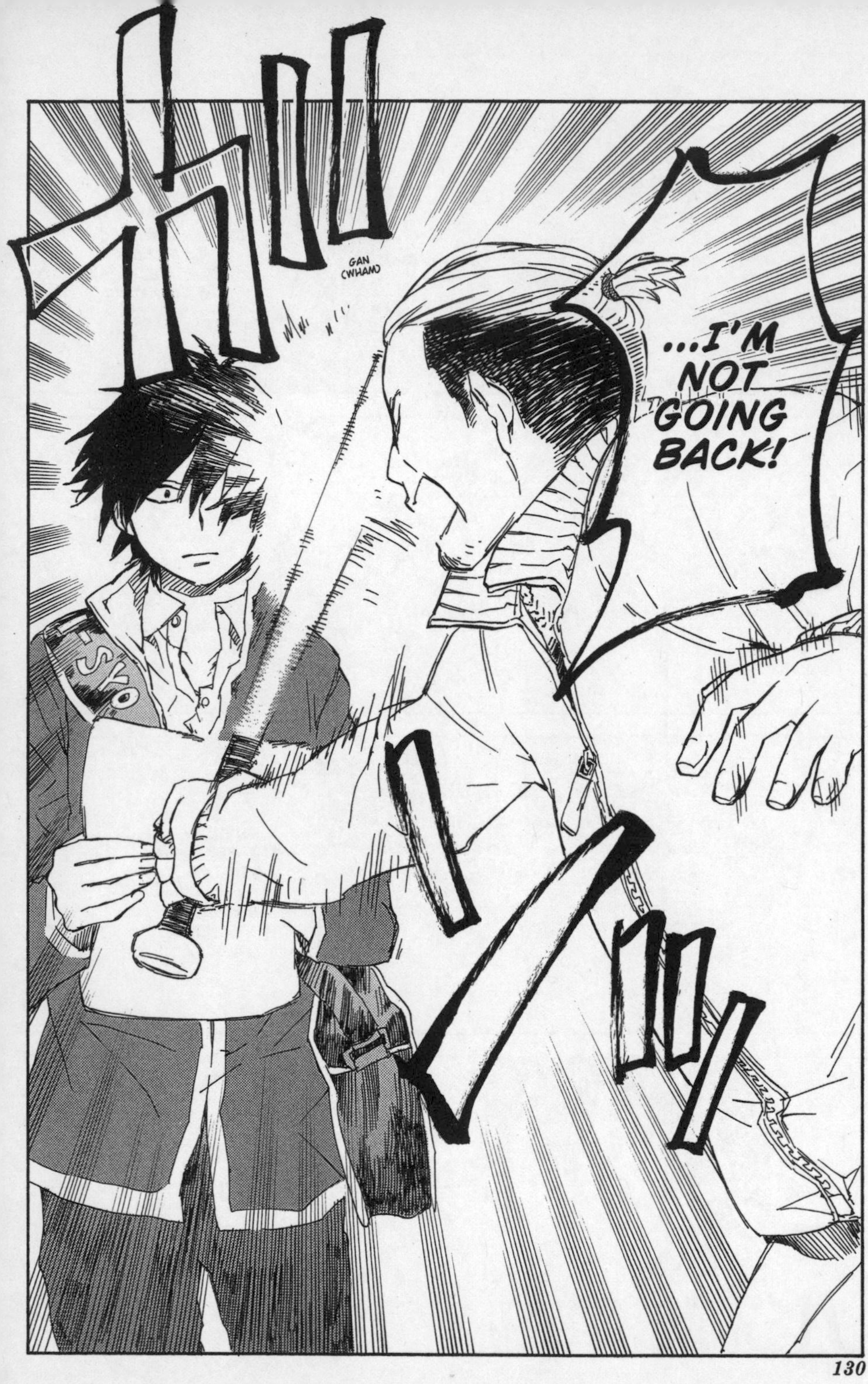

GAN (WHAM)
...I'M NOT GOING BACK!

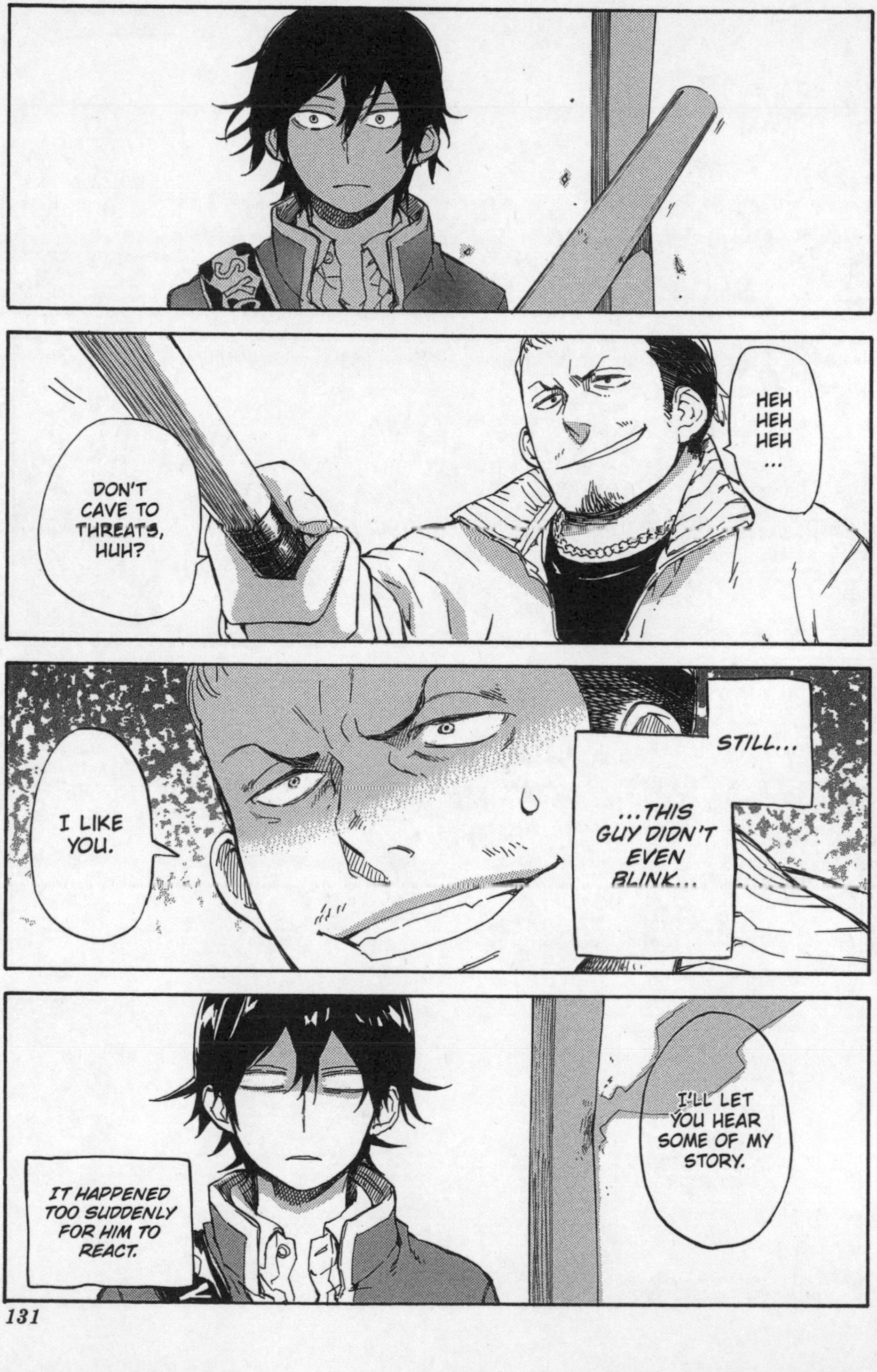
HEH HEH HEH...
DON'T CAVE TO THREATS, HUH?
STILL...
...THIS GUY DIDN'T EVEN BLINK...
I LIKE YOU.
I'LL LET YOU HEAR SOME OF MY STORY.
IT HAPPENED TOO SUDDENLY FOR HIM TO REACT.

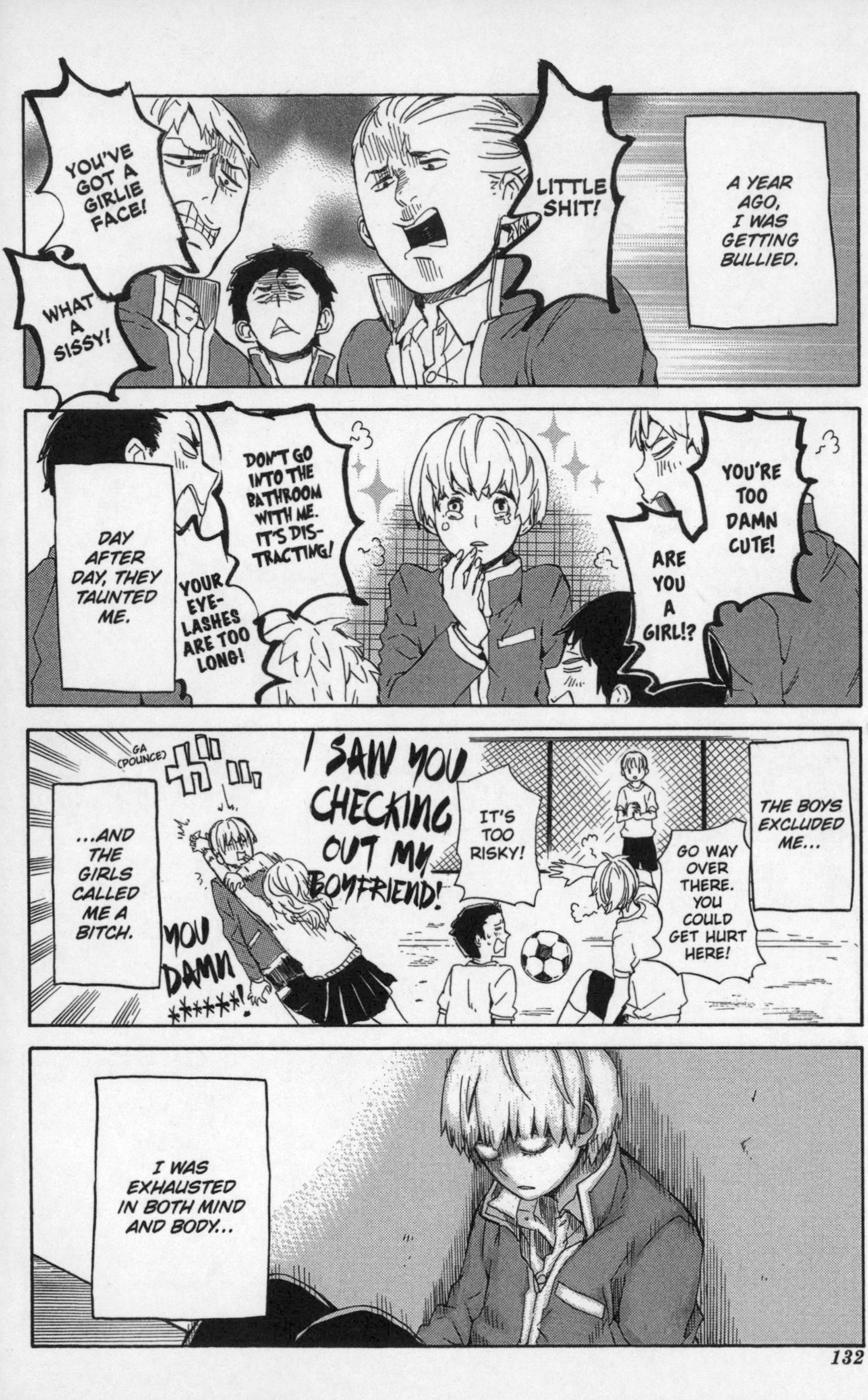
A YEAR AGO, I WAS GETTING BULLIED.
LITTLE SHIT!
YOU'VE GOT A GIRLIE FACE!
WHAT A SISSY!
YOU'RE TOO DAMN CUTE!
ARE YOU A GIRL!?
DON'T GO INTO THE BATHROOM WITH ME. IT'S DIS-TRACTING!
YOUR EYE-LASHES ARE TOO LONG!
DAY AFTER DAY, THEY TAUNTED ME.
THE BOYS EXCLUDED ME...
GO WAY OVER THERE. YOU COULD GET HURT HERE!
IT'S TOO RISKY!
I SAW YOU CHECKING OUT MY BOYFRIEND!
GA (POUNCE)
YOU DAMN *****!
...AND THE GIRLS CALLED ME A BITCH.
I WAS EXHAUSTED IN BOTH MIND AND BODY...

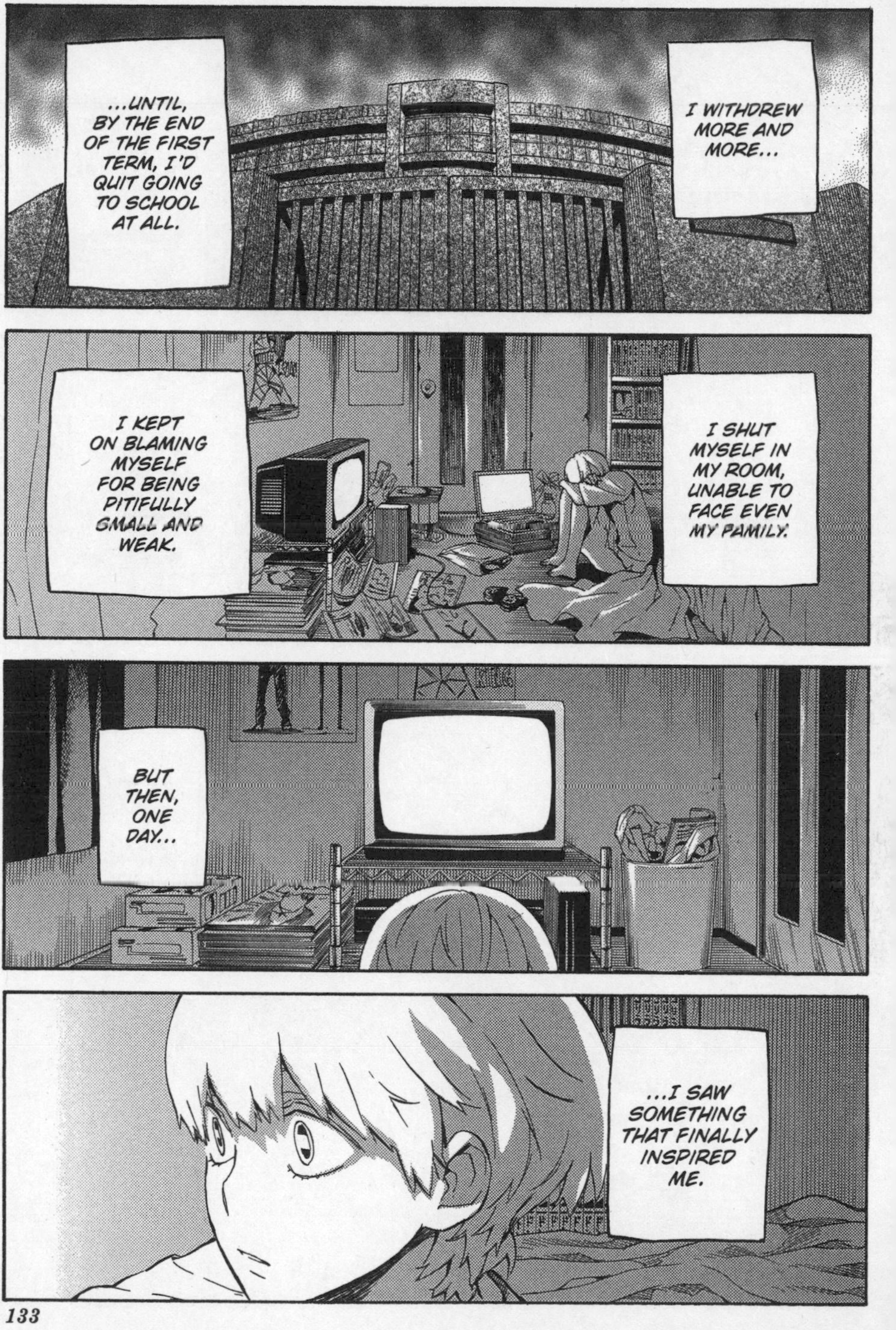
I WITHDREW MORE AND MORE...
...UNTIL, BY THE END OF THE FIRST TERM, I'D QUIT GOING TO SCHOOL AT ALL.
I SHUT MYSELF IN MY ROOM, UNABLE TO FACE EVEN MY FAMILY.
I KEPT ON BLAMING MYSELF FOR BEING PITIFULLY SMALL AND WEAK.
BUT THEN, ONE DAY...
...I SAW SOMETHING THAT FINALLY INSPIRED ME.

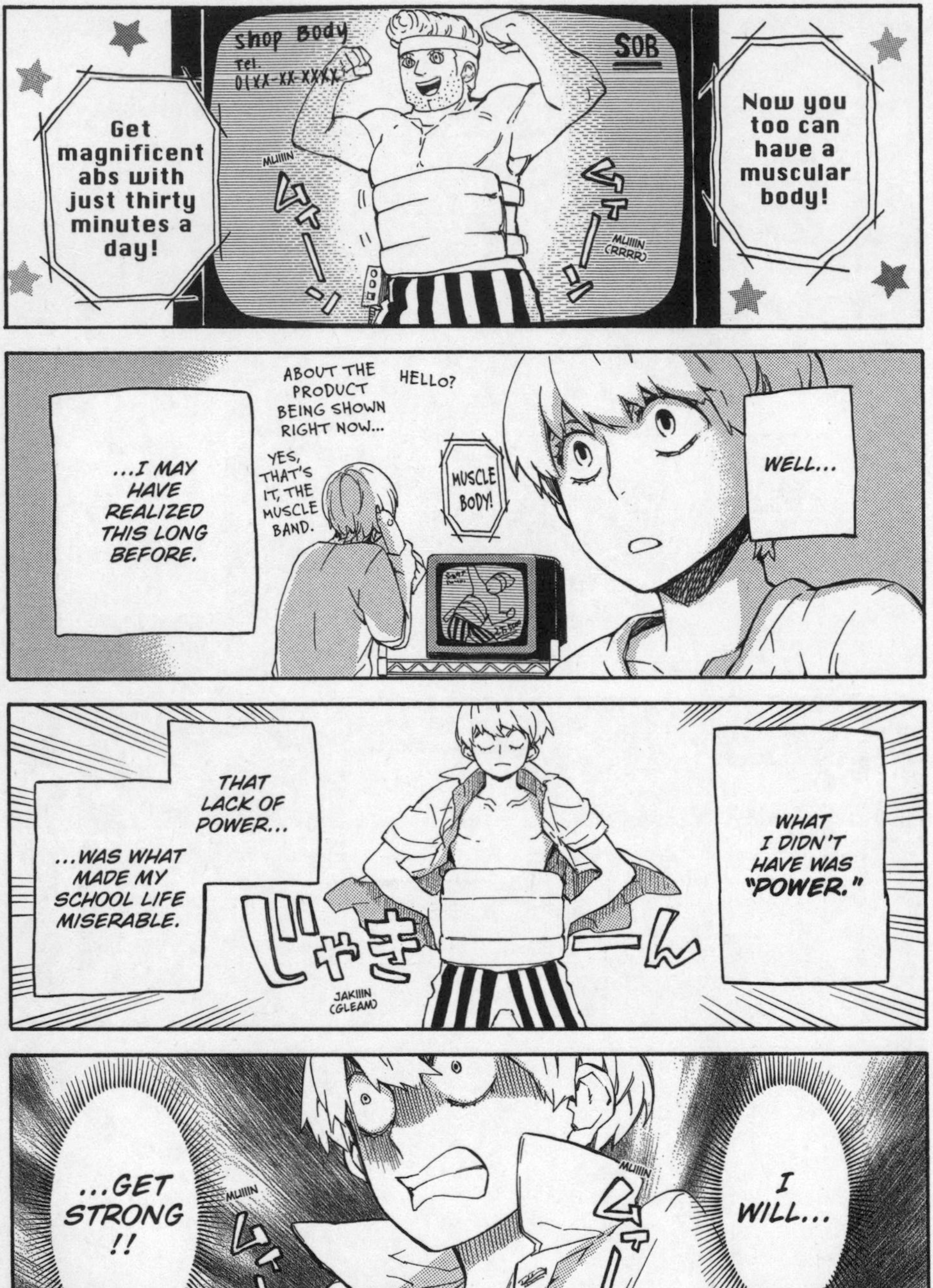
Now you too can have a muscular body!
SOB
Shop Body
Tel. 01XX-XX-XXXX
MUIIIN (RRRR)
MUIIIN
Get magnificent abs with just thirty minutes a day!
WELL...
HELLO?
ABOUT THE PRODUCT BEING SHOWN RIGHT NOW...
MUSCLE BODY!
YES, THAT'S IT, THE MUSCLE BAND.
...I MAY HAVE REALIZED THIS LONG BEFORE.
WHAT I DIDN'T HAVE WAS "POWER."
じゃきーん
JAKIIIN (GLEAM)
THAT LACK OF POWER...
...WAS WHAT MADE MY SCHOOL LIFE MISERABLE.
I WILL...
MUIIIN
MUIIIN
...GET STRONG !!

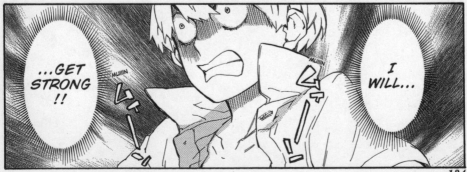

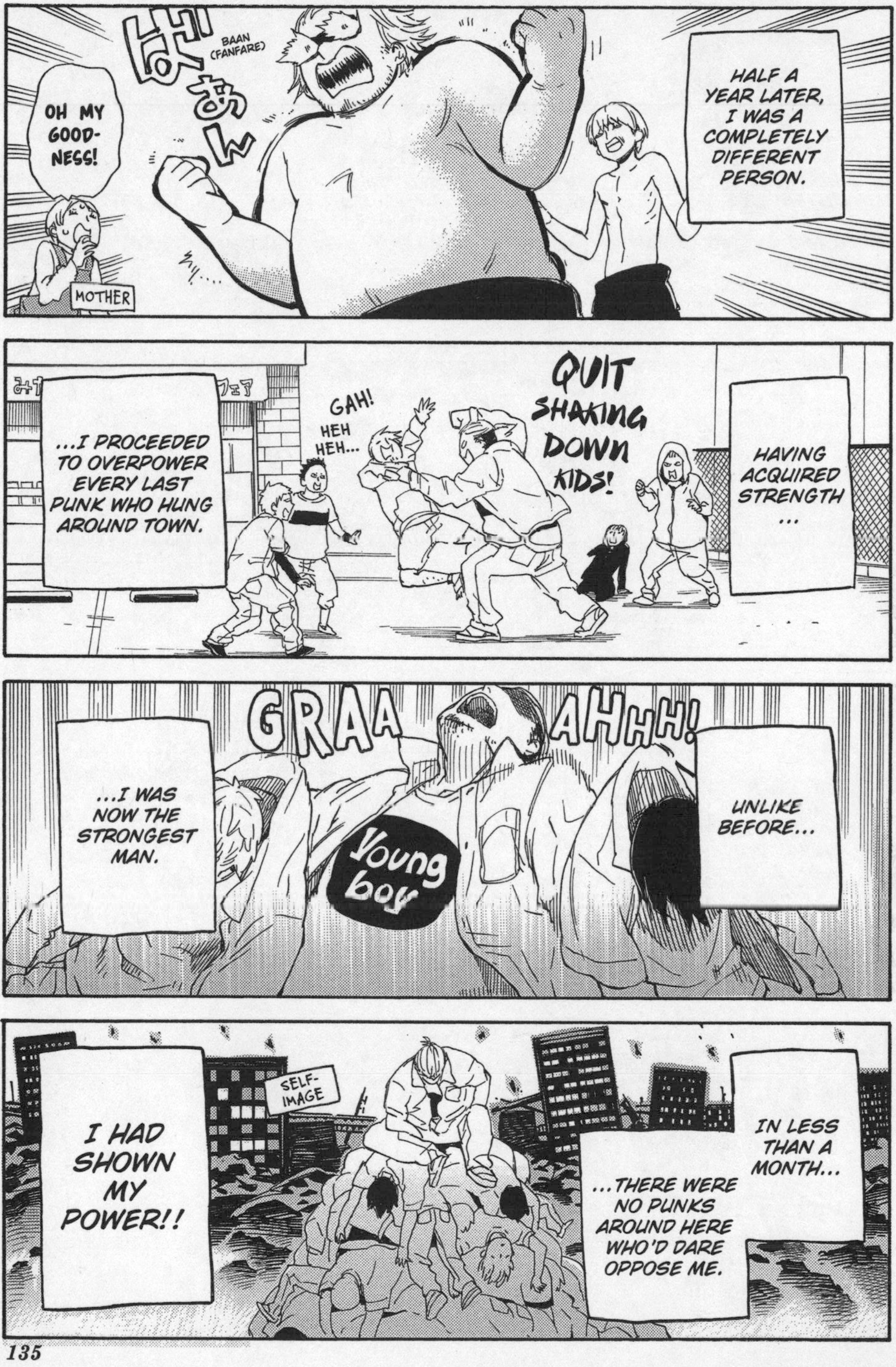
HALF A YEAR LATER, I WAS A COMPLETELY DIFFERENT PERSON.
ばあん
BAAN (FANFARE)
OH MY GOOD-NESS!
MOTHER
HAVING ACQUIRED STRENGTH ...
QUIT SHAKING DOWN KIDS!
GAH!
HEH HEH...
...I PROCEEDED TO OVERPOWER EVERY LAST PUNK WHO HUNG AROUND TOWN.
UNLIKE BEFORE...
GRAAAHHH!
Young boy
...I WAS NOW THE STRONGEST MAN.
IN LESS THAN A MONTH...
...THERE WERE NO PUNKS AROUND HERE WHO'D DARE OPPOSE ME.
SELF-IMAGE
I HAD SHOWN MY POWER!!

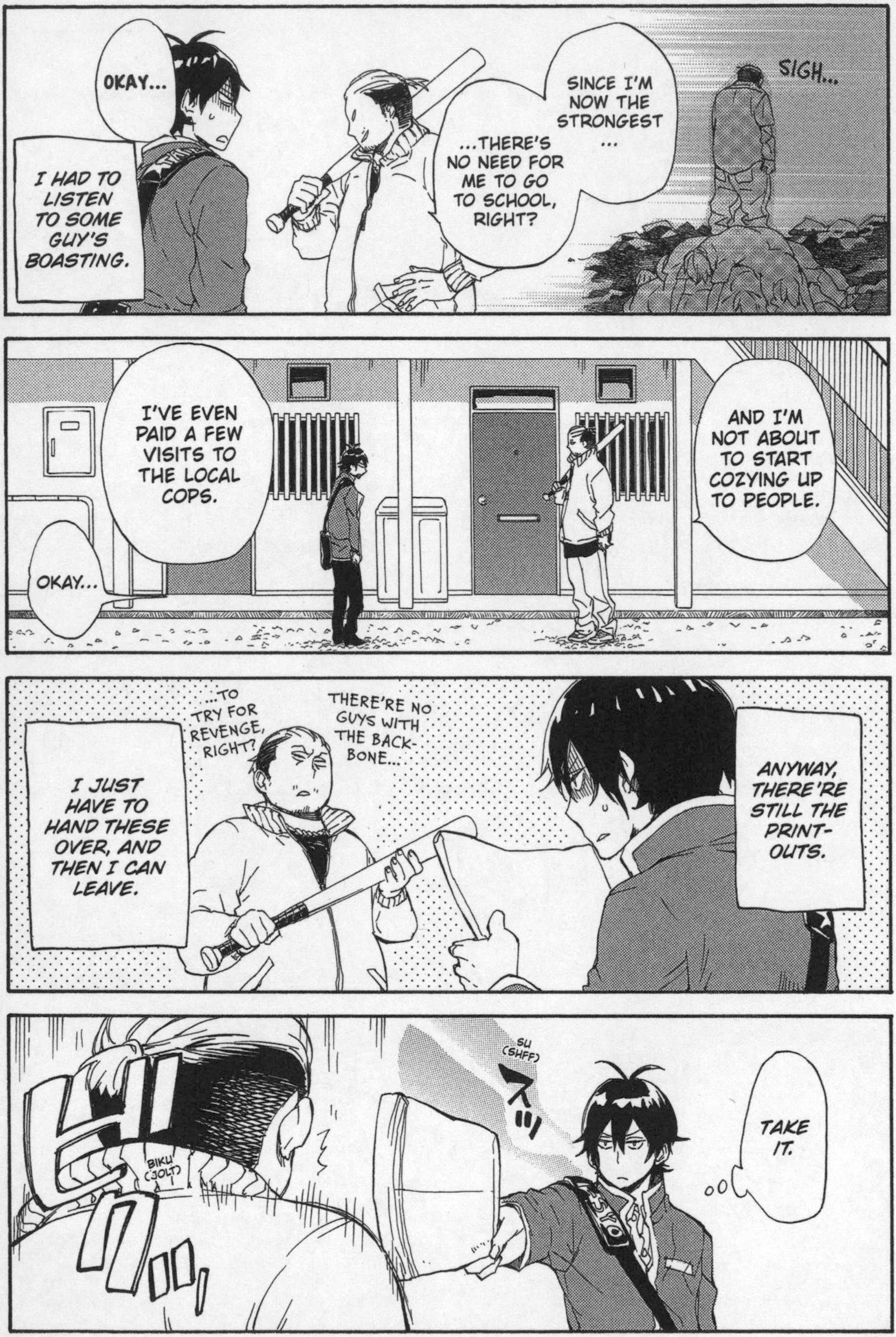
SIGH...
SINCE I'M NOW THE STRONGEST...
...THERE'S NO NEED FOR ME TO GO TO SCHOOL, RIGHT?
OKAY...
I HAD TO LISTEN TO SOME GUY'S BOASTING.
AND I'M NOT ABOUT TO START COZYING UP TO PEOPLE.
I'VE EVEN PAID A FEW VISITS TO THE LOCAL COPS.
OKAY...
ANYWAY, THERE'RE STILL THE PRINT-OUTS.
THERE'RE NO GUYS WITH THE BACK-BONE...
...TO TRY FOR REVENGE, RIGHT?
I JUST HAVE TO HAND THESE OVER, AND THEN I CAN LEAVE.
TAKE IT.
SU (SHFF)
BIKU (JOLT)

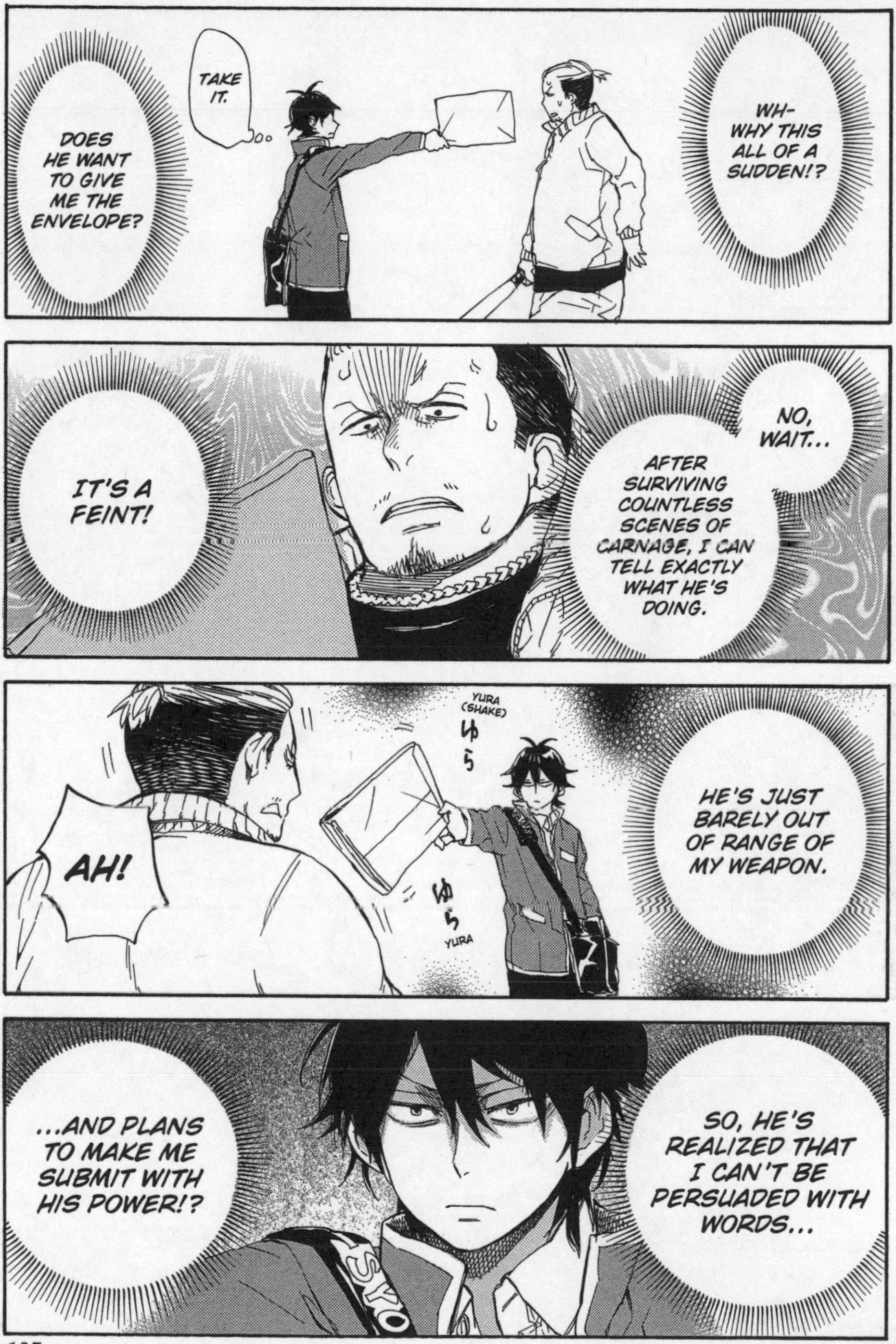
WH- WHY THIS ALL OF A SUDDEN!?
TAKE IT.
DOES HE WANT TO GIVE ME THE ENVELOPE?
NO, WAIT...
AFTER SURVIVING COUNTLESS SCENES OF CARNAGE, I CAN TELL EXACTLY WHAT HE'S DOING.
IT'S A FEINT!
HE'S JUST BARELY OUT OF RANGE OF MY WEAPON.
YURA (SHAKE)
ゆら
ゆら
YURA
AH!
SO, HE'S REALIZED THAT I CAN'T BE PERSUADED WITH WORDS...
...AND PLANS TO MAKE ME SUBMIT WITH HIS POWER!?

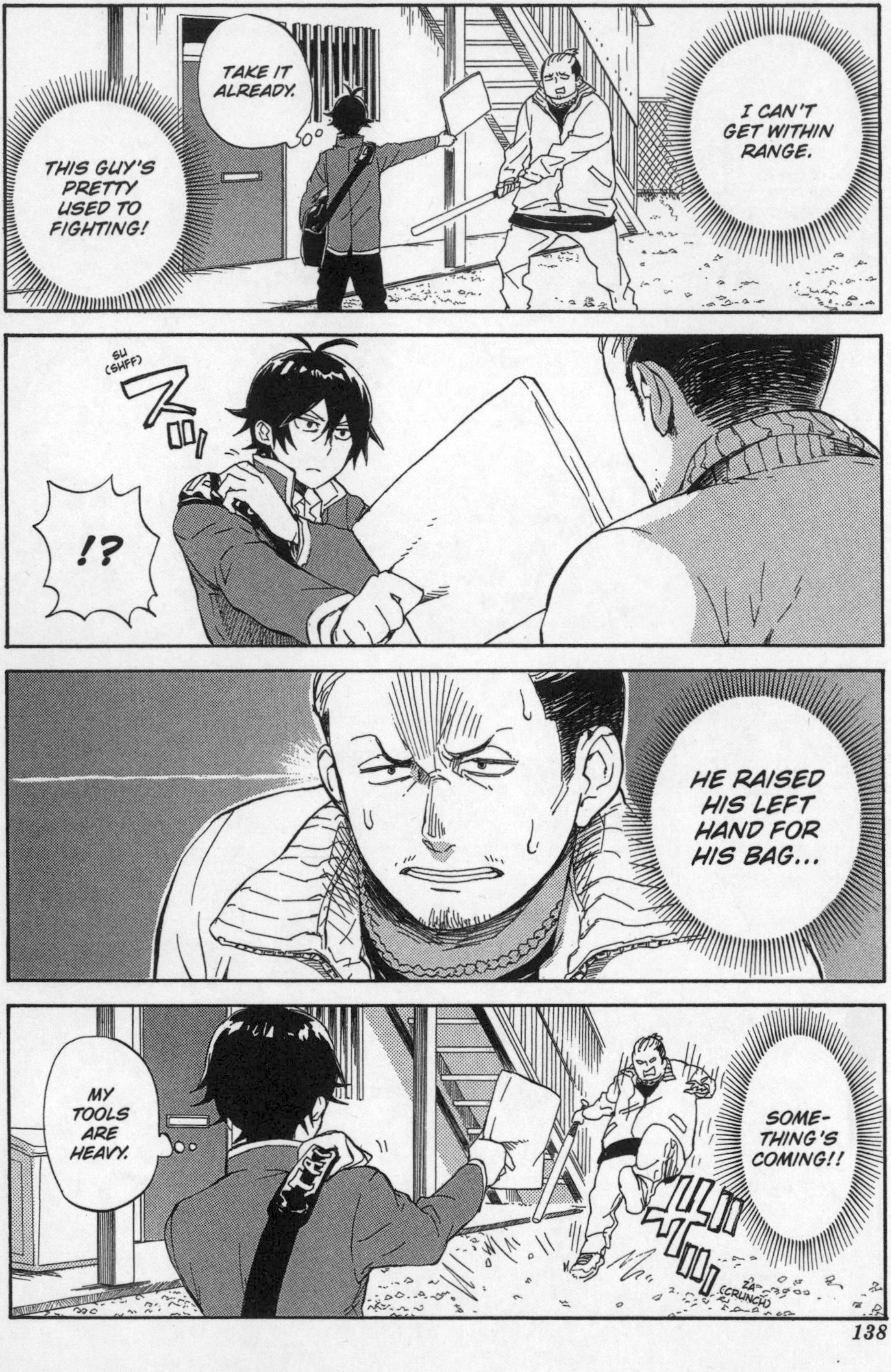
I CAN'T GET WITHIN RANGE.
TAKE IT ALREADY.
THIS GUY'S PRETTY USED TO FIGHTING!
SU (SHFF)
!?
HE RAISED HIS LEFT HAND FOR HIS BAG...
SOME-THING'S COMING!!
MY TOOLS ARE HEAVY.
ZA (CRUNCH)

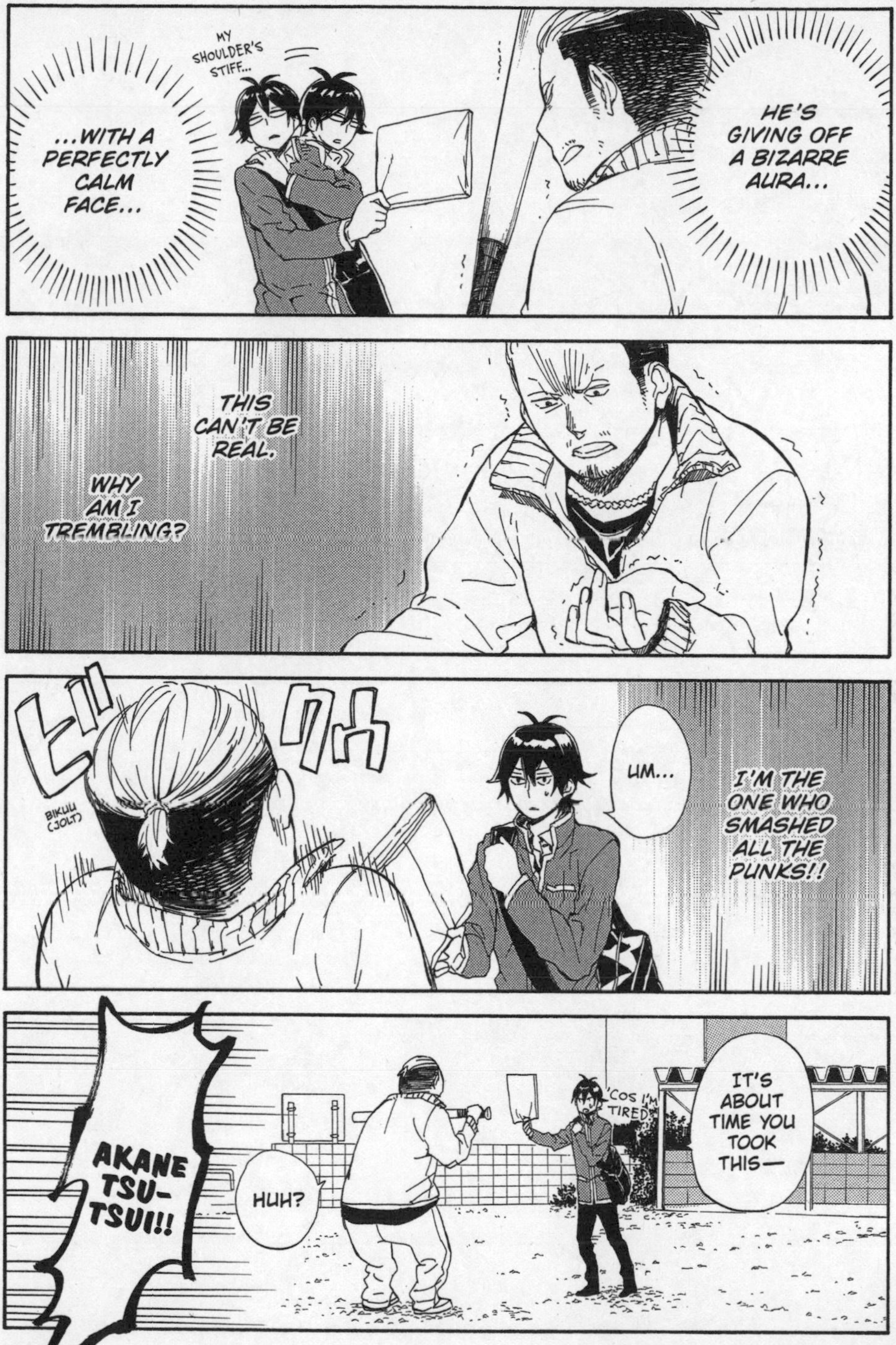
HE'S GIVING OFF A BIZARRE AURA...
MY SHOULDER'S STIFF...
...WITH A PERFECTLY CALM FACE...
THIS CAN'T BE REAL.
WHY AM I TREMBLING?
I'M THE ONE WHO SMASHED ALL THE PUNKS!!
UM...
BIKUU (JOLT)
IT'S ABOUT TIME YOU TOOK THIS—
'COS I'M TIRED
HUH?
AKANE TSU-TSUI!!!

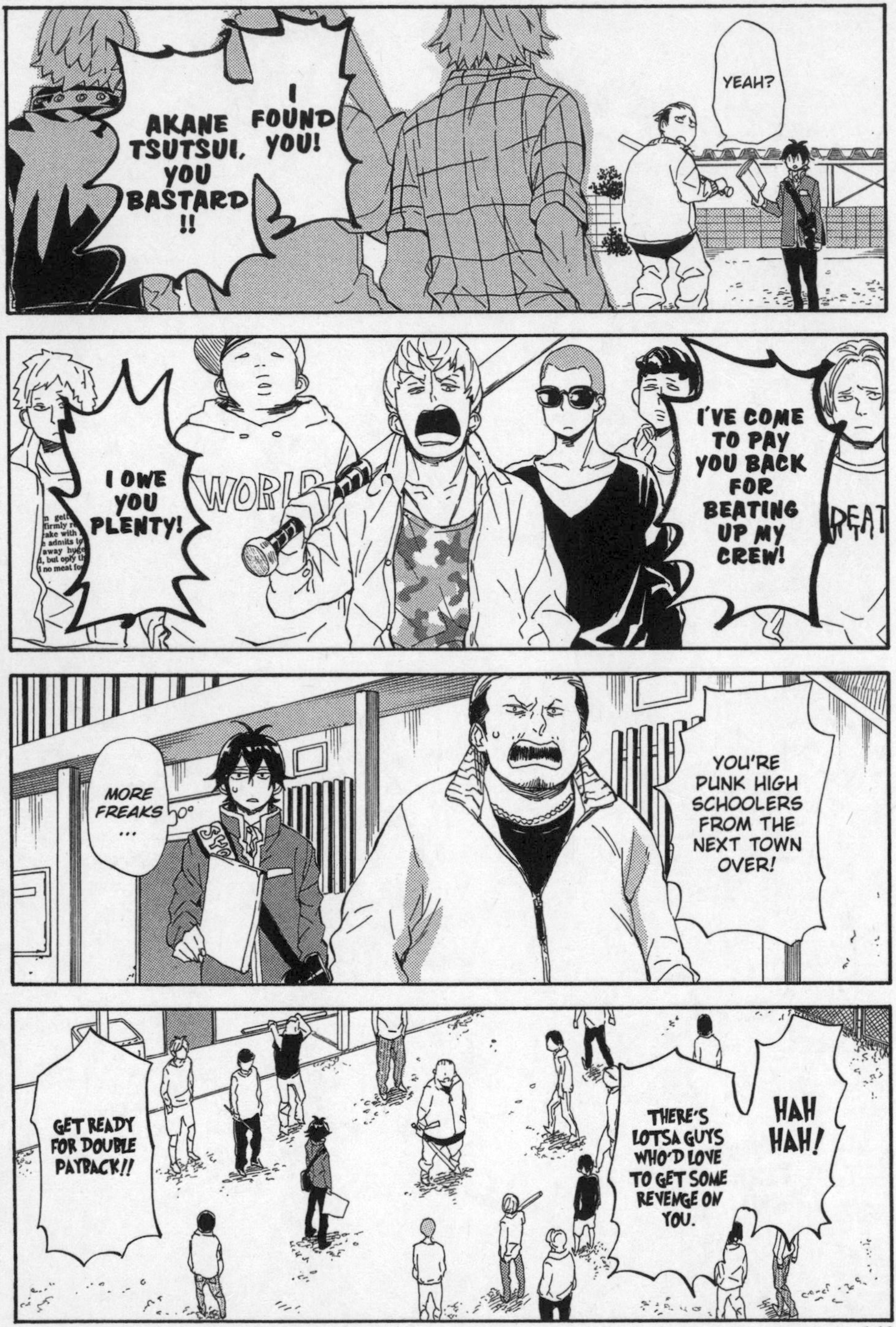
YEAH?
I FOUND YOU!
AKANE TSUTSUI, YOU BASTARD!!
I'VE COME TO PAY YOU BACK FOR BEATING UP MY CREW!
I OWE YOU PLENTY!
YOU'RE PUNK HIGH SCHOOLERS FROM THE NEXT TOWN OVER!
MORE FREAKS...
HAH HAH!
THERE'S LOTSA GUYS WHO'D LOVE TO GET SOME REVENGE ON YOU.
GET READY FOR DOUBLE PAYBACK!!

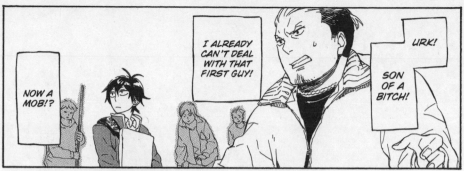

URK!
SON OF A BITCH!
I ALREADY CAN'T DEAL WITH THAT FIRST GUY!
NOW A MOB!?
WHAT THE HELL SHOULD I—
TON (TAP)
とん
!?
SU (SHFF)
ス
WHY'S HE HANDING ME THE ENVELOPE...
...ALL OF A SUDDEN?
NO WAY!! IS HE SAYING HE'LL FIGHT ALONGSIDE ME!?
KURU (TURN)
くるっ
THERE. DELIVERED.
NOW I'M GOING.

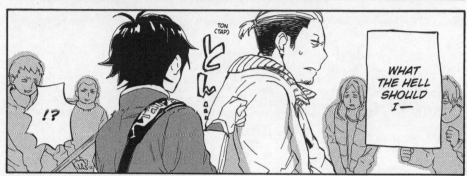

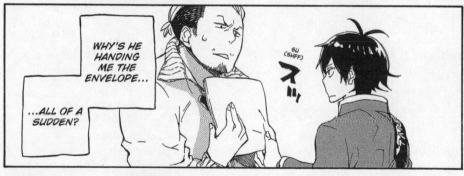

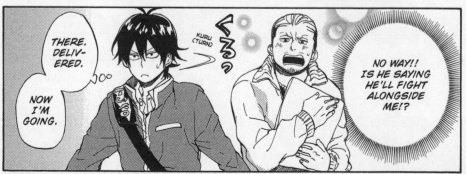

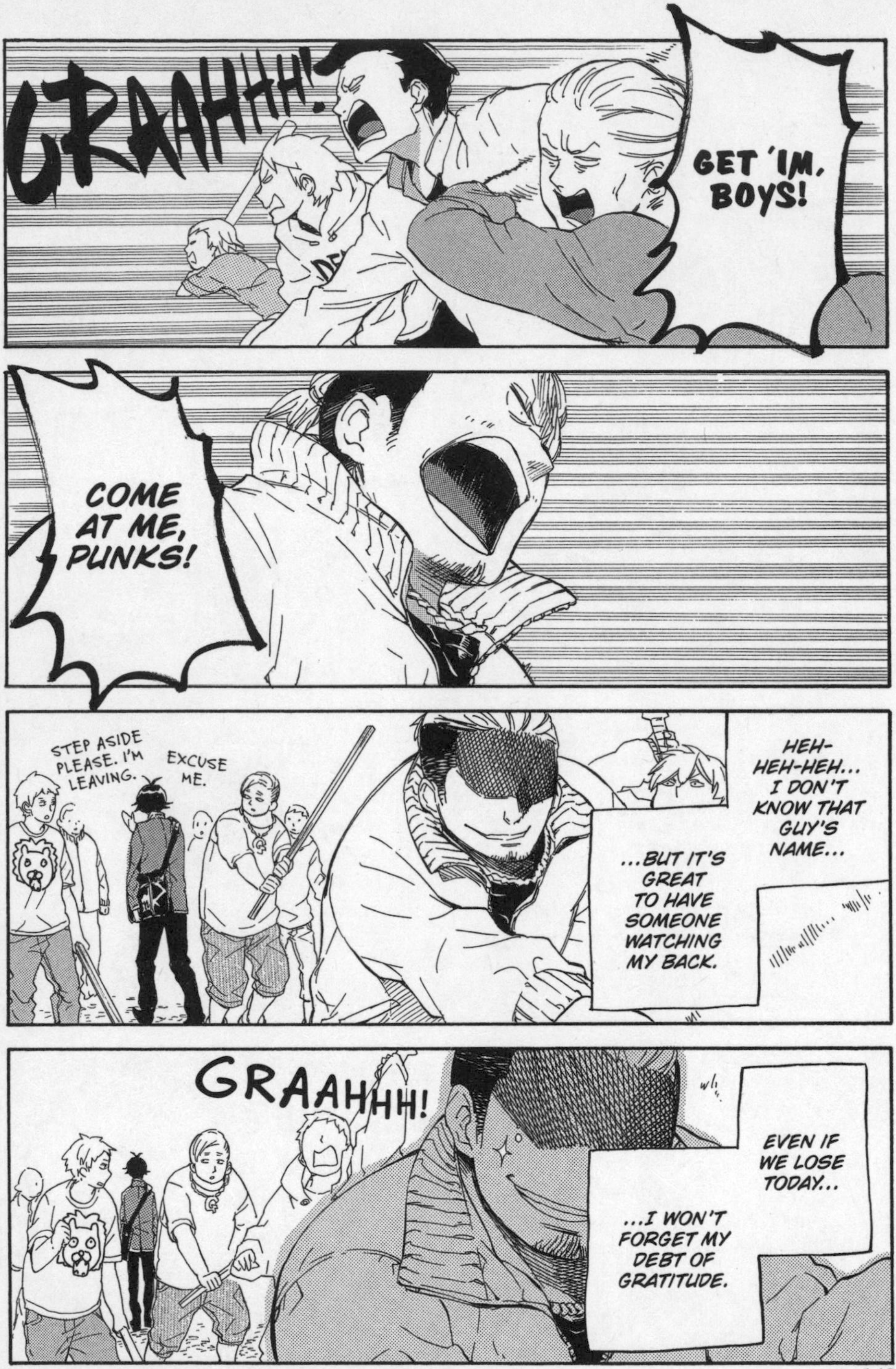
GET 'IM, BOYS!
GRAAHHH!
COME AT ME, PUNKS!
HEH-HEH-HEH... I DON'T KNOW THAT GUY'S NAME...
...BUT IT'S GREAT TO HAVE SOMEONE WATCHING MY BACK.
EXCUSE ME.
STEP ASIDE PLEASE. I'M LEAVING.
EVEN IF WE LOSE TODAY...
...I WON'T FORGET MY DEBT OF GRATITUDE.
GRAAHHHH!

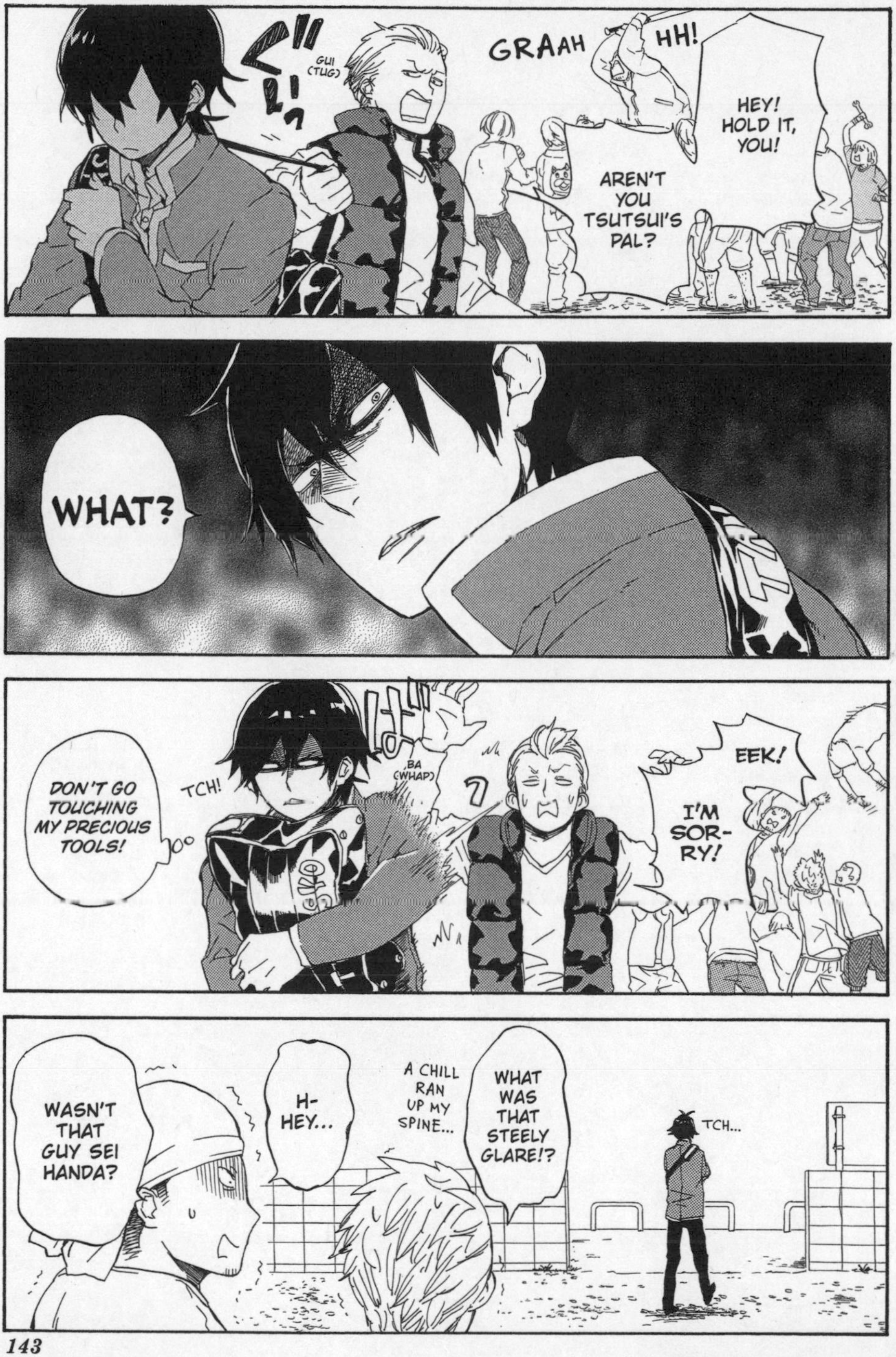

HEY! HOLD IT, YOU!
GRAAH HH!
AREN'T YOU TSUTSUI'S PAL?
GUI (TUG)
WHAT?
EEK!
I'M SORRY!
BA (WHAP)
TCH!
DON'T GO TOUCHING MY PRECIOUS TOOLS!
TCH...
WHAT WAS THAT STEELY GLARE!?
A CHILL RAN UP MY SPINE...
H-HEY...
WASN'T THAT GUY SEI HANDA?

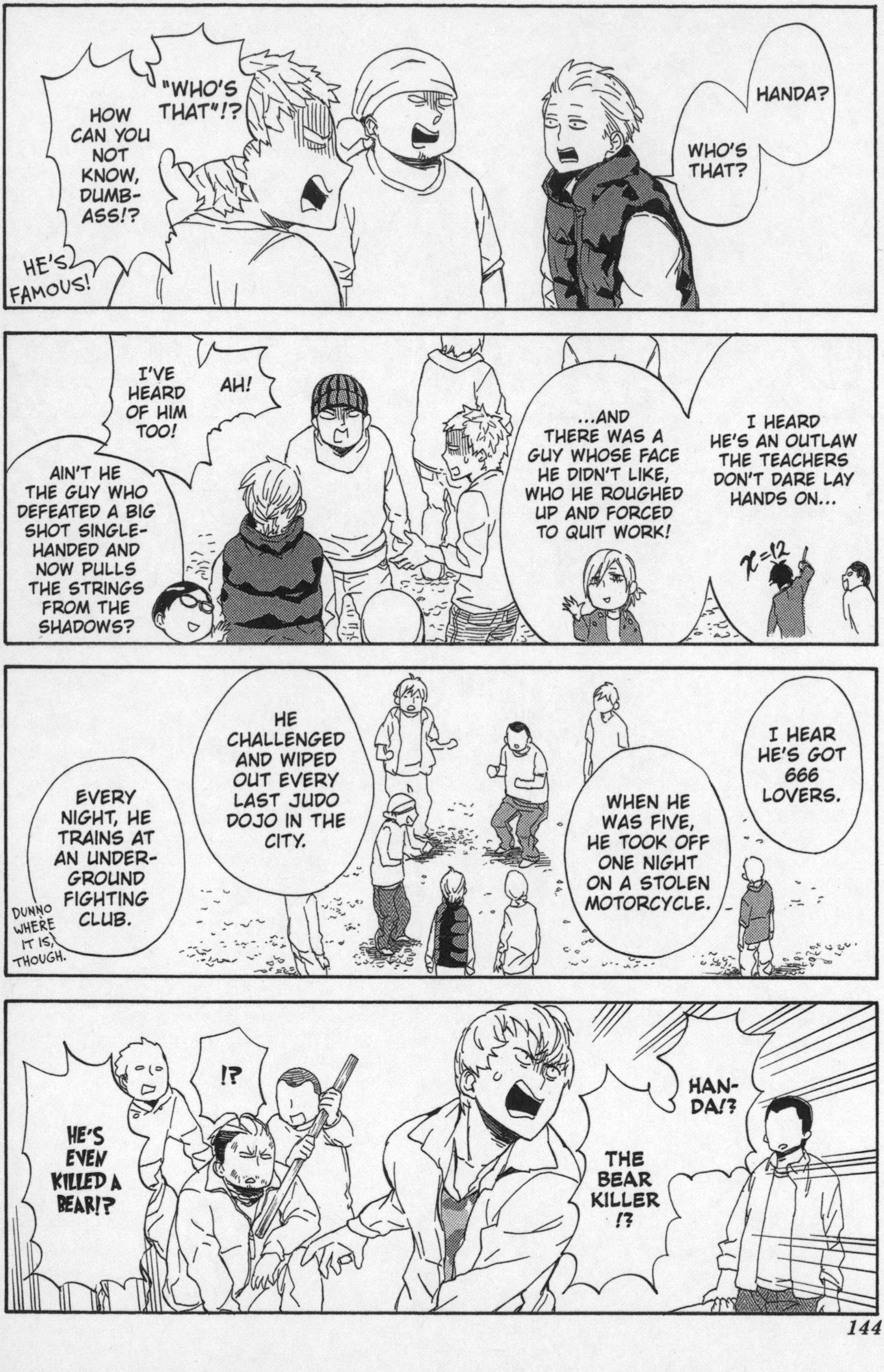
HANDA?
WHO'S THAT?
"WHO'S THAT"!?
HOW CAN YOU NOT KNOW, DUMB-ASS!?
HE'S FAMOUS!
I HEARD HE'S AN OUTLAW THE TEACHERS DON'T DARE LAY HANDS ON...
x=12
...AND THERE WAS A GUY WHOSE FACE HE DIDN'T LIKE, WHO HE ROUGHED UP AND FORCED TO QUIT WORK!
AH!
I'VE HEARD OF HIM TOO!
AIN'T HE THE GUY WHO DEFEATED A BIG SHOT SINGLE-HANDED AND NOW PULLS THE STRINGS FROM THE SHADOWS?
I HEAR HE'S GOT 666 LOVERS.
WHEN HE WAS FIVE, HE TOOK OFF ONE NIGHT ON A STOLEN MOTORCYCLE.
HE CHALLENGED AND WIPED OUT EVERY LAST JUDO DOJO IN THE CITY.
EVERY NIGHT, HE TRAINS AT AN UNDER-GROUND FIGHTING CLUB.
DUNNO WHERE IT IS, THOUGH.
HAN-DA!?
THE BEAR KILLER !?
!?
HE'S EVEN KILLED A BEAR!?

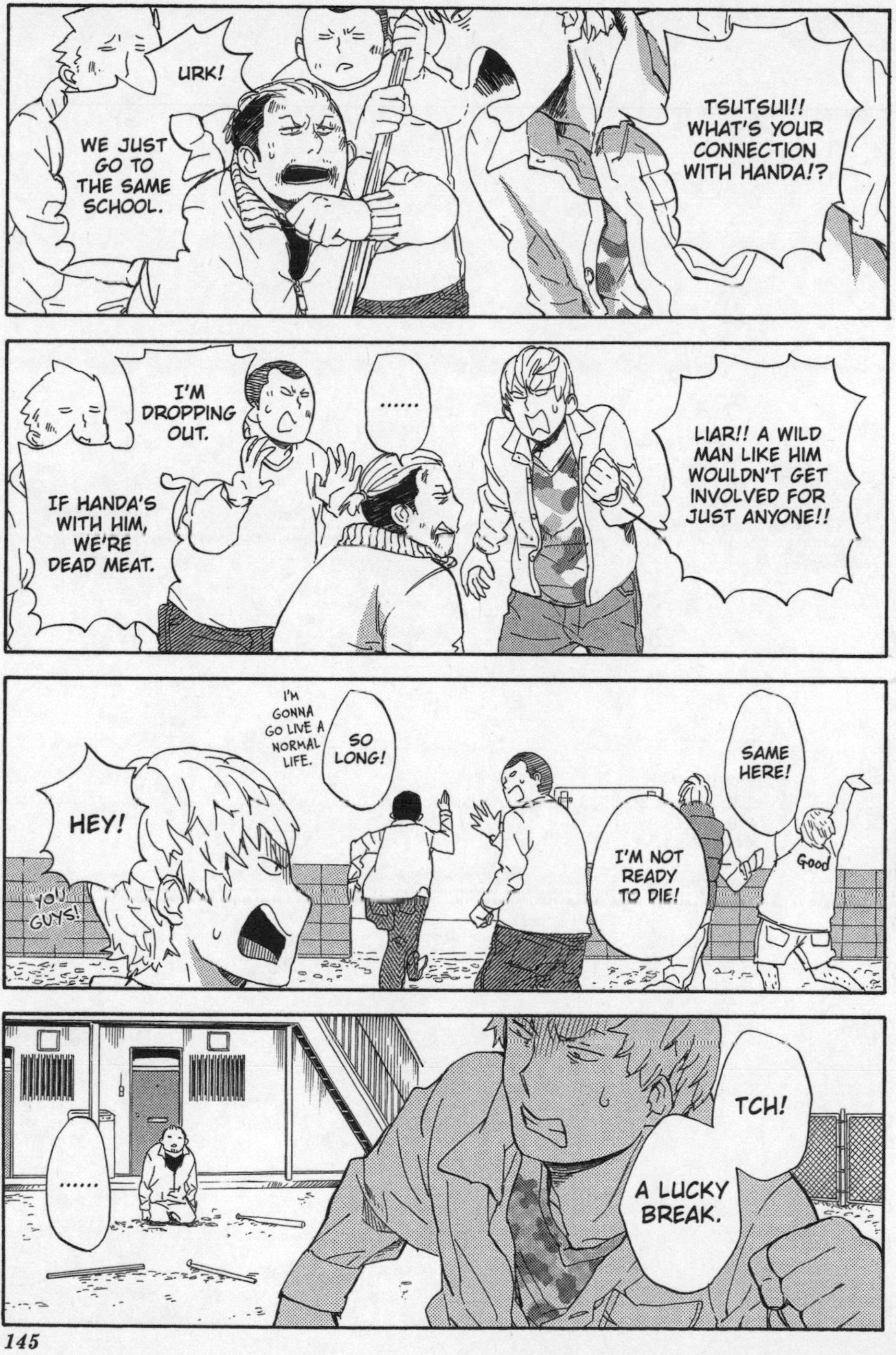
TSUTSUI!! WHAT'S YOUR CONNECTION WITH HANDA!?
URK!
WE JUST GO TO THE SAME SCHOOL.
LIAR!! A WILD MAN LIKE HIM WOULDN'T GET INVOLVED FOR JUST ANYONE!!
......
I'M DROPPING OUT.
IF HANDA'S WITH HIM, WE'RE DEAD MEAT.
SAME HERE!
I'M NOT READY TO DIE!
Good
SO LONG!
I'M GONNA GO LIVE A NORMAL LIFE.
HEY!
YOU GUYS!
TCH!
A LUCKY BREAK.
......

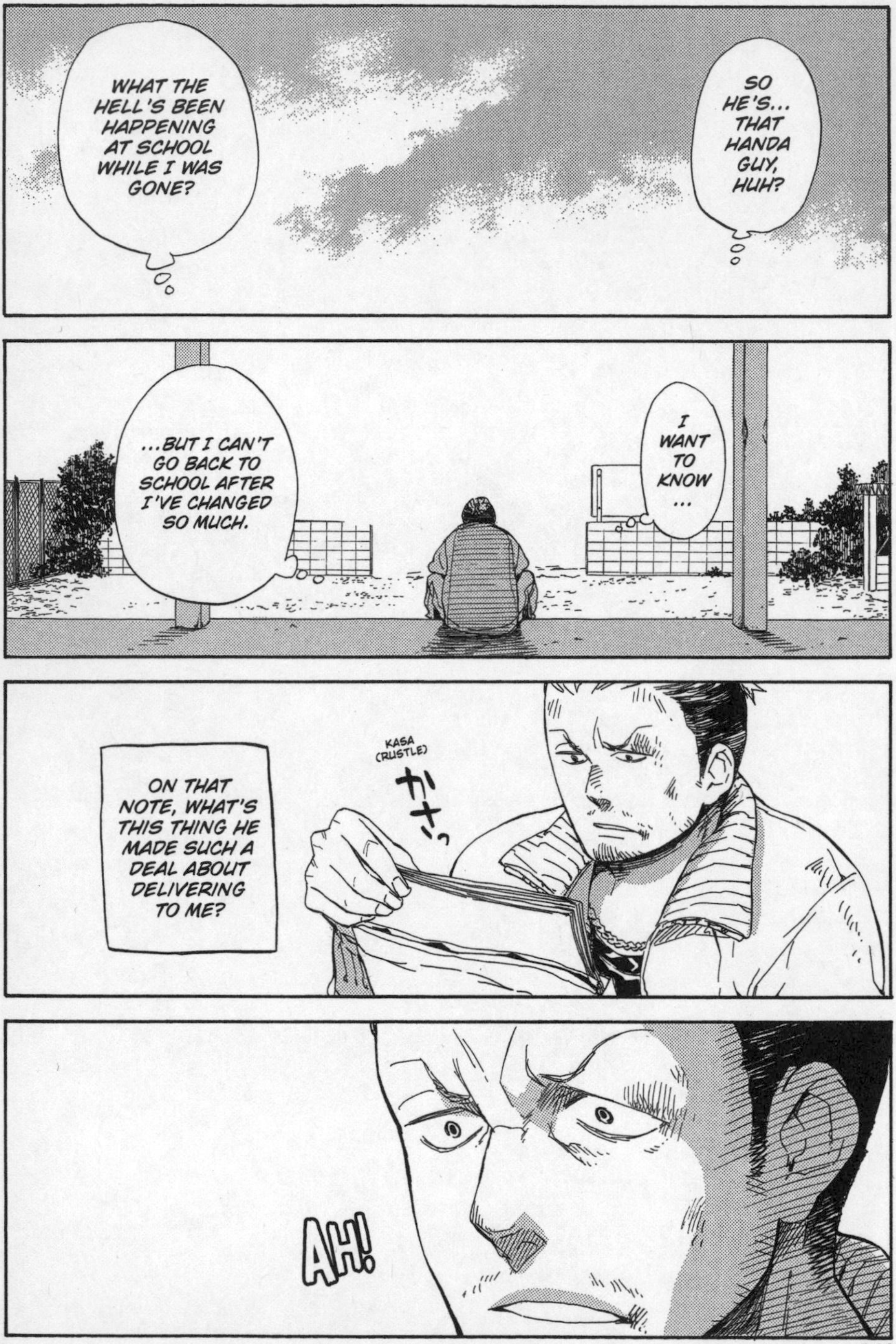
SO HE'S... THAT HANDA GUY, HUH?
WHAT THE HELL'S BEEN HAPPENING AT SCHOOL WHILE I WAS GONE?
I WANT TO KNOW...
...BUT I CAN'T GO BACK TO SCHOOL AFTER I'VE CHANGED SO MUCH.
KASA (RUSTLE)
かさっ
ON THAT NOTE, WHAT'S THIS THING HE MADE SUCH A DEAL ABOUT DELIVERING TO ME?
AH!

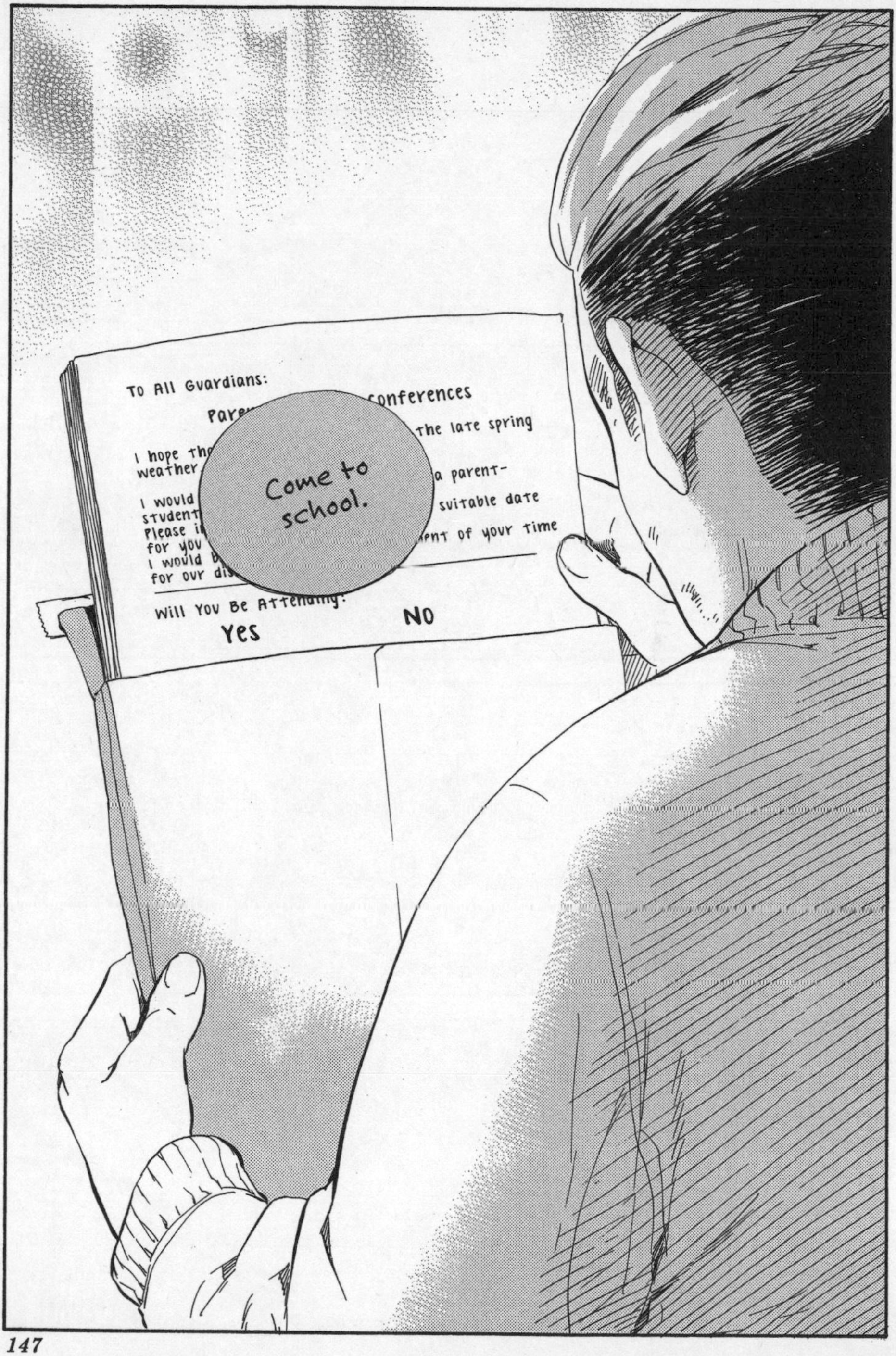
To All Guardians:
conferences
the late spring
a parent-
suitable date
of your time
Yes
No
Come to school.

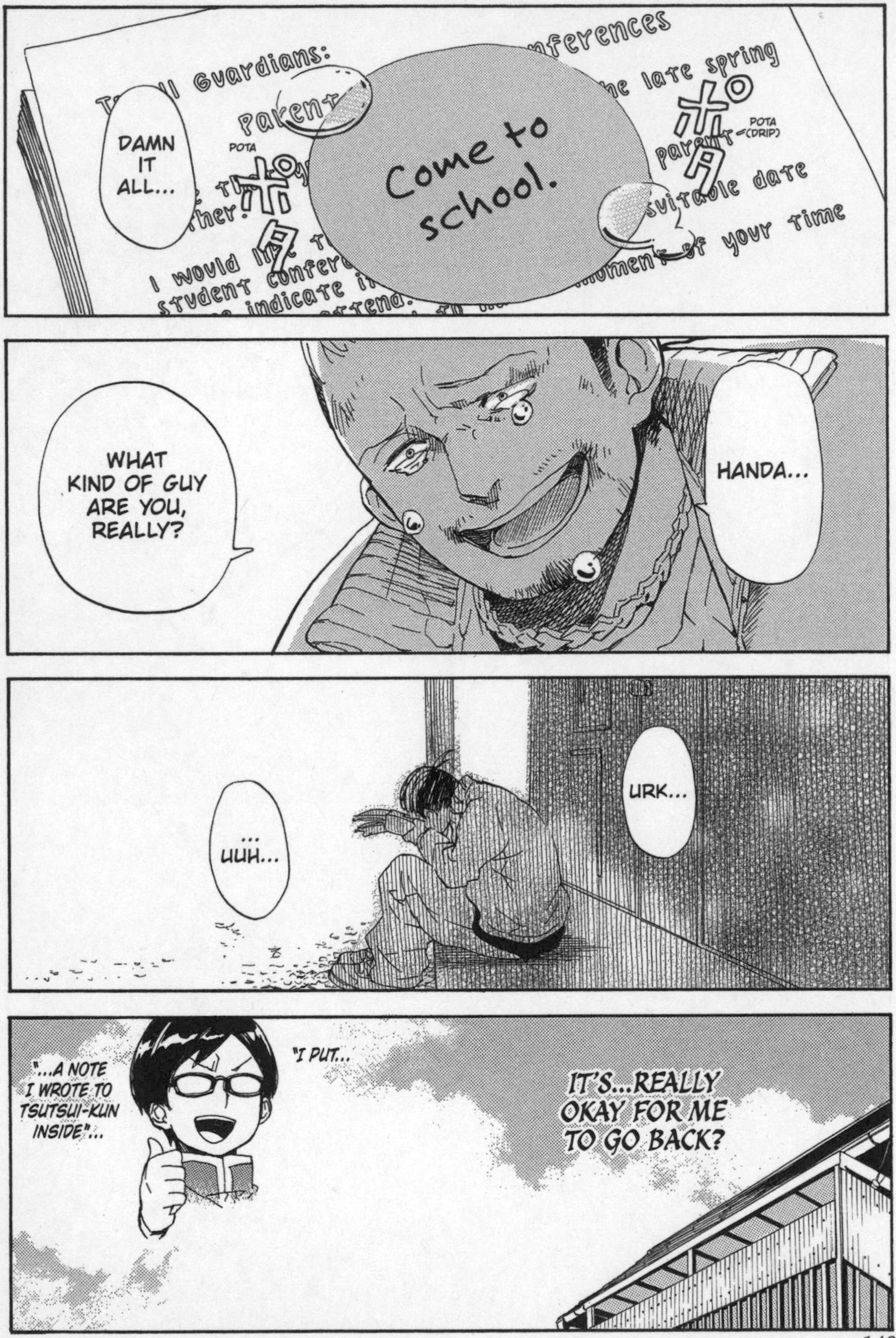
POTA (DRIP)
Come to school.
POTA
DAMN IT ALL...
HANDA...
WHAT KIND OF GUY ARE YOU, REALLY?
URK...
... UUH...
IT'S...REALLY OKAY FOR ME TO GO BACK?
"I PUT...
"...A NOTE I WROTE TO TSUTSUI-KUN INSIDE"...

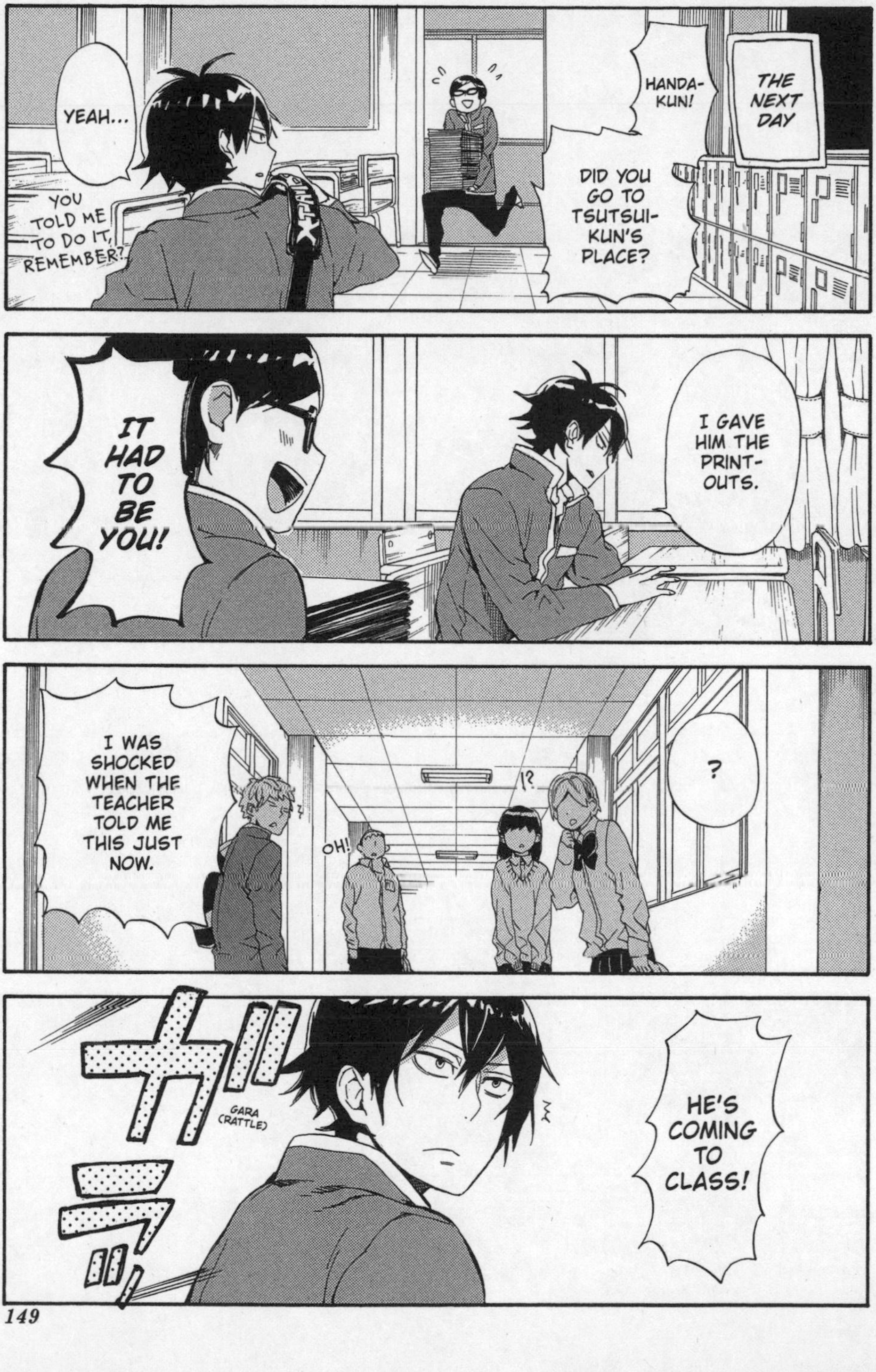
THE NEXT DAY
HANDA-KUN!
DID YOU GO TO TSUTSUI-KUN'S PLACE?
YEAH...
YOU TOLD ME TO DO IT, REMEMBER?
I GAVE HIM THE PRINT-OUTS.
IT HAD TO BE YOU!
?
!?
OH!
I WAS SHOCKED WHEN THE TEACHER TOLD ME THIS JUST NOW.
HE'S COMING TO CLASS!
ガラッ
GARA (RATTLE)

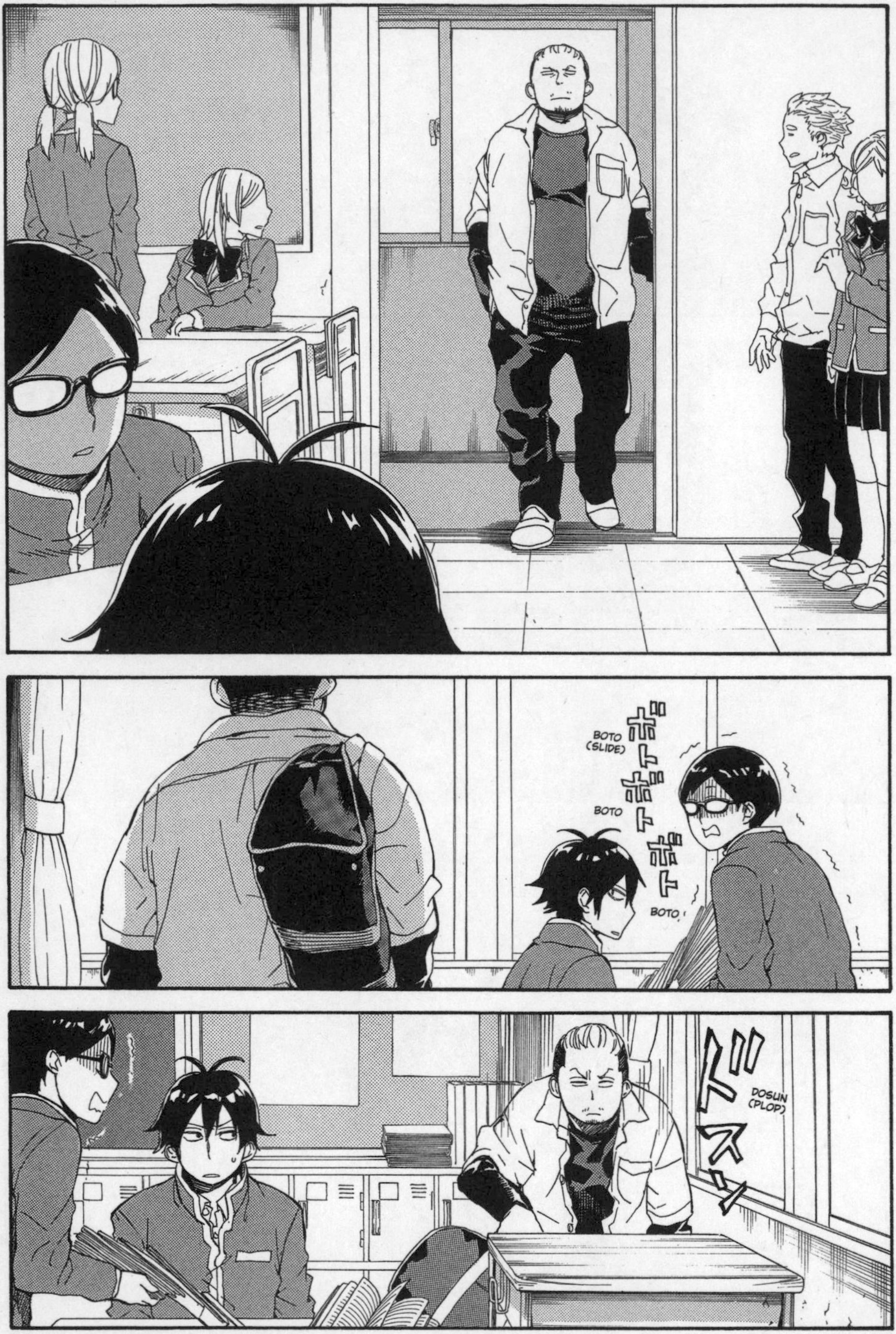
ボト
BOTO (SLIDE)
ボト
BOTO
ボト
BOTO
DOSUN (PLOP)

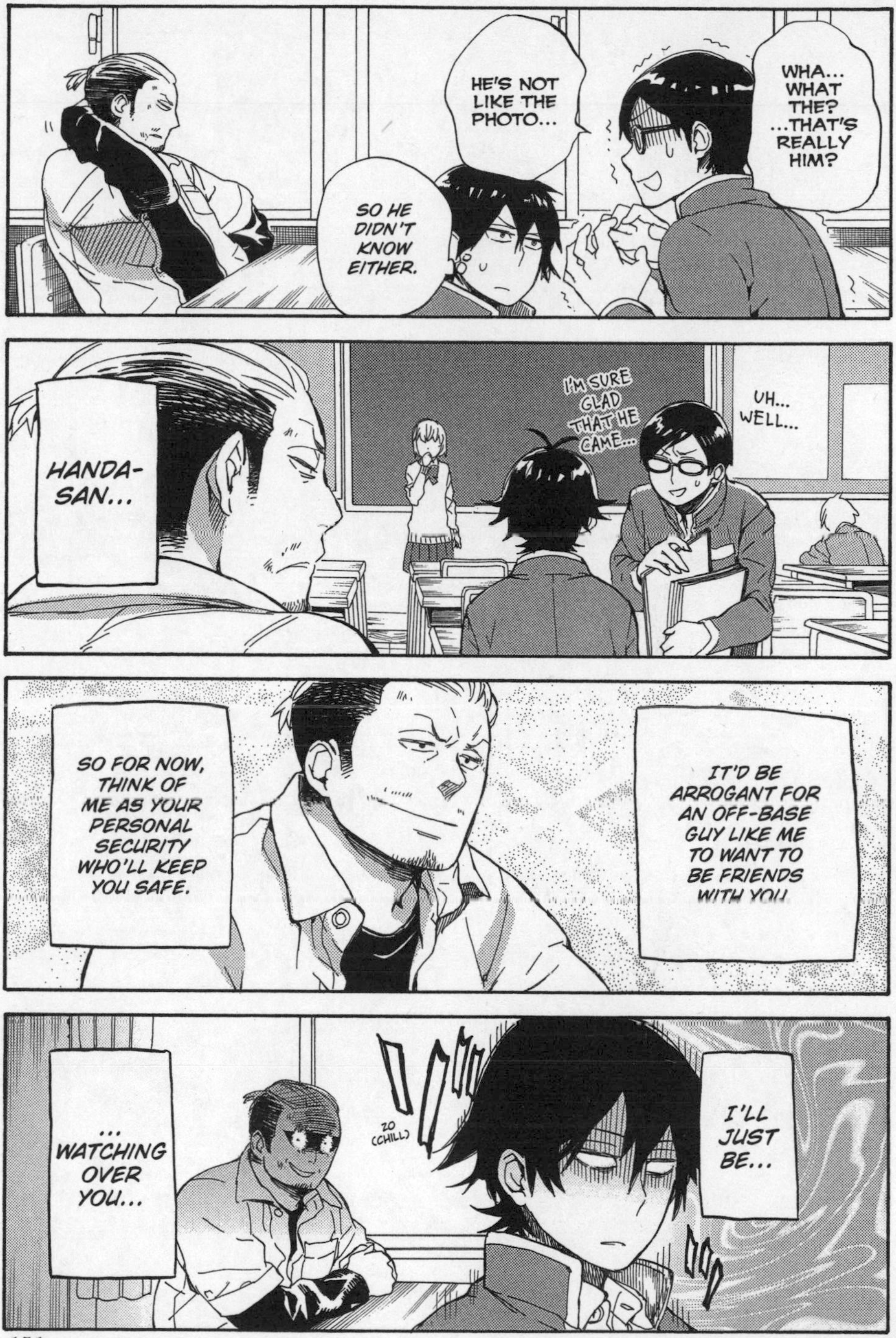
WHA... WHAT THE? ...THAT'S REALLY HIM?
HE'S NOT LIKE THE PHOTO...
SO HE DIDN'T KNOW EITHER.
UH... WELL...
I'M SURE GLAD THAT HE CAME...
HANDA-SAN...
IT'D BE ARROGANT FOR AN OFF-BASE GUY LIKE ME TO WANT TO BE FRIENDS WITH YOU.
SO FOR NOW, THINK OF ME AS YOUR PERSONAL SECURITY WHO'LL KEEP YOU SAFE.
I'LL JUST BE...
ZO (CHILL)
...WATCHING OVER YOU...

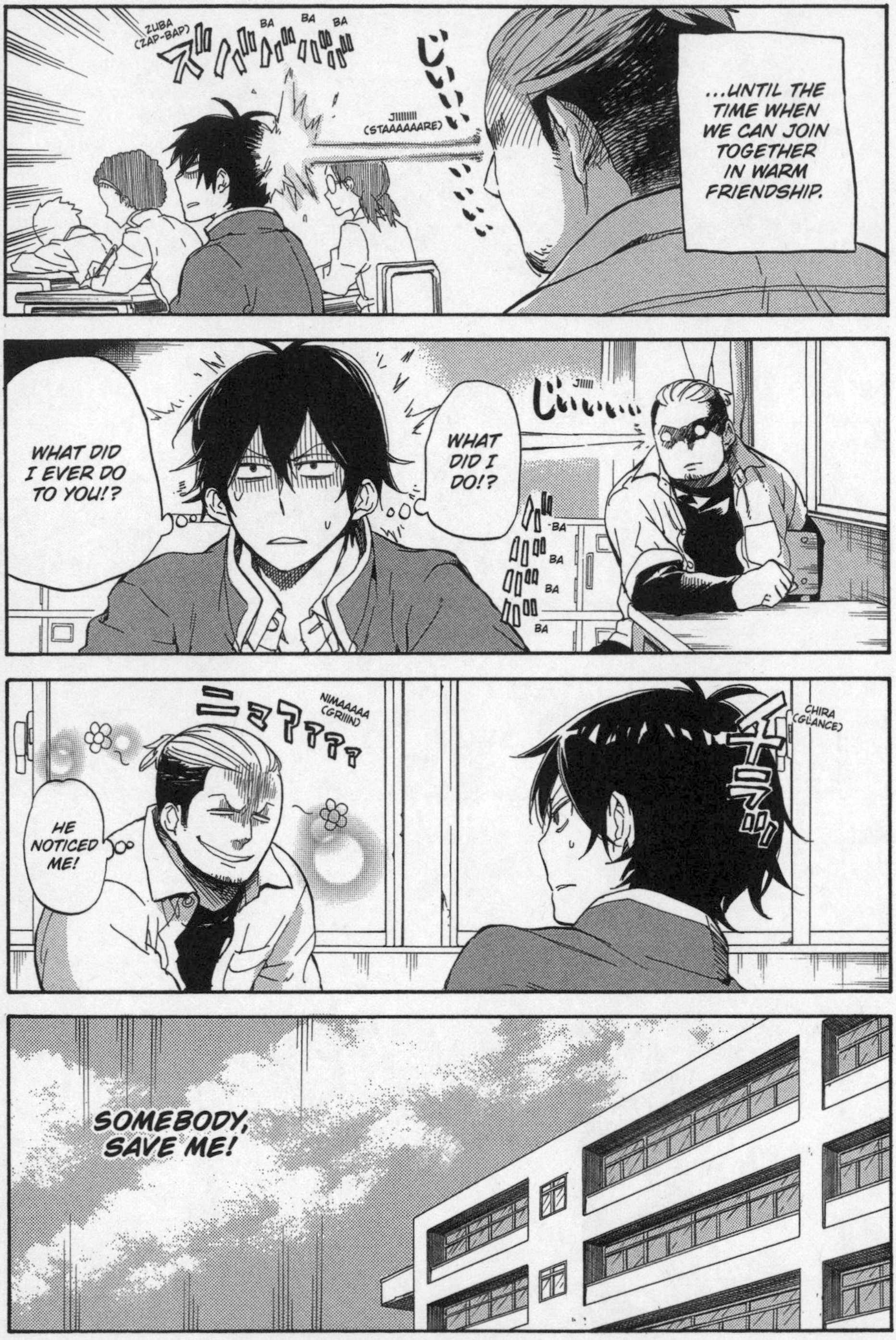
...UNTIL THE TIME WHEN WE CAN JOIN TOGETHER IN WARM FRIENDSHIP.
JIIIIIII (STAAAAAARE)
ZUBA (ZAP-BAP)
BA BA BA
JIIIII
WHAT DID I DO!?
WHAT DID I EVER DO TO YOU!?
BA BA BA BA
CHIRA (GLANCE)
NIMAAAAA (GRIIIN)
HE NOTICED ME!
SOMEBODY, SAVE ME!

TO BE CONTINUED IN HANDA-KUN 2

Handa-
kun

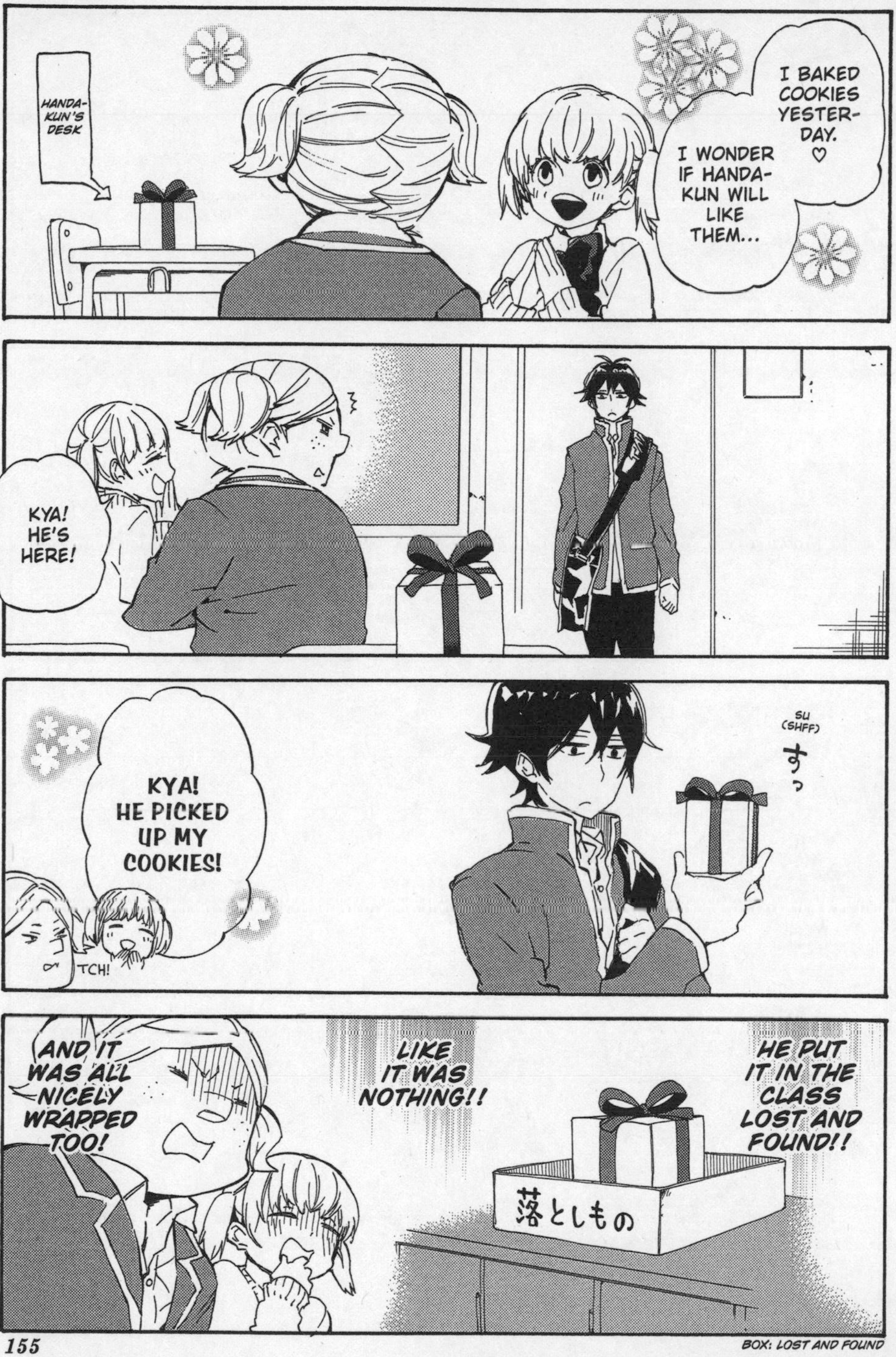
I BAKED COOKIES YESTER-DAY. ♡
I WONDER IF HANDA-KUN WILL LIKE THEM...
HANDA-KUN'S DESK
KYA! HE'S HERE!
SU (SHFF)
すっ
KYA! HE PICKED UP MY COOKIES!
TCH!
HE PUT IT IN THE CLASS LOST AND FOUND!!
LIKE IT WAS NOTHING!!
AND IT WAS ALL NICELY WRAPPED TOO!
落としもの

BOX: LOST AND FOUND

TAILING

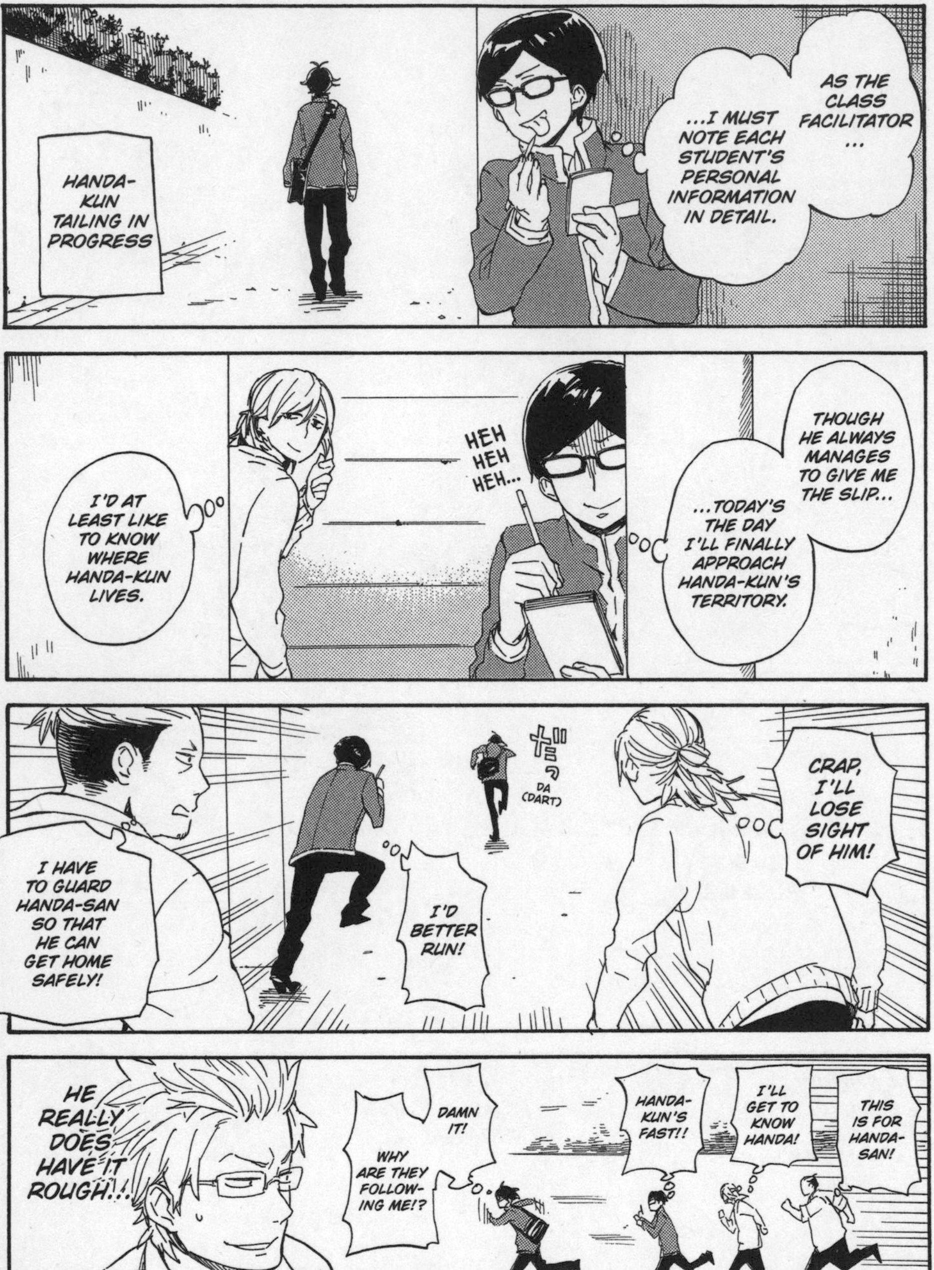
AS THE CLASS FACILITATOR ...
...I MUST NOTE EACH STUDENT'S PERSONAL INFORMATION IN DETAIL.
HANDA-KUN TAILING IN PROGRESS
THOUGH HE ALWAYS MANAGES TO GIVE ME THE SLIP...
...TODAY'S THE DAY I'LL FINALLY APPROACH HANDA-KUN'S TERRITORY.
HEH HEH HEH...
I'D AT LEAST LIKE TO KNOW WHERE HANDA-KUN LIVES.
CRAP, I'LL LOSE SIGHT OF HIM!
ダッ
DA (DART)
I'D BETTER RUN!
I HAVE TO GUARD HANDA-SAN SO THAT HE CAN GET HOME SAFELY!
THIS IS FOR HANDA-SAN!
I'LL GET TO KNOW HANDA!
HANDA-KUN'S FAST!!
DAMN IT!
WHY ARE THEY FOLLOWING ME!?
HE REALLY DOES HAVE IT ROUGH...

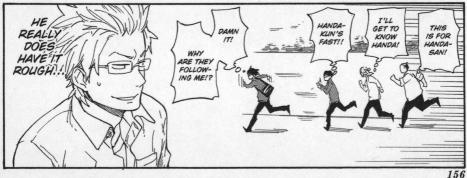

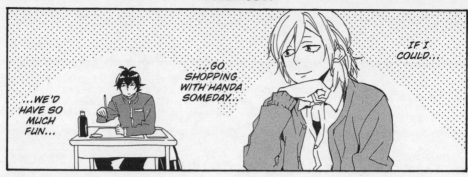

FASHION

IF I COULD...
...GO SHOPPING WITH HANDA SOMEDAY...
...WE'D HAVE SO MUCH FUN...
I'M SURE HE DRESSES WELL IN REGULAR CLOTHES, WITH HIS OUTSTANDING FASHION SENSE.
HEY NOW, REO. AREN'T YOU DRESSED A BIT TOO PLAIN?
YOU ALREADY PICKED UP THIS YEAR'S TRENDS?
THAT'S MY HANDA!
DELUSIONS OF FRIENDSHIP
YOU GUYS LOOK GREAT! ARE YOU MODELS?
KYA! IT'S HANDA AND REO COLLABING! KYA!
AHHH...
THE WORLD WOULD NEVER GET ENOUGH OF OUR DOUBLE SUPER-STARDOM!
HEH HEH...
HANDA-KUN'S REGULAR CLOTHES
HEYA!
YOU'RE ALWAYS WEARING THAT...

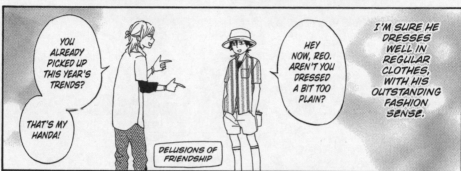

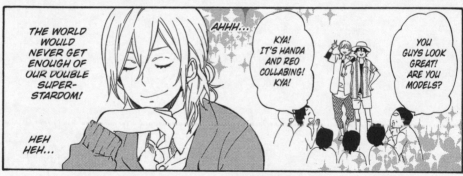

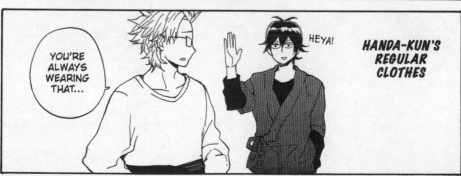

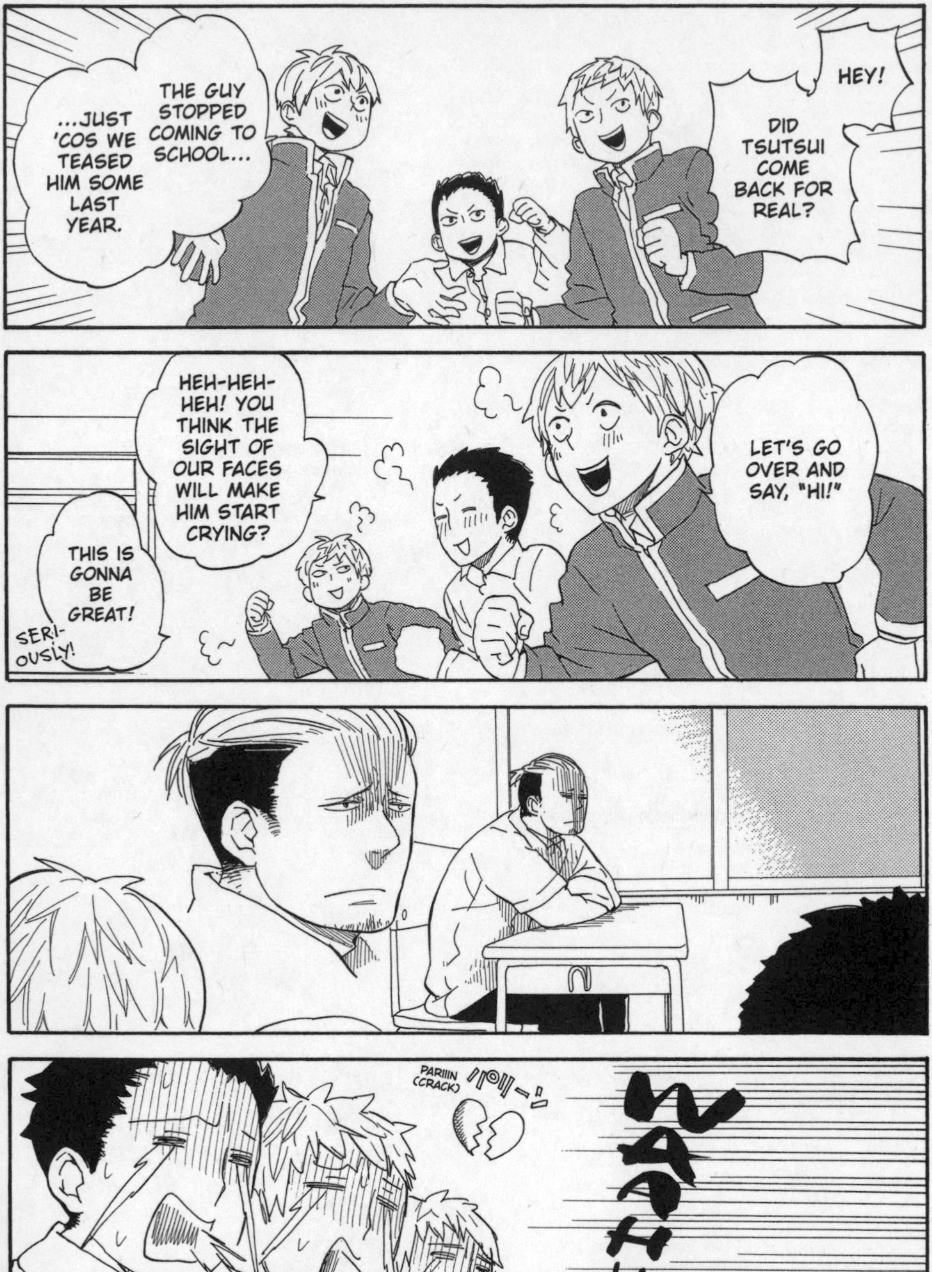
HEY!
DID TSUTSUI COME BACK FOR REAL?
THE GUY STOPPED COMING TO SCHOOL...
...JUST 'COS WE TEASED HIM SOME LAST YEAR.
LET'S GO OVER AND SAY, "HI!"
HEH-HEH-HEH! YOU THINK THE SIGHT OF OUR FACES WILL MAKE HIM START CRYING?
THIS IS GONNA BE GREAT!
SERI-OUSLY!
WAAHHHH!
PARIIN (CRACK)

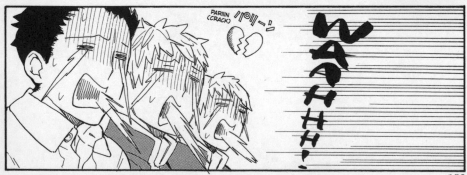

TRANSLATION NOTES

COMMON HONORIFICS

no honorific: Indicates familiarity or closeness; if used without permission or reason, addressing someone in this manner would constitute an insult.

-san: The Japanese equivalent of Mr./Mrs./Miss. If a situation calls for politeness, this is the fail-safe honorific.

-sama: Conveys great respect; may also indicate that the social status of the speaker is lower than that of the addressee.

-kun: Used most often when referring to boys, this indicates affection or familiarity. Occasionally used by older men among their peers, but it may also be used by anyone referring to a person of lower standing.

-chan: An affectionate honorific indicating familiarity used mostly in reference to girls; also used in reference to cute persons or animals of either gender.

-sensei: A Japanese term of respect commonly used for teachers, but can also refer to doctors, writers, and artists.

Calligraphy: Japanese calligraphy has a long history and tradition, with roots stemming from ancient China. One of the traditions carried over was the Chinese expression of the "Four Treasures," which refers to the brush, ink, paper, and inkstone used in calligraphy. Traditionally, an inkstick—solidified ink—is ground against an inkstone filled with water in order to produce ink with which to write. This time-consuming process helped to teach patience, which is important in the art of calligraphy. However, modern advances have developed a bottled liquid ink, commonly used by beginners and within the Japanese school system.

PAGE 10
yarou: Coarse word for "guy," written out phonetically with nonstandard kanji—literally means "wild dew/exposure." This style of writing out words is a common tough guy thing, especially using kanji with rougher and tougher meanings.

PAGE 11
Baishouen: An actual Japanese office and stationery supply company. The name also shows up in *Barakamon*.

PAGE 19
cursive: This is an actual style of speedy and connected calligraphy writing known as *tappitsu*.

PAGE 47
Handa's "TAI-SYO" bag: *Taishou* can refer to the kanji compound words "grand prize," "boss," and "object."

PAGE 53
NOMO brand eraser: A very common parody name used for the actual eraser brand MONO.

PAGE 61
Kami-sama: Silly pun on *kami-sama* (god + honorific) but using the kanji for the soundalike word for paper.

PAGE 78
vote tallies: In Japan, tallies are counted out by sets of the kanji for "correct," which uses five strokes.

PAGE 110
Wakasugi Avenue: *Wakasugi* is an actual Japanese person and place name, but it also works as a pun meaning "too young."

shushu: The Japanese word for the flower-like hair band called a "scrunchie."

PAGE 112
"Hiya": What Reo originally said was "*shaassu*," a greeting used by pop singer Nana Mizuki.

PAGE 147
parent-student conference: In Japan, parent-teacher conferences held at school are literally called "three-person conferences," because they include the student as well.

INSIDE COVER
The Giant Radish: Likely a reference to *The Giant Turnip*, an old Russian folktale the first-graders playact in *Barakamon*, Volume 7.

HANDA-KUN NEWS

Vol.HND

The highly-popular *Handa-kun* is now running in *Monthly Shonen Gangan*!

I sincerely thank you all for buying Volume 1 of *Handa-kun*! Your passionate support since the start of serialization and requests for a book release have succeeded in reaching the editorial department. And so, although only Volume 1 has gone on sale, they have planned an intense Handa Fan Club campaign for *Monthly Shonen Gangan*! Issues will include gorgeous pack-ins as well as a request form to send in for additional special items. Since these items will only be available in this premier campaign, please be sure to look for it!

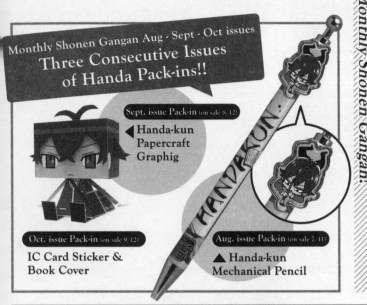

Monthly Shonen Gangan Aug - Sept - Oct issues

Three Consecutive Issues of Handa Pack-ins!!

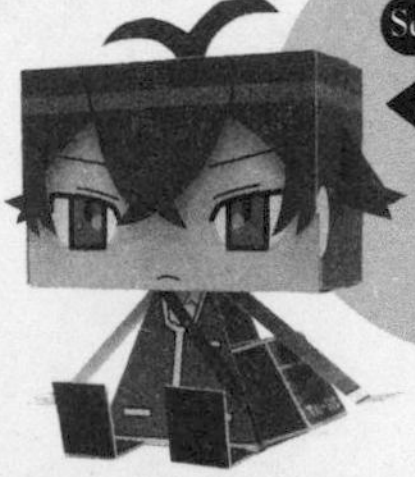

Sept. issue Pack-in (on sale 8/12)

◀ **Handa-kun Papercraft Graphig**

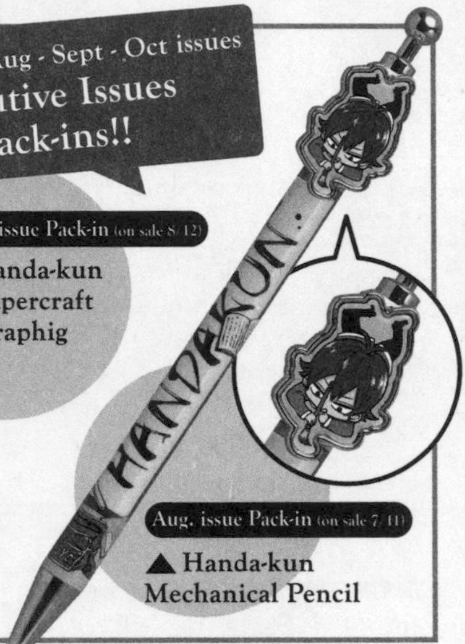
HANDAKUN

Aug. issue Pack-in (on sale 7/11)

▲ **Handa-kun Mechanical Pencil**

Oct. issue Pack-in (on sale 9/12)

IC Card Sticker & Book Cover

Handa-kun & *BARAKAMON* Beginning Double Serialization!

I believe many of you are already aware of this, but *Handa-kun* is a spin-off of the popular comic BARAKAMON.

Unbelievably, the main series BARAKAMON will now be running in *Monthly Shonen Gangan* along with *Handa-kun*, starting with the August issue! This campaign was arranged to commemorate their double serialization!

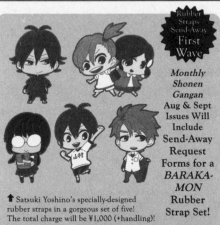

Rubber Straps Send-Away First Wave

Monthly Shonen Gangan **Aug & Sept Issues Will Include Send-Away Request Forms for a *BARAKAMON* Rubber Strap Set!**

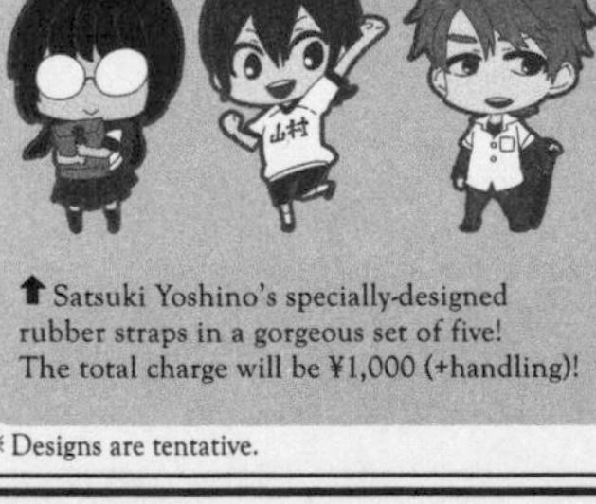
山村

⬆ Satsuki Yoshino's specially-designed rubber straps in a gorgeous set of five! The total charge will be ¥1,000 (+handling)!

※ Designs are tentative.

I humbly request that you all continue to support *Handa-kun*, BARAKAMON, and *Monthly Shonen Gangan*!

And in the ne
volume...

\ SERIOUSLY... LEAVE ME ALONE... /

Ebook
on sale now!!
Print available
April 2016!

Handa-Kun

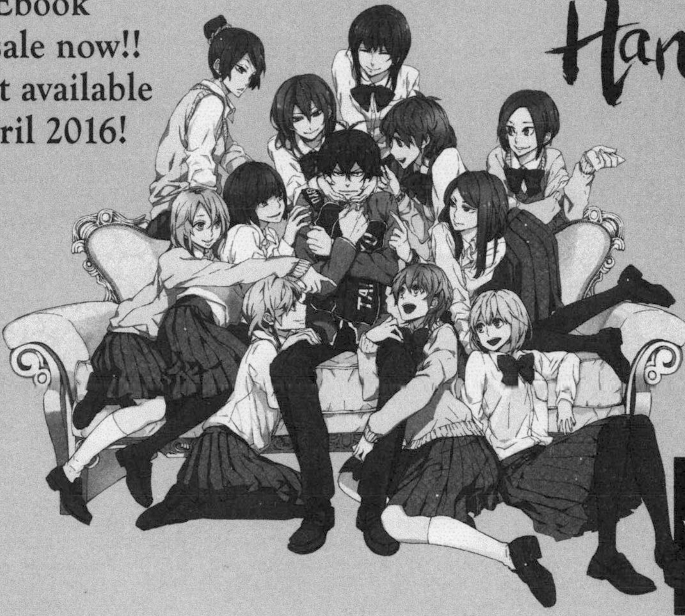

Vol. 2

In Gangan Oct. issue (on sale 9/12) & Gangan Nov. issue (on sale 10/11)

Rubber Straps Send-Away Second Wave

Handa-kun Rubber Strap Sets Available Via Send-Away Request Form!!

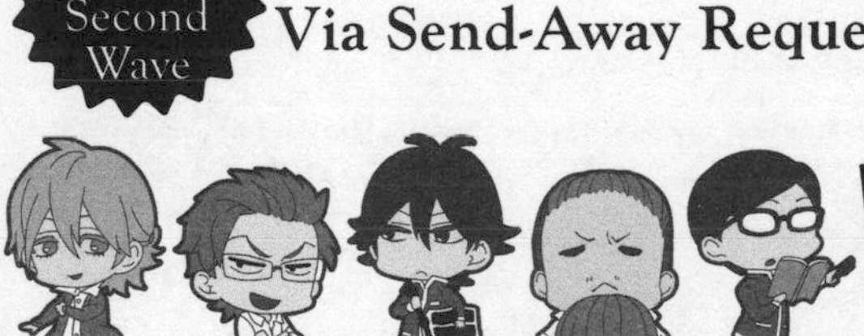

※ Designs are tentative.

Designed by Handa's Army

Superstar HND Goods Prize Campaign Slated to Commence!!

Handa-kun info is also distributed on occasion via the *BARAKAMON*/*Handa-kun* public Twitter account!

https://twitter.com/go_barakamon

※ Please note that all promotional items presented in this segment were only available to readers in Japan at the time of the original volume's release.

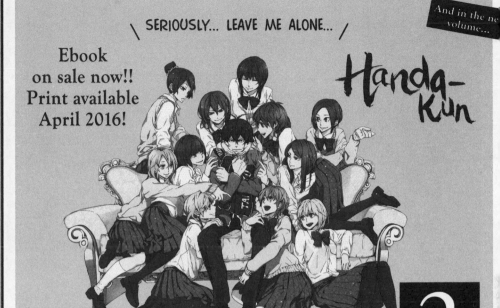

Handa-kun 1

Satsuki Yoshino

Translation/Adaptation: Krista Shipley, Karie Shipley
Lettering: Lys Blakeslee

Handa-kun vol. 1 ©2014 Satsuki Yoshino/SQUARE ENIX CO., LTD. First published in Japan in 2014 by SQUARE ENIX CO., LTD. English translation rights arranged with SQUARE ENIX CO., LTD. and Hachette Book Group through Tuttle-Mori Agency, Inc.

Translation ©2015 by SQUARE ENIX CO., LTD.

Yen Press
Hachette Book Group
1290 Avenue of the Americas
New York, NY 10104

www.HachetteBookGroup.com
www.YenPress.com

Yen Press is an imprint of Hachette Book Group, Inc. The Yen Press name and logo are trademarks of Hachette Book Group, Inc.

The publisher is not responsible for websites (or their content) not owned by the publisher.

Library of Congress Control Number: 2015952606

First Yen Press Print Edition: February 2016
Originally published as an ebook in July 2015 by Yen Press.

ISBN: 978-0-316-26918-6

10 9 8 7 6 5 4 3 2 1

BVG

Printed in the United States of America